In Pursuit of Butterflies

In Pursuit of Butterflies

A Fifty-Year Affair

MATTHEW OATES

BLOOMSBURY
LONDON · OXFORD · NEW YORK · NEW DELHI · SYDNEY

Bloomsbury Publishing Plc

50 Bedford Square   1385 Broadway
London   New York
WC1B 3DP   NY 10018
UK   USA

www.bloomsbury.com

First published 2015

'The New Forest' chapter is an adapted and updated version of an article
originally published as 'The demise of butterflies in the New Forest',
in *British Wildlife* 1996, 7 (4), 205–216.

British Library Cataloguing-in-Publication Data

A catalogue record for this book is available from the British Library.

Library of Congress Cataloguing-in-Publication data has been applied for.

ISBN (hardback) 978-1-4729-2450-6
ISBN (paperback) 978-1-4729-2452-0
ISBN (ebook) 978-1-4729-2451-3

2 4 6 8 10 9 7 5 3 1

Typeset in 11.5 pt Adobe Garamond Pro by Deanta Global Publishing Services,
Chennai, India

Printed and bound in Great Britain by CPI Group (UK) Ltd, Croydon CR0 4YY

To Sally, with thanks...

Erucam Nunquam Minoris Aestimate

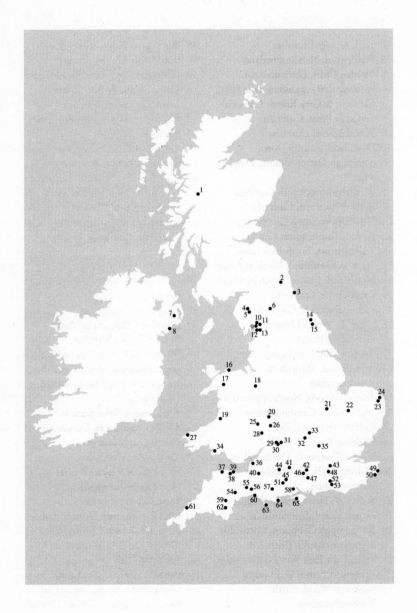

Butterflying heartlands

Contents

Foreword

For centuries, men and women who go chasing after butterflies have been, at best, belittled for their eccentricity. At worst, they have been punished for their lunacy. The title of Matthew Oates's book is taken from a memorable description of pioneering butterfly lover Eleanor Glanville, who gave her name to the Glanville Fritillary. As the eighteenth-century lepidopterist Moses Harris explained:

> Some Relations that was disappointed by her Will, attempted to let it aside by Acts of Lunacy, for they suggested that none but those who were deprived of their Senses, would go in Pursuit of Butterflies.

Perhaps some people today would draw a similar conclusion from a glance at the fifty-year butterflying career of Matthew Oates.

How many people in Britain help hoist a huge salmon into the treetops to lure the Purple Emperor? Or sell their LPs as a teenager to fund a summer chasing butterflies? Or keep a lifetime tally of rare colour variations of the White Admiral? Here is a man who befriends individual butterflies, has named his children after butterflies' Latin and Greek names and goes hunting not just for butterflies but for their eggs, caterpillars and pupae wherever he happens to be – visiting stately homes or motorway service stations or even outside prisons.

Thankfully Matthew has never been imprisoned for his singular passion, although he might describe the horrors of exam terms or having to attend incessant meetings in 'anaerobic offices' during the butterfly season as incarcerations.

Whether you know nothing about butterflies, or almost everything, you will learn a lot from this book. Unlike many obsessives, Matthew can communicate with those not in the grip of obsession, and he is also a superb naturalist with a keen attention to detail. Fascinating observations from the 1960s – when instead of butterfly collecting, butterflies 'collected' him – are remembered in exact detail, thanks to his lifelong habit of keeping a butterfly diary. For instance, he watches a pair of Orange-tips sit out five consecutive wet days before springing into action to mate as soon as the sun appears; he records how a courting pair of Small Tortoiseshells mated for eighteen and a half hours exactly; and how the Purple Emperors in the Sussex woods around Dragons Green are notably more aggressive than Emperors elsewhere.

These details are intriguing, but they illustrate wider truths: butterflies are deceptively robust and every butterfly is defined by just one impulse – to mate. More profoundly, such close observation is the basis of all scientific endeavour: all its questions, revelations and learning. We ignore the deceptively difficult skill of close observation and the precise recording of what we see at our peril.

Matthew is a particular devotee of the 'big game' of the butterfly world, the majestic, charismatic and justly celebrated Purple Emperor. But he is also alive to the most overlooked aspects of butterflies, particularly their caterpillars. He has made many discoveries about the peculiar lives of caterpillars, and can also enlighten us about the poetic and mysterious meanings of butterflies' scientific names. I certainly didn't know that 28 of our resident butterflies are named after characters in Greek mythology – including gods, demi-gods, muses, graces and a number of young ladies ravished by Zeus.

It would be a mistake to interpret all the wit and quirkiness in this magnificent memoir as a sign that a devotion to butterflies is a suitable passion for a flibbertigibbet. Matthew Oates is a new-age Romantic: he follows in the footsteps of William Wordsworth, Samuel Taylor Coleridge, John Clare, and – a particular inspiration – Edward Thomas, who have all sometimes wistfully and occasionally nostalgically described and celebrated the rapture of finding a deep connection with the natural world. He also poses some important questions for the science of ecology and for those who attempt to deny change, and loss, in nature. Conservation must be 'concerned with mending the relationship between people and Nature,' he argues. Ultimately, 'the whole show is essentially about Love.'

For *In Pursuit of Butterflies* is about far more than just butterflies. It will enthral anyone who enjoys the British countryside or adores summer, for it evokes the changing seasons in some of our most magical woods, moors, meadows and marshes. Their names dance with magic – Dogbarking Wood, Waterperry Wood, Alice Holt Forest – and we are transported to the atmospheric places that have become the author's heartland, from the spooky Savernake Forest in Wiltshire to the joyful inclines of Rodborough Common in the Cotswolds. Here, there is an ice-cream factory, walkers leave Christmas cards from their dogs to the place, and the slope bottoms are littered with lost balls and Frisbees.

Matthew is alive to the precious spirit of these places thanks to butterflies, for these insects help us discover a place and then anchor us to it. He recounts watching a female Purple Emperor feeding on the sticky buds on a young Ash tree in Madgeland Wood, West Sussex, in 1975. The ash is still there and he remembers that female every time he passes the spot. 'Butterflying does that to you,' he writes.

If you have spent any time in Britain in the last fifty years, I guarantee that this book will reawaken memories of summers past. You won't find a better account of the hot summer of 1976 (when Matthew cycled through viscous tarmac to find butterflies which had changed colour because of the great heat), or of 2003 or 2010. He believes, with John Masefield, that butterflies are 'the souls of summer hours' – and, with Tove Jansson, that the colour of our first butterfly of the year defines the character of our summer. As he puts it in these pages:

Like no other season, summer instils memories, deep and profound.
Its journey is into memory, within us as individuals and collectively.

And people collect memories, perhaps inadvertently but nonetheless, and are moulded by them. And butterflying is all about the collecting of memories in moments of time within idylls of place.

We can connect with wild places by walking dogs or watching birds, but butterflies seem a particularly powerful route to a more satisfying and intimate bond with nature. For Matthew, the immense wonder of the natural world can overwhelm us, and butterflies are a way of experiencing rapture without terror. Butterflies live so deeply in the moment of being, he believes, that they can conquer time itself. Perhaps there are lessons for us here.

In more practical terms, wandering through a wood at the most magical time of year, seeking a small, fast-moving thing, brings us alive to every possibility in the landscape – and the moment. Loiter quietly in nature and stuff happens: deer creep past or a butterfly quarrels with a bumblebee, and we become an accepted part of this world, which is a glorious experience.

I am sure that you, like me, will find the following pages beautiful, evocative, inspirational and, perhaps most importantly of all, fun. If an eccentric is someone who is unafraid of declaring his love for nature, who inspires us to follow him into nature, and who shows us how time in nature can make us happier and kinder human beings – how it can develop our souls – then Matthew Oates is an eccentric. Every one of us should be one too.

Patrick Barkham
Hoveton, Norfolk
January 2015

Introduction

Our lives have to be dedicated to something. Much of mine has been devoted to love – of British butterflies. Yet *In Pursuit of Butterflies* is as much about Nature as it is about butterflies, describing adventures in Nature, and exploring the intense personal relationships we forge with wilder places, with epochs of time, and with the seasons. It describes a journey through love and wonder. The butterflies themselves may simply be an entry point, a portal into a world so vast we need something that narrows our focus down, and so awesome we need our hand holding. Butterflies do all that, and they do it extraordinarily well.

This book is intended as an open memoir, so that others may share the experiences I have had. It is not an autobiography. Huge chunks of biographical information have been omitted, deliberately – not because they are embarrassing, though they might be, but because they do not matter.

But the butterflies and the special places they inhabit do matter, and need speaking for. What is written here is written on their behalf, that others might get to know them better, and by that I mean, know them better than me. Above all, the wondrous and captivating experiences I have had with butterflies more than merit being set down in print. It would be selfish not to share them. Please treat them as your own. They range from the sublime to the ridiculous, and back again – one tries to be serious, but cheerfulness keeps breaking through.

My essential subject is butterflying, to use the Victorian butterfly collectors' term for being out and about in pursuit of butterflies. That term is used here in a modern sense, to encompass the entire spectrum of experience from ecology and conservation through to poetics and the spiritual. The book's tone is deliberately positive, despite the fact that most of our butterflies have suffered horrendous declines and a great many of the habitats and populations described in these chapters are no more. This is because butterflies are eternal optimists and may be life's great survivors.

But why butterflies? The book will explain that, notably towards the end, but as a starting point it is worth quoting from one of the most popular Victorian butterfly books, W S Coleman's *British Butterflies,* first published in 1860. The ancient Greeks, he wrote, 'gave the same name, Psyche (ψυχή), to the soul, the spirit of life, and to the butterfly, and sculptured over the effigy of one dead the figure of a butterfly, floating away.' Psyche, who became personified as the Goddess of the Soul, lies behind all psychology – along with her butterflies. So perhaps butterflies hold some deep metaphor for a profound part of the human condition.

In Pursuit of Butterflies is a journey through time and place, amongst butterflies. Not until quite late in my career did I consider what I was seeking, or escaping from, let alone ponder why. All that came later. Sometimes the journey, the quest itself, is everything, and there may be little choice involved anyway. Sure enough, there was a thirst for knowledge, or truth even, but that was largely subjugated to a desire for experience and beauty. As Henry David Thoreau puts it at the end of his *Natural History of Massachusetts,* 'We must look a long time before we can see.' Knowledge itself can be a fickle, transitory thing, for mythology and assumption regularly dress themselves up and masquerade as truth or knowledge – even here, and even in science. Ultimately, knowledge almost invariably leads us to that most demanding of situations, a leap of faith – and abandons us there.

If you are looking for scientific truth, you may find some fragments here, but mine is a poet's mind and I have no head for statistics. These chapters may, though, help readers deepen their own perspectives on butterflies, and may strengthen the mental disciplines necessary to study and understand butterflies, and assist the development of intuitive relationships. At times I have played at being an ecologist, but essentially I am an old-fashioned naturalist, albeit one who has been privileged to work alongside, and consequently learn from, some of the country's leading ecologists. Their tuition and support is gratefully acknowledged.

Much in this book is based on detailed diaries that have been maintained since 1971, and from sketchier accounts hazing back to the halcyon summer of 1964. These diaries state what was flying when and where, and what individual butterflies and caterpillars were doing, and provide thorough descriptions of habitat and weather conditions. They even contain some useful data. I have regularly written a 2000-word account of a day's butterflying, sometimes more. The book is in many ways an attempt to justify the hours spent writing those butterfly diaries, and is a synthesis and a sharing of that effort.

Above everything else, these chapters are a celebration of a half-century of butterflying, a eulogy and a paean – and perhaps a prose-poem – on the beauty and wonder of British butterflies. It is written for anyone with an interest in butterflies and their immature life stages. No expertise or background knowledge is required. The index will assist those who like to dabble in books. Scientific terminology – please do not think it jargon, for it is a sophisticated and precise language – is largely avoided, and I hope it is all adequately explained whenever I have used it. English names for our butterflies are used preferentially.

At the end of his long, and frankly rather rambling, autobiographical poem 'The Prelude', William Wordsworth suggests, whilst musing – as ever – on the subject of Nature:

... what we have loved
Others will love; and we may teach them how.

I *Starting out*

There was no beginning, no single moment that set in motion a journey of at least fifty years, a journey through Nature. This is because Nature was central to my existence from birth. The only thing that may be remarkable here is that I did not stray away from it, as many of us do, perhaps because it had bitten too deep or because I lacked the ambition or bravery to venture elsewhere. So I journeyed with it, and it with me, and in the process I became distanced from some of the thinking and values that are prevalent in Western civilisation, together with the associated material benefits.

Someone whose first memory is of being eaten alive by red ants in a playpen might be expected to develop a pathological loathing of entomology, if not of natural history altogether. Strangely, I suffered no such reaction from that beastly experience, though it may explain why it took me nine years to get to love insects but only four to develop a passion for birds. I am not alone, however – my friend David Bullock has an early memory of being pinned to a gate by a frisky nanny goat, and he went on to become a leading mammal biologist, specialising in goats.

Yet, significantly, another personal early childhood memory is of catching, in the tender hands of infancy, a small and delicate white butterfly resting on a red rose upon that self-same wisteria-fringed veranda where the ant-biting episode had occurred, before releasing it into a brightening sky. The image – no, the very experience – remains wondrously clear. If only we could readily understand the meaning of such events, which in modern nature writing are often termed epiphany moments. Meaning, of course, often kicks in long after the event, and our understanding of metaphor is inherently poor.

These early dramas took place in Crewkerne, a bumbling small town in south-west Somerset. In those days Crewkerne specialised, if at all, in the manufacture of pyjamas. Incidents were rare, apart from a lengthy campaign of terror by a fire-raiser, who turned out to be a fireman with a penchant for torching barns and haystacks, and a serious incident when an Aberdeen Angus bull broke out and ran amok in a skittle alley, only calming down when a group of bulling heifers was cannily introduced. The town had an excellent toy shop, an autumn fair with dodgems, and seriously scary teddy boys who hung out outside a café called the Minto. The town was pronounced Crew-kurn by its few posh denizens, and variously as Cruc-kurn, Cruck-urrn or Croo-kurrn by its true natives, probably depending on for how long their families had dwelt there. Whatever, the name means the Place of the Crooked Cross, for the town had developed around a staggered cross roads on what was to become the A30, then the main highway to the far West Country. To the south lay the western fringes of Dorset, to the west the vast rural domain of Devon. All around were ridges of Lower Greensand separated by clay vales dotted with small dairy farms with thick meandering hedges, Primrose banks and dazzling streams.

My father was headmaster of the grammar school. On his staff was a young biology teacher, John Keylock, who became a leading member of the Somerset Wildlife Trust and an authority on fungi. John ran a bird nest recording programme at the school. When I was not yet five, in the spring of 1958, he showed me a Willow Warbler's nest, on a rough scrubby bank by the school fives court. The domed nest, hidden in a tussock of coarse grass, consisted of intricately woven stems of fine blades of grass – Red Fescue probably – and contained a number of tiny speckled eggs. Every now and then one discovers something for which one was unwittingly searching. Never mind epiphany moments, this was almost the blinding light on the Road to Damascus itself. The mental imprint is so great that I could show you the very spot. A Goldcrest's nest followed shortly afterwards, in a fir tree in the nearby Victorian cemetery, necessitating a heart-pulsating journey up a gigantean stepladder held firm by the mighty Keylock.

Brilliant as he was, Keylock was soon outgunned. On the wilder side of town lived a loose group of boys, led by a ten-year-old called Ronald who always wore a maroon jumper. These were serial nest hunters. Perceptions of social class, so prevalent at the time, meant that it was not appropriate for me to mix with them, or them with me, and their accents were so strong that I found them hard to understand. Nonetheless, tagging along was tolerated on a few precious occasions. Inspired, I ascended rookeries, peered into mud-lined Magpie nests in entanglements of thorn, was sworn at by irate Mistle Thrushes and stung to near-death searching for Common Whitethroat nests amongst brambly nettles. The gang's main targets, though, were nests of the Robin and what was then called the Hedge Sparrow (Dunnock), as these could hold Cuckoo eggs. Incredibly, at least a couple of these elusive trophies were found per year. Sooner rather than later, I will go a year without hearing a Cuckoo, and have, of course, long given up even dreaming of seeing one of their eggs again. But what happened to Ronald, who was seriously skilled at finding bird nests? Surely he now works for the RSPB or BTO? All I know is that he failed the eleven-plus exam and was consequently banished to the secondary modern school. Had he been examined in rural boyhood skills he would have won a scholarship to somewhere prestigious.

The boys did not avidly collect birds' eggs. The thrill was not in possession but in discovery, and they undoubtedly lacked the ability to curate eggs anyway. I never collected more than the odd addled egg, or eggs from deserted nests, being far too fond of the birds themselves. The problem, of course, is that over-enthusiastic children accidentally encourage nest abandonment by visiting too frequently. My heart still bleeds for an abandoned young Swallow I unsuccessfully tried to feed on bread and milk. That may have to be answered for on the Day of Judgement.

This might seem an idyllic childhood, but it was in many ways typical of what rural children experienced into the 1960s. The freedom they had was immense, unrestrained by the all-pervading modern fears of stranger danger and traffic. It was quite normal for children to roam around the countryside, singly or in twos and threes, with no sense of fear other than of some farmers who had gone Barking mad, become alcoholics or were simply shotgun-happy (Barking mad requires a capital B, as the term is derived from a mental asylum in Barking). There were some unwritten rules, such as never run between cow and calf and, most crucially, 'Don't tread on my (effing) mowing grass!' (uncut hay). Crucially, odd characters were well known and closely watched by the rural communities in which they lived. Children were well governed by their stomachs, and would always return for tea, and parents were concerned with recovering from a world war and rebuilding the country.

Do not for one moment think, though, that all was harmonious between Man and Nature in the countryside back then. Barbed wire fences, hedges and field trees were commonly dressed with the crucified corpses of Rooks and Carrion Crows, which were as much the victims of ignorance and prejudice as of cheap homemade cartridges. On more than one occasion I was petrified by the Otter hunt, whilst out fishing for Perch on the River Parrett. The Devon & Somerset Staghounds, up on Exmoor, were even nastier. We spent much time there, staying with Great Uncle Percy, the Reverend J P Martin, who published a series of best-selling children's books in his eighties.

It is hard to remember what I did outside the four-month heaven that was the bird-nesting season. Birds were ever-present, moving, flying, calling, but such encounters lacked the fascination and wonder provided by the hunt for nests and eggs. Wild duck and skeins of geese flew over from the nearby Somerset Levels in autumn and winter, and the Fieldfare hordes arrived to feast in untamed Hawthorn hedges. Probably, I simply roamed, picking Primroses, damming streams, exploring farms run by amenable farmers, climbing trees and haystacks, and feasting off abundant apples, blackberries and plums in season. And then, in winter, snow was a transport of delight.

There were also instances of sheer boyhood exuberance, too many of them in all probability. Notable here was the springtime practice of fishing in field ponds, with rod, line, float, leaded weights, hook and worm – for Great Crested Newts. The newts would simply ingest the loose end of the worm, and not impale themselves, and one would end up releasing a bucket full of writhing newts, hopefully none the worse for their brief captivity. The fine for such an activity nowadays could be anything up to £2000 per newt.

Farms were regarded as adventure playgrounds. Bored youth of all ages would gravitate towards these wonderlands. Farmers had to find boys something useful to do, such as feed the calves, gather eggs or help dag sheep, or boys would simply run amok, usually by creating sophisticated tunnel systems through bales stacked high in barns. In the modern utilitarian interests of health and safety, it is now almost impossible even for a farmer's own children to sample such Utopian delights.

There were also books, for it rained all too frequently; books in front of flickering firelight, and Children's Hour on the BBC Home Service. We had no television, and computers were less dreamt about than spaceships. For an undiagnosed dyslexic like me, reading was not particularly easy, but one could dream for hours at C F Tunnicliffe's illustrations in the Ladybird *What To Look For* books, which were published around 1960, price: 2/6 net. The countryside he depicted, idealised and already almost bygone, was where I wanted to be, and indeed largely was. These books taught me my first butterflies: Orange-tip, Red Admiral, Painted Lady and ubiquitous cabbage whites. Likewise, Cicely Mary Barker's *Flower Fairy* books taught the basic rudiments of botany, though the poetry often irritated. These books fired up a love of flowers, but only in their seasons, and fed an already-incipient belief that all living things have souls, alongside the feeling that places and the seasons themselves have spirits. The concept of spirit of place was obvious, and was taken for granted. Bird books abounded, but were admired more for their illustrations than for their text – apart from descriptions of nests and eggs. All these early childhood favourites survive in a bookcase today, alongside the likes of *The Chronicles of Narnia*. They are brought out whenever flu strikes. Books persist, and can set directions in life. In good books, new meanings are discovered at each perusal.

However, the idyll of childhood was shattered into irretrievable fragments by the sudden death of my father, aged 52, in March 1962. We did not merely lose a father and a husband, but the Victorian school house we regarded as home. Worse, at the age of eight I was of necessity packed off to board at the local preparatory school, which I already attended as a day boy. Never again would I visit the yew tree in the grammar school grounds in which Spotted Flycatchers nested annually. This had been the first decent nest I found unassisted. But personal tragedies can, if anything, strengthen one's relationship with Nature, and not simply by making one more dependent upon it. The problem was that boarding school equalled incarceration, albeit amongst pre-existing friends – and I could not have been amongst kinder, friendlier children. My heartland, though, was no more.

Some tentative conclusions can perhaps be reached from this opening tale. First is a suggestion that naturalists are not so much made as born – not because they are in any way special but because all people are born to Nature: we are all born as naturalists, it is just that some or many of us choose, or feel obliged, to forsake that calling, perhaps as the poison of modern materialism strengthens within our minds. Secondly, natural history was considered a normal childhood pastime, a first-nature, which raises the question of why this is no longer the case. Thirdly, but equally, the freedom to roam has been eroded from childhood. Indeed, in 2012 a study conducted for the National Trust found that the home ranges of children in the UK had shrunk by 90% since the 1970s – make that 95% in comparison with my own childhood. This is disturbing, for children fall deeply in love with their homeland, and need to explore it and live it to the full, not in the company of well-intentioned but nevertheless domineering adults but by themselves. Perhaps people establish not so much territories as heartlands, to reuse a curious word introduced at the end of the previous paragraph. It is a concept that will be developed throughout the coming pages.

2 *Laudator temporis acti*

In the early 1960s one of the junior houses of Christ's Hospital school in the West Sussex Weald was run by an ancient housemaster nicknamed Jonah. A cadaverous man, Jonah was normally quiet but like the proverbial simmering volcano was prone to sporadic eruptions of Plinian magnitude, when deliberately wound up by boys – and wound up he surely was, regularly. He taught maths, or, more precisely, dry-maths. Something exciting actually happened in one of his lessons, just once: he had the habit of storing half-smoked cigarettes in his trouser turn-ups, and caught fire, rather spectacularly, to the hysterical delight of fifteen eleven-year-olds. He also played the piano at junior chapel services, ingloriously so on one memorable occasion after someone had wickedly mistuned the skool piano. (This was of course the era of Nigel Molesworth. School was spelt 'skool' and masters were there to be pranked.)

On Tuesday afternoons in the summer Jonah did something arguably less futile than teach maths-without-humour and punish boys for having dirty shoes. It was Hobbies Afternoon, and he ran a butterfly and moth collecting group. B&M, as it was known, was nothing new to the school, having been introduced by an entomological chaplain, the Reverend L H White, in 1902, when the school migrated from London to a new location south of Horsham. Jonah continued the tradition, handing out wobbly Edwardian cane-framed nets, the bags of which were riddled with holes, along with pill boxes, breeding cages and other paraphernalia associated with the collecting and breeding of Lepidoptera. Apparently he had been inspired as a boy by no less a mortal than S G Castle Russell (1866–1955), a gloriously eccentric but deeply respected butterfly collector who had the habit of appearing randomly at public schools to instruct boys in the subtle arts of collecting. Castle Russell struggled to tell left from right, and in consequence was forever getting lost in forests, but he could tell at fifteen yards whether a male Orange-tip, in flight, possessed the small black spot in the forewing orange splash or not. He was also colour blind, which is remarkable as he was a pioneer electrician who wired up Buckingham Palace and the Admiralty. A modern equivalent of this well-intentioned and utterly innocent evangelist is much needed, but would doubtless require Criminal Records Bureau clearance.

Butterfly collecting was difficult, as junior boys were restricted to a stark expanse of playing field, on pain of extreme pain, and expeditions afield could not be arranged within a sport-orientated regime. However, Orange-tips, Green-veined Whites, Common Blues, Meadow Browns and the standard aristocrats (Peacock, Small Tortoiseshell, Red Admiral and Comma) occasionally strayed within bounds, and were vigorously pursued, netted and pinned (badly). The pride of the school's official collection was a Queen of Spain Fritillary that had been taken on the edge of the junior school cricket pitch during the great immigration summer of 1945. Boys quickly learnt how to find Red Admiral caterpillars, hiding in curled nettle leaves, and bred a profusion of Peacocks and Small Tortoiseshells, plus a few Commas and Orange-tips.

And bounds were there to be pushed, of course. Jonah once caught two of us marginally out of bounds, in a hay meadow full of Meadow Browns, and duly erupted. In blind panic I dropped the Marmite jar containing a pristine Meadow Brown. The unnecessary death of one Meadow Brown still haunts my conscience.

Moth collecting was much easier. Boys slept in long dormitories, the ends of which held ablution blocks that were brightly lit all night. The windows were jammed firmly open, turning these toilet and washing units into walk-in moth traps. There would be a stampede each morning to box the night's catch. Lime, Eyed and Poplar hawkmoths were frequent and highly treasured, the first of these breeding freely on the nearby avenue of mature lime trees. Buff Arches, Lappet, Large Emerald, Oak Beauty and Peach Blossom occurred commonly in summer, and during the early autumn the Feathered Gothic and Figure of Eight – all as intriguing as their names suggest.

The alternative wildlife hobby group, Birds, in which I dabbled, had boys tracking down nests for the British Trust for Ornithology (BTO) Nest Record Scheme. Regular highlights included Goldfinch and Treecreeper, the latter nesting behind loose bark on tree trunks, and roosting each winter in excavated hollows in bark along an avenue of *Wellingtonia* trees. But I was used to better fare, and missed water birds and warblers in particular, along with the right to roam. The junior school, or Leigh Hunt house as it was known, was a veritable prison (and alumnus Leigh Hunt had indeed spent a while in prison himself, whilst fighting for the freedom of the press). That pupils were dressed up as penguins, in a stiff Elizabethan uniform, was but a minor inconvenience. Boys were cooped up for hours on end in a small day room, where they teased and bullied each other mercilessly, largely out of boredom and the frustration of being enclosed. Boys were constantly forced to perform utterly pointless tasks, such as compulsory nose blowing each morning ('Handkerchiefs out! Nose blowing by numbers,

One, Two, Three!' – I jest not) and changing shoes a dozen times a day. Alumnus Samuel Taylor Coleridge summarised the condition through the term 'Christ's Hospitalised'. We were highly stressed anyway, for the school is a charitable institution specialising in taking into its stewardship boys (and now girls) from families which had fallen on difficult times. Most of us were from single-parent families. None of us ever talked about our backgrounds or home lives.

Sometime in the mid-1960s Jonah retired into a rhomboid or parallelogram, or wherever ancient maths masters go to lie down. Nonetheless, I owe him *Everything*, though he scarcely knew of my interest, and never openly encouraged it. One of the many curious facets of the human condition is the frequency with which people unknowingly act as catalysts for others' callings.

The school prided itself on its Spartan values. These manifested themselves in myriad ways, not all of which were based on common sense or seemed to serve any purpose. One manifestation was the absence of curtains in dormitories. The wisdom of expecting thirty small boys to get to sleep in such conditions on bright summer evenings can be called into question. In the summer of 1964 the house master of Leigh Hunt B, Mr Eagles (known, predictably, as Beaky) temporarily solved the problem by reading out *Brendon Chase*, Denys Watkins-Pitchford's captivating tale of three boys who (understandably) choose to run away and go feral in a forest at the end of the Easter holidays, rather than return to – you've guessed it – boarding school. Watkins-Pitchford, who taught art at Rugby, wrote under the nom de plume of 'BB', after a grade of shotgun pellets used for shooting geese and also as fishing-line weights. He was an old fashioned gun-and-rod naturalist.

Beaky read this book brilliantly, not least because it is a brilliant book. The heroes were seriously good naturalists, and were skilled as fishermen and hunters (having 'borrowed' the gardener's Rook rifle and ammo). They proved more than capable of looking after themselves in the forest, and, more importantly, the forest looked after them. They experienced precisely the range of adventures in Nature that I had sampled and for which I craved, but was being denied by a system hell bent on containment, rugby, simultaneous equations and making boys change their shoes. The book is essentially about freedom, freedom in Nature.

Beaky taught Geography, very well in fact. One term he taught the geography of the local area, the Horsham district, with a passion almost unknown within the teaching profession at that time. He described a treed landscape of forests, woods, shaws, copses and lags, of veteran oaks amongst buttercup fields on small higgledy-piggledy farms, of meadows and orchards bordered by outgrown hedges of Blackthorn, and of an undulating landscape on heavy Wealden Clay, dissected by the valleys of the major Sussex rivers – the Arun, Adur, Rother and Ouse. He recalled the industrial history of iron making, timber production and hammer ponds. In fact, he described a paradise, accidentally in all probability, but a paradise that any budding naturalist would readily recognise. The difficulty was that we were not allowed to venture into it – yet it was all around, calling to us.

Books can change people's lives. *Brendon Chase* changed mine, for in it I discovered the Purple Emperor butterfly. This is the passage that Beaky read out one warm evening in early June 1964, to a dormitory of restless ten-year-olds:

And then … he saw it, quite suddenly he saw it, the glorious regal insect of his dreams! It was flying towards him down the ride and it settled for a moment on a leaf. Then, as he advanced, trembling with excitement, it soared heavenwards to the top of an oak. There he watched it, flitting round one of the topmost sprays far out of reach, mocking him, the Unattainable, the Jewel, the King of butterflies! It was well named the Purple Emperor, it was truly regal in form, colour and habits. The old entomologists called it His Imperial Majesty! They were right, those old boys, it was an imperial insect, and no mistake.

Years later I had the honour of meeting the author, when he visited Selborne. I took afternoon tea with him and our mutual friend Valezina Viscountess Bolingbroke, known throughout butterflying circles by her maiden name Valezina Frohawk, for she was the youngest daughter of the wildlife artist and great lepidopterist F W Frohawk. 'BB' could talk Purple Emperors till the cows came home, but he rather resented anyone probing his imagination or adulating his work. I never met a more distant, dreamy man. Perhaps he recognised that I coveted his dreaming, his imagination and his fantasy world?

Thus The Emperor was firmly established as a dream. Bed making, cricket, something ghastly called French, and constant shoe changing and nose blowing, remained the reality.

At last the summer holidays began. Back in Somerset, a young butterfly enthusiast was unleashed on the unsuspecting countryside around the small village of Seavington St Mary, near Ilminster, armed with *The Observer's Book of Butterflies* and the equivalent volume on *Moths*. It was a hot August. The Beatles were Number One with 'A Hard Day's Night' and the Clouded Yellows were in: I caught one of these golden speedsters in a pink shrimping net outside Seavington, in a wildflower combe that has long since been converted into a cereal field. The same net also plucked a hovering Hummingbird Hawkmoth out of an azure sky at Woolacombe on the north Devon coast, during a week's holiday at the end of July. We must assume that the 'Large Blue' caught at the back of nearby Morte Point was a misidentification, but of what? Fantasy and reality are not easy disentangled, especially in childhood.

Encounters with new species are often memorable, not least because of the identification challenges they raise. Many a beginner's heart has leapt with joy before crashing with despondency on first encountering the humble Wall Brown, mistaking it for a mighty fritillary. In the summer of 1964, Comma, Marbled White, Ringlet and Painted Lady were all encountered in and around Seavington St Mary, the last of these occurring freely in old apple orchards; the Dark Green Fritillary was seen hurtling up and down Charmouth

Cliffs, elusively so; a colony of Grayling was discovered along the paths leading up to Dunkery Beacon on Exmoor; and the quarried hill fort of Ham Hill, by Stoke sub Hampden, revealed Brown Argus, identified by the bright females, and a huge population of Common Blue. Twenty-five butterfly species were identified that first summer, and the giant Old Lady moth proved to be a regular visitor to our cottage at night. None, it must be added, was killed, for I lacked collecting equipment – and the heart. If nothing else, some standards had been set, a path had been chosen or ordained. Above everything else, it was all regarded as being both normal and perfectly natural. It was part of rural life.

3 Escape to the woods

Hilaire Belloc spent much of his life at Shipley, three miles down the road from Christ's Hospital school. In the preface to *The Four Men* he writes: 'a man love(s) with all his heart, that part of earth which nourished his boyhood. For it does not change, or if it changes, it changes very little, and he finds in it the character of enduring things.' He is wrong, of course, for the landscape that we are about to explore has changed quite fundamentally. But at the same time he is absolutely right, as its spirit of place is still there – only you have to look more closely, more locally, to find it, and concentrate hard to shut out intrusions such as traffic noise.

In a dusky corridor of the junior school at Christ's Hospital hung an old 2½-inch Ordnance Survey map of the landscape between Horsham and Belloc's heartland at Shipley. By the time I was moved up to the senior school I had learnt that map off by heart – no easy task, as boys were not allowed to loiter in corridors. As a junior in the senior school one was – at last – allowed out, at least for the odd couple of hours, rugby and cricket permitting. So, at the start of the autumn term of 1967 I finally broke out, ran two miles down to the nearest block of what is known as Southwater Forest – the gloriously named Dogbarking Wood – and revelled in it, utterly. A tawny Comma butterfly ascended from a log pile, and a Lesser Spotted Woodpecker was watched probing a birch trunk. I had come Home.

Winter intervened, as it always does. Non-entomologists have no idea of the agonies suffered during the darker months, especially in boyhood. Those of us who spent part of our youth fishing will know of the angst that coarse fishermen experience waiting for the three-month close season to end. Football enthusiasts are out of season for all of six weeks, but to those afflicted with a love of butterflies autumn and winter inflict six whole months of acute mental suffering. Never mind Seasonal Affective Disorder, in itself a reality for many lovers of Nature in these islands, this is Spiritual Deprivation. We have to learn, first, how to survive winter, and then how to conquer it – the latter takes about forty years.

Fortunately, there are books. Books for escaping into, when the warmth of the summer sun is far, too far away. At Christ's Hospital, two butterfly books were favoured once we had progressed beyond the Observer's books. We fell into two camps, disciples of Richard South's *The Butterflies of the British Isles* and of Edmund Sandars's *A Butterfly Book for the Pocket*. The former contained photographs of set specimens, though these were rather dark and dingy. Sandars's book had poorly reproduced paintings, again of set specimens, but also contained illustrations of larvae and pupae, and distribution maps and life-cycle calendar charts. It lacked the rather verbose descriptions of the adults so prominent in South. I was a follower of Sandars. However, one page of South fascinated me beyond what was probably good for me: Plate 31, opposite page 63, featured the 'Black Admiral', the rare all-black colour variety of the White Admiral, and the ultimate prize, aberration *iole* of the Purple Emperor – the all-purple Purple Emperor.

The spring of 1968 started slowly, but its magic steadily grew. Any day now, something mighty was going to erupt within the world of Nature, and on Sunday May 19th it did. This was no mere epiphany moment but a life-altering day, the first day in a life's calendar of sempeternal happenings. After chapel (compulsory) I ran, in heavy nailed school shoes and dressed as a penguin, the two and a half miles to Marlpost Wood, entered the wood at the zenith of spring, and crossed rapturously into a new dimension. There, to illimitable delight that must now be shared, I found colonies of the exquisite Pearl-bordered Fritillary and what was then known as the Duke of Burgundy Fritillary. The former was undoubtedly the most beautiful thing I had ever seen, being the most graceful of our butterflies in flight, alongside the White Admiral.

The first of these colonies was found in a plantation where rows of young oaks had been inter-planted with lines of Norway Spruce, as a nurse crop. The second, across the stream gully in the wood's eastern half, was in a young Corsican Pine plantation. In both, the Pearl-bordereds searched frenetically amongst old and new bracken fronds and over patches of Bluebell and Lesser Stitchwort, pausing only to visit ride-side patches of Bugle. Speckled Yellow moths were hatching, fair-weather cumulus clouds drifted lazily above, atmospheric pressure was rising, and a Nightingale sang snatches of some Elysian song. Will people who do not recognise that Paradise exists upon this earth please revise their beliefs: it does, as this book will repeatedly attempt to demonstrate, only it tends to be transitory and episodic, and you have to be in the right place at the right time, and in the right frame of mind – you must allow Nature in.

A horribly soppy and naive song by a group called The Honeybus, who perhaps mercifully had only the one hit, was riding high in the charts that May, and was in my mind throughout and beyond that visit. There was only one thing to do: rewrite it, to give it some personal meaning, slow it down and remove the annoying castrato and counter-tenor parts. This heavily revised, sanitised and almost paganised version of 'I Can't Let Maggie Go' is my song of the Pearl-bordered Fritillary, but like so much of what one holds dearest is inappropriate for general communication. One dare not come out at that level, at least not quite yet.

Songs play a curious role within our lives. They are integral to the collection of the memories with which we fill our minds. Either we ignore the words altogether, and allow ourselves to be merely haunted by the tune, or we spin personalised meanings into the cadence of the words. Either way, they become associated with specific periods of our lives, and the original meaning is ignored. I went further, and completely rewrote the lines of many a song, to give them idiosyncratic personal meaning and relevance.

Two older boys in my house, Cesar and Longhurst (first names did not exist in boarding schools during that era), who were allowed bicycles, had discovered an even better spot, which they teasingly called Grimblings Meadow. There, they found Duke of Burgundy and Pearl-bordered Fritillary in even greater numbers. In vain I sought that place, knowing full well that it would not be a meadow. Eventually I found it, a young conifer plantation on an ancient woodland site called Northlands Wood, to the south, down the sunken Oldhouse Lane towards Brooks Green. No wonder they tried to keep the place secret, for *euphrosyne* the Pearl-bordered Fritillary abounded there.

May merged into June, the tree canopy closed over, and Bluebell scent drifted into memory. *Euphrosyne* was replaced by its congener *selene*, the Small Pearl-bordered Fritillary. In those days the Latin and Greek specific names of butterflies were still predominantly in use, and some schoolboys even knew how to pronounce *euphrosyne*. The Small Pearl-bordered Fritillary proved to be all but ubiquitous in young plantations in that woodland system, spreading along some rides, though it lacked the psychic dimension of its cousin. The Nightingales stopped singing, though the Turtle Doves continued to purr content into the world. The woods became the domain of myriad Meadow Browns and a scatter of Large Skippers, only. The equivalent of what beekeepers know as the June Gap was upon us.

Yet the Purple Emperor season was approaching, slowly, though none of us knew when, where or how to look. An older boy, Cottingham A (as opposed to his younger brother, Cottingham B), had netted a male flying low down in a ride in Marlpost Wood the previous July, only the fortunate insect had escaped whilst in the process of being boxed. The drama was witnessed by Cesar, Longhurst and McClure, and so was genuine. Had no witness been present even a wholly honest fellow like Cottingham A would never have been believed.

Also approaching, rapidly and without welcome, was the exam season. Rather inevitably, then, July ushered in a short-lived heatwave, with temperatures exceeding 30 degrees Celsius. Two superb days were consequently spent revising on the vast expanse of playing fields known as Big Side, probably for lost-cause subjects like physics. Let it be known, then, that almost fifty years on the enforced wasting of those two days is deeply resented, increasingly so in fact. Worse, this wastage was repeated exactly a year later, in identical weather. Which malicious demon determined that the exam season should coincide with the peak of the butterflying, cricket and hay-fever seasons? Pupils who experience all three stand little chance in exams, and consequently under-perform. It is obvious that the academic year should start in January, and that exams should be staged during November, so that their victims can then recover over Christmas. But we deviate.

Then, on July 3rd, the White Admiral entered into my life, and spontaneously became central to it – as if it had always been so. It is an integral part of every butterfly lover's existence, and one of the nation's best-loved insects. I have seen this gem of a butterfly annually since, searching for the first of each year in a state of pilgrimage. White Admirals were rumoured to occur in many of the local woods, so the sighting of an early male in Marlpost Wood came as no real surprise. What was surprising, or rather amazing, was the supreme grace with which the insect skimmed the ride-edge foliage, weaving secret ways in and out of sprays of horizontal leaves. A return visit in hot sunny conditions three days later resulted in the taking of a small series, and an encounter with the White-letter Hairstreak – a butterfly deemed so obtuse and elusive that none of us ever dreamt of finding it. Naturalists who have never collected butterflies will have no idea how difficult White Admirals are to catch, both in flight and when feeding from their beloved bramble flowers. Saturday July 6th 1968 remains a life red letter day – one of the top ten days I would most like to relive given the opportunity. A song, even more dreadful than 'I Can't Let Maggie Go', was in my head – a merciless melodrama sung by

Richard Harris called 'MacArthur Park', in which love is likened to a cake left out in the rain. It was hastily rewritten, and became, unrecognisable, the song of the White Admiral.

The following day I headed out towards St Leonard's Forest, east of Horsham, which I believed might be the paradise 'BB' had chosen for the setting of *Brendon Chase*, ostensibly set in the Weald. After running most of the way there, several miles, heavy rain set in. I ran back, soaked. The trouble was that we had no access to anything remotely approximating to a weather forecast at boarding school. The problem was eventually solved under the tutelage of the senior geography master, who had a profound understanding of British weather. Years later I found out that Brendon Chase was actually based on Salcey Forest in Northamptonshire, and that 'BB' had moved it to a fictional Weald because that name had a certain resonance.

The weekend that straddled July 13th and 14th was critical. It held that summer's only chance of encountering the Purple Emperor, as shortly afterwards something preposterously inappropriate was destined to occur – term would end, just when some of us actually needed to be at boarding school. Moreover, the best part of the preceding week had been lost to heavy rain. Saturday the 13th started fine. The woods to the south were calling.

Meanwhile, in another part of the Purple Emperor's empire, a Classics master from a small boarding school boarded the 6 am train from Salisbury to London, before travelling on to Huntingdon. This was I R P Heslop, lead author of *Notes & Views of the Purple Emperor*. His target was the Large Copper, which occurred only at Wood Walton Fen National Nature Reserve (NNR), where its population was artificially maintained through captive breeding and releasing. Heslop arrived at the fen at about 11.30, only to find it severely flooded. Undeterred, for he had spent 25 years in West Africa, he swam through the flood to the main flight area, collected a fine series of *dispar*, swam back, dried himself off, and caught his return train to London and Salisbury. He was 64 at the time. Such people make perfect boyhood heroes.

Longhurst and the much younger Oates were not supposed to associate, because of the age difference between them (in all-male schools such disparate associations could mean but one thing – though, needless to say, these two boys went on to father nine children between them). Undeterred, they made a strategic decision, and headed for Dogbarking Wood. One of the housemasters, Norman Fryer, had tipped me off that he had seen *iris* flying around a clump of tall oaks on the crest of the hill there a couple of years back. Norman was a reliable all-round naturalist. His revelation had been prompted by my showing him Hawfinch nests I had located in the school's neglected orchards that May. Dogbarking it was. White Admirals were skimming the ride-edge shrubs, but the crown of oaks revealed only a scatter of irritatingly high-flying Purple Hairstreaks. Then it clouded over and the day was lost.

Everything hinged on the Sunday, which turned out to be cloudy but warm with bright periods. Dogbarking Wood merited another go, but Marlpost and indeed the adjacent Madgeland Wood also cried out for visits. Chapel inflicted a delayed start, dragging on for even longer than usual, complete with Psalm 119, which is at best interminable. Again, the oaks were tenanted only by Purple Hairstreaks. In hindsight, it is likely that recent felling work had deterred Purple Emperor males from gathering over the now exposed hilltop oaks. On returning to school the worst possible news broke: a boy called Robbins, from another house, had netted a male *iris* in Marlpost Wood that morning, after committing the cardinal sin of skipping chapel. But it was too late, term finished. A year was lost in the pursuit of *iris*.

Worse, my family had moved from a peripatetic existence in the wilds of Somerset to the developing suburbia of the mid-Chilterns, where Mother had obtained a job running a conference centre. Unused to omnipresent traffic noise and houses of wealthy folk scattered intrusively everywhere, I struggled to feel even remotely at home there. Everything was Private. The countryside had been vanquished there, offering no freedom to roam. The orange glow of distant street lights obliterated the familiar stars, and the Milky Way abruptly vanished from my life. The freedom of the Somerset countryside was no more, which rendered that offered by the West Sussex countryside during term time even more important.

Mother had had enough. She sent me on a weekend butterfly course at Pendley Manor, Tring, run by Robert Goodden of Worldwide Butterflies. He introduced me to chalk grassland as a habitat, and tipped me off about various good butterfly localities in the Chilterns that could be reached by bus or bicycle. The Chalkhill Blue came into my life that weekend, as the first males were on the wing at Totternhoe Quarries close by to Tring. We also found Small Blue larvae there, an impressive lesson and eye-opener for a fourteen-year-old.

Inspired and informed by Goodden, I took the Aldershot & District omnibus service to Watlington, a small sleepy town at the foot of the Chilterns escarpment which, traffic apart, has not changed substantially since the summer of 1968. Watlington Hill (NT), on the scarp slope, turned out to hold a modest population of Silver-spotted Skipper and several colonies of Brown Argus in pockets of tall grass. The former was a devil to catch, darting at high speed low over the short fescue turf. But caught it was, by employing a turf-level version of cricket's sweep shot or by quickly dropping the net down on settled specimens. The National Trust may wish to contact me regarding the collecting of butterflies on its land, contrary to its bylaws.

On the other side of the road leading up the escarpment to the delightfully named Christmas Common was an even better butterfly site, consisting of old quarry pits and a long sunken chalk-land gully. Chalkhill Blue was abundant there, and Dark Green Fritillary numerous in a nearby abandoned field. Sadly, this whole area became enveloped by scrub within 25 years. Places change.

4 *Rebellion*

The late 1960s was above all else a time of radical social change, even within boarding schools where little had altered since Edwardian times. Lindsay Anderson's film *If* (1968) was supposed to be a parody of contemporary public school life, but to those of us who sneaked out of such places to watch that proscribed film in local cinemas it was remarkably verbatim, and unfunny. Frustration was simmering. The system was being challenged.

Change even penetrated the pursuit of butterflies. At Christ's Hospital, Jonah's retirement had brought to an end the supply of young enthusiasts entering the senior school, for no fresh-faced young master arrived down from Oxbridge to continue the hobby within the junior school. Furthermore, a generation of older practitioners, such as Cesar, Longhurst and McClure in my house, and Robbins in Lamb A, left for the real world, whatever that was. All of a sudden one was in a rapidly dwindling minority, within a social environment in which compliance to peer pressure increasingly meant *Everything*. Interest in natural history quickly became socially unacceptable in the extreme, and butterflying was deemed a gross eccentricity. Only Oates and Johnson in Coleridge A remained, and a rather fun-loving trio led by Francis Ratnieks in Lamb A (named after Charles Lamb, a contemporary and friend of Coleridge). Similar changes were doubtless taking place at that time in other public schools. Lepidoptera collecting started to become an endangered practice.

Behavioural modifications had to be made. In consequence, I gave up collecting butterflies, though not simply because of peer pressure and rising levels of testosterone. Above all, I had become too fond of butterflies. In effect, the butterflies had collected me, having infiltrated my soul. As concessions to peer pressure, bird nesting, fishing and moths were abandoned, but the power of the relationship with Nature offered through butterflying meant too much and had to remain, and intensify. The Rubicon had already been crossed (probably on May 19th 1968). The way forward necessitated bearing the cross of eccentricity. Acceptable interests in the disparate likes of Leonard Cohen, Neil Young and the Incredible String Band afforded a social lifeline.

The problem is very much alive today. Young children are fired up about Nature, wondrously, only to feel obliged to ditch that enthusiasm the moment they enter secondary school, in obedience to what they believe is expected of them by their peers. They may end up sacrificing themselves in order to be like others, or more precisely, to be as they feel others are and expect them to be. It happened, visibly, to my own children when they moved up to secondary school. Preventing this breakdown is one of the major challenges facing our relationship with Nature.

In the woods, 1969 was a year of consolidation and pushing limits back further. Okehurst Woods, way to the west near Five Oaks, were discovered, and found to be alive with both species of pearl-bordered fritillary, especially *selene*. St Leonard's Forest, to the east, was finally conquered, many of its young plantations also alive with the two fritillaries, and its buckthorn bushes stuccoed with Brimstone larvae.

At the end of a June dominated by cricket and exams the woods were alive only with myriad Meadow Browns, which were bib-bobbing everywhere along the rides. The White Admirals appeared on July 2nd in Marlpost Wood and, as in 1968, an expedition on the first Sunday of the month to far-flung *terra nova*, this time the woods around Loxwood in pursuit of reputed High Brown Fritillaries, ended with retreat in heavy rain as an unwelcome wet spell commenced. Life was repeating itself.

Yet again, *iterum atque iterum*, everything hinged on the final weekend of term. The Saturday was lost to cricket, but the Sunday was hot and clear. Marlpost Wood beckoned and received, but yielded only a goodly number of rather worn White Admiral and a Silver-washed Fritillary, then an extremely scarce butterfly in the district. Once again, term ended just as the Purple Emperor season was beginning.

Shortly afterwards, on July 21st 1969, having stayed awake all night watching the American moon landing, I R P Heslop caught a pristine male Purple Emperor aberration *lugenda* (an excessively rare and treasured colour form, or variation, in which the white bands are missing). This was close to where the main car park in Bentley Wood, in south-east Wiltshire, is now situated, a place where people gather each summer to view this butterfly. 'Never have I taken an insect more easily! It was just flying peacefully along the track at knee height,' he recalled in his diary. He had just retired from teaching Classics. A week later, close by, Heslop was to glimpse his last Purple Emperor, for he died the following spring. We will not see his likes again. But oh, that he had taught Latin at Christ's Hospital! We would have slain every gerund and gerundive in Christendom, and conquered every wood and down in the glorious land of Sussex.

Watlington Hill in the Chilterns redeemed a largely sunny but wasted summer. A male Clouded Yellow patrolled the lower slope at speed, Chalkhill Blues abounded across the road from the National Trust land, Dark Green Fritillaries feasted on thistles and Silver-spotted Skippers were out in numbers over the flinty turf. Shortly afterwards, Holly Blues became prominent, seemingly throughout southern England. Prior to this I had scarcely encountered this azure jewel. It was to erupt the following spring.

The next year, 1970, was indeed a year of eruptions. Poetry sprang into my life, inspired by a brilliant young English master who understood and taught the importance of metaphor, and who introduced me to the writings of Thoreau and Edward Thomas (W H Hudson and Richard Jefferies had already been discovered).

Girls were being courted, a trio of pretty Horsham wenches by ardent but inaptly dressed young males. Holly Blues were everywhere, for a fine summer was developing. Examinations had erupted like acne, and threatened to ruin the summer. May weather oscillated between extremes. Grizzled and Dingy skippers appeared in the woods around May 10th, Duke of Burgundy a week later, and Pearl-bordered Fritillaries on the 20th, in superb numbers. Six colonies of the latter were in existence that May within a two-mile radius of the school. Small Pearl-bordered Fritillary was well out by the end of that month, in at least eight separate colonies.

Exams generate excellent weather, and did so as usual in 1970. Relief was essential. On June 13th Barter, Last, Oates and Ratnieks consumed a considerable volume of King & Barnes bitter at the Blue Ship, a simple ale house at a lonely hamlet called The Haven in Okehurst Woods, north of Billingshurst, and sobered up by swimming noisily in a nearby lake. Small Pearl-bordered Fritillaries and Meadow Browns abounded in the adjoining young conifer plantations, but were curiously out of focus and duplicitous that hot afternoon.

White Admirals were out in numbers in Marlpost Wood by June 26th. Common Blues abounded in the more open, grassy rides. Ringlet, Small Skipper and Purple Hairstreak were well out by the end of June, and a thriving colony of White-letter Hairstreak was discovered on a tall English Elm close to the First XI cricket pavilion. A stunted Ash tree in a young conifer plantation near Dragons Green harboured dozens of Purple Hairstreaks, which had dropped down from the overheated oaks to feed on honey dew or sticky buds. Three or four could be netted with a single swipe of a net on a length of cut Hazel. The heat intensified, and resulted in another under-age drinking session, this time at the Black Rabbit near Arundel, involving a gaggle of girls. Exams rightly faded into insignificance. Something Big had to give. The anticyclone intensified, something greater than testosterone was rising.

Thursday July 9th was hot and sullen, buzzing with biting clegs and throbbing with merciless hay fever below solid stratus clouds.

The very air itself was pulsating, as if something from another dimension was seeking to break through and conquer a world begging for radical, spiritual change. And indeed it did, at 5.15 pm precisely. Having waited till the last moment before human patience broke, what the Victorian collectors called His Imperial Majesty, the Monarch of all the Butterflies and the Emperor of the Woods finally entered my life. This drama took place just north of Dragons Green, forcing me to my knees. I missed supper, roll call and half of prep (evening homework), and was consequently gated (confined to school grounds) for the remainder of term. But by now I served other masters, and was back in the woods on the following days. At this point the school rather gave up on me, perhaps recognising that my real schooling was taking place elsewhere.

The problem was, of course, that term was ending. Another assault on that bastion of recalcitrance, St Leonard's Forest, ended this time in heat stroke and a large female Silver-washed Fritillary. Nothing more was seen of *iris*, but at least He had been seen, momentarily, but forever – for some visions haunt eternally, particularly those that are real. That lone male, patrolling the high oak edge, flies on within my soul.

August was hot. Holly Blues were everywhere. Two weeks were spent on Guernsey, in the company of best friend and radical thinker Nigel Fleming, whose parents were Guernsey folk. Gatekeepers were profuse there, in multitudes, everywhere; Common Blues and Small Coppers abounded in all open places; and Pleinmont Point, on the south-west side of the island, revealed a massive population of Grayling and groups of scarlet-headed Glanville Fritillary larvae.

In mid-August time was spent in Bernwood Forest, on the clay vale north of Oxford, with Dr Roger Clarke, a retired GP, stalwart of what was then known as BBONT (the county wildlife trust) and an ardent servant of the Purple Emperor. He introduced me to Heslop's book, *Notes & Views of the Purple Emperor*, taught me how to search for Purple Emperor eggs and larvae, and indeed for the adults. He bred the butterfly annually, sometimes in numbers, for release back into the forest, in an attempt to remedy some of the damage done by a then-uncaring Forestry Commission. Bernwood that August was alive with hairstreaks, not just Purple Hairstreaks but the Brown Hairstreak, hitherto an elusive beast found only in the form of occasional eggs in and around Marlpost Wood. I have still never seen Brown Hairstreak in such numbers as in the glades of Waterperry Wood, the southernmost block of Bernwood, that August, and it is a butterfly I have seen annually since. As many as half a dozen were in view at once, high in the oaks, mingling and squabbling with their smaller and greyer cousins. Males descended to feed on bramble and Angelica flowers. It must have been an exceptional butterfly year.

But revolution was fiercely in the air. The Isle of Wight Festival at the end of August attracted 600,000 young people, including the odd one who had travelled to see the poet–songwriter Leonard Cohen and encounter the exquisitely beautiful Adonis Blue on the south-facing slope of Compton Down. Life then consisted of an unsustainable juxtaposition of diametrically opposed worlds.

By 1971, butterfly enthusiasts, and indeed naturalists, amongst the boys at Christ's Hospital could be numbered on the fingers of one hand. This indicates what a wonderful job old Jonah had done in firing up ten-year-olds, most of whom were from urban backgrounds and could not tell the difference between a Blue Tit and a Great Tit. The woods to the south were then effectively mine. Moreover, as a senior pupil one was now entitled to a bicycle (though I had already had a rickety one secreted in a thicket for a year or so). Frequent if short visits to the woods were fully enabled.

May started fine, such that the woodland fritillaries emerged early, but shortly afterwards cloud descended. The solution was simple: search for larvae, and carry on regardless. White-letter Hairstreak larvae proved to be numerous on mature Wych Elms along Crookhorn Lane, an ancient drove-way that ran straight through Madgeland Wood. Even a Brown Hairstreak larva was found, after hours of searching on unsuitable old Blackthorn. Inspired, I went for White Admiral larvae, and found them at an average of one per hour. But extensive searches during a dull early June for Purple Emperor larvae produced, insultingly, a larva of the wrong emperor – the Emperor Moth.

The weather improved at the end of June, bringing out the White Admiral on July 2nd. But it was a 'late' season. Small Pearl-bordered Fritillaries lasted well into July, especially in St Leonard's Forest, and I even saw a Dingy Skipper in Madgeland Wood on July 5th, a very late date for this spring butterfly in a wood. July intensified into brooding heat.

Again everything came down to the last Sunday of the summer term. Marlpost Wood produced a good showing of White Admiral and Ringlet, the latter then a rather local butterfly in the district. Then, in the early afternoon, a large and pristine male Purple Emperor chose to fly low along the lane past a sallow-rich copse near Dragons Green. With a twirl, he hopped over the Hazel hedge and ascended into the oaks, smashing someone's dreams in the process. There was only one option: go home, do the bored teenager act for a few perfunctory days, then return to camp out in the woods, and enter the real world.

Camping wild in the woods, though decidedly uncool in terms of teenage behavioural values, was a remarkably easy thing to do in that era. Southwater Forest was virtually unvisited, at least outside the hunting season. The few people who walked dogs in the area favoured the lanes, which at their busiest produced a maximum of one vehicle every ten minutes. These were mainly retired farm workers, gentle friends who knew how to turn a blind eye and could recognise a fellow lover of their rural idyll. Someone called Bert on a red Ferguson tractor used to mow the rides in midsummer, unnecessarily so as it merely massacred a wonderful show of Cat's-ears. The Forestry Commission rarely appeared. Armed with Thoreau and a small tent I entered my own personal Walden. 'I lived alone, in the woods, a mile from any neighbor,' began Thoreau. But that first night, long after the embers of a small camp fire had faded, a Stoat caught a Rabbit some way down the ride. The piercing screams were like those of a banshee. It took two petrified minutes to realise what was going on, and considerably longer to calm down. Then it began to rain, but there is something wonderfully calming about the patter of gentle raindrops on a tent roof. The woods had accepted me as one of their own. On subsequent evenings I watched Fox cubs playing merrily just a few metres down the ride.

The first day was largely cloudy, clearing up later, for the woods knew how I should start. Induction took the form of experiencing the evening flight of the Purple Hairstreak, for the first time. Hitherto, this had been an indolent creature of the oak tops, but now it suddenly revealed its true self, dragging the young observer into its proper world: twenty or thirty of them dancing in courting pairs or trios, and dashing about along the oak edges, in the delight of July evening air. The truth dawned: they are crepuscular, becoming quiescent during the heat of the day! That evening, lying in the dust along a stretch of baked ride I found a single blue feather from a Jay's wing. It was a token of acceptance from the woods, and perhaps from the Emperor of the Woods himself, the Purple Emperor. I fastened it to my hat band. That act established a personal tradition, for almost every July I find a Jay's feather along a ride, and wear it in my hat. Years later I found an appealing passage in an account of collecting in the New Forest

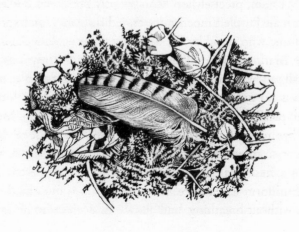

during the immortal summer of 1893: to paraphrase, the writer had stumbled into paradise in searing heat, sat down beneath a veteran oak and placed a cast Jay's feather in his hat – as a token of acceptance.

Suitably hatted, I was thus ready to be finally accepted into the realm of His Imperial Majesty on Thursday July 22nd 1971. Herself, as the Empress has become known, conducted the first initiations, flying into the crowns of two tall sallows, doubtless to lay eggs, but way out of reach. Four high-flying males were seen, aloof and far off, in a treetop world.

Saturday the 24th began wet and wild, but cleared by noon into a sunny but windy afternoon. Rather by accident on my part, but perhaps by the deliberate design of a higher authority, I discovered the high ashram of the Purple Emperor in the Dragons Green copses. There, a clump of four tall Silver Birch trees towered above a canopy of Hazel, sallow and planted Yew on a low wooded summit. Downwind, to the south-west, was a twenty-year-old conifer plantation choked with sallows, a fine breeding ground for *iris*. Two or three Purple Emperor males battled high up in the lee of this birch clump, dominated by one particularly large and distinctive male. I named him Osiris. The same weather and activity occurred the following day, then atmospheric pressure rose as an anticyclone moved in from the south-west.

At 9.15 am, precisely, on Monday July 26th, another large and perfect male Purple Emperor descended from on high to pierce the soul of one who stood by the eastern gate into Madgeland Wood, off the Marlpost Road. The hoof-printed ride there was fringed with tall sallows, leaning inwards from a young Beech plantation. This was no ordinary male, for in the corners of his hindwings were atypically enlarged and prominent pink-red ocelli. Moreover, there was no vestige of purple, or of the bright royal blue the Emperor so often displays; instead, this male possessed the light blue of a fresh male Adonis Blue, though more electric in tone and of uniform iridescence. In such situations one should simply freeze, without breathing, and allow His Majesty to settle to feed on the ride, which He usually will. But no one had told me that, and it is not an easy skill to master in such stimulating company. The Vision, for such it was, flew off in a huff, but haunts the mind still. Minds, of course, enjoy being haunted so.

Yet the spell was not broken. Further down the lane another, more typical male performed similarly. That afternoon, at least five males conducted their 'Battle Royale' (as one Victorian collector termed it) around the birch clump down towards Dragons Green. At one point three tussled together, magnificently, chasing each other high up, out of sight. Osiris himself – the same male I had seen two days earlier – led this ritual, dominating possession of the sheltered leeward side of the birch clump.

It would take something of cataclysmic importance to drag me away from that Paradise-on-Earth. And it did. A casual, celebratory telephone call home revealed that my sister was dangerously ill in hospital in London. Camp was upped, three miles were force-marched to Christ's Hospital station, and London was hastily reached. Sister duly recovered. The 1971 Purple Emperor season had passed at its peak. Another summer was over.

5 Into the green

It is a mistake to read *Notes & Views of the Purple Emperor* during one's A-level year for, unlike most A-level textbooks, it is addictive. It transports the reader into Heslop's world, a world of singular, obsessive quest deep into one of Nature's strangest mysteries – the ecology of our most elusive and odd butterfly, the Purple Emperor. But it is wrong to view the book merely as the product of obsession and rampant theorisation, which on a superficial level it surely is. It is far more than that. Proper study launches the reader on a personal journey towards the truth. No other book is remotely like it. One should be able to study it for A-level.

Nature's woods offer such a world, for forests are slow to reveal their secrets, drawing you in until they know you trust them. Once you are under their spell, forests will close around you, if you let them. They will then absorb you. They may also send you away, perhaps for years, before calling you back. Places, perhaps wood especially, can establish you as theirs.

Spring was somewhat late in 1972, May was indifferent, and June unrelentingly wet. Then, predictably, the A-level examinations at the end of the month brought with them a massive anticyclone, luring an entranced mind away from the exam hall. The hot weather actually persisted after the wretched things had finished. But by now the season was decidedly late. White Admirals did not emerge before July 12th, and then only appeared in horrifyingly low numbers. Later I learnt that White Admiral populations fluctuate acutely in those woods, erupting in fine summers (especially during good summer sequences), but imploding to token population levels after wet Junes. The high summer of 1972 was dominated by the Ringlet, which was profuse in grassy rides and pockets of rough meadowland that year. Previously it had been rather local, occurring in small loose colonies here and there.

School finally dispensed with my services on July 17th. I had failed to take in both hands most of the opportunities it offered, largely because my real schooling had taken place in the woods and lanes, and was unfinished. Make no mistake, no pupil has loved Christ's Hospital as a place more, for that may not be humanly possible. The fact that its many characters and complex rituals were perplexingly Gormenghastian is secondary here. It is a deeply beautiful place, within a landscape of intense natural beauty. Although I left school with ease, I could not leave that landscape behind – it had claimed me. The Purple Emperor calls his servants – or perhaps they are merely addicts – home. A week after leaving school I returned there by train, sped through the place like a ghost, carrying a cumbersome rucksack, heading once more for the woods. There was no alternative. Unfortunately the weather deteriorated, badly, and I was forced to return home, wherever and whatever that was. But before the abandonment one great afternoon was experienced, with three, four or maybe even five male Purple Emperors battling it out around the clump of Silver Birch trees, and the odd female skulking nearby amongst the sallows. White Admiral, though, was almost non-existent, and Purple Hairstreak numbers were about ten per cent of the previous two years' standard. 1972 was a shadow of a summer.

Strangely, only one of Jonah's boys dedicated his life to butterflies. But what happened to those other young enthusiasts? Cesar was never heard of again, a lengthy search by his close friend Longhurst failing to find any trace. Longhurst himself emigrated in 1981 and became Australian, even at cricket. Strangely, though, one thing still binds him to his West Sussex birthplace: a love of British butterflies, especially a longing for the Purple Emperor. Periodically he returns to England, in July, on pilgrimage, almost losing his Western Australian accent in the process. It was he who set up the Purple Emperor website, www.thepurpleempire.com, to maintain contact with the only thing he missed about Britain. Johnson was re-encountered briefly in the mid-1990s, professing still a love of Nature and of butterflies, but vanished again, confessing to be a lost soul. The others never resurfaced, perhaps because seventy per cent of Old Blues, as alumni are known, become top income-bracket earners – and butterflies are scarcely compatible with that sort of lifestyle, let alone with the accompanying values. Also, many of their generation simply emigrated during the Thatcher era. Ratnieks did resurface, gloriously, and sober, as Professor of Apiculture at Sussex University. Butterflies have remained an interest. Norman Fryer's son, Tim, developed a bad attack of atavism and became fundamentally Welsh, changed his name to Dafydd and worked as the Forestry Commission's landscape architect for Wales, living in Ceredigion. His interest in butterflies and other wildlife survived, and is threatening to flourish. He writes the most illegible Christmas card messages, probably in Welsh.

And what of the woods themselves?

In the late 1960s the bulk of Marlpost and Madgeland woods consisted of unsullied ranks of dense, unthinned non-native conifers, primarily Norway Spruce but also blocks of Corsican Pine and some Douglas Fir stands. The Forestry Commission had felled and replanted most of the ancient woodland during the 1950s and 1960s, leaving a fringe of old oaks around the edges, an isthmus of natural woodland along a steep-sided stream corridor and a scatter of broad-leaved trees elsewhere. Two small blocks had been replanted with oak, interspersed with Norway Spruce as a nurse crop. Felling and replanting ceased after 1967, so ending the supply of young plantations upon which the early successional stage butterfly species were dependent. Crucially, the Forestry Commission failed to thin the conifer crop, which slowly strangled itself and stopped growing. It is now well known that Norway Spruce grows well for a few years on heavy clay soils, before stopping and then slowly dying.

The broader rides were heavily poached up by the hunt, which regularly patrolled the woods during the winter. Many rides were so heavily ridden that they were rendered almost devoid of vegetation, turning from a gluey morass in the winter to ankle-twisting hoof-print-riddled concrete during dry summer weather. The wider rides were lined with tall broad-leaved sallows and surprisingly large amounts of brome and European Gorse, on which Green Hairstreaks bred. Locally, the rides held a rich flora, with much Betony, Bird's-foot Trefoil, Bugle, Common Knapweed, Devil's-bit Scabious, Primrose and Wood Spurge.

Cattle were occasionally depastured in summer along some rides by an ancient rustic who ran a smallholding in Marlpost Wood. This was Bert or Pete Rusher, depending on his mood. A gnome-like gentleman with a strong Sussex accent, he dressed in shorts and hobnail boots in all weathers, and cycled in daily from nearby Southwater. Though eccentric in many ways, with a science-fiction-orientated imagination that readily transported him to other planets, he was a seriously good stockman. He taught me cattle husbandry. He died during the 1972/73 winter, sitting against an oak trunk, contemplating the sunset. A garish and ostentatious house now stands on the site of his smallholding. Both Pete and Bert must haunt it, without mercy.

In a moment of sublime inspiration, the Forestry Commission surrendered its lease on Dogbarking, Marlpost and Madgeland woods just before the Great Storm of October 16th 1987, probably in an act of divine retribution, felled most of the ailing conifers. The devastation was wondrous – an impenetrable inter-tangled morass of prostrated trunks reminiscent of the early stages of a Great War battle. The place had had enough, and wanted to sort itself out. The purge was finished off by the January 1990 storms. Interestingly, the broad-leaved stands withstood the onslaught, incurring only incidental damage. The wisdom of large-scale silvicultural experimentation with non-native tree species on heavy clay soil had been gloriously exposed. As *Twelfth Night*'s Feste the Jester so aptly put it, 'And thus the whirligig of time brings in its revenges.' The mess was systematically bulldozed, and burnt on massive funereal bonfires that put the foot & mouth pyres of 2001 to shame.

Subsequent changes have been phenomenal, not least because the western half of Marlpost was grazed by horses for several winters, before woodland slowly reasserted itself, mainly in the form of Silver Birch, Pedunculate Oak and hybrid sallows. The place clearly wants to be native broad-leaved woodland again. The grazing seems to have helped the ground flora recover from years of needle acidification, for it is richer in the areas that were grazed. Only a single small block, at the north end of Marlpost, was replanted, with Pedunculate Oak and Ash. It became a good Purple Emperor breeding ground as sallows readily established themselves in it. Hardly a vestige of the conifers remains today. It is almost as if the woods have thoroughly purged themselves, and expunged a wretched era of their history. The eastern half of Marlpost was left to natural regeneration and is well on the way to becoming mixed broad-leaved woodland, containing much Ash, Silver Birch, Pedunculate Oak and sallows. A dozen pairs of Nightingale sing in Marlpost Wood each year, the Bluebell carpet is slowly returning, and Primroses once more line the rides.

The rides themselves have been kept open by occasional mechanical pruning. This means that the bordering sallows take a hit every few years, though they recover remarkably quickly and function as short-rotation pollards. Strangely, the stolid ranks of brome and European Gorse have not recovered, apart from along a couple of short stretches of ride. The woods are used for shooting, and are still used by the hunt, though not as freely as of yore. This means that the rides are less quagmired than formerly. Traffic hums from the east, and aircraft circle overhead whilst waiting to land at Gatwick. The biggest change is that dog walkers have penetrated in numbers, so that the woods are not the secret world they used to be. Moreover, butterfly enthusiasts now abound during the high summer period – photographers, primarily in search of Purple Emperors. This is somewhat detracting, and indeed curious, as there are many better woods in West Sussex for the Big Three – Purple Emperor, White Admiral and Silver-washed Fritillary.

Few features of bygone times remain. One of these is a small and futile water tank, sited to put out forest fires. It is the last surviving relic of an inglorious era. Inscribed in the peeling conifer-green paint is a Greek inscription, taken from Coleridge's *Biographia Literaria*: Αυριον άδιον άσω ('Tomorrow I will sing a sweeter song').

The other woods to the south, old Hazel coppices with standard oaks in the main, have largely been neglected and have closed over. Few butterflies fly there now, other than myriad Purple Hairstreaks around the oaks, as open rides and glades are few and far between. Many of the conifers in little Northlands Wood blew down in one of the great storms, but too many of the wretched things survived and reasserted their stranglehold. Its oak and Bluebell fringe was largely grubbed out in the mid-1970s for agriculture. The wood is a shadowed land now, hanging its sylvan head in shame and shade. Few if any butterflies occur there, other than canopy-dwelling species, Purple Emperor and Purple Hairstreak, which romp about overhead, unseen, and the odd shade-loving Speckled Wood, Meadow Brown and Ringlet. A passing naturalist would never know how profuse and deeply magical the Pearl-bordered and Small Pearl-bordered fritillaries were in Northlands Wood in the late 1960s and early 1970s, or that Duke of Burgundy bred there annually on the Cowslips and Primroses, or that Brown Hairstreak females dropped down to lay their eggs on the Blackthorn suckers, or that Nightingales and Turtle Doves serenaded the stars and sun, when all was well with the world. Of course, it would take only some ride opening and glade creation, or the reintroduction of coppicing for wood fuel, to reinvigorate these southernmost woods, their ground flora and their butterflies. Woods go in eras, and sleep for a while (they do that annually, each winter). The most south-westerly of the woods, Hoe Wood, a woodland of considerably antiquity, was grubbed out during the late 1970s, for agriculture. Many of the hedges intertwining within that landscape also disappeared around that time.

In terms of the butterflies themselves, four former resident species are now extinct in these woods: the three spring fritillaries and the Wall Brown. Small Heath and Green Hairstreak appear also to be lost, but residency and extinction can be very hard to prove. Several other species have declined noticeably, in particular White-letter Hairstreak and the two spring skippers, though all three of these have hung on and are starting to recover. Only Essex Skipper and Marbled White have definitely colonised, though Brown Argus is probably becoming a true resident. Silver-washed Fritillary has increased spectacularly, and is now fairly numerous around oak stands. The Purple Emperor has remained impervious to all this change. It probably flies no more in some of the Dragons Green woods, though there are still reasonable populations in Madgeland, in two areas of Marlpost, and in Dogbarking Wood. There, Norman Fryer's old 'Master Oaks' – three oaks at the ride intersection on a sheltered high point – are still used by Purple Emperor males each afternoon. There dwell the high spirits of the midsummer forest.

The simple truth is that the woods and their butterfly faunas have changed beyond recognition during the forty-plus years. Change here has not simply been gradual or iterative, for at times it has been sudden, dramatic and unforeseen. Everything changes. Everything is phase. Change is the norm.

A digression, into names

For persistent mucking about in double Latin one winter term, the master (whom we shall call Mr Kegley, perhaps because he was keg-shaped) sentenced me to double detention – only he forgot to set me anything to do. So the time was spent determining the derivations of some of the Greek and Latin names of British butterflies. This was excellent self-punishment. Armed with a huge Latin dictionary and Robert Graves's *The Greek Myths* I set upon the task. It was so enjoyable and revealing that I carried on, long after detention had ended, almost managing to work out the lot. The venture took most of a wintry term. This, rather than hours of Herodotus and Vergil, fired up some passing interest in the Classics. Kegley had no sense of humour whatsoever and consequently said the funniest things imaginable, which in front of a class of fourteen-year-olds is fatal. Double Latin on Thursday afternoons was side-splitting, painfully so at times. Kegley once caught me sugaring for moths at a midnight hour, but I managed to persuade him that I was praying to a conveniently placed water hydrant, having developed a bad attack of religion. With Kegley, there was little point in telling the truth as it would not have been believed. He was last seen, in 1975, dressed in plus-fours.

We must be grateful to the work of A Maitland Emmet (1908–2001), an Oxford classicist and keen entomologist, who dedicated his retirement to researching and writing *The Scientific Names of the British Lepidoptera: their History and Meaning* (1991). Compared with his work, my own efforts pale into insignificance, though we reached similar conclusions (in the late 1980s we fell out, amicably, over the meaning behind the genus *Apatura*).

Our butterflies have the most glorious names, both English and scientific, which are the legacy of centuries of wonder and study. Both types of name have great resonance, and influence our perception of the character of our butterflies. The names have meant an immense amount to butterfly enthusiasts over time and are an essential part of what appeals to us about these creatures. However, the names are not fixed in tablets of stone, having always been subject to alteration, following changes in taxonomic knowledge and fashion. Changes are regularly made to the scientific names, so much so that at present the English names tend to provide better stability, though they themselves are also subject to occasional modification.

The English (or common, or vernacular) names of individual species attempt to be descriptive, though in a rather idiosyncratic language. Skippers skip in flight, swallowtails have long forked-wing tails, hairstreaks have fine hair-like lines on the hindwing undersides, tortoiseshells are tortoiseshell-coloured, and the name fritillary may be derived from the Latin *fritillus*, the chequered dice-box of a popular Roman gambling game. The assonance is superb. Without doubt, the English names capture the characters we attribute to our butterflies, especially in conjunction with the Greek and Latin of the scientific names.

It took decades for the English names of our butterflies to be agreed, as different names were assigned by different pioneer authors. For example, the Silver-washed Fritillary was originally recorded (in 1699) as the Greater Silver-streaked Fritillary, and eleven years later another author named it the Silver-stroaked Fritillary. Then, in 1717, the sexes, which differ visibly, were named as separate species: the Greater Silverstreakt Orange Fritillary (males) and the Greater Silverstreakt Golden Fritillary (females). In a book of

1769 the insect was recognised as a single species, called the Great Fritillary, just after the names Silver-washed Fritillary and Silver-wash Fritillary, a variant, had been introduced by another author. The Victorians finally opted for the Silver-washed Fritillary, and we should be grateful to them for settling matters down. Only now it all too often appears as the silver-washed fritillary, for the lowercase is in vogue – wrongly so in my opinion, as it hinders or confuses adjectival use.

Since the late Victorian era the English names have remained relatively constant, bar a few shifts and changes. For example, what I learnt as the Duke of Burgundy Fritillary has since reverted to an older name, the Duke of Burgundy. Additionally, the Small Mountain Ringlet became the ordinary Mountain Ringlet, and the Hedge Brown became known as the Gatekeeper. No one knows how His Grace the Duke of Burgundy received that name in the first place, any reasoning being lost in the mists of entomological antiquity.

If anything, the common names of moths are even more capti-vating. Many of the family names are wonderful: there are families of footman moths, hawkmoths, hooktips, pugs, underwings and wainscots. Many of the individual species names are remarkable, often in the extreme, with the Clifden Nonpareil and Death's Head Hawkmoth being unforgettable. Other truly wondrous British moth names include The Alchymist, Brussels Lace, Chimney Sweeper, Double Kidney, Emperor Moth and Feathered Gothic. Merveille du Jour and True Lover's Knot are also impressive, but the pick of the bunch has to be the Setaceous Hebrew Character, a thoroughly boring common grey moth that irritates moth enthusiasts by being annoyingly abundant in moth traps in late summer. This was also the nickname of Baron Charles de Worms (1904–1980), on account of his Austrian-Jewish ancestry and him being distinctly hairless and notably eccentric. The Baron will make a spectacular entry into this book in due course.

The scientific names of the bulk of our butterflies were determined by the father of scientific nomenclature, Carolus

Linnaeus (1707–1778). Greek and Latin were used by the likes of Linnaeus in an attempt to find a universal language. Scientific names can be rather a mouthful, especially for anyone who was, perhaps mercifully, not taught the Classics. And as if two names in a strange tongue are not enough, sometimes there is a third, identifying the subspecies.

In the scientific names of British butterflies, Greek dominates amongst both the genus and the species names. Some of our butterflies have a Greek genus and a Latin specific name, such as *Thymelicus* (Greek) *sylvestris* (Latin), the Small Skipper. Occasionally, a hybrid word between Greek and Latin is used, to the deep chagrin of true Classicists, and a few of our butterfly names are non-Classical in origin (some are Biblical).

In terms of individual species names, 28 of our resident butterflies are named after characters in Greek mythology. These include four gods or demi-gods: Cinxia (Glanville Fritillary), Iris (Purple Emperor), Paphia (Silver-washed Fritillary) and Palaemon (Chequered Skipper). In addition, Thalia (Heath Fritillary, known as *athalia*), Euphrosyne (Pearl-bordered Fritillary) and Aglaia (Dark Green Fritillary) were Muses and/or Graces. Also, Lucina (Duke of Burgundy) was the Roman goddess of childbirth and of the spring.

On the debit side, three of our butterflies are named after young ladies who were ravished by Zeus: Antiopa (Camberwell Beauty), Io (Peacock) and Semele (Grayling). Poor Io had a particularly hard time of it: Zeus took a fancy to the wench but Hera, Mrs Zeus, who was also his older sister, objected and turned the poor girl into a heifer. Not to be outdone, Zeus transformed himself into a bull and, to complete the agricultural allusion, served the heifer. Worse befell hapless Semele, who mothered the god Dionysius (Bacchus). Jealous Hera persuaded the girl to ask Zeus to appear before her in his full splendour. This proved too much for a mortal girl, who spontaneously combusted.

Several other characters met sticky ends, notably Actaeon (Lulworth Skipper), who, whilst out hunting, came across the goddess Artemis bathing. Fatally, he chose to watch, voyeuristically, and was spotted, then duly chased and eaten by his own hounds. Tithonus (Gatekeeper) was a Trojan youth to whom Eos, the goddess of the dawn, took a fancy; she persuaded the powers that be to grant him everlasting life, but stupidly forgot to ask for everlasting youth, so that the boy withered away and was last seen hopping about as a grasshopper or a cicada (depending on the source).

Other celebrities include Argus (Silver-studded Blue), a hundred-eyed monster who failed to protect Io from the ravages of Zeus after being instructed to do so by Mrs Zeus; Arion (Large Blue), a singer–poet who was thrown overboard, for singing and/or reciting long after being asked and then ordered to stop, and was rescued by dolphins who actually liked hearing him; Atalanta (Red Admiral), a famous beauty and athlete who raced her suitors and killed them if they lost, until one cheated and won her; Icarus (Common Blue), an early and unsuccessful pioneer of flight, who used waxed feathers that melted when he flew too close to the sun; and Machaon (Swallowtail), a Greek doctor in the Trojan wars, who may possibly have existed.

Some of our butterflies are named after particularly obscure Greeks. Most notable here are Hyperantus (Ringlet) and Pamphilus (Small Heath), two of the fifty sons of Aegyptus, who did little other than beget those fifty sons. They were betrothed to, and slaughtered on their communal wedding night by, their female cousins, the fifty daughters of Danaus. Why any of this took place remains unclear, as are the connections with two of our more mundane butterflies.

Thirteen of our butterflies are named after plants with which they are supposed to be associated. These are mostly Latin names, such as *cardui* (Painted Lady), which simply means 'of thistle'; *rubi* (Green Hairstreak), which means 'of bramble'; and *quercus* (Purple Hairstreak), the Latin for oak. These three butterflies are all associated with these plants, weakly so in the case of the Green Hairstreak. A few of our butterflies have been seriously misnamed after inappropriate plants, notably the Wood White, which is wrongly named *sinapis* after the mustard family, with which it has no association, and the Brown Hairstreak, which is inappropriately named after the Latin for birch, *Betula*, whereas it breeds on Blackthorn, *Prunus*. It is downright absurd that these two erroneous names remain in use when so many other names have been altered by zealous taxonomists.

The names of six of our butterflies are derived from words that supposedly describe their appearance, habit or habitat. Thus *sylvestris* (Small Skipper) means 'of the wood', which is odd as it is a grassland insect; *lineola* (Essex Skipper) is a descriptive term meaning a small line, referring to the male sex brand on the forewing upperside; whereas the Clouded Yellow, Large Tortoiseshell and Scotch Argus are named after colours – *croceus* (saffron-coloured), *polychloros* (pale green) and *aethiops* (dark-coloured). Neither Emmet nor the youthful Oates was able to determine the origins of the names of the Brown Argus (*agestis*) and the humble Meadow Brown (*jurtina*).

The names of the genera (plural of genus) have similar origins. Ten generic names are derived from Greek or Roman personages. These include Cupid, the Roman god of love, after whom we have the genus *Cupido*, which includes our Small Blue, though in Latin the word *cupido* is the verb for desire. The Dingy Skipper belongs to the genus *Erynnis*, derived from the Erynyes or Greek Furies, a gang of nasty winged creatures that mercilessly harried wrongdoers. This is an appropriate name for this belligerent butterfly. *Pieris*, the genus of the true whites, is named after one of the Muses, and *Aricia*, the genus of the brown arguses, is named after the stepdaughter of Theseus, a Greek hero. Some of the generic names are pure biological description, such as *Carterocephalus* (genus that includes our Chequered Skipper), which means strong-headed; *Anthocharis* (genus that includes our Orange-tip), which effectively means 'grace of a flower' in Greek; and *Lasiommata* (genus that includes our Wall Brown), which means hairy-eyed. The genus *Thymelicus* (Small and Essex skippers) comes from one of the chorus members in Greek drama, a dancer. Finally, and importantly, the genus *Papilio* (swallowtails) uses the Latin noun for a butterfly.

Aberrations (or variations) that have been formally described have a more varied name base. Again, many are derived from classical figures or from Greek or Latin terms, but many have been named after entomologists, and a few after places. You cannot name an aberration after yourself, but an aberration can take your name if given it by someone else – for example, if created in your memory. The term aberration is almost invariably shortened to ab., as in ab. *nigrina*, the rare all-black colour form of the White Admiral. Aberration names, like specific names, always take the lowercase, even when named after a person or place, and are italicised. Some aberration names are clearly designed to generate serious angst amongst teenage Latin scholars. For example, ab. *lugenda*, the nearly all-purple form of the Purple Emperor, is an example of one of the nastiest devices in language – a declined gerundive (feminine), the sort of thing that is used as a weapon of mass destruction by Classics teachers. *Lugenda* here means mournfulness.

Taxonomists (Whom God Preserve) will not even leave the names of aberrations alone. What I learnt as ab. *iole* has largely been replaced by the name ab. *lugenda*, and rather downgraded in the process. Iole was indirectly responsible for the death of Heracles (Hercules), the ultimate Greek hero. Heracles set out to win Iole, a princess of excessive beauty, even though he was already married to the ageing Deianeira. Iole resisted, totally, even after Heracles had won her fair and square in an archery contest and had slain her family in front of her, and she had thrown herself out of the window. Chaste, lovely beyond bounds and utterly unattainable, she was eventually wedded and bedded by one of Heracles's sons, after Heracles himself had been accidentally poisoned by Deianeira. Heracles died in agony and Deianeira committed suicide. The lesson is simple: do not on any account aspire after the likes of Iole, as attaining the unattainable brings disaster. Technically, ab. *iole* of

the Purple Emperor still exists, although it is now not allowed to have any vestige of white on it whatsoever, such that I am unsure whether any true specimens exist in museums. Nonetheless, true ab. *iole* is the main thing I am seeking on this earth. As Heracles appreciated, one needs targets.

Only a few aberration names readily make sense, such as ab. *obscura* (the dark version of several species), and many make little if any sense at all. Sometimes, especially with some of the blues, a specimen may be an example of more than one aberration. Thus, in the Chalkhill Blue, of which over 400 aberrations were listed by Bright and Leeds in their 1938 monograph of this highly variable species, multi-variation specimens exist which are described as being ab. *fowleri + alba* and ab. *antiextrema + postalba + limbojunct*. The record is undoubtedly held by a specimen H A Leeds named as ab. *infrasemisyngrapha + grisealutescens + albocrenata*, which involves a staggering 44 letters. The old entomologists took language into pastures new. They also knew their Latin and Greek, having been exceedingly well taught by the likes of Emmet and Kegley.

The scientific terms for the four stages of a butterfly's life cycle are borrowed from the Latin. You would therefore think that the terms ovum (plural ova), larva (larvae), pupa (pupae) and imago (imagines) are from the Latin words for egg, caterpillar, chrysalis and butterfly. Sure enough, *ovum* directly translates as egg, but *larva* is the Latin for a ghost or mask, *pupa* means a doll, and *imago* means what it looks like, an image or appearance. It is hard to determine why these odd words were chosen. For the record, the Latin for a caterpillar is *eruca*, for a chrysalis is *chrysallis*, which is borrowed from the Greek, and for a butterfly is *papilio*.

Classicists get rather worked up over the way science has transmogrified and bastardised the languages of Homer and Vergil for its own convoluted purposes. Taxonomists now change the scientific names with surprising regularity, so frequently in fact that it is small wonder that people choose today to use the English names. But in the 1960s even schoolboys tended to use the Latin or Greek names, with relish, not least because it provided some justification for the hours spent learning two dead and seemingly impossible languages. The truth is that these names are an integral part of the butterflying experience, as they have acoustic resonance and are genuinely musical. They also assist the natural tendency many of us have to anthropomorphise about butterflies beyond the bounds of reason. Above all, butterfly enthusiasts become strongly attached to the names, English and scientific, which they learn as beginners – a point apparently lost on taxonomists in museum underworlds or university research blocks. This must surely be because the names themselves are integral to the precious memories that butterflying engenders.

6 *Desperately seeking Rima*

In the high summer of 1973 the Sussex woods provided a most necessary haven from the unreality of student life. July, however, was wild, wet and windy, matching what was going on in my mind. During the winter some bright spark had constructed a slurry lagoon in one of the better Purple Emperor woods in Southwater Forest, down towards Dragons Green. By mid-July the lagoon was half-full of glistening, stinking dairy slurry. Had the weather been hot and sunny this might have constituted a gigantean attraction for Purple Emperors, which – like many tropical butterflies – do not feed from flowers but are renowned for favouring unsavoury substances. But the hot weather had been and gone, and had in part been spent on an expedition into the Highlands west of Fort William, in pursuit of what proved to be the last Chequered Skippers and Pearl-bordered Fritillaries of the year, and a multitude of Small Pearl-bordered Fritillaries. I was lucky to find the skipper, for in those days there were no books, let alone websites, telling of localities. Indeed, localities for the rarer species were kept as closely guarded secrets. One had to explore, and explore one did. With the Pearl-bordered Fritillaries, it was odd to see familiar butterflies in such unfamiliar terrain, in this case no longer creatures of young conifer plantations in clay woodland but of lightly grazed bracken hillsides above a loch-side path along which the Bonnie Prince had fled after Culloden. The fritillaries looked different too, with darker spots on the hindwing undersides. Strangely, this expedition was not recorded in my diaries, so the memories are vague.

But the Emperor was calling, and would be dutifully recorded. I arrived in my old woods on July 14th, to find a Jay's feather lying on the ride for me and the Emperor emerging in remarkably good numbers. In keeping with the weather, the males were in a foul mood that season, vicious and violent, chasing each other, and small birds, around with malevolent intent, especially around the shrubby fringes of the slurry lagoon. There I witnessed a Great Spotted Woodpecker shriek in fear, and a Chiffchaff panic like Piglet pursued by a heffalump. Over Osiris's birches there was even an assault on a passing Heron, which croaked in surprise. The Dragons Green Emperors remain the most violent I have encountered, though their numbers are now considerably reduced. That season, the males were repeatedly searching the tops of the sallows and birches that fringed the pungent lagoon, especially during the mid to late morning period. If you could put up with the smell the lagoon was an amazing place to watch their antics. Years later I realised what they were up to: they were searching the sallows for freshly emerged females in need of male services, 'sallow searching' as I termed it. This they do in some if not all localities, until all the females are out and mated.

By 1973 I had gone through the stage of wanting to find which butterflies were out and about, where and when, and was critically observing what they were doing, and asking why. Why on earth did it just do that? What is it seeking? Had I been a science student, rather than a failing English scholar, I might have done much better. But in terms of depth of experience the ten days spent in the woods during the height of the 1973 Purple Emperor season were profoundly memorable.

I even netted my very first Purple Emperor, my first specimen of *Apatura iris*. Previously, I had only had one genuine chance, by the Madgeland gate on July 26th 1971, which I botched badly, for in those days the Emperors seldom flew lower than 4 metres in Southwater Forest, and then only momentarily and at speed. During that era in those woods they fed high up, in the trees, and seldom if ever sought minerals from the forest floor. But now, pleased with my success, I carefully carried the male in my binoculars case up to the old school to be photographed by a delighted Norman Fryer, then released it back home. Later I netted a second, older male. In contrast to the established custom, these specimens were released unharmed – raising the question of why catch them in the first place? The truth is that this butterfly had entrapped me, rather than the other way round. I also watched a female feed from sap running from a wound where two oak branches had rubbed together. That sap run was utilised for the following two years. The branches remain today, fused together, but have long since died. In the near future they will descend to earth together, perhaps in an autumn gale. And as for the slurry lagoon, it was never used by farmer or Emperor again. Doubtless the taxpayer had funded it. In time it scrubbed over, with sallows, and was reclaimed by the Emperor as a breeding ground.

The White Admirals were up to something that year. On July 16th I spotted my first 'Black Admiral', what is now known as ab. *obliterae* but was then called ab. *semi-nigrina*. This is the aberration (or variation) with significantly reduced white bars. The diary recalls: *It looked very small and black in flight, for the white bars give* L. camilla *its size.* Indeed, I almost mistook it for an odd-flying Ringlet. Two more specimens were seen in other parts of

Southwater that summer. I had never dreamt it possible to see such a beast, though an Old Blue I once met out collecting in Marlpost Wood had informed me that both ab. *semi-nigrina* and even the much rarer ab. *nigrina*, the all-black Admiral, had been collected by boys at the school there during the Second World War.

As the Emperor season was on the wane, I migrated on to the South Downs and walked the length of the West Sussex downs from Harting Downs to the Adur, a young man with long hair, a rucksack and a small tent, furtively watched by locals in quiet rural pubs and giggled at by teenage girls at bus stops. I had no agenda and took no particular route, following my intuition or being guided by the spirit, Holy or otherwise. I even spent a comfortable night, alone, on Chanctonbury Ring, naively oblivious of its status as one of the most haunted places in Britain. All I knew about it was that the young Laurie Lee had slept there, time ago, when he was walking out one midsummer morning. It was a rather peaceful star-filled night in fact, but then I wore a Jay's feather in my hat. Marbled Whites were everywhere, often in clouds, though ageing fast. Here and there were Chalkhill Blue colonies, whilst Dark Green Fritillaries battled against the wind on downland crests. But this was not a butterflying expedition, it was an exploration of a previously unknown hinterland, a pushing back of bounds, and a celebration of summer in the south country. I took with me W H Hudson's *Green Mansions*, one of the strangest books in the English language, an allegory on humankind's relationship with Nature. It tells of a young man's discovery of, and love for, a tropical forest bird-girl, Rima, who dresses in a smock of spider webs. As he penetrates further into the jungle – no mere forest this – he loses his European identity and falls in love with Rima, who of course embodies Nature. She is a shape-shifter – girl, bird, butterfly, flower, jungle monkey, the lot. She falls for the young man, of course, for she loves all things, and even more predictably he kills her, in one of her animal manifestations, whilst out hunting. Finally, and symbolically, he returns to civilisation bearing Rima's ashes in an ossuary. I had planned to visit Hudson's grave, in

Worthing cemetery, but went off the idea after accidentally leaving the book behind in a pub somewhere along the way. Of course, *Green Mansions* was not on my university course reading list, little that I read was. I could never have written a critical essay on it anyway, for it spoke above the academic level, to the human soul itself. And as for seeking Rima, I had already found her, only her name was Iris, or was it Iole? Years later I discovered that Edward Thomas's mentor, the great Victorian nature writer Richard Jefferies, is buried in the same Worthing cemetery. Years later still, I visited to scatter rose petals on both graves.

Life was directionless in 1974. I was supposed to be contemplating Heidegger's 'Yet poetically man dwells upon this earth', but it was too blindingly obvious for lengthy consideration, especially when Keats's 'The poetry of earth is never dead' is added. Fortunately, the butterflies held firm, and held me firm with them, though the Purple Emperor was rather a shadow of himself that year. Perhaps I arrived in the woods too late in the Emperor season, having hitch-hiked and wandered around the Highlands in search of the Mountain Ringlet, that dusky denizen of the high hills, who flies only in the warmth of the sun and vanishes into tussocks when mountain clouds come scudding over. By the time I found a colony, high on Ben Lawers, a greater butterfly was calling. But foolishly, I took a lengthy detour, via the New Forest. I had only visited the Forest briefly and superficially once before, passing through en route to the Isle of Wight, and knew little of it, other than that it was the spiritual home of British lepidopterists and that it had been even more ruthlessly vandalised by the conifer revolution than the West Sussex woods. Despite seeing, for the first time, Silver-washed Fritillary in numbers and some impressive High Brown Fritillaries feeding on tall Marsh Thistles around Ramnor Inclosure, north of Brockenhurst, I did not feel at home there at all. The sallows were absent, the very soil itself seemed wrong – too acidic – and much of the vegetation was grazed and browsed to obvious entomological detriment. I was not ready for the New Forest. I belonged elsewhere, somewhere that was still itself.

Eventually arriving at Southwater, I found it was the year of the Purple Hairstreak. They abounded, in far greater numbers than before, putting on spectacular evening flights high up along the wood edges, even well away from their beloved oaks. On July 23rd, around 5.30 pm, the diary records that forty or fifty could be seen in a vista along one short stretch of oak edge, a vista less than 80 metres wide. Finally, on the 26th, I cracked what they were up to on those warm, still early evenings – doing their courtship and mating. At 6.30 pm that evening, after a damp day, I watched a pair join and mate, staying paired, motionless, wings closed, within an oak leaf spray, until separating fifty minutes later at 7.20. So that's what they were up to!

There were 'Black Admirals' again, two of them, though this time I instantly recognised them for what they were. However, the Emperor was aloof and distant, having forsaken his slurry lagoon. With the wondrous benefit of hindsight I can suggest why: I had arrived just a little too late in the flight season, after all the females had emerged and been mated, and had missed the period during which the males search the sallows. But they nonetheless put on some good shows. At last I watched females laying eggs inside the sallow bushes, and again watched a magnificent display of battling males around Osiris's birches. I even discovered that after hot days, during which they take a lengthy siesta, they may indulge in an evening flight, mingling with, and often attacking, Purple Hairstreaks. Holly Blues were on the increase again, having vanished during the rotten summer of 1972, and White-letter Hairstreaks were popping up all over the place, even in the George & Dragon down at Dragons Green.

I found my first Sparrowhawk's nest, which sounds ridiculous until it is remembered that the bird was then only beginning to recover from the effects of DDT poisoning and decades of predator persecution. Indeed, I think I saw my first ever Sparrowhawk in 1972. The adults were incredibly wary, and utterly silent, nesting high in an old oak above a woodland pond, rearing two young. These left the nest on July 28th, but remained in the nearby oaks for a couple of days. It is strange to recall that prior to 1974 I had seen far more of the Hobby, itself a rarity then, which had nested annually in the lonely Brooks Green woods since at least 1971.

The remainder of the good summer of 1974 was spent working in a factory that made plastic lipstick holders, talking cricket with migrant workers from Pakistan. Students do a lot of utterly pointless things, but then a great many people have to perform generally pointless tasks in order to earn a living. The lipstick holders were sent to the other side of the country, where lipstick was inserted, before they were transported 200 miles in another direction to be packed into boxes, only to be winged to a distribution centre near to where they had started out. In due course, the firm went burst.

Evening flight (ψυχή)

Where the evening sky hangs still,
Shafts of July sun stretch softly
Warm along the wood edge oaks;
Living dust ascends within the heat,
In particles, miasmic and opaque,
To greet the climax of the day;
For there, just there, entirely there,
Within the sun's last radiance,
Grey sprites of frenzied vibrancy
Circle dance the living air,
In celebration of Midsummer's days;
Engulfed within the moment that is all
And everything to those in courtship
Of a life beyond an evening of eternity.
Then pray, my spirit, deftly pray
That you might join the dance of Psyche,
And these small butterflies that worship her,
In tones of iridescent purple and of humble grey,
Before they drift into the forest night
To mate for now, and for eternity.

7 *Walden*

Anyone with an interest in British butterflies in the mid-1970s would have seized the opportunity to move to East Hampshire. My mother, who had backed me through thick and very thick, provided me with such an opportunity. John Heath's *Provisional Atlas of British Butterflies* had recently been published, indicating that over forty species occurred there. This was due largely to the varied geology and habitat diversity, but also to assiduous recording by Dr J W O Holmes, a retired GP and good all-round entomologist who moved to Linford, near Bordon, in the mid-1960s. The district was eulogised by no less a mortal than the Baron de Worms, in his regular jottings in *The Entomologist's Record* which I had studied in the university library, whilst failing to research an essay on Dickens or whatever. Selborne, the birthplace of natural history, was close by, though on perusing Gilbert White's *Natural History* it was disappointing to discover that he only once mentions butterflies, and then only to describe a vagrant Swallowtail bumbling down Selborne High Street. Consequently, Gilbert should be mentioned just this once in these chapters. More importantly, I now lived close to Edward Thomas's heartland. I knew Thomas more as a superb writer of rural prose than as a poet, and relished the prospect of getting close to him in spirit. So the decision was easily made, though first university had to be completed – and although it was in theory a privilege to be there I was in fact bored, intellectually, senselessly so at times. That was not at all unique in those days.

The winter of 1974/75 was mild and wet, and the spring late. Heavy snow fell in southern England at the end of March. The sallow blossom was behind, though the Willow Warblers arrived on time in early April. I visited Alice Holt Forest, just south of Farnham, on April Fools' Day, enticed there by de Worms's accounts of stirring Doings (to introduce a Victorian collectors' term) involving *iris*, *paphia* and *camilla* – Purple Emperor, Silver-washed Fritillary and White Admiral.

Southwater Forest was in striking distance, somewhere along the dreamy A272, and was visited during the second week of April in calm, largely cloudy weather. The woods were starting to dry out, in anticipation of summer. I camped out in some secret place in the woods and was woken abruptly at dawn. A cockerel started it all, a clarion some way off to the west, sounding off at 5 am. At 5.15 the misanthropic Wood Pigeons commenced their daily prophecies of doom, in massed ranks. Fifteen minutes later the woods erupted with a vibrancy almost beyond human understanding as a multitude of joyous Blackbirds and Song Thrushes announced the day. The whole experience was Sublime, in the true Picturesque meaning of the term. The dawn chorus is indeed best heard from within the sanctuary of a sleeping bag within a tent, otherwise one is simply too cold to appreciate its rapture.

The larger part of two days was spent searching for White Admiral larvae. These were still in hibernation, concealed within their winter hibernacula – the brown withered remnants of Honeysuckle leaves spun up into a crude tent with caterpillar silk, and fastened to the stem with more silk. Mostly, the hibernacula dangled down by a silk thread from the stem, drifting aimlessly in any breeze. The secret is to search in steady light, and watch for movement caused by the breeze or your breath. As I watched, one larva, a tiny brown and grey spiny creature, emerged from his tent, crawled up his silk thread and commenced to feed on an unfurling leaf. Shortly afterwards, an early Red Admiral flew down Crookhorn Lane. A good omen, as in that era early spring Red Admirals were distinctly rare. A summer was being born.

Returning, after university ended, on Midsummer Day, there was only one thing to do – lose myself in the woods for the duration of the Purple Emperor season, and record every detail. I had sold my album collection to fund it. There were no plans beyond that, for beyond it little mattered. Thoreau was to be my guide: 'Not until we are lost do we begin to understand ourselves,' he wrote. I was utterly lost in the wonder of that summer; and seriously lost, in that I knew – and had known all along – precisely what I wanted, and perhaps needed, to do in life, but knew not how to do it, let alone how to resource it. That is an issue common to many young people. But all that could wait. Time alone created problems and time alone could resolve them. One thing I had determined was that I would never again allow the exams system to spoil a summer, for May and June had been good, too good, and had been wasted. More pertinently, the first Silver-washed Fritillary was seen in Alice Holt Forest on June 25th and the first White Admiral on the 28th. There I met John Clarke, a young biology teacher who at that time collected butterflies in a modest manner, but shortly afterwards converted into an ardent birder. He filled my mind with impressive tales of *iris*, *paphia* and *camilla*. We drove to Jubilee Hill, a heathland summit near Aldershot, where Silver-studded Blues were emerging in great numbers. A day or so later John returned, and collected no fewer than five halved-gynandromorphs – excessively rare specimens wherein one pair of wings is male and the other female, royal blue and dull brown in this case.

In three days I explored Alice Holt, a mix of oaks mostly planted around 1820 and younger conifer plantations, then moved east to Southwater. There the butterfly season was a couple of days more advanced, and was promising great things. A blue Jay's feather was promptly found, lying on the ride for me. There were hairstreaks in the air, but not so much the Purple Hairstreak, the previous year's butterfly, and denizen of the oaks, but the White-letter Hairstreak. Hitherto, this had been an elusive creature, seen only in some years, usually high up over the tall English Elms or sprawling

Wych Elms that were scattered about the district, but 1975 was its *annus mirabilis*. It was also its death knell, for Dutch elm disease was burgeoning. Elms, which had previously been secreted away as singletons or scattered clumps within a well treed landscape dominated by mature oaks, suddenly sprang to prominence, made salient by the intrusive autumn-like foliage of premature death. Early signs of Dutch elm disease had been evident in that part of West Sussex during the hot summer of 1970, but it only rose to prominence there in 1975. In other landscapes, of course, elms were the dominant tree and the transformation was acute, but here the dying of the elms went largely unnoticed, except by resident naturalists.

The small dark White-letter Hairstreak butterflies dispersed, in search of nectar in the early July heat and also in search of healthy trees. Throughout that wondrous July I witnessed their efforts to find safe havens, but there was none. In scores they fluttered first around, then away from the dying elms at Southwater, Christ's Hospital and Coolham in West Sussex, and along the Upper Greensand hangers in East Hampshire. I have not seen them since in such numbers, or with such regularity within a landscape, and never will again. I learnt that they were most active in mid-morning, before the day heated up fully, and then became quiescent. The males would squabble over the elms or the crowns of adjoining Ash trees, whilst in search of receptive females. Periodically two males would meet up in flight over the tree canopy, and spiral up together in a vertical dog-fight, before separating and dropping back down to the canopy again. With four of our five hairstreaks, and Emperors of course, one looks up, not down. They had favoured bramble patches too, where each afternoon they could be found, crawling around in search of – was it simply nectar, or something else? – for the flowers they visited had often dropped their petals. (Holly Blues behave similarly.) Their favoured brambles were often sparse, shaded patches that attracted few other butterflies.

The July weather was largely benign, with weakening bands of rain coming across at night, prolonged spells of gentle undemanding sunshine by day, and atmospheric pressure wanting to build. Butterflying, and Emperoring in particular, does not entail hours of walking, but eternities of standing about, watching and waiting. Patience is everything, and those of us who have spent our youths fishing will have mastered this essential skill. Sitting down is no good, as it narrows the field of view too much, as any hunter will appreciate. So, butterflying is more akin to game angling than to coarse fishing. One of my favourite standing places was in a young conifer plantation, where I would loiter for hours, gazing up at the adjoining oak edge in wait of Purple Emperors and their attendant knight, the Purple Hairstreak. But the conifers were growing and the vista was narrowing. Early in July I found a rusty milk churn in another wood, and laboured it on my shoulders to where it was needed. Nowadays, of course, such a venture would involve embarrassing interactions with several dog walkers. It was surprising on that day to encounter a lone woman walking a dog, a pioneer of the impending hordes: 'The Lord hath need of it,' I announced, which left the lady speechless. She was not seen again in those woods. I stood on that milk churn for hours and hours, gazing up at the oak edge. No one ever saw me. It was an excellent vantage point. The churn stands there still, a forgotten monument to times gone by, but woods are strewn with the features of personal memories. They collect them.

The first Purple Emperor appeared out of an altostratus sky on July 5th, in the Straits Inclosure of Alice Holt Forest, at 12.23 precisely.

Diary, July 5th 1975: *A momentary spectre of a large black-looking insect appeared near the top of a 50-foot oak about 50 yards away ... This was my first Alice Holt iris. It was pecking at a spray for a split second before vanishing as mysteriously as it had appeared: Was it a vision or a waking dream?*

It was the first of a massive emergence, for this was, without doubt, the year of the Emperor. The following afternoon, with an anticyclone stationed over Scotland, the butterflies put on a breathtaking display in Southwater Forest. At least half a dozen males were viewed, from the milk churn, partaking of an entertaining evening flight. Around 7 pm, four went to roost in oak sprays close together, squabbling up to the last minute. They were still there early the following morning, tucked well in. This was my first encounter with their roosting behaviour.

In the early hours of the 8th a thunderstorm slowly brewed from the south. It began at around 3 am with an hour or so of edifying sheet lightning. Then the rumbling began, quickly intensifying into storm force ten. Nature is at its most powerful during a thunderstorm. There was only one thing to do, join in, and Bob Dylan's *Blood on the Tracks* was album of the summer. One of the most powerful tracks on this most personal of albums is called 'Shelter from the Storm', and another is 'Idiot Wind'. At approximately 4.20 am, though by then time had become an irrelevance, a gust of wind hurried up the ride, carrying my tent with it. As Thoreau put it, 'As you simplify your life, the laws of the universe will be simpler.' Seconds later the deluge began. But that did not matter, for the Purple Emperor puts on a notably fine performance after a thunderstorm, and did so that day. The following day's flight was even better, doubtless because more had emerged, including the first females. The Emperor's polite and distinguished courtship flight was then duly witnessed.

Each day was a journey into the timelessness of Nature, as the weather slowly intensified, each day lovelier than its predecessor. I constantly checked to see that the Jay's feather was still in my hat, for to lose it might be to lose the summer. The stillness of the evening saw a celebration of what had been, and each night was lit by a small camp fire and glow worms along the rides. As Thoreau puts it in his *Natural History of Massachusetts*: 'Think of ... the myriads of insects ushered into being on a summer evening ... the nonchalance of the butterfly carrying accident and change painted in a thousand hues upon its wings.'

And the Emperors were everywhere, by their aloof standard. Each canopy glade revealed one or two, usually two, for this butterfly is indolent when alone but boldly, even aggressively active when a rival male is about. This was the July to search the whole woods, to find out how widespread they actually were. Each canopy gap along the oak-lined Marlpost Road, between Marlpost and Madgeland wood, held at least one male, and the journey into wonder continued down Oldhouse Lane, which wound its sunken way down past the dense trees of Netherwood and round towards Brooks Green.

Was I lonely? Thoreau once again springs to our aid here, stating in his famous treatise on 'Solitude' in *Walden*: 'I love to be alone. I never found the companion that was so companionable as solitude. We are most lonely when we go abroad among men.' Indeed, only in society is the naturalist, the lover of Nature, lonely, and then only within the growing elements of society divorced from or in denial of Nature. And for voices, there were the birds, the hum of a million insects, and *Test Match Special*, for this was the summer when Lillee and Thomson terrorised English batsman and a streaker, gloriously named Michael Angelo, straddled the sanctity of the Lords wicket. The Ashes were duly surrendered.

It could not last, and it did not. Gradually the Emperor males burnt themselves out. First their regal glory faded, then their physical strength and levels of activity. Late in the day on July 26th

I watched an aged male fly low and slow over a field, into the sunset, seeking eternity. That was the first time I saw an Emperor take a deliberate last flight off into the sinking sun. But first, on the 22nd, I experienced a vision of a dark form that could only be the most elusive and cherished of all British butterfly varieties, the all-purple version of the Emperor, ab. *lugenda* – or was it even the impossibly rare ab. *iole*? I disturbed it low down in a glade below the mighty Osiris's birches where, daily, half a dozen or more males battled amongst themselves whilst their ladies skulked amongst the coppiced sallows. The females slowly took over, secreting their eggs in sallow trees during the middle part of the day, but always high up out of reach or on wispy coppiced branches that could not be brought undamaged to the ground, and which therefore remained uninspected. One morning, the 25th, one particular female glided in to feed on the sticky buds of a young Ash tree at the Crookhorn Lane junction in Madgeland Wood, the buds of 1976. She fed there for twelve minutes, wings closed except to flash away a pestering bee. That tree is still there, a handsome Ash capable of growing into a veneer butt. I remember that female each time I pass the spot. Butterflying does that to you.

On July 26th a massive area of high pressure came over. The Long Hot Summer of 1976 was born that day in 1975, for thereafter anticyclonic conditions dominated our weather for precisely a year, a month and a day. The Empresses laid their last eggs, then wilted in the intense heat that also accounted for the last of the White Admirals and White-letter Hairstreaks. I saw the year's final Purple Emperor on August 2nd, a ragged female wandering aimlessly down a favoured ride. I waited around for two more days, but the midsummer party was over, and my energy levels were depleted. Peacocks, Common Blues, Small Coppers and, especially, Wall Browns were everywhere instead. Another party had begun.

On August 7th, my 22nd birthday, I entered a new dimension of existence, in the form of Noar Hill, to the south-west of Selborne. In that era it was a rundown sort of place, consisting of large areas of rank False Oat-grass and brooding patches of Hawthorn scrub, and surrounded by a thick band of impenetrable Blackthorn dotted with Ash and Beech trees. Not many people visited, and I had the place to myself that day. Marbled Whites and Small Skippers were abundant, though ageing fast in the heatwave. Common Blues were everywhere, as is their practice there in good summers. Wall Browns were numerous. The diary states: *I saw one settle in the shade down a Rabbit hole and display.* Later I realised this was an egg-laying female, for Wall Browns often deposit their eggs on root hairs protruding through the roofs of Rabbit burrows. It must also be added that within a decade the butterfly disappeared from Noar Hill and from the entire East Hampshire district, inexplicably, and that it was my duty to record that loss.

Selborne was duly explored, and the wooded hanger system that wound its way down towards Petersfield – Edward Thomas country – and the hazy South Downs. But it was all too leafy, too shaded in late summer; it would come into its own in spring, when the lanes would dance with Orange-tips. The central tangle of twisted Blackthorn growth on Selborne Common was clearly the haunt of Brown Hairstreaks, as was the perimeter of Noar Hill, if one had the energy to work a butterfly even more elusive than the Purple Emperor. In open places, along grassy roadside banks and even on old lawns sloping down to the lanes, Wall Browns were frequently encountered, for this late summer belonged almost exclusively to them. Towards the end of August they petered out, only to be replaced by a prolific third brood that lasted into early November. The Small Copper reacted similarly.

I spent a glorious autumn picking apples in Blackmoor Estate's orchards, below the hanging woods of Selborne, in an attempt to earn some pennies without sacrificing my relationship with Nature, and in good company. Red Admirals were abundant, feeding profusely and at times drunkenly on fallen apples, alongside a scatter of Comma, Speckled Wood and Small Copper. Wall Browns frequented the sunny banks, but I had lost the will to record butterflies: the ending of that summer was simply too sad. The butterfly diary petered out early.

8 *The long hot summer of 1976*

Having weaned himself off opium, Coleridge mused in his 1814–1815 notebook: 'If a man could pass thro' Paradise in a Dream, & have a flower presented to him as a pledge that his Soul had really been there, & (if he) found that flower in his hand when he awoke – Aye? And what then?' Those of us who have passed through paradise are left, perhaps indefinitely, with the question Coleridge poses. We find ourselves wanting to get back, somehow, anyhow, rather than move forward. Such, for me, was the summer of 1976. Part of me still wanders, sunburnt, through that parched land of relentless sun, droughted trees and brown, cracked lawns, haunted by its omnipresent butterflies.

The winter of 1975/76 was largely mild and dry, as if the power of the late summer and autumn of 1975 had never really left. By late February sallows were blossoming and some were even in leaf, Lady's Smock was flowering along the East Hampshire lanes and the Bullfinch was singing his summertime song. The last eleven months had been the driest on record, and in the South-east the last six had produced only 60% of the average rainfall.

Good summers tend to be heralded by an anticyclone at the start of March – seemingly, the stronger and more prolonged that anticyclone, the greater the summer. Sure enough, March 1976 began with a light frost that was quickly burnt off by shafts of sun strengthening through misted fields, promising glory and tempting the lark to ascend. By noon the magic temperature of 12 degrees Celsius had been reached, and the first butterflies of the year appeared. Early in Tove Jansson's childhood classic *Finn*

Family Moomintroll it is revealed that, 'if the first butterfly you see is yellow the summer will be a happy one. If it is white then you will just have a quiet summer. Black and brown butterflies should never be talked about.' Her story continues, 'But this butterfly was golden ... Gold is even better than yellow.' Certainly, the male Brimstone that danced through St Matthew's churchyard in Blackmoor, and off and away down a path through silvered birch trees, appeared as a golden butterfly, and in golden light. The early March anticyclone intensified, peaking on the 4th, a day when chimerical Skylarks ascended en masse through early-morning mists over the nurseries and orchards of Blackmoor estate, between Selborne and the heaths of Woolmer Forest. I had worked there through the winter, reconnecting with rural people who had a profound relationship with the land, the weather and the seasons. The issue here is that the more time one spends outdoors, the more one lives under the thumb of the vagaries of our climate, the weather and seasonal extremes.

The four standard hibernating butterflies – Brimstone, Comma, Peacock and Small Tortoiseshell – were all out and about in unusually high numbers. I had determined to throw all caution to the warm summer wind and spend the season butterflying, having saved a paltry sum of money by working on the land and writing the odd article. But sometimes one develops an intuitive feel of faith in a summer, or even in an entire year. Great summers are not merely planned, however assiduously, but are faithfully dreamt and prayed for during the winter. Moreover, great butterfly years are not one-offs, but the second or even third in a sequence of good summers, which allows butterfly populations to build up incrementally and spread to establish new colonies. I had no objectives other than to relish each sunlit moment, explore the promised land of East Hampshire, experience an entire Purple Emperor season again, see some of the few remaining British butterflies I had not yet seen, record each sighting and each event in diaries, and learn as much about our butterflies and their habitats as was humanly possible. For relaxation, I would play some cricket and woo pretty young ladies, until they realised I was living in another spiritual dimension and deemed me unsuitable. My parameters were limitations in funds and transport, the latter often restricted to a bicycle.

In those days it was rare to see the Orange-tip, that quintessential harbinger of spring, before mid-April, even during the great spring of 1976. The lower hanger system between Selborne and Empshott, where the Upper Greensand gives way to heavy Gault Clay, is an especially rich area for Orange-tips and Green-veined Whites, as one of their favourite larval foodplants, Lady's Smock, grows profusely in the damp woods there, whilst another, Garlic Mustard, occurs commonly along the lanes. Sure enough, the first Orange-tip of the year was seen in a lonely winding part-wooded combe below Selborne on April 16th. Shortly afterwards the first Cuckoo of the year, a sleek dark male, flew silently off into a copse there, perching barred chest on-high in a leafing Ash tree, having been disturbed whilst feeding on the ground. Minutes later, he called, clear and deep, and in that very moment winter, and all the tedium it epitomises, was forgotten. Within three days Orange-tip males abounded around drifts of Lady's Smock in the young conifer plantations of Hartley Wood, between Oakhanger and Selborne, a sizeable Gault Clay oak wood then in the process of being replanted with non-native conifers. What surprised me, during that spring of discovery in East Hampshire, was how small Orange-tips are in that district. I have never worked out why. Perhaps the majority of them breed on Lady's Smock there, a relatively small plant that perhaps produces small underfed adults.

Over in Southwater Forest, the Nightingales were in. Two nights were spent with them – more precisely two sleepless nights, as two birds sang close by from 9.30 pm, non-stop. I lay in my tent pondering how dear Keats had managed to turn the lightning storm of the Nightingale's explosive song into a soporific. Had he, a Cockney with no natural history knowledge, actually been listening to the right species of bird?

May stuttered at the start, then quickly mended its ways as another anticyclone moved in from the south-west. Cuckoos seemed to be everywhere in the East Hampshire countryside, especially in Hartley Wood, where a knot of five was seen on May 6th, four loud males and a 'bubbling' female. The following day what was still called the Duke of Burgundy Fritillary was beginning to emerge at Noar Hill, a somewhat late start for this butterfly in such a fine spring, but in those days this and other butterfly species emerged later than is now considered normal. Azure-winged Holly Blues were by then almost ubiquitous around clumps of flowering Holly bushes in the Selborne lanes and gardens, and migrant Red Admirals were starting to appear. On the 11th, Pearl-bordered Fritillaries began to emerge in Alice Holt Forest, in a young plantation close to Bucks Horn Oak. A great butterfly summer had been born.

In mid-May, two lengthy searches of Southwater Forest revealed that both Duke of Burgundy and Pearl-bordered Fritillary had died out there during my three-year enforced springtime absence. This hurt, and was hard to believe, especially with the former, for it is a tiny butterfly which can subsist at very low population levels and is easily overlooked. Nonetheless, despite suffering five near-sleepless nights on account of the incessant tongues of the wanton Nightingales a double blank was drawn, and a heart-wrenching conclusion reached: I had seen the last of the Southwater Duke of Burgundies and Pearl-bordered Fritillaries back in 1972. Their lifeblood, the supply of young plantations from broad-leaved fellings, had ceased. There was nowhere for them to move to, for in woodland systems these butterflies follow the woodcutter, and the woodcutter had stopped work here. A fatal break in continuity of habitat supply had occurred.

The loss was rubbed in by the discovery of huge colonies of Pearl-bordered Fritillary in several places in Alice Holt Forest, and more modest colonies in the Oakhanger woods. Pearl-bordered Fritillary had emerged in wonderful numbers that spring. There were three sizeable colonies alone in the Lodge Inclosure of Alice Holt, and others in Goose Green, Abbots Wood and Willows Green inclosures. This most graceful of springtime butterflies almost abounded along the rides there, feasting communally on patches of Bugle flowers, fulvous amber on gentian blue. Wall Browns, today a rarity in most districts and all but extinct throughout Hampshire, were very common that May. In Alice Holt's Lodge Inclosure I counted over fifty in two hours on the 23rd. I had not seen this grassland insect so numerous in a wood, and have not since. This was 1976.

Monday May 24th was cloudless and hot, with a vestige of breeze emanating vaguely from the south-east. I cycled, some twenty miles, to the Chiddingfold Woods, in search of a species new to me, the Wood White. A male bumbled out of the entrance to Fisherlane Wood as I arrived after an hour and a half of cycling over undulating terrain. Crossing the arduous heights of Haslemere proved to be worth the effort. I fell instantly for this fragile white butterfly that flutters perpetually just above the rough ride-side grasses, forever threatening to alight on some choice plant yet changing its mind at the last millisecond and continuing in perpetual motion, ever onwards, at a constant speed, in dithering flight. I watched the females laying eggs, found other eggs and even some tiny young larvae on the leaves of Greater Bird's-foot Trefoil growing along the ride-side ditch margins. Pearl-bordered and Small Pearl-bordered fritillaries abounded in a young fir plantation at the southern end of the wood, where male Grizzled and Dingy skippers fought each other almost manfully. That evening, I took my young cat, Thomas Mouse, for his customary amble through the apple orchards to a Beech cathedral on a promontory along the greensand hanger system. There, I scratched the name of the Wood White in the dust – *sinapis* – whilst my cat, a highly confident long-haired black with white trimmings, played merrily with a clan of young badgers, dashing in and out of exposed tree roots, overhangs and hollows on a steep earthy bank with his mutually coloured counterparts. There is a better reality than the one we continually subsist within, Nature's.

The weather wobbled at the turn of May, producing a short spell of indecision between pulses of high pressure, as if Nature was taking a deep breath before the immortal June of 1976 commenced. The abundance of butterflies was making the news, with eulogies appearing in several newspapers. An expedition to the Moulsford Downs by John Clarke and myself somehow generated a spate of indignant letters in *The Times* concerning butterfly collecting. In early June 1976 the Adonis Blue was a seriously rare butterfly outside Dorset, the Isle of Wight and Wiltshire. In Hampshire only a single colony was known, at Martin Down NNR in the extreme west of the county. In Surrey it was known only from Denbies Hillside (also and wrongly known as Ranmore Common) near Dorking. In Berkshire and the Chilterns there were colonies only on the Moulsford Downs just west of Streatley. Clarke and I had travelled there as much in search of Stone Curlew, an even greater rarity, as Adonis Blues, which I had seen there back in August 1970. Despite much agricultural damage to the downs during my six-year absence we found the Adonis still present. A couple of old collectors were also present, and a spate of critical letters started. Clearly, perceptions and values were changing. Indeed, 1976 was the last year of widespread butterfly collecting in this country, a watershed year in our attitudes towards butterflies. Thereafter collectors converted to photography, switched to collecting abroad, went undercover and became paranoid, or simply gave up – most of the collectors I encountered in 1976 were never heard of again. In the ensuing sequence of poor summers Clarke hung up his net and converted to birding.

At the end of June, a Mr John Lodge wrote to *The Times* claiming to have rediscovered the Large Blue 'in the Cotswolds', supposedly near Cheltenham. At that time, the butterfly was known only from a single, top-secret site in south Dartmoor. Three years later that colony, and with it the British race, was formally declared extinct. Sadly, Lodge's claims were never substantiated, as he insisted on keeping the locality secret, but years later it was reported that a credible source knew of a colony in existence in the southern Cotswolds that persisted until after 1976, so perhaps Lodge had after all found something. We will never know. But this was 1976, and it was that sort of year.

Meanwhile, in early June the spring butterflies started to burn themselves out. The Pearl-bordered Fritillaries were replaced by a massive emergence of Small Pearl-bordered Fritillary. In the East Hampshire woods, as in West Sussex, this proved to be an even more widespread butterfly than its congener. A large population was discovered in the Oakhanger woods, which produced two acute aberrations, one of which was probably ab. *vanescens*. Only a verbal description exists, in my diary, as I had no camera then and was not prepared to take them as specimens. Had I done so, and they were worthy of collecting, the summer would doubtless have died on me. In brief, the wing undersides did not look remotely like a Small Pearl-bordered Fritillary, and the uppersides, scarcely.

Another long cycle ride, past Edward Thomas country, to the sheep-grazed slopes of Butser Hill and Ramsdean Down south of Petersfield, on a stultifying hot day in mid-June, is memorable for what may be the best flight of the humble Small Heath I have ever seen. In those days, long before it showed any sign of decline, it was such a commonplace insect that one took little notice of it. The general attitude was that it got in the way of better quarry. Little Butser Hill also held a sizeable colony of Duke of Burgundy, though this spring butterfly was by then finishing for the year.

The following day I returned to Southwater Forest, in search of Small Pearl-bordered Fritillary. But none was found. It too had apparently died out there. I had seen the last of the Southwater Small Pearl-bordered Fritillaries the previous year. The Nightingales were still vocal, though, at night, and White-letter Hairstreaks were emerging, somehow, from dying elms. Farmers had been hard at work, grubbing out hedges and cutting back wood edges that had encroached decades ago. The heat built steadily.

June 19th was a Saturday, and the Saturday of the Lords Test match to boot. Not a ball was bowled. I know, for I was there. Snow and Underwood had dismissed the mighty West Indies for a mere 182. Snow was a man of Sussex and of Christ's Hospital school (a few years earlier I had slept in his bed, and by that I mean only that the bed I occupied in the senior school had formerly been his, for his name and dates were etched into the headboard). Contrary to the weather forecast, light but steady rain fell from midday, ceasing mid-morning on the 20th. By then, Clarke and I had travelled up to the Oxfordshire woods in search of the elusive Black Hairstreak. I had unfinished business with that butterfly, having looked for it in past years with at best only paltry success, being miles away at boarding school during much of its flight season. Returning to Rushbeds Wood north of Brill, the scene of a failed expedition in 1971, this most evasive of hairstreaks put on a stupendous performance. I have only once seen it in better numbers since, during its *annus mirabilis* of 2010. It is very much a boom or bust butterfly, experiencing many lean years punctuated by occasional years of plenty. In 1976 it was abundant along the east edge of Rushbeds Wood, which was then a neglected and thoroughly forgotten tract of broad-leaved woodland that had been clear-felled during the Second World War and then forsaken (some years later Rushbeds was acquired by the county wildlife trust, and became a managed wood). *Pruni*, as the Black Hairstreak is known, was still flying actively when Clarke and I left at 6.30. It had started its day late, at around 1.30, due to the unforecast rain, and had been making up for lost time.

From June 22nd the weather intensified, the famous Long Hot Summer had truly begun. Britain, or the UK, or whatever it was called at the time, had just capitulated bizarrely to Iceland in the third Cod War, indicating that something was out of kilter. Clouds became almost as rare as Large Blues. In the Hampshire woods Meadow Browns had emerged in myriads and were jostling for position on every bramble flower. They had started to emerge in the meadows and along the road verges as early as June 2nd and were now threatening to reach plague proportions. But minds were on mightier, loftier matters: would it be possible to equal or even beat Heslop's record for the earliest Purple Emperor, on Midsummer Day? I failed, though not for want of sweat and effort. Later I found out that *iris* commenced that year in Alice Holt Forest on the 25th. Had I visited Southwater Forest, where flight seasons are a little earlier, I might have beaten that Midsummer Day record, but it mattered little.

Over the last weekend of June, Clarke and Oates staged an expedition to the Lake District. The journey north on the Friday afternoon was memorable, in that there seemed to be an overheated car every three or four miles up the M6, bonnet up, radiator steaming. The summer of 1976 was nothing if not exacting. We slept in Clarke's car, along a quiet lane near Witherslack, and were unkindly woken at 5.30 the following morning by a passing farmer: 'Good morning, you queer bastards!' he shouted from the safe haven of a tractor cab. Little did he know that the occupants had lulled themselves to sleep by discussing girls. Undeterred and unbreakfasted, we found Large Heath males well out on Meathop Moss, once we had stumbled upon a way into this most hidden of places, a world within a world. The Large Heath is the grey pilgrim of the peat hags, drifting about aimlessly in the breeze. Oddly, the last Pearl-bordered Fritillary of the season was seen flying over the wet heath vegetation there, a stray from the surrounding limestone hills. In those days the moss was still genuinely wet, such that even at the height of the 1976 drought Wellington boots were essential, and were regularly overtopped. Not too much had changed, then, since an Edwardian collector writing in *The Entomologist's Record* advised: 'Great care is necessary in moving about, as one's leg frequently disappears well above the knee, either into a large hidden crack or into a bog hole, in either case a highly dangerous occurrence if on the run.' Similar recommendations were made by an earlier entomological visitor, who for many years ran the 'lunatic asylum' at Lancaster, and escaped from there to entomologise around Arnside and Witherslack. After 1976 I witnessed the moss, a wonderful domed raised bog, dry out such that first Wellingtons became unnecessary, and then, prickles apart, even walking boots as the water table was lowered by drainage ditches cut along its boundaries to facilitate agriculture in the surrounding fields.

Massive conservation effort by the Cumbria Wildlife Trust is now remedying that situation.

The mountains were calling, and even revealed a cloud or two, one like a ring of dragon smoke around the summit of Blencathra. On Fleetwith Pike, above the Honister Pass youth hostel, the Mountain Ringlets were just starting to emerge, revealing an iridescence on their wings like that of a Starling in breeding plumage. Herdwick sheep panted and bleated pitifully in the heat. Arnside Knott was also visited, but it seemed that the High Brown Fritillary season there had not yet begun and we failed to locate another target species, the Northern Brown Argus. All we saw was yet another proliferation of Small Pearl-bordered Fritillary before duty called us back south. Clarke had to return to his teaching job, for it was the exam season, and I to the Emperor.

But something was wrong with the strength of the sun, it had become if anything too strong. During a fifteen-day period, from June 23rd to July 7th inclusive, the temperature reached 32 degrees Celsius somewhere in southern Britain. Clouds were all but absent, restricted to wisps of high cirrus, often in curious shapes. Roads melted such that the tarmac became and then remained viscous. Cycling through, rather than over it, was arduous in the extreme, with the tyres making a curious dragging, sticking sound. Almost daily I cycled to Alice Holt Forest, through nine miles of melting tarmac. My nose burnt, peeled, burnt again, peeled, before giving up in abject resignation. One by one the East Hampshire heaths caught fire, seemingly by design rather than by genuine accident, for the disaffected youth of places like the military town of Bordon had problems sleeping on those warm nights. Palls of smoke rose high, before bending and drifting in some high-altitude wind. There was a searing inevitability about it all.

The Purple Emperor at last exploded onto the scene, adding iridescent purple to a world of azure and gold. It was a short but extremely sweet season. I saw my first, a brace of battling males, in Alice Holt's Straits Inclosure, early on June 28th, saw two more, and met someone out rough shooting who had earlier watched one settle and display on a rickety old wooden gate that stood at the wood's western entrance. I knew the spot – it caught dappled morning sun, framed between tall oaks. I coveted that sighting. I discovered a thriving colony in Hartley Wood, by Oakhanger: large, bold and aggressive males that threatened to rival their Dragons Green counterparts in belligerence.

On July 1st there was a mass emergence of females. I must have seen at least ten that day, whereas in previous seasons I had never seen more than three in a day. That morning, a huge ancient silver Bentley drew up at the entrance to one of the Alice Holt inclosures, and a gnome-like man emerged, clad in a string vest, Boy Scout shorts of considerable antiquity and hobnail boots – and proceeded to rub rancid Danish Blue cheese into a Forestry Commission gatepost. This was the Baron de Worms, close friend of my boyhood hero I R P Heslop and the most respected lepidopterist of the era. He swore by rancid Danish Blue as a bait for *iris*, but had retreated to a local hostelry by the time the first male descended. The bait was duly consumed by wasps. That morning I made a fool of myself, though mercifully there were no witnesses. A huge dark butterfly flew at 3–4 metres above ground along a heavily shaded ride. Immediately I gave chase, convinced this was a rare dark colour form of the Empress, ab. *iole* perchance. Whooping with delight I eventually cornered my first ever Silver-washed Fritillary form *valezina*, the strange dark-green colour form of this normally orange species that is found only in the female and seems to prefer heavily shaded rides, at least in heatwaves. Black Admirals were around too: I saw on average one a day in Alice Holt that season.

Two days were then spent in Southwater Forest, but the woods felt oppressive in the sweltering heat. Worse, I did not belong there anymore, for the poetic spell was broken. The signs were ominous: I found a dying Emperor, hit by a car along one of the quiet lanes, whilst a scatter of White-letter Hairstreaks fluttered round the last of the dying elms, in the knowledge that there were no living elms left for them to seek and in recognition of their doom. Huge hexagonal cracks were everywhere in the Wealden Clay. Here dwelt the ghosts of last year. The present year lay elsewhere. The sense of belonging was broken. I left after two difficult days and two sleepless nights. It was many years before I was able to return to those woods; or perhaps, until they invited me back.

Back in Alice Holt early on July 6th, the Emperors put on a truly majestic show. I had moved home, or home had moved itself. I even saw four females in a vista, which remains the most I have ever seen of Herself at once, and at last saw eggs laid in a place I could actually reach. The latter represented a major breakthrough. The butterfly was at peak season. Each morning, both sexes would descend to the grassy rides to seek whatever vestige of moisture they could find, with the bulk of this activity taking place between 8.30 and 9.30. On occasions there were three or four down at a time along my favoured 75-metre stretch of ride. The White Admiral behaved similarly. But by mid-July much of the White Admiral's Honeysuckle had wilted.

By July 8th I had been butterflying all day, every day, in intense heat, for over three weeks, and pursuing young ladies or playing cricket (or both) in the evenings – and so I failed to wake up that morning. A shame I did not manage to last another day because on the 9th the weather broke, sort of: it actually rained, a little, then stayed dull and only reached a maximum of 17 degrees. At Old Trafford, Michael Holding bowled England out for 71.

On July 10th I was back in Alice Holt, reinvigorated. There was no mistaking the *valezina* Silver-washed Fritillary that greeted me at the main gate at 8.30, not this time. Then at 9.40 I saw the real thing, an Empress ab. *lugenda*, a black Empress. Three of us watched her for twenty minutes. She even laid eggs in front of our eyes. The prominent white bands that normally run through the middle of the wings were absent, the hindwings being uniformly dark; on the forewing uppersides there were a few small white markings; the undersides lacked any white, being predominately grey and brown. At the time I considered this a once-in-a-lifetime experience. I was wrong: years later I photographed a similar female in Fermyn Woods, Northamptonshire.

The following day I and two others, Peter and Joan Baines of Farnham, witnessed the courtship flight of the Purple Emperor. Now this was ground-breaking stuff, for many of our butterflies are rarely seen courting and mating, especially those which dwell up in the canopy. At 2.45 a male was seen closely following a female, as if they were playing follow-my-leader, the male mimicking the female's every move – White Admirals do this when courting, weaving in and out of foliage in synchronised motion. The Emperors settled high up on an oak and immediately joined, wings closed and motionless, tucked into a leaf spray. They remained *in copula*, as scientists put it, for three and a half hours, before separating and flying off into the concluding pages of a D H Lawrence novel, or wherever over-amorous butterflies go. Incidentally, it cannot have been the lady's first mating, for she was clearly worn.

Thereafter the Emperor season rapidly burnt out, though it was evident that they had deposited a large number of eggs and set themselves up well for 1977. The Alice Holt females had taught me how to look for their eggs and larvae. By July 18th the Emperor was all but over, but not before I had seen the aberrant female again, on the 14th, in the same glade. She still flies within my mind. Graylings and Silver-studded Blues were appearing in strange places, displaced from their beloved heaths by wanton fires. As the brambles and thistles finished flowering in the woods, so Silver-washed Fritillaries dispersed in search of pastures new. A roadside flowerbed of African Marigolds attracted quite a host of them, until that too succumbed to the drought. Purple Hairstreaks were regularly encountered probing for moisture on the parched ground. In the evenings they were almost too profuse to describe – an order of magnitude greater than I have experienced at any other time, and their evening flight lasted till 9 pm. At times they moved around in droves along wood edges. Their eggs later proved to be abundant: I found 225 along a 75-metre stretch of drooping oak boughs in Hartley Wood, but only twelve there the following year.

In Bernwood Forest and in the Chiddingfold Woods the Wood White produced a sizeable second brood. A spur-of-the-moment translocation was made, of six females and two males, to the Straits Inclosure of Alice Holt, as a thank you for producing such a great Purple Emperor, White Admiral and Silver-washed Fritillary season. Butterfly enthusiasts did things like that in that era. Later I found out that the butterfly had spread naturally to Alice Holt that year anyway. It took there quite well, only blowing out in 1981 when its favoured rides were pulverised when timber was extracted during wet weather.

A day of torrential thunderstorms on the 20th failed to relieve the drought. About an inch of rain ran straight through the parched ground, even on clay soils. Then another anticyclone established itself over Britain, heralding a major August drought. In the Straits Inclosure, on the Gault Clay, a huge crack had opened in the main ride, some 6 metres long and at least 2 metres deep and perhaps 30 centimetres wide. Slowly, during the late summer and early autumn, that crack gradually vanished. It has never reappeared. By now, the nation's lawnmowers had gathered cobwebs and dust in garden sheds, all lawns having been brown for weeks. In early August a stupendous gaff letter, on official paper, was issued to a number of Southern Water's customers in north-east Hampshire. It complained that they had been squandering water profligately, advised that in addition to placing the by-now obligatory brick in the loo cistern they should place another in the loo itself, and told them to bath with a friend or next door's teenage daughter. It was signed 'R Sole'. Apparently some of Southern Water's customers took it seriously. Doubtless someone got the sack. The heat was getting to the nation.

August dragged on in sullen heat. The downs turned a pale shade of grey as the vegetation wilted, south-facing slopes even turning brown. On the thinnest soils, much vegetation frazzled away. Elsewhere, farmers took advantage of the dry conditions to drain wetland pockets and meadows for more productive agriculture. Noar Hill revealed a good population of Brown Hairstreaks, active early in the morning before entering a heat-induced stupor for the rest of the day. It was hard not to join them. Graylings and Silver-studded Blues appeared there off the blackened heaths, and Chalkhill Blues and Brown Argus from the distant downs. Wall Brown produced an even more prolific brood than it had managed in early summer, occurring along almost every sunny bank in the district. But the most interesting feature of the month was the frequency of dwarf specimens, of many species, presumably induced by larvae cutting short their feeding time and pupating prematurely as their foodplants wilted. In particular, numerous Common Blues and Chalkhill Blues were significantly undersized that August.

One late summer day, I discovered that a new track had been bulldozed along the northern edge of Noar Hill, through Blackthorn entanglements beloved by Nightingales, Turtle Doves and Brown Hairstreaks. Ancient pollard Beech trees were being felled willy-nilly and for no obvious reason in the adjoining hanger. The contractors told me they were dangerous trees and had to come out. I was not fooled. Trees are seldom if ever dangerous. My protestations culminated in me becoming a warden for the reserve, which at that time lacked any practical input. A conservationist had rather suddenly been born. It was pay-back time.

At the end of August two cataclysmic things happened, almost simultaneously. The government appointed an official Minister for Drought, and the Hindu community brought over a Holy Man to pray for rain. Within three days of the Minister's appointment and even less after the Holy Man's arrival, the weather broke, spectacularly; so spectacularly that an excessively wet autumn ensued, and Britain did not experience any sustained hot or dry weather again until the spring of 1980. Once more I retreated to the apple harvest on Blackmoor Estate, where Red Admirals feasted on fallen fruit between the deluges. In early October they drifted away south, seeking warmer climes. Weekends were spent searching for Purple Emperor larvae in and around woods in East Hampshire and into West Sussex. I had cracked how to find them, and located over a hundred. One weekend in late September, when the sun actually shone, I returned to Southwater Forest, only to find that many sallow trees there had succumbed to the drought.

The Butterfly Monitoring Scheme (BMS) dataset does not show how abundant butterflies were that year. Analysis of all the years within the scheme places 1976 some way down the hierarchy of excellence. Scientists are well aware of how inadequate Year One datasets often are, and the scheme was launched in 1976, with just a few places contributing. The truth is that reliance on BMS analysis sells the Long Hot Summer of 1976 terribly short. Hopefully this account goes a little way towards remedying that situation.

9 *The legacy of 1976*

It is difficult to determine the impact of the great drought of 1976 on our butterflies, as those effects were muddled up with those of the subsequent wet summer. Certainly, populations of several species declined severely in localities where their foodplants had succumbed to drought. On many southern downs, for example, populations of the Adonis and Chalkhill Blue butterflies collapsed, as their vetches had desiccated. On Noar Hill, Duke of Burgundy numbers in 1977 were half those of 1976, doubtless because a great many of the Cowslips on which its larvae feed had wilted; the Grizzled Skipper colony there vanished, for the Wild Strawberry plants it bred on frazzled up early on in the drought.

In 1977, spring ran late, though it produced a couple of good spells. May started promisingly but soon became plagued by convective cloud spreading across from the west mid-morning after clear cool nights. However, from the 18th high pressure developed, and dominated the remainder of the month. This proved to be the best weather of the whole butterfly season. During this period, it became clear that spring butterflies were nothing like as numerous as they had been the previous year, that they were emerging decidedly late, and that many colonies had simply vanished.

Most salient by its absence was the Speckled Wood, which normally started around April 20th in that era. Although I saw a singleton on April 27th the butterfly did not appear in any numbers before late June. Larval development had been hampered either by the drought or by the excessively wet autumn, or by both.

Even more delayed was the Small Copper, which I did not see before August 11th – a good ten weeks late.

Butterfly of the spring in Hampshire was undoubtedly the Holly Blue, which appeared in even greater numbers than it had done the previous year. At one point I watched two pairs of Holly Blues mating some 20 centimetres apart on a Holly bush, whilst two other females were busy placing their eggs on nearby flowers. That was impressive, but the second brood, in August, was almost non-existent, the victim of an atrocious June.

During May, several hours were spent following Green Hairstreak females on Noar Hill, in the far chalk pit, up against the Beech hanger. The conclusion was that individual females of this distinctly polyphagous or catholic butterfly, which utilises a wide range of foodplants, were each selecting only a single species of plant: a couple of females laid only on Common Rockrose, after testing and rejecting other plants within the foodplant range, whilst others laid exclusively on Bird's-foot Trefoil. It might be worth someone developing this little study further, to explore the hypothesis that individual female Green Hairstreaks behave somewhat akin to female Cuckoos – or maybe this behaviour was merely the trait of an odd year?

June was dire, memorable for the rains that marred the Queen's Silver Jubilee. Punk rock was all the rage, led by the Sex Pistols' nihilistic 'Anarchy in the UK'. We were perhaps fortunate: the hit song in Maoist China was a ditty entitled 'How I Love to Carry Dung up the Mountainside for the Commune'. June was the fourth wettest on record, and one of the coolest and cloudiest. By its end, buttercups were still well in bloom in the meadows, whilst in the woods brambles and thistles were only just budding up. Large Skippers and Meadow Browns emerged decidedly late, not appearing in East Hampshire until late June. Marbled White, Ringlet and Small Skipper only commenced at the end of the first week of July, whilst White Admiral and Silver-washed Fritillary did not appear in Alice Holt Forest until July 10th.

High summer belonged to the White Admiral, which emerged in superb numbers – despite the fact that its larval foodplant, Honeysuckle, had dropped its leaves the previous August, and despite the fact that Dr Ernie Pollard's research had found high levels of mortality amongst the pupae during cool wet Junes. Somehow the tiny larvae had survived the great Honeysuckle wilt of August 1976, and somehow the woodland Honeysuckle itself had (largely) recovered. But doubtless White Admiral numbers in 1977 would have been even greater had June been less inclement. Above all, this was the year in which the White Admiral produced a great number of variations, or aberrations. I personally saw 18 'Black Admirals' in the Straits Inclosure of Alice Holt, at least two of which were the excessively rare all-black version, ab. *nigrina*. Well into August White Admirals were skimming the edges of each and every glade in Alice Holt, often in twos and threes, summoning each other from afar, and meeting up briefly before continuing their lone pilgrimages.

That July R W (Robert or Bob) Watson, the last of the great New Forest collectors and a glorious eccentric, appeared in Alice Holt Forest in pursuit of Black Admirals. A Forest man born and bred, he worked as a milkman and even as a prize fighter before becoming an accountant. Women, though, were his nemesis. He married five times, each time unsuccessfully. Early in March he would hold an open weekend at his house, at Sandy Down near Brockenhurst, for anyone with an interest in butterflies or wider Lepidoptera. Other doyens of the final era of New Forest collectors gathered there, notably the butterfly artist A D A Russworm and Rear Admiral A D Torlesse. Watson was a most generous host, if a little over-interested in escorting young men's girlfriends around his garden, on the pretext that he wanted to show the young ladies his plums (or was it grapes? Either way they were seriously out of season in March, and at least one young lady stated that the experience was akin to an outing with Benny Hill). He was obsessed with pigs, naming his house Porcorum, after the Latin for pigsty. He passed away, rather spectacularly, in 1984. One should not promulgate rumour, so the following account must be offered as fact, safe in the knowledge that Bob himself would thoroughly approve. Having being advised by his doctors in the strongest possible terms to avoid alcohol (his personal intake consisted of a bottle at lunch and at least one at supper) he partook somewhat splendidly at the Royal Entomological Society's annual Verrall Supper, only to pass out on the steps there, supported by two fellows' wives. That is precisely how Robert Watson would have wanted to depart this mortal coil. His immaculate collections were bequeathed to the nation.

For the most part, a veil needs to be drawn over the 1977 Purple Emperor season. It appeared absurdly late, scarcely getting going before July 24th. Larval development had been retarded by the wet June – I found a full-grown larva on Midsummer Day. The Emperor season did produce some magic moments, however: notably a frenetic few minutes on July 30th when half a dozen males were seen in a vista, attacking anything on wings, whilst two Black Admirals, including a full ab. *nigrina*, floated innocently by. In Alice Holt, a few females lingered into September, the last being recorded there on the 7th, a record for the modern era.

If the Purple Emperor was poor in 1977 the White-letter Hairstreak was even worse: I saw none all season, for I knew of no surviving mature elms. More curiously, the Ringlet was scarce for several years on Hampshire's downs after the 1976 drought. Somehow, though, the Brown Hairstreak emerged in exceptional numbers at Noar Hill in September, almost redeeming a rotten summer.

Alice Holt Forest

People need trees, though whether trees need people is another matter. We have a special relationship with forests, for we were once forest people – though we have largely cleared our forests away. That relationship has a metaphysical dimension, which often extends to particular forests and wooded places – the sacred grove of Greek mythology.

In the 1970s much of Alice Holt Forest, an 851-hectare (2100-acre) expanse of woodland on the Hampshire/Surrey border, was a secret and shadowy place. Public access was tolerated in most of it, but was by no means encouraged, and naturalists had to apply for an annual access permit – to be shown on demand. The Forestry Commission, which runs the forest, wanted primarily to grow trees, shoot deer and meet financial targets imposed on it by the Treasury.

Historically, entomological activities in Alice Holt concentrated on the Lodge Inclosure, in the north-west of the forest. 'The Lodge', as it was known in butterfly-collecting circles, lies close to Bentley Station, which enabled field-meeting parties from London to descend on the place. Baron de Worms himself started to lead excursions of the British Entomological Society there before the Second World War.

By the mid-1970s a few butterfly enthusiasts had explored beyond Lodge Inclosure and discovered Straits Inclosure, in the south-west part of the forest. Straits Inclosure was by far the wildest and least frequented part of the forest. It lies on Gault Clay, a heavy thug of a clay that turns to cracked and fissured concrete during summer droughts and intractable glue in the wet. It grows good-quality oak, but timber extraction is extremely difficult. In effect, forestry operations are only viable there during periods of sustained drought. The surfaced main ride, 'New Ride', now frequented by butterfly photographers each July, was installed early in 1987 to facilitate the Forestry Commission's thinning and harvesting programme. But throughout the 1970s there was only one L-shaped grassy open ride, which was opened up in 1970, and some narrow linear glades along overhung rides. These rides were dominated by huge tussocks of Tufted Hair-grass that rendered walking difficult. The place hummed with clegs and other biting flies in high summer. Bramble patches were frequent, though mainly in dappled shade. The understorey of Hawthorn and Hazel was draped in vast tangles of Honeysuckle. Tall sallows lined many of the rides, and were profuse amongst the younger blocks of oak woodland. Turtle Doves purred in the distant shade. Traffic noise was absent. It was a world apart. The inhabitants of nearby Frith End were largely ex-colonial types who did things colonially, like mass fly-mowing on Sunday afternoons, and seldom ventured into the wood.

The inclosure is some 80 hectares (200 acres) in size. It had been replanted extensively with oak during the 1930s, though some curious narrow bands of Norway Spruce were added, which blew down spectacularly in the great storms of January 1990. The mess was cleared, and the bands left to natural regeneration. They are now choked with sallows and other young broad-leaved trees. A small plantation of Corsican Pine, established in 1965, survives on the west edge. Efficient deer management has meant that the growth of the Hazel and Hawthorn understorey is vigorous. It is this shrub layer that holds the Honeysuckle tangles on which the White Admiral breeds.

The Gault Clay also comes to the surface in Goose Green Inclosure, across the Frith End road from Straits Inclosure, and further east across the busy A325 in Abbots Wood Inclosure. These inclosures too are primarily oak country, holding remnant stands of oaks planted in the 1820s for navy timber. At the southern end of Abbots Wood Inclosure is an area of some 10 hectares that was clear-felled in 1981 and replanted with oak, much of which failed or was out-competed by broad-leaved natural regeneration. For many years this clearing held sizeable colonies of the two spring-flying pearl-bordered fritillaries, along with Dingy and Grizzled skippers, before sallows grew up and converted it into a massive Purple Emperor breeding ground. The Gault Clay also extends northwards along the western edge of the forest into Lodge Inclosure.

Much of the forest lies along a transition line between the Gault Clay and the Tertiary sands. The northern and north-eastern inclosures lie on former heathland. These sandier areas have been vigorously exploited for growing conifers, though old oaks still fringe the inclosure margins. The butterfly interest is primarily associated with the more clayey areas. Clearings and young plantations on the sandier soils tend to be utilised more by Nightjars than by butterflies.

In the late 1970s the Forestry Commission designated the Straits Inclosure as a Conservation Area, primarily for the Purple Emperor and other butterflies. That internal designation did not actually mean much, as few funds were available for conservation work, though some ride widening and glade creation was carried out in the late 1970s and early 1980s, and a large pond was created along the southern edge during the 1977/78 winter. The pond failed to contribute towards the conservation of the existing wildlife interest, and drained the conservation budget. In time it will silt up and grow sallows, and Purple Emperors.

My diaries document the highs and lows of 'the Straits' over nearly forty years, and record some of the most wonderful events of my life as a naturalist and butterfly lover. They chronicle the highs and lows of three butterfly species in particular, Purple Emperor, White Admiral and Silver-washed Fritillary. I have kept a record of every sighting of Purple Emperor, whilst White Admiral and Silver-washed Fritillary have been monitored through rough timed counts during their peak season periods along the more open sections of ride, which have of course changed from era to era due to ride creation, widening and canopy closure. The problem with such data is that route, time and distance have varied considerably between different epochs.

In effect, there have been four distinct monitoring phases: the period 1975–1982, during which there was only some 300 metres of open L-shaped ride; 1982–1987, after the open ride system had been extended to the wood's centre; from 1987, when 'New Ride' was cut out, to the late 1990s, when there was a triangular route of open ride that extended for almost a kilometre; more recently, parts of this system have closed over, only to be reopened. Above all, my records track massive and often horrendous change, whilst illustrating the difficulties of consistently monitoring butterfly populations in dynamic woodland environments.

It is probable that I discovered the Straits at the end of its golden era: would that I had known it during the 1960s, when Purple Emperor and White Admiral must have abounded! Duke of Burgundy and Pearl-bordered Fritillary, Dingy Skipper and Grizzled Skipper all died out from the west-edge conifer plantation after 1976, though Small Pearl-bordered Fritillary lingered on until 1980. A small colony of Wood White, established in July 1976, lasted until 1981. It might have thrived had its favoured ride not been pulverised by timber hauling associated with pond creation during the 1977/78 winter.

Major ride widening took place in August 1982, to prepare the site for timber extraction. In late July 1983 heavy thinning work started in the eastern half of the wood, and an era of entomological greatness ended suddenly. This work was hugely exploitative and took no obvious account of nature conservation interests. Most of the mature sallows in the wood's eastern half were felled during three summers of thinning and harvesting. The impact on the Honeysuckle tangles beloved of the White Admiral was equally acute. Purple Emperor and White Admiral populations collapsed, despite a sequence of three good summers.

Tufted Hair-grass increased strongly when the oaks were thinned. This could have adversely affected the Silver-washed Fritillary, which breeds on violets beneath the oaks. Yet, the opposite occurred, for after modest seasons in 1984 and 1985 *paphia* exploded in the wood: the 1986 emergence is still the best on record for the Straits. Also, Essex Skipper invaded the open grassy rides in numbers, before dying out in the 2000s.

The Straits showed impressive indifference to the 1987 'hurricane', and sallow regeneration was encouraged along the newly cut-out broad New Ride. However, thinning work got into full swing in the remote western half of the wood during the summer of 1988, at a time when July butterfly populations were falling due to bad midsummer weather. By the end of 1988 nearly all the mature ride-side sallows had been felled – long before they would have been out-competed by taller-growing trees.

After a short lull, thinning work returned with a vengeance in 1991 and I wrote mournfully in the diary: *I think I've seen the last of* iris *here*. I was wrong, of course, for the following year thinning ceased and the sun shone. I saw my first Straits Emperor for six years. Even better, White Admiral resurged in the eastern half, which was recovering nicely from collateral damage incurred during thinning works. Matters improved further in 1993, especially for Silver-washed Fritillary, which had a bumper year. The following year brought the first Black Admiral for eleven years, and an encouraging flight of Purple Emperor.

But heavy thinning work returned with a vengeance in 1996, and Straits Inclosure was abandoned as a conservation area and de-prioritised for nature conservation by the Forestry Commission as it was not a Site of Special Scientific Interest (SSSI). Again, White Admiral and Purple Emperor populations collapsed; the former to the point of near-extinction, whilst the latter became dependent on the young New Ride sallows. At this inapposite time, the Purple Emperor was adopted by the Forestry Commission as the symbol of its new commercial creation, Alice Holt Forest Woodland Park. A visit in perfect weather on July 17th 1999 revealed a wood almost void of butterflies, as populations of both White Admiral and Silver-washed Fritillary had plummeted. The Straits entered the new millennium at an unprecedented nadir, especially as the harvesting work had failed to open any of the overhung rides. I could scarcely visit, the experience being too painful, the desecration of spirit of place and personal memory too great.

There then began seven peaceful years, during which vegetation and butterflies recovered from the maelstrom inflicted by Euroforest, the Forestry Commission's contractors. Of course, vegetation conditions recovered ahead of the butterflies, which meant that 2001 was a particularly bleak year for Silver-washed Fritillary and White Admiral – the latter was not recorded at all, and only produced a singleton in 2002. Yet all the while the Emperor population was rebuilding. The great summer of 2003 saw Purple Emperor breeding in the New Ride sallows. Populations of other butterflies were recovering too. The only gremlin was an infuriating bleeping machine, erected on a pole in the centre of the wood by Forest Research, contributing data to the Forestry Commission's Environmental Change Monitoring Programme. The good people of Frith End raised such a rumpus that the wretched thing was switched off, permanently.

By 2006 the Straits Inclosure was once again rising towards its old dizzy heights, though it had changed vastly in appearance. That summer saw a great July. Black Admirals reappeared, indicating that the White Admiral population had recovered. Purple Emperor was impressive, especially around the New Ride sallows. The wood even made it on to a primetime BBC1 television programme.

The next round of timber harvesting took place after the wet summer of 2007. But something had changed, wondrously, and despite difficult ground conditions the work was sensitively conducted during the autumn, with fair regard to conservation principles. A new approach was adopted: small groups of trees were felled in smash-and-grab raids along a herringbone access system. This method left numerous pockets of understorey intact, such that the White Admiral breeding grounds were not devastated, and three new glades were cut out along New Ride. Unforeseen allies had rallied to the butterflies' cause, for that August stringent new measures for the conservation of European Protected Species were imposed on the UK by the European Union. The Forestry Commission realised that forestry operations would have to take the ecological requirements of bats and the Hazel Dormouse firmly into account. A corner seemed to have been turned.

The Straits produced a great flight of Purple Emperor in 2009. The BBC Natural History Unit descended to film Emperors and captured some immensely impressive footage, notably of four males searching sallows for freshly emerged females. Sadly and surprisingly, early in 2010 the Forestry Commission, in a moment of supreme *lapsus*, felled nearly all the sallows along New Ride, ostensibly of necessity in order to resurface the ride, leaving a scatter of token specimens. No consultation had taken place. The Forestry Commission received a large number of complaints.

It is, of course, unwise to write an account of one of the seven Alice Holt Forest inclosures without adequate reference to the other six, but as is the case with so many of our larger butterfly sites, one part has absorbed a disproportionate percentage of recording effort. However, casual observation elsewhere in Alice Holt has recorded similar highs and lows; the pattern is the same, and the causes similar.

This account shows that the three key species of butterfly have experienced huge vicissitudes in this wood over the 39-year period, with the main drivers being tree-felling operations and the opening up and closing over of rides. Above all, it shows that within a large woodland system butterflies can experience dynamic fluctuations in population size, though in this case the lows were human-induced and need not have been so acute. The practices that have adversely affected butterflies and butterflying in the Straits Inclosure hopefully now belong in the buried past. The Straits now seems to stand at the dawn of a new, more enlightened era. Perhaps with forestry, as with so many other countryside management practices that impact on wildlife, it matters not so much what you do, but rather *how* you do it.

10 *Out of the seventies*

The final two years of the 1970s were characterised by cold, snowy winters, late springs and what a cynic might deem 'typical' summers. We were in the shadow-land of 1976, some sort of doldrums before the next sequence of good summers materialised. Butterflying requires the patience of Job at the best of times, but during poor summers it also requires the ability to use fine weather spells as and when they come along. The motto is simple: *carpe diem, quam minimum credula postero* – or more simply, seize the day.

Five of our butterfly species pass the winter as hibernating adults – Brimstone, Comma, Peacock, Red Admiral and Small Tortoiseshell. Almost every year one of them comes through the winter better than the other four, and establishes itself as the butterfly of that particular early spring. Until recently the usual contenders in these rites were the Brimstone and Small Tortoiseshell, with the Comma and Peacock occasionally claiming the honours. On just a few occasions there was no discernible winner. Until around 2000 relatively few Red Admirals were successful in overwintering, so it seldom figured in this competition before then.

In 1978 the Small Tortoiseshell was the butterfly of the spring, at least in and around Hampshire. My first butterfly of that year was indeed a Small Tortoiseshell, seen feeding on Snowdrop flowers in West Worldham churchyard, near Alton, on March 3rd. Shortly afterwards Small Tortoiseshells were evident everywhere. March, such as it was, belonged to them, then they seized April and made it imperiously theirs. By early May they were laying eggs on the fresh growth of sunlit nettle patches that fringed the wasteland around Farnham Art College. I observed some fifty individuals there on May 7th, feasting on Dandelion flowers, seeking mates in the case of still-ardent males, and in the case of some half-dozen females laying batches of bright green eggs on the underside of Stinging Nettle sprays. What surprised me, though my new friend Ken Willmott had already observed this, was that females were adding fresh eggs to pre-existing batches. In one instance fresh eggs were added two days after the first batch had been laid. Of course, it was impossible to tell whether this was the same female returning to add to her own clutch, or some opportunism by another. Since then I have on several occasions observed Small Tortoiseshells adding to pre-existing egg batches.

Spring was backward, so backward in fact that Orange-tips did not begin to emerge before St George's Day and may not have laid any eggs during April that year – which is one of the characteristics of a genuinely late spring. Also, I saw no Green-veined Whites or Speckled Woods that April, and heard of none elsewhere. May commenced with the coldest and wettest May Day since 1940 and wobbled for quite a while. The diary for May 8th states: *The ambition of today was to rain. For nineteen hours it tried desperately, eventually succeeding at 7 pm when a tedious drizzle commenced.* But then May sorted itself out, even ending strongly. The Small Tortoiseshell led the way. On the 15th, when the first Duke of Burgundy of the spring was seen at Noar Hill, I at last observed Small Tortoiseshells mating, in the nettle beds bordering the lane that leads past Charity Farm up to Noar Hill. Oh, that's a common butterfly, it's always mating, you may think; but some butterflies are incredibly secretive, retiring well away from people to conduct their personal business. Such is the Small Tortoiseshell, though their lengthy chase-me-about courtship flights are frequently observed, particularly in late afternoon. At 3.40, as I was about to find out whether my motorbike was going to start or not, a pair was seen playing follow-my-leader.

Diary, May 15th 1978: *They settled quickly on a nettle leaf, wings open, the male below the female, sometimes touching her with his forewings and antennae ... the same thing happened on another nettle leaf. Then the female flew down at the edge of the nettle patch amongst 6-inch tall nettles and grasses. They crawled well into the nettle patch and were promptly in cop, resting on grass, in deep shade, wings closed. I left them there.*

I had left them at 4 pm, and they were still there, still joined together, early the following morning. Gentlemen, ladies even, we are outdone: they mated for eighteen and a half hours.

Inspired, on May 19th I proposed to the young lady I had been courting at Farnham Art College, exactly ten years on from my life-altering *dies mirabilis* in Marlpost Wood. The Duke of Burgundy was again present, though no longer a Fritillary by name, for that epithet had been removed by a committee in some powerhouse of taxonomy somewhere. My own personal drama took place on a Yew log in the top chalk pit on Noar Hill, up against the Beech hanger. There was an azure haze about the sky that day, which juxtaposed and mingled curiously with the verdant yellow-green of young Beech leaves, and a poignant stillness hung within the air. The colours and intensity of light were right. Holly Blues and Green Hairstreak males darted about along sunny wood edges, whilst Dingy Skippers and Duke of Burgundy males squabbled over territorial rights down below. There was magic in the air, not all of it entomological. The young lady, incidentally, agreed to my proposal, though I had little to offer her other than love and the promise of a life of wonder within the world of Nature.

Much of that early summer was spent studying the Duke of Burgundy, particularly by following the fastidious females and recording precisely where they deposited their eggs. That, as I had learnt from Professor Jeremy Thomas, our foremost butterfly scientist, provided the main route towards understanding a butterfly's ecology. I also started systematically counting them on Noar Hill, and searched for new colonies elsewhere on the western South Downs. Holly Blues and Green Hairstreaks were also studied, the former being observed depositing eggs, unusually, on the buds of Dogwood and Purging Buckthorn on Shoulder of Mutton, the down dedicated to the memory of Edward Thomas above Petersfield. On Shoulder of Mutton Hill I studied Grizzled Skippers, watching them lay their eggs on the undersides of Common Agrimony leaves. I searched hard there for the Duke of Burgundy, and in suitable habitat patches on nearby Wheatham Hill, but found none. It should have been there, for everything was right. This was a disappointment, as unoccupied habitat is often a sign of a butterfly in decline. Edward Thomas, my poetic hero, had rather let me down.

The Marsh Fritillary colony on Bartley Heath, near Hook, was also tracked down. The butterfly had been introduced to an open expanse of humid heathland here by Peter Cribb of the Amateur Entomologists' Society in 1970, when its original location was being converted into the Hook interchange of the M3 motorway. The Marsh Fritillary fared well there in some years, but usually managed merely to subsist from year to year. In the early 1990s, Bartley Heath was heavily grazed by ponies, and the Marsh Fritillary quietly disappeared.

Worse was to befall a much larger and entirely natural population at Foxlease Meadows, near Fleet, which I first got to know in 1978. Here, the butterfly regularly abounded in a series of marshy meadows that were owned by the Ministry of Defence and grazed by cattle run by its tenant farmer. Melancholy Thistle grew in several of the meadows and Water Violet in the ditches. On Saturday June 23rd 1979 England was playing the West Indies in the cricket world cup final at Lords. The proceedings were broadcast live all over Foxlease Meadows via a small transistor radio in my breast pocket. But the news was bad, the main Marsh Fritillary breeding area had been planted up with conifers and Collis King and the invincible Viv Richards were flaying the English attack all around the ground. Let it be known, that each time a boundary was conceded a batch of conifers was wrenched angrily from the breeding ground. The brilliance of the West Indian batting that afternoon ensured that a sizeable area was cleared. These efforts made no difference, for after a major population explosion during a fine summer sequence during the early 1980s the Marsh Fritillary spiralled into a terminal decline there. The M3 ripped through its heartland and the town of Fleet expanded onto much of its habitat. Several of the best meadows were preserved as token nature reserves, rather pointlessly as the necessary grazing proved all but impossible to implement in these isolated fragments, and the butterfly's foodplant was quickly swamped by rank grass.

Back in early June 1978, an expedition was launched in pursuit of the Chequered Skipper in the western Highlands. In many ways this was a typical southerner's expedition after this most distant of our butterflies, for a spell of fine weather ended the day we set off and much time was spent waiting for deluges to end, and then for hanging mists and vapours to clear. The mountains regularly disappeared, and at times even the loch surfaces. Grey was the dominant colour in the landscape. It was all so different to my previous expedition to that region, which had been an ecstatic romp in quintessential late spring weather only four years previously. The Small Pearl-bordered Fritillary, a species that is very common along the loch sides there and which, crucially, has a lower weather threshold than the Chequered Skipper, completely stole the show. As soon as the weather began to relent they appeared in myriads, everywhere, courting, mating, laying eggs, feeding on Bird's-foot Trefoil and early bramble flowers, and doing everything a butterfly ought to do, to perfection. The Chequered Skipper, however, was scarcely in the giving vein, but did appear, reluctantly, whenever the sun made more than a transitory appearance. The weather became so dreich, to use the wonderfully apt Scots term for foul and abusive weather, that in desperation we visited that most dysfunctional of Highland tourism venues, the Aviemore rubbish dump. This was a renowned site for the Kentish Glory moth, whose eggs and larvae could be found on young birch bushes around the fringes of the tip. None was found, we caught colds and were eaten alive by assorted biting Diptera (flies).

Yet, on our final day the sun shone strongly, albeit after a wet morning. Chequered Skippers were duly found in several places along the northern shore of Loch Arkaig, particularly on a promontory jutting into the loch just east of Auchnasaul and in a young conifer plantation that later became part of Butterfly Conservation's reserve at Allt Mhuic. The following week Ken Willmott visited this area, in lovely weather, and fared considerably better. My diary reads:

> We must have seen getting on for a thousand C. selene [Small Pearl-bordered Fritillary] along the three-mile stretch from Clunas house to Auchnasaul today. It was worth coming all this way for them alone.

That was quite some statement. We had driven over 800 kilometres (500 miles) each way to see them in Scotland, when all along there was a huge colony in Hartley Wood, back in Hampshire, right next to where I was then living.

Back on Noar Hill, the Small Blue was having a good year. Its larval foodplant, Kidney Vetch, had proliferated there after the drought of 1976, and the butterfly was tracking its foodplant. The vetch is primarily a biennial, and seedlings that germinated there in 1977 were beginning to flower. The plant spread further in subsequent years, peaking on the reserve in 1980, and the butterfly population followed its host plant, almost doubling in 1979 and again in 1980. Strangely, though, the plant decreased there following the hot summers of 1983 and 1984. I know not why.

Midsummer butterflies were late in appearance in 1978, though they were blessed with much decent weather. For some reason or other the Black Hairstreak had one of its periodic good years. On June 30th I saw some fifty individuals at Drunkard's Corner, a solitary but deeply evocative place where a forgotten ancient drove-way winds around the south-easternmost corner of Bernwood Forest, through caverns of ancient Blackthorn stems. On a second visit there ten days later I encountered females laying their eggs, the first time I had witnessed this – only the eggs were so superbly camouflaged that they were almost invisible, especially when tucked into a striation in the Blackthorn stems or placed in the node of a thorn spike. Wood Whites were bumbling idly by, for in those days this butterfly was well established in Bernwood Forest, as was the agile Dark Green Fritillary in large grassy clearings.

White Admirals emerged in stupendous numbers in Alice Holt Forest. Strangely not a single 'Black Admiral' variation was recorded all summer, though a few appeared the next. I even saw them mating, for the first time. This took place high up in an oak in Alice Holt after a lengthy follow-my-leader courtship flight. It was not until 2012 that I saw this species pairing again, and then only when a pair was blown out of the oak crowns by a strong wind. Quite simply, some butterfly species are seldom if ever observed mating.

The Purple Emperor waited until mid-July before appearing, but then put on a fine performance. The males were very wound up that year, perhaps because there were enough of them around to aggravate each other into activity, and also because their activities did not get suppressed by hot weather. Occasionally in butterflying one goes back in time, momentarily but iteratively. This happened to me on July 29th 1978 when I observed a female of the ab. *semi-iole* variety (with significantly reduced white markings) laying eggs and skulking around in the very same Alice Holt glade where I had observed an almost identical female back in 1976.

Noar Hill produced an acute aberration of the Marbled White, a black and tan beast with little white. It then went further, producing the first of a series of blue Small Skippers. To describe them as blue is no exaggeration, and the term was used in accounts of this remarkable occurrence in the *Entomologist's Gazette* and *The Butterflies of Hampshire*. Fresh specimens of these Small Skippers possessed bright blue body hairs, akin to those of a fresh male

Chalkhill Blue. The wing uppersides were steely blue when viewed at certain angles, though at other angles or in poor light they were more of a bluish-buff colour. This aberration has yet to be formally described, not least because I never had a net on me when one appeared (though I may have lacked the heart to catch and kill one anyway, even though in the interests of science I should have). When it is described, it could perhaps be called ab. *noari*, after Noar Hill. It is certainly far more extreme, and distinctly bluer, than the very pale variety ab. *pallida*, which also appeared occasionally on the reserve during that era.

August 1978 also produced a Queen of Spain Fritillary, which landed at my feet on Kingsley Common, one of the sandy heaths near Bordon, on the 14th. There was sufficient time to blink twice, expostulate loudly and verify the vision before it flew off rapidly, and was not seen again. This was an odd sighting, as 1978 was not a good year for migrant butterflies and this was the only Queen of Spain recorded then, and far inland too. I had only gone there to watch Graylings and Gatekeepers laying eggs, but then butterflying specialises in producing the unexpected.

The year then ended as it had begun, for the Small Tortoiseshell was very much the butterfly of the autumn, gathering in numbers in gardens to feed up on nectar prior to hibernation. Outside my front door they fed on an old variety of *Calendula* grown in large tubs. It was my first butterfly of that year, and my last.

There then began the infamous Winter of Discontent. The diary describes the winter of 1978/79 in some detail:

> *The autumn of 1978 was dry and mild until mid-November when it became very cold. Snow fell just prior to Christmas and some parts of southern England had a White Christmas. That was just the prelude. Heavy snow fell on the last day of the year and the New Year began with four to five inches on the ground in East Hampshire, though further west and north it was measured in feet.*

I spent that New Year's Day brushing snow off the rafters and bedroom ceiling of the primitive cottage in the woods in which I was living – it had drifted in as snow dust on a brisk wind, and settled there an inch deep. The diary continues:

The third coldest January this century materialised (after 1942 and 1963). Snow lay in Hampshire all January ... Hardly a night went by without a noticeable frost and the maximum temperature recorded all month was 6°C. No Snowdrops were noted. February started dry and comparatively mild but the second week saw the return of the very cold weather, with a St Valentine's Day Massacre in the form of six inches of snow that was again loath to melt. More fell during a cold but otherwise wet final week. A few catkins appeared right at the end of the month. March saw a change in the weather, but not for the better: the sun hardly shone at all during the wettest March on record, and more snow fell on the 21st, the First Day of Spring.

Suffice to say that a cold, wet and sunless April ensued. The whole nation struggled, not just its naturalists.

I was living in a cottage deep in the woods, at the end of 2 kilometres of rutted lane that plunged suddenly down the East Hampshire Hangers escarpment between East Worldham and Oakhanger, on the edge of my beloved Hartley Wood. The cottage lacked electricity, loft insulation and double glazing, and indeed any modern comforts. Water was obtained from a spring, in containers. I had dug out a cesspit system and installed a simple toilet. Heating, as such, was provided by a Calor gas stove and open fires. Dead elm trees were in plentiful supply, though they were incredibly hard to saw and chop, and then burnt too fast and gave off little heat. The country was in turmoil, culminating in the collapse of the Labour government and the surge to power of Margaret Thatcher. Alton, my nearest shopping centre, was the first town in the UK to run out of sugar in a nationwide wave of panic buying and hoarding. All this mattered little to one whose windows iced up nightly, both inside and out. Existence degenerated into subsistence. Serotonin levels were dangerously low. The sun disappeared into the pall of winter, seemingly for weeks on end. It was all akin to the apocalyptic world that Byron describes in his poem 'Darkness' –

I had a dream, which was not all a dream.
The bright sun was extinguished, and the stars
Did wander darkling in the eternal space,
Rayless, and pathless, and the icy earth
Swung blind and blackening in the moonless air;
Morn came and went – and came, and brought no day ...

But spring, when it eventually arrived, was all the sweeter. The bird life around the cottage had to be experienced to be believed, though it rendered sleep difficult. Nights pulsated with the songs of a dozen Nightingales, far and near, and reeled softly with the constant whirr of Grasshopper Warblers. At the first sign of dawn the Cuckoos started up, meeting noisily for courtship in a nearby prominent tree, their gathering tree. Minutes later the full dawn chorus began, such that the living air itself actually vibrated – certainly, the noise rattled my windows. Lesser Spotted Woodpeckers nested in a hole in the old sallow tree at the end of my washing line. In mid-May, I watched a female Cuckoo lay an egg in a Dunnock's nest concealed amongst the Ivy jungle on the edge of the adjoining garden. The egg better resembled a Robin's than a Dunnock's, but it hatched and the youngster was successfully fostered. I followed the development of the young Cuckoo, which eventually flew in late June. The following year I found what may well prove to be my last ever Cuckoo's egg, in a Tree Pipit's nest in Hartley Wood.

The butterfly season was late, and with one or two exceptions distinctly poor. Orange-tips hardly got going before May, again laying no eggs in April, and my first Speckled Wood was not seen until May 12th. Pearl-bordered Fritillaries did not begin to appear before the end of May. Then June was so indifferent that they almost lingered into July. The Small Pearl-bordered Fritillary delayed its appearance until mid-June and lasted well into July. It was a year of record latest sightings, with the Orange-tip being the pick of the bunch: I saw the year's last on July 8th, the day after my wedding day. There was no contest for the title of Butterfly of the Year. The Purple Emperor won it fair and square, emerging in considerable numbers in late July, squabbling incessantly and at times violently, and laying eggs in the sallow tree at the end of my washing line. In one glorious moment I saw a posse of seven in a vista.

And as for the cottage in the woods, that little piece of Walden? The following winter the landowner had no proper work for his farmhands to do, so he instructed them to clear the Nightingale's (and Brown Hairstreak's) Blackthorn scrub. The year after that, much of the adjoining ancient oak woodland was felled too, and a rye grass field was duly created, where sheep developed foot rot. The farm workers were then made redundant, ending their lives in council flats in Alton and Basingstoke. The 'ethnic cleansing' of the rural poor had begun. Their cottages were sold off as second homes – a fate that also befell my little cottage, but only after all the necessary utilities had been installed. I have never been back, for the place I loved has gone.

Winter

Be near me when my light is low,
When the blood creeps, and the nerves prick
And tingle; and the heart is sick,
And all the wheels of Being slow.

Alfred, Lord Tennyson, from 'In Memoriam'

For lovers of sunshine, and of butterflies, our winter constitutes a spiritual prison sentence of sixteen weeks of non-existence. Think of your nightmare school-timetable day (for me, double maths, double French and double physics), and grind that out, in mindless repetition, day after wretched day, for four interminably long months: that is precisely what our butterfly lovers suffer, annually. They scarcely belong in this country, and perhaps should be migratory beings, wintering on the shores of the Mediterranean.

Winter begins in November, sometime, normally late on, depending on how unkind the Fates are feeling. Of course, we deny it for as long as possible; not least because it takes a while for winter to erase the memories of warmth and sunshine, for such pleasantries are keen to linger. December gets away with it, just, because of the helter-skelter rush that has become Christmas – that takes our minds off the dying of the light, and of the year. But when Christmas has passed we are left alone, bereft. New Year is a mirage. We should be in hibernation.

It is curious that most of our so-called country sports are winter-based activities. Perhaps they are so keenly defended because they help their practitioners endure winter, for without precious days out with hounds or gun surviving winter might prove too difficult? The humble butterfly lover survives on paltry fare, of searching for the eggs of Brown Hairstreaks on Blackthorn shoots, or Purple Hairstreak eggs around clusters of oak buds, or White-letter Hairstreak eggs placed, symbolically, where the old and new wood meet on elm twigs. The bravest search for White Admiral larvae, in tiny spun-up Honeysuckle leaves, or prospect new places. But this is subsistence fare: a bolder strategy is required. First, I shortened winter by studying Marsh Fritillary larvae, which emerge from hibernation in mid to late January; and then slew it altogether by following Purple Emperor larvae through their five-month-long period of hibernation. Once winter is placed under the spell of the Purple Emperor it is rendered impotent.

Yet winter remains at least one month too long, and that month is January. It is the slowest month of the year, with time outworn, almost still. Throughout this shadow-land of transience the sun angles remain dangerously low, and we may suffer day after day of

opacity. We are in the Underworld. There is no lucidity in January skies, the days of so-called 'crisp winter sunshine' are at best a sad parody of the real thing, summer. No changes of any note occur in the countryside that long and pallid month, bar the mustard-haze yellowing of catkins in clouded drab copses and hedges, whilst Snowdrops apart the gardens remain soulless. We are entombed, under winter's pall.

One of the most important, and little used, words in the English language is 'apricity'. It means the warmth of winter sunshine. The secret is to sit in it, behind a pane of glass, and allow the warmth of the light to reach the eyelids. That will help you through, but in true desperation visit a butterfly house.

Yet winter has its magic: its blood-drained sunsets, a tranquillity and calmness of air that is so seldom experienced in summer, days of embalmment when the light fades stealthily from noon, its wakefulness. It is a period of meditation, and of dreaming.

We all, as pilgrims, look out for the signs of spring – yet they are not signs, or even tokens of hope, but actualities. It is February that brings most hope. February is much maligned, yet it is the shortest and often the driest month of the year; and apart from in severe winters it is a month of transition, into spring. In a mild winter it is indeed the first month of spring, for spring begins when the Rooks start to build, which is normally around Valentine's Day. February is also the month of many firsts – Coltsfoot, Primrose, Celandine, sallow blossom, bumblebee and butterfly – and the slow inexorable lengthening of days. A good February will issue a new sign of spring almost every other day, making it a month of immense hope. Then, at the end of the month the Blackbirds begin to sing, and they sing of spring.

Early on in his rural prose-poem 'The South Country' (1909) Edward Thomas muses: 'It is not Spring yet. Spring is being dreamed ...' He then loses his thread, badly in fact (he later regretted writing the book, knowing that he could and should have ventured deeper); but what he had almost stumbled upon is the concept that spring needs to be dreamed up, ideated. Surely that is precisely what the sleeping trees are doing? In which case there may be a role for us too, in the meditative conjuring up of spring; so maybe we need winter after all, though it certainly needs shortening.

> Over the land freckled with snow and half-thawed,
> The speculating rooks at their nests cawed,
> And saw from elm tops, delicate as flower of grass,
> What we below could not see – Winter pass.

Edward Thomas, 'Thaw'

11 *In and out of war: the early 1980s*

After three lousy summers we were due some serious sunshine, and we got it in 1980 – for a while. After a mild and dry winter, a distinctly warm and dry spring developed. Virtually no rain fell during April or May, with day after day of hot sunshine. It was the driest May in England for fifty years. Butterflies emerged early, and in pleasingly good numbers, with core populations recovering well after being suppressed by three dire seasons. At Noar Hill, the Duke of Burgundy began to emerge on May 4th, which at the time constituted its earliest known appearance there. Pearl-bordered Fritillaries and Wood Whites started to appear soon after. Sprinklers were in use on lawns, hose-pipe bans were being introduced and two-thirds of Ludshott Common, a vast expanse of heather and gorse heath near Hindhead, went up in flames on May 12th. It felt like 1976 was returning.

The drought coincided with an attempt to restore grazing to Noar Hill, after an absence of some thirty years. We (being the Hampshire & Isle of Wight Naturalists' Trust) borrowed 34 sheep from the Nature Conservancy Council at Old Winchester Hill NNR, in the Meon valley. On the advice of various experts, notably Dr Francis Rose, who lived nearby at Liss, Lady Anne Brewis, a gloriously eccentric but brilliant botanist and dearest of friends, and the Nature Conservancy Council's wardens from the Martin Down and Old Winchester Hill NNRs, Paul Toynton and John Bacon, it was decided to graze a quarter of the reserve that spring. The objectives were to eliminate scrub and reduce the dominance of coarse grass. Much later I learnt that grazing can only ever succeed with the latter aim. Bacon masterminded things. I had met him for the first time the previous year, on a sheep-handling course, where he was engagingly teaching a small group of volunteers how to dag sheep: 'Sheep need dagging out, and you need to learn how to dag 'em,' he preached. He and I instantly forged a partnership which explored various new directions in nature conservation over three decades. But this first venture was a disaster. In the absence of perimeter fencing the sheep were contained within electric flexi-netting, which was not easy to erect or maintain on Noar Hill's undulating topography of chalk pits and spoil heaps. There was also no water supply, so we ferried water up to the animals in large containers, in heat that seemed to stupefy sheep. The inevitable happened: the sheep broke out, or were otherwise released, and wreaked havoc in Farmer Vining's barley field. Mercifully, Vining and I both emanated from the same corner of Somerset, and so had some form of understanding, in that at least I could understand him when in the heat of the moment he lapsed into deep West Somerset brogue. It took several years to get grazing back on the reserve, as we had to raise the necessary funds for perimeter fencing and a water supply, for in those days there was little in the way of grant aid.

That May I cracked how to find the larvae of the Dark Green Fritillary, at Stockbridge Down and Broughton Down in west Hampshire. Their larvae either take the upper third of the leaf or remove the basal lobes, producing distinctive and fairly diagnostic 'eating marks'. Later I learnt that I had not discovered anything new, for many of the old butterfly collectors had developed that particular skill – as far back as mid-Victorian times. Whilst the Dark Green Fritillary is one of our boldest butterflies, relishing a battle with the wind on a downland crest, its larvae are the most frightful cowards, curling up into a tight, paranoid ball when disturbed.

In early June the Painted Ladies showed up in numbers, for the first time since 1969. We had hardly seen this loveliest of migrant butterflies during the late 1970s, even during the great summer of 1976, when I recorded less than twenty. But no sooner had they arrived, along with a pleasing number of Red Admirals and the West Indian cricketers, complete with a battery of fast bowlers of Richter scale magnitude, than the weather collapsed, badly. We suffered the wettest English June since 1912. It was also cold and sunless. The problem was that the high-summer butterflies, including Purple Emperor, Silver-washed Fritillary and White Admiral, had all pupated early because of the fine April and May, which provided excellent conditions for rapid larval growth. They then got stuck for ages in the vulnerable pupal state, and seemingly suffered high levels of mortality. Certainly White Admiral and Purple Emperor populations collapsed badly.

But what the Emperor lacked quantitatively he made up for qualitatively. On the last day of July, a visit to Shortheath Pond, a small acidic lake on one of the East Hampshire heaths, produced a most edifying encounter with this most memorable of butterflies.

Diary, July 31st 1980: *A lovely male was spotted settling on the bare sand on the pond's east side. We watched him feeding firstly on Rabbit droppings and then on damp sand. He had obviously just emerged since his wings were perfect and still soft, and he was of above average size as well. We watched him as he fed for about fifteen minutes, crawling over the sand and occasionally taking off and swooping down again a few yards away, flicking his wings at various flies and regularly showing his wonderful purple. He fed mainly with closed wings due to the wind but when possible he opened them. Of course I had only four shots left in the camera, and when I'd just changed the film he took off for good and began flying rather erratically over the pond westwards into the wind. He had not quite mastered the art of flying. He soon learnt, for a few yards out he encountered a male Emperor Dragonfly* Anax imperator *and the great Battle of the Emperors ensued. The dragonfly pitched into young butterfly with much wing rattling. For a full minute a wonderful battle was watched as the butterfly escaped west over the pond, rising to 60 feet, pursued by his tormentor. Suddenly, he turned on the dragonfly and explained concisely and conclusively who is Emperor of All Insects in this country. The* Anax *immediately returned to patrolling his reed bed, duly chastened.*

Almost a year later Shortheath was the setting of another memorable occasion, though this time the entomology played second or even third fiddle. We are all supposed to be able to remember precisely where we were and what we were doing when seminal moments in world history occurred. I was listening to *Test Match Special* on a small transistor radio and studying Grayling butterflies during the dramatic conclusion to the famous Headingley Test match of 1981 when, inspired by Ian Botham, Bob Willis and the late Graham Dilley, England came back from the dead to trounce Australia. What is worth recording here is that several anglers, who had been fishing placidly around the pond, suddenly went berserk when Willis took the final wicket. One slipped into the lake and half a dozen independently danced jigs, to the (hopefully perpetual) bemusement of a couple of lady dog walkers. For the record, I was butterflying at Denbies Hillside (NT) near Dorking during

Botham's stupendous innings at Old Trafford in the same series, when cricket proved rather a distraction from a fine display by the Chalkhill Blue. It is, of course, against National Trust bylaws to listen to radios on Trust land – but it is unlikely that anyone has infringed that particular bylaw more than me, for I have butterflied intensively on NT land and *Test Match Special* is the perfect accompaniment to a day's butterflying.

Back in the summer of 1980, a belated honeymoon took place, along the Purbeck coast in late July. The weather was right, cloudless and almost calm; time itself stood still. We walked from east to west, and in consequence got sunburnt along the left side of our bodies. Lovers do things like that, but naturalists should know better. The Winspit, near Worth Matravers, is one of the most famous butterflying spots in the UK. Collectors used to work the downland slopes here, particularly looking for aberrations of the Chalkhill Blue, finishing the day with a well-earned beer in the Square & Compass at Worth Matravers. The area is also renowned for the pride of Purbeck, the Lulworth Skipper, though butterfly collectors tended not to trouble it much as it rarely varies from the norm in colouring or markings. It gathers in numbers on favoured flowers – Marjoram, knapweeds, scabiouses and, where available, Viper's Bugloss. Perhaps it rather lacks what used to be called moral fibre. The diary states: *The males are seemingly a trifle over-sexed. At 11.35 a pair met over some flowers and within 30 seconds were in cop... the receptive female was grabbed by the male without any preamble.* Some butterflies have elaborate courtship displays, many do not, and the Lulworth Skipper falls comfortably into the latter bracket. That same day produced a spectacular aberration of the Small Skipper, with prominent canary-yellow veins on the wing undersides.

We wandered westwards, past tussocks of Meadow Clary, drifts of Pale Flax and patches of exotic Viper's Bugloss and, best of all, some clumps of Yellow Vetchling. Our aim was to find the Long-winged Conehead, a cricket which at the time was confined to a mere nine populations along the coast of central southern England.

After hard endeavour we found it at Chapman's Pool. We need not have bothered, though, for within five years it had erupted out of its coastal strongholds to colonise spectacularly much of central southern England, including our garden at The Lodge, in the hamlet of Binsted Wyck near Alton. Butterflies have such powers too, though they need triggering, kick-starting.

But 1980 was a damaged summer, punctured by a rotten June, and butterfly populations were further harmed by other, shorter pulses of poor weather. The Painted Lady and Red Admiral immigrations of early June resulted only in a scatter of home-grown specimens in late August and September. They were certainly around and about, in twos and threes here and there, but a great many more home-bred specimens would have graced the turn of summer had June been less inclement. A few Clouded Yellows appeared inland, though again as only a shadow of what might have been, for a fair few had arrived in early June.

❧

1981 was designated Butterfly Awareness Year by a consortium of entomological societies, the World Wildlife Fund and the Nature Conservancy Council. The Large Blue had recently been declared extinct in Britain, and it was feared that the Heath Fritillary would follow. Interestingly, the Large Tortoiseshell had managed to sink into oblivion without anybody actually noticing, presumably because it was suspected of being partially migratory. But it was time for action, so Butterfly Awareness Year was announced, though the diary mused, *This is tempting providence, it's bound to rain all summer.*

It did rain all summer, or for most of it. March set the scene, being the second wettest on record. April started mild, producing early Orange-tips and Speckled Woods, but then fell apart: heavy snow fell over much of the country of the 24th and 25th, in an unseasonal blizzard, and then persisted on the ground into May. Many trees in leaf were caught out by the blizzard. May failed to redeem things, being the dullest since 1932, and one of the coolest.

The only golden moment was on the evening of the 10th when, after countless hours of searching over several years, I found my first Small Pearl-bordered Fritillary larva, feeding on Early Dog-violet leaves along the ride edge in Hartley Wood, Oakhanger, which at the time supported a genuinely large population of this local butterfly. Some British butterfly caterpillars are relatively easy to find in the wild, but many are not – and none more so than the Small Pearl-bordered Fritillary. The triumphant diary entry concludes, *I don't intend looking for them again.*

Another triumph of 1981 was finally seeing Commas mating. Like the Peacock, Red Admiral and Small Tortoiseshell, this familiar butterfly is seldom seen *in flagrante delicto*, though courting pairs and duos of battling males are regularly observed (and the latter readily confused with the former). The action occurred in our garden at The Lodge, Binsted Wyck, at the end of July. The Lodge was the most loveable if dilapidated of houses, the gatehouse to a crumbling Victorian edifice owned by one of the most remarkable, and eccentric, personalities of the twentieth century, Lady Charlotte Bonham-Carter. She was by birth a Wykeham, and Binsted Wyck was the family seat. Charlotte was a serious patron of the arts and of nature, and was my sponsor. We lived at The Lodge for ten glorious years. The garden was cared for with butterflies and birds firmly in mind, alongside flowers, fruit and vegetables. Although in a hilltop position, it was well sheltered, being surrounded on two sides by an outgrown Beech hedge and on the others by entanglements of Laurel, Privet and other shrubs. Each high summer Comma butterflies would gather in the west-facing corner, especially in late afternoon and early evening. This was clearly an established assembly point for a butterfly that must have a highly sophisticated mate-location strategy, as it occurs at low population density. The diary recalls that in the late afternoon of July 29th two pairs of Comma were courting in the garden, the males pursuing the females around in a frenetic spiralling flight before losing them. Occasionally, a female would settle on shrub foliage, where the attendant male would seek to join her, body to body, only for the minx to change her mind at the last moment and fly off. Eventually, at 4 pm, a female led a male high into an Elder bush, where she settled receptively. They joined, in cop, instantly, before crawling out of view into the bush. Mating must have lasted only a little over an hour, as the successful male, with distinctively torn hindwings, was back in the courtship territory at 5.20, wanting more. Gentlemen, please …

Also that year, I was taken to a wood midway along Hampshire's northern boundary which held the vestiges of a colony of the rapidly declining High Brown Fritillary. These were hurtling about at speed within an ailing conifer plantation that had been adversely affected by the 1976 drought, and intermingling with a much larger population of equally frenetic Dark Green Fritillaries. I only positively identified one, a large female resplendent on a Marsh Thistle head, but felt at the time that that species was calling me. I had received The Call before, of course, by no less a being than the Purple Emperor, but he seemed to be dispensing with my services. This sighting near Kingsclere, and further sightings that summer on Arnside Knott in south Cumbria, constituted the beginning of a long personal journey, into the realm of that most wondrously named of our butterflies, the High Brown Fritillary.

But 1981 is most memorable for the Wildlife & Countryside Act (1981). The Thatcher government had inherited it as a bill from its predecessor, which it watered down heavily – but it did nonetheless produce it as an Act. Although diehard nature conservationists such as young Oates ardently believed at the time that the Act did not go anything like far enough, hindsight has to label it a success – simply because it was backed by an effective government agency, the Nature Conservancy Council. NCC, as it was known, actually had teeth, as well as strongly motivated and highly competent staff who were not bogged down by bureaucratic targets and reporting systems. We owe that generation of NCC staff a considerable amount. Of course, government soon realised that NCC was unhelpfully effective, and systematically neutered it.

One of the less widely recognised aspects of the Wildlife & Countryside Act was its impact on butterfly collecting, which it effectively drove underground. A small number of butterfly species were afforded full legal protection, and became untouchable, but many more were listed under preposterously bureaucratic trading restrictions. The 'trade-only' restriction, as it became known, annoyed everyone involved in butterflying: it angered the conservationists, who wanted to ban all collecting and the breeding for release into the wild of most species, and completely disaffected butterfly breeders, dealers and collectors. This schism has not been bridged, and the butterflying fraternity remains horribly divided, with a shadowy subculture. Furthermore, as most quality butterfly collecting grounds became Sites of Special Scientific Interest (SSSIs) under the Act, collecting became a decidedly risky business.

The spring of 1982 saw Britain at war, against unforeseen adversaries. Prior to April 2nd that year hostilities between us and Argentina had been limited, sensibly, to the football and rugby fields. Then, completely out of the blue, Argentina invaded a forgotten remnant of Empire called the Falkland Islands. This drama occurred as spring was getting going at the end of a challenging winter which had brought two spells of sub-zero temperatures and a snowy December.

Naturalists need strategies for surviving the British winter. I had surveyed the distribution of Brown Hairstreak in the Selborne area and had found that the butterfly liked young, dynamically growing Blackthorn stems that were grey in colour, and scarcely used the older, shiny red-stemmed variety. I had also determined that nearly all the eggs laid in hedges were pulverised by hedge trimming, making study singularly depressing.

The solution was to follow the larvae of the Wall Brown through the winter in the wild, on Noar Hill. Now, these are fun, yes fun. Following them is utterly fascinating. In that era Wall Browns were considered rather commonplace, though their adult populations were prone to great fluctuations, according to the vicissitudes of summer weather. Consequently, no one had really thought about studying them, there were higher priorities. During the mid-1980s, though, Wall Browns began to decline. We are still far from sure why. At Noar Hill, in August, the females tended to lay their eggs on grass roots protruding through the roofs of Rabbit holes or the overhangs of tractor ruts along the tracks bordering the reserve. The eggs look like tiny pearls, though they are greenish when first laid. I used to find little Aladdin's caves, containing as many as half a dozen eggs, as August merged into September. Following larval development seemed a natural thing to do, though larvae resulting from eggs laid in late summer have to make it through the winter. Fortunately, they do not wander far, living sedate lives close to where they had started off as eggs. I discovered that these tiny larvae, grass-green in colour, have the habit of basking in the sun on mild winter days when the vegetation is dry. That in itself is remarkable, as most butterfly books state that they are nocturnal. I also found that they begin feeding on very fine, soft grasses, such as Red Fescue and Yorkshire-fog, but graduate on to broader-leaved and coarser grasses, such as False Oat-grass and Upright Brome grass, as they grow bigger. Then, they will even feed on coarse-leaved sedges, notably Glaucous Sedge, a common downland sedge. My main discovery was that when fully grown the larvae return to the Rabbit-hole ceilings and tractor-rut overhangs to pupate – some pupated within a few centimetres of where they had started out as eggs, on the same substrates! There I found that there are two colour forms of the pupae, green and black.

Early in 1982, I found Wall Brown larvae out basking as early as January 23rd, only a week after a lengthy sub-zero spell. On the last day of the month, when it was almost warm enough for butterflies to fly, a good dozen were found, basking and even feeding a little. So much for larvae that are reputed to be nocturnal! In late March they changed skins for the last time, then fed slowly but steadily before beginning to pupate in mid-April, during a prolonged spell of fine weather. The first adult butterfly appeared there on May 10th.

Lest you think that following these larvae during the winter and early spring was easy, think again. It regularly took half an hour to find one, even in a known spot, for the larvae are wondrously cryptic, matching the grass blades perfectly. Also, I was forever finding Marbled White and Meadow Brown larvae, which closely resemble Wall Brown larvae in colour, though in spring the Wall Browns grew faster than their cousins and quickly became distinct. So, that is where my mind was when Britain went to war.

But, distant war apart, the spring of 1982 was fine, and spring butterflies thrived. The Duke of Burgundy put on a fine show at Noar Hill. I followed egg-laying females and staked out 317 eggs, with the intention of studying the larvae. Incredibly, 85 of those eggs (27%) were devoured by snails, mainly by the Kentish Snail (*Monacha cantiana*), which was feeding heavily on Coswlip leaves that year. Help was readily to hand in the nearby Gilbert White & Oates Museum (named after two explorers, Oates of the Antarctic and another Oates who got eaten by cannibals) – for the museum's curator, June Chatfield, had conducted her PhD research on that very species of snail. I stormed into the museum with Lettres of Fyre & Sworde:

'Your snail has been eating my butterfly eggs!' I exploded.

'I'm sure it didn't mean to,' June gently replied.

She was right. This snail is exclusively a herbivore and had been consuming eggs by accident, whilst grazing on Cowslip leaves. Its population was unusually high on Noar Hill in 1982, having increased during a sequence of wet summers. In the following two summers snail predation rates declined to 18% and 15% respectively, before subsiding to an insignificant 7% in 1985, as snail populations declined following a run of three hot dry summers – great for butterflies, but bad for molluscs: swings and roundabouts.

The Marsh Fritillary was on the move, forming new colonies in west and north Hampshire, and indeed in many other counties. Marsh Fritillaries are renowned for having occasional periods of expansion, and 1982 was the start of a major expansion phase for it. Please do not think that the status and distribution of our butterflies is remotely stable; they are forever expanding and contracting, and above all seeking to push limits – weather permitting.

That year brought a genuinely good summer, the first since 1976, and one that ended a long sequence of summers that were disappointing or worse. Butterflies, being tremendous opportunists, largely bounced back. But I was hefted to Noar Hill and Alice Holt Forest that year, seldom venturing further afield and visiting only a few new places. Money was in short supply, which meant that journeys of discovery had to be rationed.

Also, in 1982 much time was devoted to establishing the Hampshire Branch of what is now Butterfly Conservation, but was then the sleepy British Butterfly Conservation Society. I had joined as a life member in 1977, for a paltry £15 which was indicative of the society's lack of ambition. Along with several like-minded folk I was determined to help transform, even revolutionise the society. The Hampshire Branch, which was founded late in 1981, came together largely on account of the energies and abilities of Pat Torrie, whom I had first met in Alice Holt back in 1976, and Christopher Holt, an old Etonian who had recently retired from being the Queen's banker and stockbroker. A gangly man with a mischievous sense of humour and the ability to communicate with anyone, Christopher had a remarkable knack of making money. To his considerable embarrassment he was forever winning the raffle at Branch events. He magnetically attracted money, and was remarkably well connected. Many a useful deal was done for butterflies whilst he was out shooting pheasants on various Hampshire estates. He had, of course, collected butterflies as a boy, but now regarded butterfly photography as a country sport every bit as challenging and enthralling as pheasant and partridge shooting, salmon fishing and even deer stalking, all of which he practised. My role was to set up field and indoor meetings, produce a newsletter, and attract new members. A great many were recruited on Noar Hill. Holt and Torrie conducted the real business: they pulled strings.

Prior to the metamorphosis of the British Butterfly Conservation Society into Butterfly Conservation, butterfly enthusiasts were essentially loners, socialising at best in pairs or as loose associations. It was the development of the county and regional branches that revolutionised the society, and the world of butterflying with it. Without Butterfly Conservation, butterfly enthusiasts would still be isolated loners, and their cause alienated from wider society. More than anything, Butterfly Conservation has made butterflies socially acceptable.

Noar Hill

Noar Hill, to the south of Selborne, may well be Britain's best-loved butterfly site, rivalled only by Arnside Knott in South Cumbria and Bentley Wood, on the Hampshire/Wiltshire border. It has long been a place of pilgrimage for admirers of butterflies and orchids. Butterflies have been studied there since 1975, and closely monitored since 1983, when a butterfly monitoring transect walk was established. Incredibly, only two people have ever walked that transect route, having become hefted to the place, part of it.

Noar Hill lies within a landscape of arable farming and hanging woodland, and adjoins an ancient woodland hanger (from the old English word *hangra*, meaning steeply sloping woodland). It has been a Hampshire Wildlife Trust reserve since the late 1960s, under a leasehold agreement from Rotherfield Estate. The reserve was scheduled as a Site of Special Scientific Interest (SSSI) in 1951, early on in the designation process. It is listed as a Grade 2 SSSI in Derek Ratcliffe's seminal review of important nature conservation sites in Britain (1977), failing to achieve Grade 1 status simply on account of its small size (about 10 hectares). More recently it has become included within a large, mostly wooded, Special Area for Conservation (SAC), which means it is part of an area of European importance for nature.

Essentially, Noar Hill is an intimate mosaic of short-, medium- and long-turf chalk grassland, scrub of various sorts, and developing woodland over ancient chalk pits. These pits are considered to be of medieval origin, though it is decidedly unclear what the material was used for, as extraction pre-dates the use of lime in agriculture. Soil depth varies, with skeletal soils on the pit floors supporting short-turf plant communities and deeper soils longer turf.

Little is known of Noar Hill's wildlife or management history prior to the 1950s. Gilbert White scarcely mentions the place, as it is situated just outside his parish. It was known by lepidopterists by the time of the First World War, though it lay in the shadow of a better-known butterfly locality at Selborne Common, where Brown Hairstreak and Duke of Burgundy occurred in good numbers. It appears that the butterfly interest gradually transferred from Selborne Common to Noar Hill during the second half of the twentieth century. The hill was grazed by cattle until about 1950, then lost the Rabbit population and became dominated by coarse grasses – primarily False Oat-grass.

Since 1975 no fewer than 46 species of butterfly have been recorded at Noar Hill. Although it is likely that no site of comparable size has surpassed this tally during that period, it must be emphasised that the figure in part reflects the butterfly richness of East Hampshire together with the intensity of butterfly recording. The maximum number of butterfly species that has been recorded on Noar Hill in a day is a staggering 30 – half the UK fauna!

All told, it is probable that 36 species of butterfly have bred on or adjacent to Noar Hill since 1975, though the tally was seldom in excess of 31 at any one time. The term 'adjacent' is important, as several common species breed only intermittently or in low numbers on the actual reserve, though they breed annually on the surrounding land. This category includes Peacock, Small Tortoiseshell, Large White, Small White, Green-veined White and Orange-tip, all of which are seen on the reserve annually, sometimes in numbers. Some species are intermittent residents on Noar Hill: as examples, Dark Green Fritillary and Brown Argus, which seem to colonise during good summer sequences, only to vanish during runs of poor summers.

The main finding of forty years of study is that Noar Hill's butterfly fauna has been in a state of flux throughout that whole period. There has been little constancy, despite and sometimes because of nature reserve management. Nearly all species have been subjected to significant population swings, and nearly all the true resident species have experienced population fluctuations of an order of magnitude or more. This may be the norm for butterfly faunas at site level, for status and distribution are dynamic.

Only Essex Skipper has become truly established since 1975, colonising spectacularly during the mid-1980s, though Purple Emperor may now be breeding regularly there at a low population level. The latter can be viewed as a negative indicator species for a chalk grassland site, being a scrubland species! Silver-washed Fritillary has also increased in frequency on the reserve, breeding in the adjoining hanger since major changes were inflicted by the great storms of 1987 and 1990.

These gains can be countered by some losses. Grizzled Skipper was resident up to 1976 but then died out, seemingly because of the adverse impact of the 1976 drought on its Wild Strawberry foodplant, which frazzled up and never recovered. The butterfly has scarcely been recorded since. In keeping with much of inland central southern England, the Wall Brown, which was moderately frequent on the reserve in most years until 1985, disappeared as a breeding species then and now occurs very rarely. In addition, Small Pearl-bordered Fritillary bred successfully in low numbers on Noar Hill between 1981 and 1983, when there was a large population in the nearby Oakhanger woods.

This last example reflects the butterfly wealth of the general area during the forty years, as do records of four Hampshire resident species which have only been recorded at Noar Hill as occasional strays (Silver-spotted Skipper, Pearl-bordered Fritillary, Marsh Fritillary and White-letter Hairstreak). In addition, I was accosted by a Large Tortoiseshell on the reserve in 1985, at a time when the butterfly had some form of status in the nearby hangers. Furthermore, several Silver-studded Blues were recorded in 1976, after major fires on the nearby heaths, and Grayling was recorded as singletons in 1976 and 2000. But Noar Hill's greatest moment occurred in 2013, when Tony James recorded a specimen of the continental subspecies of the Swallowtail whilst walking the weekly butterfly transect! The insect was almost certainly an immigrant, as several others were seen in the South-east during that memorable summer.

Some important butterfly foodplants are either absent from, or rare on, Noar Hill. Horseshoe Vetch and Devil's-bit Scabious, the main foodplants of three key butterfly species strongly associated with chalk grassland (Chalkhill Blue, Adonis Blue and Marsh Fritillary), are absent, and there is barely sufficient Common Rockrose and Honeysuckle for their associated butterflies (Brown Argus and White Admiral). Nonetheless, Chalkhill Blue does appear sporadically, mainly as solitary adventive males during hot summers. Also on the debit side, scarce migrant species are recorded only uncommonly at Noar Hill, doubtless due to its distance from the coast. Clouded Yellow does, though, appear intermittently and occasionally produces a weak summer brood.

The SSSI citation states that Noar Hill is of particular importance for populations of Duke of Burgundy, Brown Hairstreak and Small Blue. For such a small site, Noar Hill is unique in supporting populations of these three species. Noar Hill's butterfly species assemblage is, in effect, strikingly unusual for both species-presence and species-absence.

During the 1980s and for much of the 1990s, Noar Hill supported the largest known colony of Duke of Burgundy in Britain. It still supports one of the strongest. Admittedly, management between 1981 and the early 1990s favoured this species, with a third or quarter of the grassland area being grazed during the autumn and winter period, on rotation. With hindsight, this regime may well have exacerbated the pace of scrub invasion, though that was tempered by clearance work, and the grazing regime probably also allowed the Rabbit population to increase during the mid-1980s, to the temporary discomfort of the Burgundy and several other butterflies. The Rabbit population was duly reduced. Transect and

other data show that the Duke of Burgundy population peaked in 1990. After 1992 the butterfly went into steady decline, associated with a reduction in Cowslip abundance under different grazing regimes. But in 2011 the Burgundy resurged wondrously on Noar Hill, largely because of ideal flight-season weather.

The Brown Hairstreak persists in the district despite having been restricted to the immediate environs of Noar Hill and Selborne Common since the late 1970s. It remains to be seen for how long such a small area can sustain a population of a butterfly which normally occurs over large tracts of land, as it formerly did in East Hampshire. However, the Brown Hairstreak has the potential to expand strongly around Selborne, given positive changes in hedge management practice in the landscape, which are now starting to happen under Environmental Stewardship. On Noar Hill, this butterfly was for a long time greatly assisted by short-rotation coppicing of Blackthorn, but recently the reserve has become less suitable for it as a result of efforts to remove encroaching scrub from the chalk pits. There have been occasional years of relative abundance, notably 1977 and 1995, but the Brown Hairstreak is, in truth, highly vulnerable in the Noar Hill district. Its survival there is an example of a butterfly's sheer tenacity.

The third of Noar Hill's special butterflies, Small Blue, was always scarce and vulnerable, apart from during the late 1970s when its foodplant, Kidney Vetch, increased spectacularly following the great drought. The butterfly seemingly died out, and was not recorded during the years 2002–2004, before reappearing in 2005. This is curious, as the nearest known colonies are more than 15 kilometres distant and there is no other site within that radius where Kidney Vetch occurs. Small Blue seems to have died out and recolonised there before, for it was not recorded between 1968 and the second brood of 1976. Extinction can, of course, be very hard to prove.

Despite great and laudable conservation effort, the long-term future of Noar Hill's butterfly fauna is by no means secure. The site is probably too small to sustain permanent populations of most of its significant butterfly species and is inexorably moving towards woodland. Indeed, the sustainability of small, intimate mosaic habitats is highly questionable. The conflicts between the grassland and scrub interests are rampant here, and many of the features listed in the SSSI citation are associated with scrub, not grassland. The challenge of halting or reversing the pace of succession here may well be, with all due respect, beyond the capacity of today's conservationists. The real challenge is to enlarge the reserve significantly, most logically by returning much of the surrounding arable land to downland, and by seeking better ecological linkage with Selborne Common. The latter is being planned.

In terms of conservation lessons, the following are apparent from forty years' experience of Noar Hill. First, the cutting of scrub during the winter only encourages it – scrub loves being cut; once a scrub patch is cut for the first time, it ceases to be slow-moving and becomes fast-moving. Second, grazing only controls coarse grasses, which are actually highly susceptible to it (with the exception of the unpalatable False Brome); at Noar Hill, Red Fescue takes over instead – which supports fewer butterfly species. Third, grazing does not control scrub invasion, rather it encourages it by reducing the cover of competitive grasses that hinder scrub seedling establishment. Also, modern herbicides are surprisingly ineffective against some scrub species, especially regrowth. At present, like many nature conservation sites Noar Hill is trapped within an ever-increasing spiral of frenetic conservation management. It is as if nature conservation is trying to deny change; yet conservation, like life itself, is primarily about change, and especially about how we handle change. Everything changes, if it has not already changed.

But never mind any of that, for it is all of secondary importance. Understand the *genius loci*, the spirit of the place, and everything else follows. Above all, Noar Hill oozes an intense sense of its spirit of place, which absorbs and transforms the visitor. It is a place of pilgrimage, and a place where experience runs deeply. Yet it is being loved to bits, by visitors and conservationists alike, and is now looking badly worn out. The spirit of place is being compromised, eroded. Noar Hill is too small to maintain its wildlife interest, or sustain current visitor pressure. It needs to break out from its confines, and expand within the landscape. There are still unique aspects of the place: vistas out and views in, hidden worlds within worlds contained within each individual chalk pit, secret places where lovers can lie, banks where poets can dream, and perhaps Cowslip bells wherein freed spirits lie; it is an intensely poetic fragment within a landscape that is now well etched upon the national poetic map. Yet, strangely, Edward Thomas never wrote about it, though he wandered through it. Perhaps he died before he could eulogise it. He was saving it, perhaps. However, the opening lines of his poem 'Home' say it all:

Often I had gone this way before:
But now it seemed I never could be
And never had been anywhere else;
'Twas home; one nationality
We had, I and the birds that sang,
One memory.
They welcomed me. I had come back ...

(Steep, Hampshire, April 1915)

12 *The return of the wanderer*

The first Hawthorn leaves were spotted on an early-leafing bush at the Chawton roundabout on the A31, in East Hampshire, on February 3rd 1983, indicating how ridiculously mild the winter had been. Providence, of course, resents being tempted, and a bitter February ensued. Heavy snow fell on the 10th and 11th, and sat there, in stolid occupation of the land, only thawing late in the month. March was kinder, even producing a minor influx of that incessant wanderer from sunnier climes, the Painted Lady, along with a scatter of immigrant Red Admirals. That month belonged to the Small Tortoiseshell, logically so as this butterfly had been numerous throughout the summer and autumn of 1982. April wobbled, badly, being the wettest on record, though it gave a scatter of good days. Once again, the first Orange-tips emerged in Hampshire on April 16th, the day the first Cuckoos arrived. Then, there was even a heavy thunderstorm at the end of the month, a precursor of things to come.

May was so wet that Common Toads bred in the tractor ruts on Noar Hill, for the first and only time. The Duke of Burgundy flight season commenced late there, on May 11th, ushered in by a windswept individual which was rapidly blown away. Over in Alice Holt Forest, by mid-May White Admiral larvae had scarcely grown following their long hibernation, and Ash trees were starkly bare. Things were so late that the Pearl-bordered Fritillary was not out in the Chiddingfold woods on the 22nd, when the first Wood Whites were emerging. Frustrated away from conducting an experimental mark-and-recapture exercise on Duke of Burgundies on Noar Hill, I was forced first to study Wall Brown larvae again, as a consolidation exercise, and then to move on to White-letter Hairstreak larvae on the undersides of Wych Elm leaves.

Spring failed, but only for summer to burst through spectacularly and produce three hot dry months, before being blasted away by gales in early September. June commenced with a bang, literally, for a series of heavy thunderstorms crossed the Channel in its earliest hours, as if to obliterate a dismal spring and usher in a most hegemonic summer. Sunday June 5th started bright, though with a sultry and distinctly ominous breeze from the south-east. I had cycled the 8 kilometres to Noar Hill, into a stiff headwind, to count Duke of Burgundies in the chalk pits, knowing that the butterfly had emerged in goodly numbers there and would that day be at peak season. I counted 229 of them in two hours before all butterflies stopped flying. From noon, individual Dukes were seen flying into the tops of low trees, which they do just before the advent of seriously wet weather. I never finished my count. Nonetheless, 229 was the highest tally I ever managed on Noar Hill. Perhaps I would have totalled around 260 had the weather not deteriorated. Had I conducted a mental risk assessment I would have abandoned the count before noon, but I didn't; instead, I carried on in the greater interests of science and passion. Thunderstorms enliven me, electrifying the mind, and I relish them. I arrived home in the midst of a cataclysmic storm that lasted until mid-evening.

On the following day, which was cloudless, several immigrant Clouded Yellows were reported from the Isle of Wight and the South Downs. Seemingly, the butterflies had flown in on the back of the storms. These reports were difficult to comprehend, for I was part of a generation of naturalists who believed that Clouded Yellow invasions were a thing of the past. The butterfly had scarcely graced our shores during the 1960s and 70s. The thinking was that agricultural intensification in central and northern France deterred them from invading the Realm of Albion. There was some justification for this view, as between 1950 and 1983 the butterfly had only shown up in anything approaching reasonable numbers in 1955 and 1969. Even the great summer of 1976 produced only a handful. But 1983 changed all that: at least 15,000 individuals were recorded that year, by perhaps a quarter of the number of butterfly recorders active today.

In Hampshire, Clouded Yellows arrived in pulses during early June. Evidence suggests that they used the major river valleys, spreading onto the adjoining downland slopes. Having dedicated that period to studying the Duke of Burgundy and overseeing the reintroduction of the Marsh Fritillary to Conford Bog, near Bordon, at the request of the National Trust, I could only receive others' records, and wait in hope. The wait ended with a scheduled trip to the Isle of Wight on June 15th. Magic was evidently in the air, for the ferry trip over to the island was sublime, with the whaleback downs shimmering alluringly in an azure haze. There is only one way for the naturalist to cross over to the Isle of Wight – on the Lymington-to-Yarmouth ferry.

At Compton Chine we found the Glanville Fritillary numerous, seeing in the region of a couple of hundred of these hyperactive orange butterflies, skimming swiftly over the crumbling sandy cliff face and feeding greedily on the flowers of Bird's-foot Trefoil and Thrift. One particularly splendid individual fed for a while on a purple Southern Marsh-orchid spike, a memorable sight for those entranced by beauty. When a dark cloud came over they hid in grass tussocks. By Compton's Glanville Fritillary standards this was a good show, but this butterfly was comprehensively outgunned by another, for that afternoon I more than doubled my life tally of Clouded Yellows, which were arriving low over the sea in ones and twos. By the happiest of chances my dear friend Ken Willmott had also been lured over to the island: 'It's laying eggs!' he shrieked in delight, as a female flew in off the sea and halfway up the cliffs before commencing the all-important task of egg laying. Indeed, the females were depositing two eggs a minute on the leaves of tiny plants of Bird's-foot Trefoil and Hop Trefoil situated in pockets of bare sand, in the hottest spots. Two females were of the pale *helice* form, a rare colour form that occurs only in the female of the species, in which the gold is replaced by pale white. The Clouded Yellows were not alone, for a few Painted Ladies also arrived from distant shores.

Another batch of heavy thunderstorms hit central southern England on Midsummer eve, but these may have knocked out more Clouded Yellows than they brought in. But the influx had laid a mighty number of eggs, and had spread right the way up the country – and the weather was set fair, suggesting that there could be a sizeable emergence of home-grown Clouded Yellows later in the summer.

July dawned hot and fair, and then intensified in heat, exceeding 30 degrees Celsius for the first time since July 1976. The White-letter Hairstreak, which had had the worst of possible times following the demise of most of its elm trees during the mid-1970s, staged a most welcome comeback, having miraculously colonised the beginnings of a new generation of elms. White Admirals emerged in stunning numbers in Alice Holt Forest and elsewhere, including a couple of 'Black Admirals' – the rare ab. *nigrina* variety – followed by a mighty emergence of Silver-washed Fritillary and then Purple Emperor. The latter began to emerge in Alice Holt on the 11th, and went on to have one of its most monumental seasons. At Bookham Common in Surrey, Ken Willmott saw a string of eleven in the favoured male territory there, including a dark male of the *lugenda* or *iole* variety. This is the highest number of Purple Emperors seen in a single vista that I know of – ever. I have never exceeded seven myself, though I have managed that tally on several occasions. Ken became known as The Blessed Willmott after this veritable blessing, though no one has had the effrontery to tell him, for he is a man of impressive modesty.

I missed much of the 1983 Purple Emperor season, for NCC contracted me (ably supported by Mrs O) to survey the Carboniferous Limestone hills of the Morecambe Bay area for butterflies. Rather incredibly, they had little information on the butterfly wealth of these hills, as there were no active butterfly recorders in the region and those who travelled up from the south visited only a few well-known localities, notably Arnside Knott. I had visited the region before, having stayed with a cousin of Mother's in Grange-over-Sands in August 1967, and having visited Arnside Knott and Witherslack in 1976 and 1981, but this expedition felt like a pilgrimage into a new world, a promised land. Our journey up north took two days, in an old but intrepid Morris Minor (registration NCG 67F, Oxford blue) as we were delayed by punctures at Warwick and Preston. But the weather held, fantastically, which is what matters. For ten days we arduously searched the grey limestone hills on both sides of the Kent estuary, under sunny skies and in temperatures in the mid-twenties. Each place we visited revealed its own intense magic in its own particular way. At each, I left part of my soul behind, for such is the nature of our love for special places. Even the walled limestone massif of Whitbarrow revealed its secrets – it is a haughty place at the best of times, belonging more in the foothills of the Pyrenees than northern England, and it wishes to be treated with respect. We decided to storm it, like Joshua Son of Nun when he took the Promised Land.

We had been set two main target species, High Brown Fritillary and Duke of Burgundy. The former is not a beginner's butterfly, being hard at first to separate from the similar-looking and equally fast-flying Dark Green Fritillary, with which it almost invariably occurs. But I had already cut my teeth with this butterfly, both in the New Forest and up here, on the Morecambe Bay limestone hills. The latter species was easier, for I had developed a sound method of surveying for it – by searching for the near-diagnostic peppering and panelling holes that its larvae make in Cowslip leaves. We found huge colonies of High Brown Fritillary on several of the hills, north and south of the Kent estuary, and some just east of the M6 motorway. Whitbarrow proved to be a bastion of this magnificent fritillary. His Grace the Duke of Burgundy was more elusive, but south of the Kent we found small colonies on the summit of Arnside Knott, on nearby Heathwaite, at the delightful

Fairy Steps near Beetham, in two places on Gait Barrows NNR, and at Heald Brow in Silverdale. North of the estuary we found colonies on Yewbarrow, the lonely hill above Witherslack, along Brigsteer Scar, and a massive colony above the hamlet of Howe on the east flank of Whitbarrow.

Our main finding was that the area was clearly of national importance for both High Brown Fritillary and Duke of Burgundy, and probably for some other butterfly species too – and that we needed to return the following summer for further surveys, for the job was only half done. One interesting finding was the discovery that the Northern Brown Argus bred on both Common Rockrose and the rare Hoary Rockrose, for we found numerous ova and many young larvae on the latter plant along the crag and scar system that runs north to south due west of Kendal. The expedition was so successful that we were promptly contracted to return the following year.

Returning south, this time without vehicular vicissitudes, I found that butterflies had enjoyed a July even hotter and, localised thunderstorms apart, drier than that of 1976, and were consequently profuse. The Brown Hairstreak began to emerge at Selborne at the beginning of August, producing a relatively strong brood, though days quickly became too hot for this lethargic butterfly, the males of which are active only until the day warms up properly, after when they tend to become comatose high up in Ash trees. The hot weather had ensured a large second brood of the Wall Brown, a plethora of Common Blues, and a scatter of rare second-brood specimens of the Dingy Skipper, an early-summer species which will produce a few August specimens in hot summers. The downs turned grey, as is their wont in drought summers, clay soils developed hexagonal cracks, and the few dry heaths that had not been incinerated in 1976 went up in flames (heaths that had burnt up in 1976 had not yet regrown into a combustible condition).

A sizeable home-grown brood of Clouded Yellows started to emerge, from about July 23rd, probably augmented by fresh arrivals from across the Channel. Like the Painted Lady, this insect is a fast breeder, which in hot weather can metamorphose from egg to adult in six or seven weeks. There were reports of a swarm of them in a Lucerne field near Radlett in Herts. Every south-facing downland slope in southern England was graced by half a dozen or more of these living jewels, the males ceaselessly patrolling in search of freshly emerged females. There were at least ten on Noar Hill on August 4th, and I even saw a male flying down Selborne High Street, right outside the Gilbert White & Oates Museum. The females were again seen laying eggs on tiny semi-isolated plants of Bird's-foot Trefoil and other vetches in hot bare-ground situations, such as along the south-facing sides of tractor ruts. Numbers peaked during the second week of August, but remained high throughout that wonderful month. I followed another generation of larvae through in the wild, on Noar Hill and at Broughton Down in west Hampshire. The tiny larvae lay along the mid-ribs of the trefoil leaves, but the larger ones tended to hide away amongst the foliage.

September commenced with a thunderstorm, which augured well, but then fell apart as a deep Atlantic gale came over on the 2nd, persisting for three days. Butterflies were decimated by this, and were then annihilated by cold weather coupled with pulses of heavy rain mid-month. Consequently, the second home-grown brood of Clouded Yellows all but failed, for only a few individuals were seen into the autumn. I saw my last on October 6th – a female busily laying eggs on clover leaves in the lawn of a garden near Alton. Warm sunny weather during October came too late, for the bad September had stopped the 1983 butterfly season in its tracks. But three ecstatic summer months, following on from a generally good season in 1982, had set butterflies up very nicely for 1984.

Arnside Knott

The clitter of footfalls,
softened on scree paths,
past sun-straw heads of
Blue Moor-grass that wave
the July breeze, and blow

From here to here alone;
for there is nowhere else
to journey, just this place
of warm grey-stone paths,
and clear intensity of light.

Estuarine sands, stretch
silvering into distanced haze
where mountains far off fade;
whilst here, on this lone hill,
the wind and trees are one.

13 *Nineteen eighty-four and all that*

To many naturalists New Year's Eve is a special time, not to be wasted singing *Auld Lang Syne* at parties. Naturalists want to be out and about, amongst the morass of dark trees, under the starlight, bidding adieu to the old and welcoming in the new; or saving their energies for a dawn raid or a day out somewhere special. To naturalists, New Year is all about promise, the promise of the coming year, and it has to be launched, properly. Welcoming in the New Year is therefore part of their spirituality, if not their religion, though non-naturalist spouses may struggle to understand this – and drag them off to parties. My spouse did understand. Thus, I saw 1984 in on Noar Hill, on a clear, mild and windy night, and felt the New Year roar in on a treetop wind that whisked away a mild December. A vicious gale arrived on January 2nd, from the north-west, blowing tiles off The Lodge roof and wrecking the nylon sleeve in which a few Purple Emperor larvae were hibernating. The Lodge liked shedding tiles. The Emperor was in decline in my life; it was almost as if he had cast me out, whilst the Duke of Burgundy and High Brown Fritillary were in ascendancy. Perhaps I had been placed out on loan, for development?

Winter was mild and forgettable. The more memorable parts of it were spent searching for White-letter Hairstreak eggs on the new generation of elms that was springing up. One wood, at Blacknest on the northern end of the East Hampshire Hangers, revealed eggs on three species of elm – English, Smooth-leaved and Wych Elm. Now that presented interesting opportunities for study.

Spring was in danger of bursting through too early, especially when the first day of March brought out the first butterflies of the year. I opened the season with a male Brimstone in the far chalk pit on Noar Hill, up against the beech hanger. However, the rest of March was cold and dull, and spring ended up running late.

April drifted in on a bitter northerly wind that carried spells of spring-like sunshine punctuated by snow showers borne by towering clouds, the temperature alternating accordingly. It was a memorable day, hinting that April meant business. At last the Chiffchaffs arrived, in April's second week, and the White-letter Hairstreak eggs I had marked out on elm twigs, using coloured pipe cleaners, began to hatch. The larvae quickly buried themselves into expanding leaf buds, or ageing flowers, and disappeared. The wind veered from north to south, and a truly wondrous April ensued. Spring caught up with itself, then rushed gleefully ahead with riotous abandon, such that each day, almost each hour, saw monumental change. Brimstones, Commas, Peacocks and Small Tortoiseshells were all out and about in unusually good numbers. Holly Blues appeared out of nowhere, as is their wont; the males wandered about incessantly from bush to bush, searching for freshly emerged females. At The Lodge, half a dozen males ceaselessly explored the contours of the laurel bushes, now with upright panicles of pale flowers that scented the air. The Cuckoos arrived. Each morning, at the flush of dawn, they would meet up in the giant Beech tree that towered above the house, noisily, for Cuckoos mate with gusto. After mating, and waking the inhabitants of The Lodge, they would fly off to feed in the nearby hop gardens.

In such conditions limits can be pushed, and butterflying is at its best when limits are being pushed. At Noar Hill, the first male Duke of Burgundy emerged on April 25th. At the time that sighting appeared to be the earliest the butterfly had been recorded anywhere in England since the amazing spring of 1893. That appearance, and the accompanying record, boded well, for

I had just secured a useful grant from what was then the World Wildlife Fund (now the World Wide Fund for Nature) to study the ecology and conservation of the Duke of Burgundy. Of course, the wretched butterfly then emerged early, and caught me in Ethelred The Unready mode.

The fine April weather, on top of two good summers, was surely an omen of a third good summer to come. The previous two had been good, even very good, and butterfly populations had built up incrementally. I was back in the dizzy heights where I had wandered so joyously in the Long Hot Summer of 1976, only now there was work to be done – butterflies needed conserving.

At the end of a sunny and dry April Mrs O and I spent a memorable hour watching a huge female Large Tortoiseshell flying about high over a large stand of Smooth-leaved Elm in the hanger near Blacknest where I was studying White-letter Hairstreak larvae. Presumably, this giantess was seeking to lay eggs, though I failed to spot any of the gregarious larvae later. During the late 1970s and early 1980s this butterfly held some sort of exiguous existence along the Upper Greensand system of the East Hampshire Hangers, that sinuous band of scarp slope woodland that runs northwards from the South Downs near Butser Hill before eventually petering out into Alice Holt Forest. This butterfly was almost the size of an Empress, and behaved similarly, aloof and incompliant. She was, though, one of a kind that was supposed to be extinct in the country at the time. The half-dozen sightings in the hangers during that era suggested otherwise, for no one had released the butterfly there – no butterflyers even knew of the hangers.

Much of May was plagued by nagging convective cloud, the sort that develops quickly in the morning but dissipates at the end of the day to allow cool, clear nights. Butterflies had some flying time most days, but would have liked more. The month was all a-stutter.

I had experimented with mark-and-recapture work on Duke of Burgundies at Noar Hill during 1982 and 1983, having been taught by the likes of Jeremy Thomas and Keith Porter, scientists who between them had marked several thousand butterflies. This technique enables one to determine how long individual butterflies live, how far they move and, for sedentary butterflies like Duke of Burgundy, the population size. It is, though, rather addictive, and one can spend too much time marking new specimens and not enough time seeking recaptures.

Originally cellulose paint was used, but by 1984 quick-drying oil-based felt-tip pens were available. By placing two small dots on the wing undersides, one for tens and the other for digits, each butterfly is given its own unique number, by means of something called the clock method. The butterflies do not seem to mind, but one needs to handle them with care. Most of the male Burgundies I marked flew straight back to their chosen territories, resuming their never-ending hunt for receptive females, and fighting each other in the process. I had one minor accident, when a purple felt-tip leaked badly and covered one unfortunate male almost entirely: he lived for at least another ten days, twice the average lifespan of a male. Aged seven days, and still covered in purple, he was seen mating with a fresh female, and a particularly pretty wench she was at that. Out of a total sample of 348 males marked, the longest 'life' measured for a male was 22 days (marked when freshly emerged), with three others living for at least 20 days. Not bad for a thumbnail-sized insect.

Burgundy males are wonderfully territorial, simply because this is their way of finding mates. Males establish territories in sheltered spots which warm up early in the morning. There they perch, low down, flying up to intercept any small dark flying object that passes by, in anticipation of it being a virgin female. Green-veined Whites and Orange-tips are ignored. At Noar Hill, favoured territories at the foot of ancient chalk-pit banks are occupied annually, often by more than one male – which means that a lot of male infighting takes place. Most of the primary territories in use when I first saw the butterfly there in 1976 are still utilised today, though some have been lost to scrub invasion.

Mark-and-recapture work found that males tended to live their lives in their favoured territorial patch, only moving to a new patch when the wind increased or changed direction and their original locality became exposed – for this minuscule butterfly seriously hates wind. More recently, I have found that males change territory when disturbed by people, a lesson some over-ambitious butterfly photographers need to learn. At Noar Hill, males occupying the better (primary) territories were considerably more successful at finding mates than those in the lesser (secondary) territories. The record is four matings by one particularly fortunate male, whom I named Byron.

One fine day back in May 1982, I had watched one particular male for six and a half hours. For 70 per cent of that time he was inactive, particularly from mid-afternoon, after the day's emergence of females had finished. But he did spend 46 minutes patrolling his tiny patch, a few square metres, and another 23 minutes intercepting 30 winged intruders. He squabbled with eight other Duke of Burgundy males, three Dingy Skippers, singletons of Small Copper, Small Heath and Wall Brown, and a number of flies. Best of all, he saw off a Willow Warbler that flew low overhead. He went to bed at 4.45, high up in a Hawthorn bush. I repeated this vigilance in 1984, with highly comparable results. However, about 10 per cent of Burgundy males behave differently, being almost nomadic. One male was recorded on six different territories on four different days over an area of a couple of hectares – positively peripatetic by Burgundian standards.

Burgundy females, by contrast, are at best highly uncooperative. One female followed continuously for more hours than I care to relate was comatose for 80 per cent of the time. Her longest period of inactivity lasted 53 minutes. She took twelve flights, totalling some 30 minutes. She had three sessions feeding from flowers and five sessions, totalling a mere eleven minutes, indulging in the all-important act of laying eggs, depositing seven. She was then lost, just before 4 pm, when she suddenly took off after a lengthy period of quiescence, and disappeared over a block of scrub. Other 'stalkings' of individual Duchesses were less successful, for these females have the habit of suddenly making off at fair speed after sitting around doing precisely nothing for lengthy periods. This is quite normal for female butterflies generally, who tend to follow a behaviour pattern of bask – fly – feed – bask – fly – lay eggs, etc. In 1984, I marked 89 females on Noar Hill, but recaptured a mere seven. Five of the seven had travelled more than 250 metres, suggesting that the females are considerably more prone to disperse than their male counterparts.

Suffice to say that I could not possibly follow butterflies like this had I not spent a fair proportion of my youth fishing. That taught me patience, and watching a butterfly is rather akin to watching a fishing float. Also, I am particularly grateful to the *Test Match Special* commentary team for maintaining my sanity during these incredibly intense and demanding vigils. In 1984 the West Indies were over here, and at the very pinnacle of their might, with the most fearsome battery of fast bowlers ever assembled – today's health and safety standards would have prevented them from playing.

At the end of May, after a wet Whitsun bank holiday, I entrained for Silverdale on the Cumbria/Lancashire border, and spent four vernal days studying Duke of Burgundies and their friends and relations at Gait Barrows NNR and at Heathwaite, by Arnside Knott. May 1984 had been good in that district, far better than down south, and butterflies were in superb numbers. Spring in Silverdale is something special, for there is an intensity of light in that region of low Carboniferous Limestone hills that is unique within the UK and is at its lucid best in late spring. Some day a vibrant artists' community will develop there, and change the world of Art for ever. Deep poetry also lies there, undiscovered. Sure, Edward Thomas visited and wrote one of his poems there, but someday a great poet will dwell there, whose writings will change the world of Poetry for ever.

Gait Barrows became a National Nature Reserve after NCC compulsorily purchased it to prevent further quarrying of the limestone pavement. The damaged pavement areas soon became good for butterflies, and the reserve was colonised by the Duke of Burgundy in the early or mid-1970s. I was asked to solve the riddle of why it was there at all, as Cowslips and Primroses, on which the larvae feed, were decidedly localised, and also to advise on its conservation. But this is the most tenacious of our butterflies, capable of subsisting at low population level on just a scatter of suitable foodplants. A thorough search in sublime weather on May 30th revealed thirteen individual Burgundies, a reasonable tally, and a total of 83 eggs, 66 of which were in two small areas of scrub that had been coppiced two winters back. Fifty-seven of these eggs were on Cowslip, twenty-two on Primrose, and four on the 'False Oxslip' hybrid. We learnt that coppicing and widening rides in areas where primulas were growing under trees could really help this little butterfly, but the primula-rich areas had to be located first. Suffice to say that since 1984 the Duke of Burgundy has slowly but surely improved its status at Gait Barrows.

But the Pearl-bordered Fritillary completely stole the late May show around Silverdale that year. I saw hundreds at Gait Barrows, probably the best flight I had seen of this living jewel at the time. It was also numerous on Arnside Knott and on the slopes of the adjoining hill, picturesque Heathwaite. But the lasting memories are twofold: first, a trio feeding on a patch of pink Bird's-eye Primrose flowers growing along the edge of a lonely sedge-flanked mere called Haws Water and, secondly, of the butterfly going to roost in numbers high in scrub on Arnside Knott at 6 pm one evening. A naturalist's mind can photograph such near-divine experiences far better than any camera. A poet can place them in words.

There was time, too, to search for the spectacular larvae of the High Brown Fritillary. Now these were new to me; indeed, there may have been no one alive at the time who had actually found High Brown Fritillary larvae in the wild, for the insect had become both rare and neglected. The larvae are of a golden-brown colour, and are heavily and gloriously spined. They were found basking

close to Hairy Violet plants growing in warm spots as the sun was coming out after cloudy spells, or during periods of thin cloud through which a pale sun shone. The feeding marks on the violet leaves were quite distinctive, with basal lobes and/or leaf tips being removed, though Dark Green Fritillary larvae leave similar tell-tale signs.

Back in Hampshire, the Duke of Burgundy was on the wane. Much time was spent endeavouring to track dispersing females, but they proved to be uncooperative minxes and my endeavours, though honest, were largely thwarted. It was not a single-person job. But up near Farnborough the Marsh Fritillary had exploded, at least metaphorically, at Foxlease Meadows near Cove. I visited a little on the late side, judging by the ragged and worn state of the many hundreds that were flying, and by the frequency with which dead specimens were found in funnel-trap spider's webs. It was the third consecutive good year for this butterfly, during which time populations had increased phenomenally, enabling the butterfly to spread far and wide. Indeed, it turned up in many places on the west Hampshire chalk in that era. Similar range expansions were recorded during this period in Dorset, Wiltshire and the Cotswolds.

Over on the Isle of Wight in mid-June, Clouded Yellows were not flying in off the sea, as they had during the previous June. But, like the Marsh Fritillary across the Solent, the Glanville Fritillary had produced a bumper brood, for similar reasons. They were so profuse that I started spotting emerging specimens crawling out of tussocks of grass, then hanging upside down on a sturdy stem to expand and harden their wings. Sure enough, the vacated pupal cases were promptly located within deep matted tussocks of Yorkshire-fog grass. A number of unhatched pupae were also found, and another useful jigsaw-puzzle piece of butterfly ecology was put in place.

The White-letter Hairstreak also revealed some useful secrets, back in Blacknest Copse on the edge of Alice Holt Forest. My pipe-cleaner experiment, so called because I had bedecked several elms with multicoloured pipe cleaners, marking egg and larval sites, had come to fruition. The study suggested, strongly, that the butterfly bred most successfully on flowering Wych Elm, followed (some way behind) by flowering English Elm and flowering Smooth-leaved Elm, though a few larvae developed successfully on non-flowering Wych Elm. Larvae failed to develop from eggs laid on non-flowering English and Smooth-leaved elms. The problem here is that Dutch elm disease tends to infect trees as they become mature enough to flower.

June intensified, and brought out a huge emergence of Small Tortoiseshells. These home-grown butterflies were perhaps augmented by immigrants from the continent. Their gregarious larvae were almost commonplace on nettle patches in sunny places, and batches of Peacock larvae were also fairly frequent. The summer was building up well. Drought conditions were developing: hose pipes had been banned in several districts, lawns and weeds had stopped growing, and farmers were relishing the prospect of a bumper and early harvest. The only blemish was on the cricket field, where the imperious West Indies steamrolled a cocky England side in the first two Test matches, to be two–nil up by the start of July.

It was time for something silly, and the Duke of Burgundy provided the silliness. The larvae are nocturnal, hiding at the base of Cowslip leaves during the day and only venturing out to feed after dark, often on the under surface of Cowslip leaves. A vast amount of effort was devoted to looking for them at night, though I never stayed later than 3.30 am. They fed only on warm dry nights, when the temperature was at least 10 degrees and the vegetation dry, ceasing to feed when dew wetted the foliage. Lowlights included being tripped over by a Badger that hustled out of a bush unexpectedly, and stumbling into a courting couple who had progressed rather beyond courting.

The planned apex of the summer was to be a return visit to the Morecambe Bay limestone hills, to finish off surveying rare butterflies there for NCC. A friend with a malicious sense of humour had recommended a small hotel in Arnside as a good B&B establishment. We duly booked in to what turned out to be the most preposterous B&B I have ever visited (out of well over a hundred). Offensive features included nylon sheets, a grandfather clock on the landing that struck quarters loudly, a bath without a hot tap, cheap self-assembly furniture with non-opening drawers and doors, and an average of four notices on each room wall forbidding guests from activities that no one in their right mind would contemplate doing anyway. Worse, breakfast was served from 9 am, table by table, by room number – and we were the last room – and one was obliged to stay for a minimum of two nights. We fled after one night, and discovered a superb B&B at Witherslack, where Red Squirrels visited the bird table each morning. Years later the Willowfield Hotel at Arnside changed hands and became, and remains, an excellent establishment. Places go in eras.

We visited many small fringe sites, but some of the larger hills, notably Whitbarrow, required more work, and some hills north of the Kent estuary were visited for the first time. The region was in the grip of severe drought: much of the vegetation was frazzled beyond recognition and many of the Silver Birch trees and Hazel bushes had dropped leaves. However, the drought was ending, and we saw less of the High Brown Fritillary than during the previous July, but found a few more Duke of Burgundy colonies by searching for larval damage on *Primula* plants, notably a thriving colony on

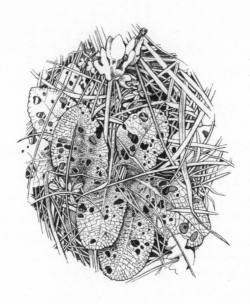

a lonely hill above Grange-over-Sands called, ignominiously, Wart Barrow. After three weeks, we were flooded out, and retreated down the M6 in a deluge.

August was hot, and belonged to the Small Tortoiseshell, which seemed to be everywhere that summer. There were always twenty or so in our garden at The Lodge and huge aggregations on many downs. Absent, however, were the main migrant butterflies. Not a single Painted Lady was recorded in Hampshire all year, and by the end of August I had seen, nationally, a mere two Red Admirals, and a lone Clouded Yellow. Migrant moths were equally scarce. But August 1984 was most memorable for its cereal harvest, the first four-tonnes-to-the-acre harvest. British agriculture had become obsessed by cereal production, even though much of the harvest ended up in costly grain intervention stores. To a young nature conservationist, George Orwell's prophetic warning about that year was more applicable to agricultural values than to wider society. That summer, numerous lengths of hedge throughout the cereal lands were burnt out by wanton straw and stubble burning. A few years later burning was at last banned, mercifully so, for on dry August and September days the sun over Hampshire would be obscured by a pall of acrid amber smoke that stained the sunlight brown and poisoned the sunset. It became impossible for rural housewives to hang washing out to dry, whilst asthmatics simply had to stay indoors.

In mid-July I had introduced 25 full-grown Duke of Burgundy larvae to a carefully re-created plot of rough downland in our garden, which was then carefully proofed with fine nylon netting, dug well into the ground. At the end of August it was time to dissect out this contraption, known as HM Prison Wyck, in an attempt to discover where the butterfly pupates. Ably assisted by my cat, Mouse, and to the trance-like accompaniment of *Test Match Special*, the task took two painstaking days, involving archaeological investigation with a table fork. Only seven pupae were found, suggesting either that some larvae had managed to break out of the contraption, which seemed doubtful, or that mortality is high around the pupation process. Crucially, five of the seven were found 5–8 centimetres above soil level in tussocks of fine-leaved grasses containing many dead blades. One was found lying on the ground within one of these matted tussocks. The seventh was discovered inside an empty beechnut case lying on the ground amongst a patch of Beech litter. The good news is that none was found on the netting, in contrast to how the insect performs in breeding cages.

Nonetheless, the experiment inspired me to search for Duke of Burgundy pupae on Noar Hill. The following day I actually found a wild pupa, 8 centimetres above ground in a tussock of rank Red Fescue grass containing many dead blades. This was only 25 centimetres from a Cowslip plant which had supported a full-grown larva. However, that proved to be the limit of my achievements, even though two days were spent examining tussocks of Red Fescue and other grasses where a large number of larvae had been followed earlier in that summer. Eventually I cracked the mysteries of where the Duke of Burgundy pupates, at least on Noar Hill, by searching for freshly emerged adults and then digging down to discover the vacated pupal case. This revealed that HM Prison Wyck had been a useful exercise, for the species appears to specialise in pupating 4–8 centimetres above ground in matted tussocks. The lessons for conservation grazing here are obvious.

Autumn slowly waned into winter, by means of a veritable tempest in late November that demolished the roof of one of The Lodge's outhouses. Right till the end of the year I surveyed for Duke of Burgundy colonies on downland fragments in and around Hampshire, searching for larval damage on Cowslip leaves. The last colonies were found on Boxing Day, near Buriton and Finchdean on the western South Downs.

14 A time of discovery

Church bells reverberated off the houses and chimney smoke drifted low across Selborne High Street as I cycled up to see in the New Year on Noar Hill. Then, at midnight, a host of burgundy-coloured rockets ascended from a nearby farmstead. Meanwhile, down near Winchester the year's first conservation drama was being played out: a landowner needed to enlarge his farm by an extra ten acres in order to qualify for an EU grant towards a new grain store, only to find that the grant stream was terminated as he finished grubbing out a rather good Duke of Burgundy colony. Please do not think that these were halcyon days: Hampshire was a battlefield, with woods, hedges, marshes and downs disappearing under buildings or agricultural intensification.

Snow descended in early January 1985, primarily on Kent and East Anglia but reaching as far west as Wiltshire. The fallen snow promptly turned to ice and was added to by further falls during a sixteen-day spell in which the temperature scarcely reached zero. At The Lodge, we retreated into one room, heated by a small wood burner. Habitually, we took the battery out of our Morris Minor overnight and kept it in the house. January 16th was London's coldest day for thirty years. The following day the thermometer peaked at −5°C, and the South-west was subjected to a blizzard which buried Cornwall. In the midst of this chaos the year's first butterflying expedition was launched, to search for White-letter Hairstreak eggs at my study site at Blacknest, near Alice Holt Forest. The previous year had been an excellent one for this tiny treetop butterfly, and the egg lay was prolific, even if one's toes

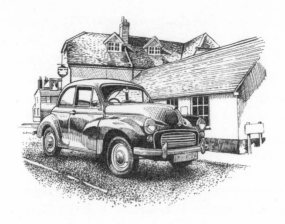

and fingers took a long time to thaw out. A rapid thaw kicked in but the land promptly became saturated and rivers flooded. At the end of January there was even a vestige of a dawn chorus. Diary: *A Song Thrush with a sore throat, a couple of sparrows and something unrecognisably out of tune.*

A second heavy fall of snow descended on February 9th, covering each twig with 5 centimetres of crystallised snow. On Noar Hill, the Yews and Junipers were weighted way down, some broke; and the sheep had to be dug out of a drift and fed hay. Then, whipped up by an easting wind, the snow blew into the lanes, cutting villages off. Snow ploughs came through, and turned road surfaces into ice rinks, as salt and grit were limited commodities in that era. For eleven days the temperature struggled to reach zero, though the sun shone effortlessly. Then, towards the end of the month, the weather improved, enabling the first butterflies of the year to take to the air on February 24th. Hampshire Conservation Volunteers were working with me on Noar Hill that day, cutting scrub in the Top Pit, the Holy of Holies up against the Beech woodland. My first butterfly of the year was a male Brimstone, which (diary) *danced right up to me out of the sun* in exactly the same spot as where the first butterfly of 1984 had been seen. Could history repeat itself, in the form of a replicate summer? Later that day, a Small Tortoiseshell came out to play, and a few days on, a Red Admiral appeared, having miraculously hibernated. The year was up and away, and winter was forgotten – only to return with a vengeance in mid-March, as two further snowfalls occurred, including one on the first day of spring, March 21st. Spring was now running late, and running scared.

March ended wet, then April roared in on a south-west wind. Incredibly, that wind ushered in an immigration of Painted Ladies. A great number were seen on the South Devon coast. By mid-April more Painted Ladies had been seen in Hampshire than during the whole of 1984. I saw my year's first in Dorset on April 8th, a small grey male along a ride at Lydlinch Common, near Sturminster Newton. By the 10th they had reached the north of England. On the 14th I saw one in Selborne High Street and three on Shoulder of Mutton, the hillside dedicated to Edward Thomas above Steep.

I drove over to the Cotswolds, on a Duke of Burgundy fact-finding tour, by way of Oxford and Bernwood Forest. In Bernwood the Pearl-bordered Fritillary was responding well to recent ride widening and coppicing work at ride junctions – Caroline Steel and I found larvae along a ditch margin in York Wood. But this apparent panacea proved to be short-lived, for coarse grasses soon took over in these opened areas and choked out the butterfly. That was the last Caroline and I ever saw of this illustrious spring butterfly in Bernwood, despite laudable conservation effort. By no means everything that is done in the name of conservation works, or if it works it works only for a while, as in this case. Deer numbers rapidly increased in Bernwood, and their browsing rendered the forest even more unsuitable.

The Cotswolds were interesting, for here the Duke of Burgundy had experienced a boom era after the Rabbits succumbed to myxomatosis and tall grasses and scrub grew up. The poor Large Blue and Adonis Blue died out, though for a couple of decades or so His Grace thrived in their stead. But by the mid-1980s the vegetation on neglected Cotswold grasslands was becoming too coarse even for this long-sward specialist, though some large colonies still survived. At all these rough grassland sites, Dark

Green Fritillary and Small Blue occurred in numbers. Also, the Marsh Fritillary had enjoyed a major expansion phase, and was present on many grassland slopes in the southern Cotswolds. Soon afterwards, it retreated during a run of poor summers.

At last spring broke through, and the first Orange-tips and Green-veined Whites took to the wing, on April 22nd. They were late. Painted Ladies were still batting about, but nights had become cold and spring was stalling. At Noar Hill, the first Duke of Burgundies and Dingy Skippers emerged, and promptly squabbled. I was determined to look for emerging Duke of Burgundies in order to find the empty pupal cases. The trick worked, for a recently vacated pupal case was found 5 centimetres above ground level amongst a thick matt of dead grass. Later I found another amongst deep moss, again 5 centimetres above ground. These findings were crucial, as the insect spends at least nine months in the pupal stage, and we need to know just where the pupae occur. At this point, two weeks of dry (but cold) weather ended in rain, and the weathermen kindly pointed out that the country had just suffered eleven sunless Saturdays in a row. Gloom descended, day after day of it, and at the height of the Duke of Burgundy flight season. But one huge colony was discovered, on a rough grassland slope near the curiously named village of Vernham Dean in the extreme north-west of Hampshire. Here, I counted 85 in less than an hour. It doesn't need to be a rare butterfly, and didn't used to be.

May ended well, though the spring species had been decimated by diverse forms of adverse weather. One surprise was in store, on Noar Hill:

Diary, May 29th 1985: *A colossal Large Tortoiseshell buzzed me at 3.25, in the north-west corner. I suspect it was a wild insect, rather than a bred-and-released specimen, on account of its size (bred specimens are almost invariably undersized) and behaviour – it beat me up then glided away majestically. An amazing beast – I'm sure it is resident (just) in this area.*

But that was the last Large Tortoiseshell recorded in the East Hampshire Hangers. Two days later a Pearl-bordered Fritillary sauntered through the reserve, and a week afterwards a Marsh Fritillary, probably a wanderer from the introduced colony at Conford, to the north-east. Such were the riches of the Selborne area in that golden, now bygone and almost forgotten era.

Flaming June came in, ablaze, then descended into darkness. One of the tasks that unmerry month was to show a party of American butterfly enthusiasts, from the Xerces Society, around butterfly sites in Hampshire and on the Isle of Wight. An eclectic group, under the leadership of beer-loving biologist Robert M Pyle, they visited Noar Hill where it rained heavily, Old Winchester Hill NNR where they saw a paltry few Adonis Blues, and Compton Chine and the adjoining downs on the island. At Compton the sun shone wondrously and the Glanville Fritillary was in goodly numbers, and looked and behaved like some of the American Checkerspot butterflies. But the highlight of the trip was up on the downs. There, in a moment of inspired serendipity, I led a group of twenty Americans laden with cameras through a gap in the gorse bushes, straight in upon a hyperactive pairing of *Homo sapiens*. 'Don't stop for us!' my American visitors shouted; 'You two have fun while you're young,' they advised; and best of all, 'Hold it right there! I crossed The Pond for this shot!' It was the highlight of their trip. The rest of June was an afterthought, though I did record my latest ever Duke of Burgundy, at Noar Hill on June 26th.

July began promisingly, seeking to redeem a weather-spoilt season that was running late. In perfect weather, on July 7th, our wedding anniversary, we joined a party from Butterfly Conservation Hampshire Branch on a field visit to Porton Down, the MOD's Chemical Defence Establishment site near Salisbury. This 1458-hectare (3600-acre) expanse of chalk grassland, scrub and woodland is one of the country's top butterfly sites, boasting some 43 species, many of which occur in huge populations over vast areas of landscape. I was bowled over. *Quite ineffable*, I wrote in the diary. It was the scale there that was so impressive.

Diary, July 7th 1985: *The day belonged to the Dark Green Fritillary which was omni-present and omnipotent. We must have seen thousands, and it was hard to go a minute without seeing at least one. Regularly we saw, five, six or seven together. Mostly males quartering low over the ground in search of emerging females, but also some egg-laying females around the numerous Hairy Violet patches.*

Above all, Porton illustrates the scale of what we have lost in this country, where quality butterfly habitats are reduced to fragments hither and thither. It also demonstrates the value of large-scale habitat mosaics.

In mid-July Mrs O and I set off up north for what was to be the highlight of the butterfly season, a ten-day survey of butterfly sites on the North York Moors, concentrating on the Duke of Burgundy. If the weather was indifferent down south it was positively vile in Yorkshire. That did not matter too much, as for the bulk of the time we were searching for the distinctive larval feeding damage on *Primula* leaves. His Grace was in trouble up here, struggling with issues of neglect and abandonment, heavy Rabbit and sheep grazing, and coniferisation – not to mention a less than clement climate. We concentrated on visiting sites in the valleys where the butterfly had been recorded in the recent past, but dabbled a little in *terra nova*, looking for new colonies. At Ellerburn Bank, in Thornton Dale, the butterfly was lingering on nicely – we found 46 Cowslip clumps supporting larvae on this nature reserve and others nearby. We were shown round by a black and white tom cat, out rabbiting. Shortly after our visit the Rabbits took over severely, and the butterfly died out. More tom cats were needed. At the south end of Newton Dale, above Pickering, a small but thriving colony was present in a young conifer plantation. Shortly afterwards, the conifers grew too tall and the colony was lost. There was also a scatter of tiny relic colonies dotted about further north, along the North Yorkshire Moors railway line. What was worrying was the presence of suitable but unoccupied habitat. There was no reason, obvious or otherwise, why the butterfly had died out from Gundale, from where it had been known for over a hundred years. An abandoned quarry system near Silpho was even more perplexing. This site, above a wooded dale delightfully named Whisperdale but full of screaming Girl Guides for our visit, looked to be in perfect condition for the butterfly, which was clearly absent. Presumably, there was no colony nearby from which colonisation could be sourced. At last, as the rain increased, we found a thriving colony amongst a few acres of scrubby limestone grassland above Rievaulx. There we counted 269 breeding sites (eaten Cowslip clumps), perhaps equating to 25–30 butterflies on a fine day in early June.

On the limestone grassland slopes the Northern Brown Argus was almost omni-present, though for much of the time these butterflies were to be found at roost on the grass heads, jewelled with raindrops; but being hardened northerners, they sprang to life immediately the sun glimmered. The Dark Green Fritillary was present in modest numbers on many of the open grasslands, but was loath to take to the air due to the cold temperatures. In the valley bottoms some sizeable colonies of the Small Pearl-bordered Fritillary were found, based on Marsh Violets growing in wet flushes. Everywhere, Ringlets abounded. They, almost alone, relish a damp summer. The Small Skipper and Marbled White were moving in, as recent colonists, and we also found a couple of White-letter Hairstreak colonies, based on Wych Elms which abound on the valley slopes. We also visited Fen Bog, the famous Large Heath site along the North Yorkshire Moors railway line below Goathland. In this valley fen and mire system the middle race of the Large Heath occurs – the moderately spotted race. They were bobbing up from in front of us and allowing themselves to be carried away downwind. I found a freshly emerged female and located the vacated pupal case. However, tired out that evening, I failed to describe where the pupa occurred in my diary, and cannot for the life of me remember anything about it now. This may well be the only record of the pupa of the Large Heath being found in the wild, and it is useless – and there is no excuse for bad natural history recording.

Perusal of the weather forecast suggested that Yorkshire was going to be plagued by endogenous cloud whilst the western fringe of Britain bathed in glorious sunshine. There was only one thing to do: abandon the Moors and spend a couple of days on the Morecambe Bay limestone hills. High Brown Fritillaries leapt to greet us on Hutton Roof, a partially wooded limestone pavement east of the M6, the nearest High Brown site to Yorkshire. But after one glorious day Yorkshire's weather crossed the Pennines. The M6 southbound enveloped us in motorway spray, all the way back to a sunny Hampshire.

Down south, a reasonable August and September were spent surveying new territory in and around Hampshire – primarily chalk downland fragments trapped within vast acreages of arable farmland. Many of these places, remnants of the extensive tracts of downland that had characterised Hampshire, were surprisingly rich, supporting colonies of Chalkhill Blue, Small Blue, Brown Argus and the like, and even tiny relic populations of the Duke of Burgundy. The season was running so late that many of the high-summer and August species lingered unusually long, usefully extending the surveying season. The problem was that many of these newly found sites were tiny, isolated fragments, too small to maintain their butterfly faunas indefinitely and, above all, neglected because they were too small to be viable as grazing units or because the farms had converted to arable farming. They were last-ditch stand places, tiny corners into which butterflies had been pushed by wave after wave of agricultural intensification, backed up by afforestation of downland fragments. In effect, this was depressing work.

Outside Hampshire, a number of sites for His Grace the Duke of Burgundy were visited, localities known to support sizeable populations, primarily to advise on habitat management for this rapidly declining butterfly. Judging by the abundance of eaten Cowslip plants, Edge Common in the Cotswolds and Ivinghoe

Beacon in the north Chilterns threatened to rival Noar Hill for the privilege of holding Britain's premier Duke of Burgundy population. I was somewhat blown away.

Women, especially wives, can choose their moments carefully, such that Mrs O chose the precise moment when I was being blown away by the scale of the Burgundy population at Ivinghoe to announce that we were going to become parents in May.

❦

Some redemption was necessary after the deprivations of the previous year, but 1986 started wet and cold, with widespread flooding. The last thing the country needed was February, but we got it, big time, for we were subjected to the second coldest February of the century (after 1947). Snow arrived in the South on the 6th, and remained on the ground for over ten days as temperatures struggled to rise above zero, boosted by a biting wind from Siberia which dominated the whole of the second half of a loathsome month. At The Lodge, we again retreated into a single room, the toilet froze and our beloved resident cock Blackbird, a partial-albino called Percy Bysshe, died on the windowsill. On Noar Hill, the sheep and Rabbits were both reduced to stripping Ash bark, as the grass lay buried. The beginning of March saw no improvement, but then, quite suddenly, at the end of the first week something approximating to spring arrived: Snowdrops immediately popped up, Robins began to trill and a Small Tortoiseshell appeared in the garden, thought better of it and retreated back to hibernation in a densely foliated conifer.

March concluded with a vicious gale, borne on a very deep depression, which took a while to blow itself out. Worse, Easter came early, at the end of March, and as the diary bemoans: *Why is it that every time Easter comes early the weather is Vile?* The omens were not looking good: there was still no sign of a Chiffchaff, and England's cricketers were getting pulverised in the West Indies.

April started ominously – perishing cold in fact. By mid-month I had seen a mere ten individual butterflies, of just two species, and had yet to hear a Chiffchaff. Some improvement then occurred, bringing in the migrant birds and, on the 30th, the first Orange-tips – some two weeks late. April 1986 later won the accolade of being the coldest in southern England since 1922. The first leaves only started to appear on the Beeches and oaks in early May, though within a week they were well in leaf and the early Bluebells were starting to flower. Mid-month the first Duke of Burgundy males appeared on Noar Hill, two weeks late. They then struggled, as the weather found diverse ways to irritate – rain, wind, convective cloud cover, the lot. The month was, however, redeemed by the birth of our first child on May 27th. We named her Lucina, after the Roman goddess of light, and of course after the Duke of Burgundy (*Hamearis lucina*). The name could readily be shortened to Lucy. It was.

First-time dads go off on an adrenaline rush, especially if blessed with a daughter. This one went off searching for Duke of Burgundy colonies in obscure parts of Hampshire. The insect was, though, suffering from the effects of a poor May. At Noar Hill, its numbers were decidedly substandard, partly on account of the weather and partly on account of rising Rabbit numbers. The Rabbit is probably this rare butterfly's Number One enemy, for Rabbits graze too close to the ground, lowering the sward height such that the Cowslips on which the larvae feed become stunted and the leaves turn yellow before the larvae are fully grown. Something had to be done about the rising Rabbit population on Noar Hill. Done it was, by means of dawn shooting with a .22 rifle and silencer, aiming safely down at targets in the chalk pits. My cat, Mouse, also helped – just as, on other occasions, he also helped by discovering Yellow-necked Mouse and Harvest Mouse on the reserve. Later, after fifteen happy years, he was buried there.

Spring and early summer were so poor that I did not see the first Red Admiral of the year until June 10th, when it suddenly arrived in modest numbers, borne on some reasonable weather. A disappointing June ended well, though by now the butterfly season was running decidedly late, so late that the Orange-tip lingered into early July and butterflies such as the Marbled White, Ringlet, Silver-studded Blue and White Admiral did not appear before around July 7th.

A change in the weather was due, and we got one. It was ushered in by the following event:

> Diary, June 22nd 1986: *An excellent thunderstorm. It began at 11 pm with a 45-minute preamble of distant sheet lightning, after an evening of eerie pallid light. Around midnight rolling thunder came over, in waves, accompanied by both sheet and forked lightning and some torrential bursts of rain.*

There are people, like me, who just have to be outside in a storm like that – to be amongst it, and within it, and to absorb its energy.

In mid-July ten days were spent surveying for High Brown Fritillary colonies in the Malvern Hills and the Wyre Forest in the West Midlands, commissioned by the NCC. Simon Grove, a young Hampshire naturalist of considerable ability, joined me on this venture. He was recovering from university finals, and from a broken heart. I was temporarily escaping from fatherhood. To make the money run further, and to escape deep into Nature, we took tents and camped in Eastnor Park, an ancient pasture woodland below the west flank of the southern Malverns, adorned with veteran oaks and grazed by sheep and a long-established herd of Red Deer. Incredibly, the weather was set fair; our noses burnt and then peeled.

We knew that the High Brown had strong colonies at the southern end of the Malverns, based on Swinyard Hill and over to Eastnor Park, via Gullet Quarry, but had little other information. Those were the places which the West Midland butterflyers of the time visited, but few ventured beyond those safe havens. Swinyard Hill is a steep Bracken-covered slope on the east flank of the southern Malverns, directly above Castle Morton Common. A large number of sheep then grazed on the common and roamed onto Swinyard Hill. It was particularly important that they grazed off the soft grasses that grew amongst the Bracken in spring, to ensure the warm microclimate conditions required by High Brown larvae. In the process, these animals trampled down the dead Bracken and so enabled the necessary violet leaves to abound. Gullet Quarry, with its deep blue lagoon water, naked swimmers, naturalised goldfish and exposures of ancient rocks, was little more than a staging post for High Browns flying between Swinyard and Eastnor, stopping by to feed on its bramble and Buddleia flowers.

The place of most interest was Eastnor Park, particularly the south-facing Bracken slope below the obelisk. That slope was a revelation. It had recently been used as a venue for ad hoc four-wheel-drive training events, with the vehicles following no fixed course through the Bracken and regularly changing route. By happy chance, this rather mindless activity produced the best breeding conditions for the High Brown I have ever seen, for the trackways consisted of an open, knee-high Bracken cover with huge drifts of violets amongst the masticated remains of the previous season's Bracken fronds and stalks. Grasses had great difficulty coping with all this and were consequently sparse – and the High Brown requires drifts of violets amongst broken Bracken litter, without the grass that cools the microclimate down. On this slope the High Brown Fritillary abounded, such that I counted 90 in an hour one afternoon. Best of all, a muddy puddle along one of the trackways attracted a dozen males one hot and humid afternoon, to imbibe moisture. The photograph had to be carefully lined up, requiring lying down prostrate, elbows in mud. But coming towards me was a jogger. 'Please! Go left! Slow down! Let me take this photo.' But no, he ran straight through, scattering the host of golden butterflies, and splashing me. A paltry four High Browns returned, and were duly photographed. Forgiveness can take a long time to materialise: nearly thirty years on, there is no sign of it arriving yet.

Perhaps that jogger was an outrider of the Four Riders of the Apocalypse, because soon afterwards the High Brown Fritillary collapsed at Eastnor. First, the four-wheel vehicles were persuaded to keep to an established route, which produced wholly unsuitable

High Brown breeding habitat. Second, the number of deer and sheep declined greatly, and no longer ventured onto the obelisk slope. Finally, Bluebells increased dramatically and ousted the violets, and provided microclimate conditions that were far too cool for this heat-loving butterfly.

Simon and I searched almost the entire length of the Malverns, though avoiding the high northern summits where soil conditions were too acidic for violets to grow. We found small colonies on and around all the southern hills, places with haunting names like Ragged Stone Hill, Chase End Hill, Midsummer Hill (where several ley lines converge), Hangman's Hill and British Camp. The butterfly was thriving there. But we could see that it was highly vulnerable, dependent on high levels of commoners' stock and threatened by neglect and abandonment. Within a few years those fears were fully realised.

We searched northwards along the Herefordshire/Worcestershire border, discovering dwindling populations on Bringsty and Bromyard Commons, above Bromyard. These Bracken-invaded commons were grazed by large numbers of sheep, but even so conditions were deteriorating rapidly, as the sheep were not penetrating the Bracken stands adequately and the commoners were giving up the practice of periodically burning blocks of Bracken, on advice from the fire brigade. The butterfly was lost from these two sites when grazing animals were culled during the 2001 foot & mouth outbreak.

Finally, we spent two days looking for the High Brown Fritillary in the Wyre Forest, on the Worcestershire/Shropshire border. Two days to search a 3333-hectare (8200-acre) forest is clearly inadequate, but we were assisted by Mike Williams and other members of Butterfly Conservation's West Midlands Branch. All told we saw thirteen High Browns, some of the last ever seen in Wyre, but little suitable was habitat found. Our conclusion was that the butterfly was lingering on in Wyre through inertia, breeding in tiny fragments of suitable habitat dotted about amongst open-grown trees on south-facing slopes. Shortly afterwards, the Wyre race of the High Brown Fritillary became extinct. They were the largest High Browns I have ever seen, the size of Silver-washed Fritillaries. Of course, the High Brown Fritillary stormed its way to win Butterfly of the Year for 1986.

Inspired by what was clearly a very good year for High Brown Fritillaries, I searched yet again in the New Forest for the butterfly, but failed to find it. At the end of July I journeyed up to South Lakeland to search for High Browns there, but on crossing the Cumbrian border I found that foul weather was moving down from the north. In five rotten days I managed a measly five High Browns, during glimmers of watery sun. But I did discover a Large Heath colony new to science, and on a National Nature Reserve to boot. Incredibly, it seemed that no one knew that the Large Heath occurred on Rusland Moss NNR, in the Rusland valley south of Windermere, despite it being one of our oldest National Nature Reserves. I had only gone there because I wanted to see Arthur Ransome's grave in the nearby churchyard. Finally, a lone fine day on Arnside Knott produced a scatter of soggy High Browns, drying out, and the first Scotch Argus males of the summer. Then, yet again, I was flooded out of the Lake District.

But after a rotten start August worked hard to redeem itself. The year's first Painted Ladies appeared, late. The July species were lingering on, due to the late start to the season. Silver-studded Blues were flying on the north-east Hampshire heaths well into the second half of August, whereas normally they are gone by late July. The year's Peacock hatch did not commence until August 9th, at least around Selborne, and the Brown Hairstreak did not appear there before mid-August. Small Whites abounded, until they got blasted away by an excessively wet August bank holiday.

We then entered a lengthy spell of benign weather, with day after day of gentle mild Septemberine sunshine, punctuated by an occasional day of unchallenging drizzle. In such genial weather conditions individual butterflies can live unusually long lives. Having emerged late, because of the poor spring, Gatekeepers and Small and Essex skippers lasted well into September, and Graylings into October. One Gatekeeper was seen as late as September 18th in the garden of The Lodge, the latest I have seen the species. At Old Winchester Hill NNR in Hampshire's Meon valley the Silver-spotted Skipper lasted into early October, remarkably late for that species, although it does fly distinctly later in the Meon valley than elsewhere. The pleasant early autumn weather carried on well into October, allowing me to see a faded Brown Hairstreak on Noar Hill as late as October 16th. This remains my latest sighting of that species. Small Heaths and Meadow Browns persisted until the end of the month. They might have lasted longer, only the autumn rains then arrived with a vengeance, and the country degenerated into flood and quagmire.

Autumn

While barred clouds bloom the soft-dying day,
And touch the stubble-plains with rosy hue;
Then in a wailful choir the small gnats mourn
Amongst the river sallows, borne aloft
Or sinking as the light wind lives or dies.

From John Keats, 'To Autumn'

Summer gradually burns itself out, rather like the human body. But it does so gently, almost imperceptibly. August is a descending month, and the subsequent vitiation into autumn is most gradual – until the oak leaves fall and we find ourselves stranded in early winter. Autumn, like winter, descends from the north, reaching the far south coast last. You can find touches of autumn in middle England in mid-August, and earlier further north – if you look.

There are autumn broods of Comma, Red Admiral, Small Copper, Small Tortoiseshell and occasionally some fresh Painted Ladies and a partial third brood of the Wall Brown. Rarely, a few other species produce autumn broods, such as the Holly Blue and White Admiral. The Speckled Wood is usually at its most numerous in early or mid-September, when its autumn brood emerges, and after warm summers late emergences of the Green-veined White occur, at least down south, and very locally. Small and Large

Whites can also produce a few fresh adults in October during mild weather. Later, on warm late autumn days a few hibernating Brimstones, Peacocks and Small Tortoiseshells wake up to enjoy the last of the sunshine, before returning to hibernation.

There are early autumns, precipitated by gales in September or frosts at the start of October, middling autumns, and late autumns when the frost and rains hold off. There are also Indian summers – periods of warm fine weather during September or October – though, strictly, an Indian Summer comes after the first pulse of frosts (like 'decimate', the term 'Indian summer' has transmogrified). Whatever, our butterflies seize upon Indian summer weather and make it their own, but it is their last stand. They are doomed, and they know it; for above all else autumn tears summer's leafy temple down.

Gradually butterflies diminish and retreat as autumn advances: the number of species on the wing declines, and the individual survivors age and head south or gather in sheltered warm places, such as gardens, valley bottoms or the foot of south-facing hillsides, where they become more and more dependent on late flowers. They are pushed towards warmth, and seek out the warmest

microclimates where summer lingers longest, and so become increasingly localised. The last of the year is often seen fluttering around the south-facing edge of a building, a Red Admiral usually, or a Small Tortoiseshell.

But gradually the strength of the sun wanes and the sun angles become too low in the sky, so that the temperature fails to reach the 12-degree threshold that butterflies require for activity. It is this diminution that ends the butterfly season, rather than night frost or even the autumn rains. Consequently, it is unusual to see a butterfly on the wing after November 5th – the sun has sunk too low. By the end of October the sun angles are comparable to those of mid-February.

Perhaps autumn is loved so much by people, not so much because of the colours – yellows, browns, oranges and some reds – but because it gives us a last chance to value sunshine before the pall of winter descends. Also, those final sunlit days allow us to say goodbye to summer, properly.

November is the grim reaper, the Avenging Angel of Death, which strips the leaves off the trees, casts the sun into shadow, sends forth the driving autumn rains which blow before the emptying of time, and subdues the colours of the land to the drabbest shades of brown. It is a reign of terror. We can only rage against the dying of the light, and retreat into the memories of summer gone – and start dreaming of spring.

November, the crucifixion of the year,
Spread-eagles my soul upon a naked land.
Bereft of leaves, the flail-maddened hedge,
Cut with thorns, bereft of hope.
The furrowed land where no bird flies,
But for waif-like blackened crows
Whose cries are wraiths of summer gone,
Borne on the wind that drives the rain.
The pheasant struts, there but to be shot,
And die on winter's waste of thorns.

Dismember, there is no colour here:
The blood has drained through nail holes,
In palm and heel, within the mind itself,
And in the earth, through heel and palm.
Then in the brambles, stripped by wind,
An empty warbler's nest, of twisted grass,
The makers long away in sun-tilled lands,
Their song a memory, remote, alone.
My soul flew with them time ago,
Leaving but something lost behind.

(Selborne, Hampshire, autumn 1975)

15 *High-blown years: the Great Storm and afterwards*

Our winters are largely unmemorable, and when we do recollect them it is seldom for positive reasons. The winter of 1986/87 was memorable, for a lengthy freeze-up. The cold weather moved down from the north at the start of the year. It was well forecast, so I removed the sheep from Noar Hill early. January 12th was one of the coldest days on record nationally, with maximum temperatures in central southern England around −5°C. Snow then fell on several consecutive days, a powdery snow that cannot be moulded into snowballs and which blows around in the wind – call it fairy snow. It blew off the fields on a bitter wind and accumulated in the lanes, cutting off villages. Around The Lodge, 20 centimetres of snow in the fields blew to form drifts more than 2 metres deep in the lanes. We were cut off for three days, during a ten-day freeze-up in which the temperature failed to rise above zero. Once again, we retreated to a single room in the house, with three cats and a baby – and survived. A slow thaw began on January 21st, generating three days of fog. All told, the nation suffered a spell of fifteen sunless days.

February brought a change, to mild and grey weather – day after day of thoroughly mindless weather. Mid-month, the sun broke through, but with it came the return of the cold. At least it was dry and the first butterflying expeditions of the year could be launched, in search of Brown Hairstreak eggs in north-west Hampshire, to the south-west of Andover. This was *terra nova*, a vast undulating expanse of arable landscape – Edward Thomas called it ploughland – over Clay-with-Flints overlying the chalk. There were 'old' records of the Brown Hairstreak in this district, but no one had looked in recent years. Sure enough, the butterfly was still present, breeding along green lanes flanked by Blackthorn and on the few roadside hedges that were not flail-cut to smithereens annually. Major epicentres were discovered on MOD land around Shipton Bellinger, on the Wiltshire border, and at Cholderton, where an enlightened landowner, Henry Edmonds, manages his estate with butterflies, moths, birds and flowers firmly in mind. Henry is in touch with Nature, and with the land in his sound stewardship.

Early March brought more snow, this time the wet variety that settles on the grass and decorates trees nicely, but melts on roads. So we did not get cut off. Spring was long in coming, and the entire nation was becoming decidedly Fed Up. Then, on March 27th we suffered a violent storm, the fiercest spring storm I had known. Nationally, twelve people were killed and a large number of trees were blown down. It was perhaps a foretaste of what was to come.

Spring then broke through – on Passion Sunday, April 5th. Chiffchaffs flew in from the south and butterflies took to the air. My first butterfly of the year was, unusually, a Comma. The Comma was the butterfly of that early spring, outnumbering the Brimstone and Small Tortoiseshell. But no sooner had spring started than the weather got into the wretched habit of clouding up for the day and clearing for the night. Anyone with an eye for butterflies will understand the frustration that this weather pattern instils, especially in spring and after a long numbing winter. Nonetheless, the first Orange-tip appeared in East Hampshire on April 14th, bang on time. Once again, the species had timed the start of its emergence with the flowering of the Lady's Smock, one of its two main foodplants.

St George's Day, April 23rd, finally sorted things out. The weather was perfect, many Orange-tips hatched and an immigration of Red Admirals occurred – they had to be migrants, for the winter must surely have been too cold for this butterfly to have hibernated successfully. Holly Blues, Green Hairstreaks and Speckled Woods all quickly followed. Five reasonable, or even good, weeks ensued, allowing our spring butterflies to enjoy a successful season. It did, however, prove to be the best spell of weather of a difficult season. It brought out the first Duke of Burgundy of the year on Noar Hill on April 27th, a freshly emerged male launching itself at passing hoverflies from a perch in one of the chalk pits. By the end of April the vegetation was some ten days ahead of the norm, with the Beech, birch and oak trees well in leaf. By mid-May the Hawthorn was in flower, bedecked with snow again. Somehow, a bitter winter had led into an early spring.

The Forestry Commission arranged for a survey of the Pearl-bordered Fritillary in Alice Holt Forest. We were worried it was dying out there, as the Forestry Commission had (rightly) stopped felling blocks of oak woodland. This meant that there was a shortage of suitable new clearings and young plantations for the butterfly to colonise. The news was better than expected, but still worrying. I found two thriving colonies, at either end of the forest, both in experimental areas used by Forestry Commission Forest Research. In these plots, each of about 1 hectare in size, trees were planted, grown on for a few years and then grubbed out and replaced. The objective was to study how well saplings of different species established themselves. Crucially, Bracken, bramble and coarse grasses were controlled, by cutting and spraying, enabling violets to abound. Sure enough, in one of these research plots, in Lodge Inclosure at the north end of the forest, many Pearl-bordered Fritillaries were on the wing. I spent an afternoon catching, marking and recapturing them. All told 65 were netted and marked, and one was recaptured as many as six times. Jeremy Thomas kindly analysed the data and reported that there were between 128 and 182 individuals flying on the day. This represented an annual emergence of about 450 Pearl-bordered Fritillaries. Sadly, soon afterwards these experimental plots were abandoned, and the butterfly died out in Alice Holt.

There was nowhere new for them to colonise. The Small Pearl-bordered Fritillary, which also utilised these plots, lasted a while longer, then followed suit. Alice has been a shadow of herself since.

June started poorly, with a deep depression which gave vent to a fully fledged autumn gale. The month sagged, then recovered briefly, only to fall apart when the Lords Test match started. The spring butterflies, together with the immigrant Painted Ladies, were knocked out, and the high summer species were prevented from emerging. The sun returned towards the end of the month to bring out the Silver-studded Blues on the East Hampshire heaths, and the Ringlets and Marbled Whites on the downs.

The new month began promisingly, with the first Silver-washed Fritillaries and White Admirals appearing in the woods and another electrifying display of Dark Green Fritillaries at Porton Down, north-east of Salisbury, on July 5th. The latter was emerging in numbers that day, and a group from Butterfly Conservation's Hampshire Branch encountered several pairings amongst the grasses – limp, soft-winged females at the mercy of amorous males who were quartering the breeding grounds, low, picking off virgin females as soon as they had emerged. As the day progressed and the heat intensified they moved on to Viper's Bugloss – large orange butterflies with silver pearls on their undersides, feeding avidly together on plumes of mauve and blue flowers, under a cloudless sky. Send for an artist, or a poet.

The following day – July 6th – was National White Admiral Day, and The Lodge excelled itself. The previous July we had noticed a female White Admiral showing an interest in the old Honeysuckle which covered much of the southern front of the house, but assumed she would not lay eggs there. But at 5 pm a year later we spotted a freshly emerged, soft-winged White Admiral sitting on the Honeysuckle. The butterfly had bred there after all! I took it down to the local wood, a kilometre away, and set it free. Later the vacant pupal case was found, high up on the Honeysuckle tangle. Such was The Lodge, and such was my contentment and depth of belonging there.

The fine weather held. Ringlets erupted on Noar Hill, with the Marbled Whites appearing soon after them. Over at Bentley Wood, I R P Heslop's old heartland on the Hampshire/Wiltshire border, butterflies were massing. The wood, a small forest really, had been sold by the Forestry Commission to the Bentley Wood Trust, a charity set up by the Colman (mustard) family with the objectives of promoting nature conservation, public access, sustainable forestry and the Christian faith – four things that blend wondrously together. The Trust set about steadily removing non-native conifers and preserving the wood's flora and fauna. They have done a superb job, for Bentley Wood to this day remains England's best site for woodland butterflies. Only one butterfly seems to have been lost from there in the last thirty years – the High Brown Fritillary, which was on its last legs, or rather wings, when the Trust acquired the wood. On July 8th 1987 I saw a magnificent female feeding on a tall Marsh Thistle, and a couple of males amongst a plethora of similar-looking Dark Green Fritillaries in what is known as the Eastern Clearing, an area of former meadowland where planted conifers had died during the 1976 drought.

The fine weather then ushered in the Purple Emperor season, with a magnificent male feeding on fresh horse manure in one of the East Hampshire Hangers near Hawkley, before capitulating horribly – just as I was setting off for two weeks surveying for the High Brown Fritillary in Herefordshire and Worcestershire. The expedition could not have been more unfortunate, with day after day of cloud, drizzle and at times precipitous rain. The weather mattered little in the main, for many of the Bracken-filled commons I had been asked to visit had ceased to be suitable for the butterfly, though they might have supported populations in the not too distant past, before they became neglected. I found that the High Brown had gone from the Abberley Hills in west Worcestershire, and saw one of the last High Browns ever recorded in lovely Haugh Wood, south of Hereford. The one success was at Bircher Common and Croft Ambrey, on the National Trust's

Croft estate north of Leominster. Here, between downpours, a thriving cluster of colonies was discovered, flying over Bracken on a sheep-grazed common. The National Trust was delighted that this rare and rapidly declining butterfly was present there and a major conservation initiative began. Scratched, bruised, storm-battered and suffering from foot rot and incipient trench foot, the 1987 High Brown Fritillary Roadshow was abandoned.

Of course, soon afterwards the weather improved, for a while. Hampshire welcomed me home, with a magnificent flight of Purple Emperors at Coxmoor Wood near Odiham and the news that the Essex Skipper had at last colonised Noar Hill. The latter is all but impossible to separate out from its cousin the Small Skipper in flight. I was not looking forward to separating them out during the weekly butterfly transect count there: *Heaven help me*, I wrote in the diary. Time was spent in the New Forest, searching for High Brown Fritillaries amongst a plethora of Dark Greens in Hawkhill Inclosure, and admiring an excellent show of Silver-washed Fritillaries in Pondhead Inclosure, the most famous of the old Forest collecting grounds, near Lyndhurst.

The summer of 1987 had fallen apart, and not even the first Clouded Yellows could redeem a blighted season. These were seen in a conifer plantation near Bramshill in north Hampshire, which was threatened by a new town development. The nature conservation interest of this former heathland site managed to stave off the threat, not least because the insect fauna turned out to be distinctly rich. Over on the Isle of Wight a public inquiry was to be held to determine the future of the coastal road that cuts over the chalk downland ridge east of Freshwater. The road, known as the Military Road, is destined to disappear as the sea gradually eats into the chalk cliffs. The county council proposed to reset the road further back into the chalk ridge, cutting through one of the richest areas of downland in the country, and one of our best butterfly sites. Evidence had to be gathered to present to the inquiry. This involved surveying and counting the butterflies – several thousand Chalkhill Blues for a start. Suffice it to say that the inquiry was won, and that discussions over the future of the road along the west coast of the Isle of Wight are ongoing to this day.

August was up and down, but mostly down. On one of the better days I visited Watership Down, famous for its Rabbits. This proved to be one of the most disappointing stretches of Hampshire downland I have visited, with much flowerless Red Fescue grassland and few butterflies other than a modicum of Common Blues and Small Heaths. The Rabbits had over-grazed it, prior to leaving, perhaps in disgust.

The first autumn gale came over on September 6th, though in truth we had had several during the summer. Somehow, the Small Tortoiseshell came good, very good – so much so that it wrested the title of Butterfly of the Year 1987 away from the Pearl-bordered Fritillary. Perhaps the poor weather had hindered the larval parasites more than the host. At least 25 were present in our garden at The Lodge each sunny day, feeding up prior to hibernation. Some fresh Painted Ladies joined them too. Then there was another autumn gale, this time on September 12th. Unabashed, the Small Tortoiseshells continued to emerge: on September 17th over 50 were counted in The Lodge garden. Then the Red Admirals appeared in numbers, feasting drunkenly on rotting apples and pears. Another gale came over, and a precipitous deluge on October 9th. The weather was winding itself up, the rivers were swollen and the ground saturated.

Diary, October 15th 1987: *Heavy rain from early pm. Very deep depression. Had to attend evening meeting in Hants County Council underground chamber in Winchester. Walked out into and then drove home in a tempest. Switched engine off going up Arlesford bypass and was blown uphill for two miles. Went for walk under swaying dancing trees until I was bowled over and decided it wasn't time to meet my Maker – limbs were crashing down ...*

Diary, October 16th 1987: *Hurricane during night, with heavy rain, gradually easing off at dawn with wind dying down, exhausted, in pm. The Great Storm of 1987, an intensifying Returning Polar Maritime Depression moving up from Biscay, only the weather men hadn't forecast it. Seventeen people lost their lives.*

It began at midnight and peaked around 5 am here. London recorded a gust of 94 mph, but many spots along the south coast had gusts in excess of 100 mph. It was even more devastating than the March 27th storm, with myriad trees falling – the leaves were still on and the ground saturated. Our local environs looked like one of those haunting photos of shell-damaged woodland from the Great War: hardly a tree had survived unscathed. The towering Beech to the immediate east of The Lodge was rent asunder, like the temple veil in Jerusalem. It took us most of the morning to clear the drive.

The Lodge escaped rather miraculously, merely losing a coping tile, the electricity (for nine days), telephone (five days) and water supply (four days). Luckily The Lodge didn't present much of a solid object and the apocalyptic wind just howled through it, billowing the curtains and blowing out decades worth of dust from under the floor boards – this hung as a miasma for days. In the garden the sweet peas disappeared into orbit. All the colour was washed out of surviving oak leaves, as if blanched.

Managed to get up to Noar Hill (to check the sheep), expecting to find the electric flexi-netting up in the trees. Two rolls had vanished, blown utterly away. The hanger looks as if it has been clear-felled. The sheep hadn't noticed.

The following day the picture of devastation throughout central southern and south-east England became clear. Myriad mature, but drawn-up and spindly, Beech trees had been uprooted, like dominoes. A visit to the Selborne hangers revealed (diary): *A scene of near-total devastation, probably only one in every 20 trees left standing along Noar Hill Hanger, and many of those are damaged. The hanger was impenetrable, looking as if it had been bombed. Arboreal carnage.* This picture was repeated all over the south-east quarter of the UK. Over a million trees were lost. I never found the flexi-netting.

Incredibly, on that day of sunshine and easing showers, I saw a Small White in our garden at The Lodge at noon, and then a Small Tortoiseshell and a Brimstone. Later, on Noar Hill, a Red Admiral was active. Somehow, some butterflies had survived the maelstrom; but that's butterflies all over for you, they are life's great survivors. A few days later I managed to get to the hangers above Petersfield. From Shoulder of Mutton Hill, the hillside dedicated to Edward Thomas, I counted blue smoke rising from 27 wood fires dotted across the Sussex Weald. The great clear-up had begun. But on the summit a superb Beech grove, a natural cathedral fit for a great poet, was lying horizontal, uprooted. Nearby, the road down Stoner Hill was so badly blocked that dynamite was needed to clear it. As around Selborne, it was not so much the veteran Beech pollards that had come down – though many had – but the densely grown and drawn-up maiden trees.

A massive germination of young trees took place, and within twenty years the scars had healed. Time creates these issues, and time solves them. Woods think long term, we don't.

And the Great Storm did some good. It uprooted countless acres of ugly arboreal slums which should never have been established in the first place. Mile after mile of dense, non-native and poorly maintained conifer plantations were blown down, creating a wonderful opportunity to resolve some of the worst excesses of the twentieth-century forestry revolution. The storm proved to be a pathfinder towards the Forestry Commission's laudable Plantations on Ancient Woodland Sites (PAWS) programme, which removes conifers from ancient woodland. Above all, many of our woods were far too dense prior to the storm, having been neglected for decades. The storm opened them up to the benefit of much wildlife, notably the butterflies.

In the short term, the storm provided great opportunities to look for the eggs of the Purple and White-letter Hairstreaks, which breed high up in oaks and elms respectively. In Hampshire, Andy Barker, Adrian Hoskins and I spent much time searching for these eggs, finding that Purple Hairstreak eggs were profuse in what had been the high canopy of dense oak stands, and on several different species of oak too. I was finding a Purple Hairstreak egg about every three minutes. In the New Forest, north-east of Brockenhurst, the beleaguered Pearl-bordered Fritillary benefited greatly from mass wind-blow and the resultant clearance, and in the medium term the Purple Emperor benefited from mass germination of its foodplant, sallow trees.

October remained wet to the last, achieving its ambition to be one of the wettest on record. Mercifully, November calmed things down, by being cold and dry. Finally, the Christmas period was remarkably mild: Red Admirals appeared out of hibernation, and a small influx of Painted Ladies was noticed by birders along the south coast. The *Daily Mail* even published a letter reporting a Painted Lady at Ventnor on Christmas Day.

A clear and mild night, with a three-quarter moon and a host of stars, ushered in 1988. However, it was not long before rain started.

In contrast to its predecessor the winter was mild, ridiculously so, but horribly wet. Aconites and Snowdrops were well out by mid-January. At the end of the month we left our beloved Lodge and moved in to a small and rather loathsome house we were purchasing in nearby Alton. The ending of our tenure at The Lodge, with its pantiles and Pipistrelle Bats, Death-watch Beetles and condensated windows, severely damaged my relationship with Nature – by distancing me from the countryside and, less obviously, from the weather and the night sky. I have not felt genuinely at home in any house since. There one could dwell, not just close to Nature, but as part of it – for the place was so primitive that there was little choice.

Looking after the sheep and organising scrub bashes on Noar Hill, with occasional sorties into the far west of Hampshire to survey the Brown Hairstreak population, maintained some vestige of sanity. In mid-February, with the rookeries in full repair and Primroses blooming, the first butterfly of the year appeared – a yellow Brimstone weaving its way beneath bare trees at the foot of Shoulder of Mutton Hill, by Petersfield. By mid-March the vegetation in both town and countryside looked a month ahead of the norm, with sallows in flower and Hawthorn hedges leafing commonly. The year was running ahead of itself, in what was to be the start of a long run of absurdly mild winters.

April started well, and it was holiday time. A week was spent walking the coastal path between Hartland Point in Devon and Bude in north Cornwall, with a small daughter in a back-pack – up and down, from combe to combe, stopping to play on wooden bridges over helter-skelter streams lined with mosses and Golden Saxifrage. The slopes were heavily scented by the heady coconut aroma of gorse blossom. Incoming Swallows skimmed by in loose groups.

This coastline is steeped in butterflying history, for this had been Large Blue country. The butterfly had been discovered along this coast around 1891, in the mysterious Millook valley. Later, during the 1940s, it was found to occur in most of the sea combes between Bude and Hartland Quay. Then myxomatosis eliminated the Rabbits, and the heavily grazed and sparsely vegetated slopes proved to be the perfect seedbed for gorse and Blackthorn, not to mention rough grasses. The gentler slopes lost their butterflies through agricultural improvement. It is not possible to walk these valleys today without immense sadness for what has been lost, especially amongst the Blackthorn and gorse entanglements of the Millook valley, where some lingering pathos tells of paradise lost. Clearly, though, the old collectors must have sweated buckets collecting their specimens on the near-precipitous slopes, though presumably they were not carrying toddlers.

In mid-April the Orange-tips started to appear, and some Painted Ladies. There were reports of huge numbers of Ladies in Spain, Portugal and southern France. April had been reasonable, and had brought out the first of the Noar Hill Duke of Burgundies as early as the 26th. After four poor days May righted itself, and a fair scatter of Painted Ladies appeared. I saw 20 in a week in various places in Hampshire. In theory the arrival of the Painted Lady augured well, though its previous two invasions – in 1980 and 1985 – had been thwarted by poor summer weather.

The Forestry Commission had set up an experimental programme to enhance butterfly populations in Cheriton Wood, near Arlesford in mid Hampshire. Originally a coppice-with-standards wood on Clay-with-Flints overlying the chalk, Cheriton Wood had been felled and replanted with conifers, neglected, and leased out to an intensive pheasant shoot. Annoyingly, it had escaped the 'Hurricane' unscathed. Early in 1987, rides had been widened and a series of bays created, the object being to see how these simple measures would benefit butterfly populations in a coniferised wood. I was tasked with studying butterfly population changes there, and learnt much from the five-year programme. One of the immediate beneficiaries was the Brimstone, the females of which homed in on Purging Buckthorn bushes that were regrowing strongly in the coppice bays. So that is what makes Brimstones tick! Coppice the buckthorns, for like the Brown Hairstreak and its Blackthorn, this butterfly favours dynamically growing bushes. The practice on nature reserves at the time was to leave buckthorn bushes well alone. Inspired, I coppiced some of the buckthorns on Noar Hill, with dramatic results. In Cheriton Wood, Brimstones thrived on first-, second- and third-year coppice regrowth, then forsook the maturing bushes.

Some of the most wonderful, memorable days of one's life occur in mid-May, when spring is at its best. Such was Saturday May 14th 1988. Liverpool was playing Wimbledon in the FA Cup Final, under a shimmering sky. Down in Bentley Wood, towards Salisbury, the Pearl-bordered Fritillaries were emerging in numbers, pilgrim Painted Ladies were visiting Bluebell flowers along with ageing Peacocks, and all were being busily and bossily intercepted and seen off by male Duke of Burgundies and equally irate Dingy and Grizzled skippers. These were all thriving in the Eastern Clearing, which was being carefully managed by the Bentley Wood Trust. I was supposed to be surveying the hoverflies there but had got badly hijacked by the butterflies, especially the Pearl-bordered Fritillary, of which three distinct colonies were found, and the dark woodland race of the Duke of Burgundy which was breeding on Primrose plants along the mown path edges. A return visit to Bentley Wood took place on June 7th, by which time spring had merged into early summer and the Pearl-bordereds, Burgundies and spring skippers were all but over. Instead, Marsh Fritillaries were emerging in a clearing in the centre of the wood, a large and lovely race too, taking nectar from Bugle and Tormentil flowers. Best of all, a huge emergence of the Small Pearl-bordered Fritillary was taking place, and the brassy males were skimming and fluttering low over the bracken and rushes. For years now, Bentley Wood has been our best and most loved site for woodland butterflies. It can lay on the most magical of days, not least because its butterflies make an essential contribution to the immense sense of place that is assiduously preserved there.

Taking another stab at surveying the Herefordshire commons for High Brown Fritillary colonies was going to be the highlight of the 1988 butterfly season. The previous July's attempt had been a weather-spoilt teaser. It was clear that the butterfly was in trouble in what had almost certainly been a stronghold county, but there was still the very real chance of turning up some sizeable colonies. The big find of the 1987 survey had been Bircher Common, on National Trust land north of Leominster. It needed visiting in early summer, to assess habitat conditions. One of the problems with surveying for High Brown Fritillary during the butterfly's flight season is that by then the bracken canopy has closed over: one can see the adult insect, but it is very hard to read breeding conditions. So in mid-May the old 1986 Malverns High Brown partnership of Grove and Oates was dusted off and dispatched to north Herefordshire, to look at violet densities amongst dead Bracken litter, search for the distinctive but elusive caterpillars, and identify and map breeding areas.

The weather was good, probably too good, for High Brown larvae are relatively easy to find during thin-cloud conditions, when they bask openly, but during hot sunshine they hide. Fortunately, patchy cloud came over during the afternoon to produce a magical half hour during which eleven of the bronze spiny caterpillars were found, basking on dead Bracken fragments. By caterpillar-hunting standards that's Mega, especially as High Brown larvae cryptically match the pieces of dead Bracken stems and fronds on which they sit. We found that the butterfly had two distinct breeding grounds on Bircher Common. Better still, we found that the High Brown was breeding in a few discrete patches on the ramparts of the Neolithic hill fort of Croft Ambrey, a place haunted by the spirits of autumn, and also on the sheep-grazed west-facing slope of Yatton Hill below. In other words, there was a cluster of colonies, each with distinct breeding areas, within a couple of square kilometres of landscape. Additionally, several other areas of potential habitat were spotted across the valley from the Croft Ambrey ramparts. We were looking at what conservation biologists call an intact metapopulation, a loose cluster of habitat patches within an area of landscape. I could not wait until July.

June was indeterminate, then in early July we were subjected to the deepest July depression since 1902. The White Admirals were blasted away. A few days of indifferent weather followed, before another depression came over, followed by a return to sunshine and showers. But I could wait no longer, the assault on the Herefordshire commons was launched. It could not possibly suffer worse weather than I had experienced there the previous July. It did. The expedition started reasonably, with days of long cloudy periods interspersed with short sunny spells. Such conditions are workable: the trick is to explore during cloud, keeping an eye out for developing sunny breaks, and make sure you are in the best-looking spots when the sun deigns to come out. I started on Swinyard Hill, a known 'good site' at the southern end of the Malverns, in order to get a measure of what numbers were like. They were far from impressive. Then, three days on slopes around Symonds Yat in the Wye valley and on Bracken-filled commons in the Hay-on-Wye and Dorstone areas drew blank. Few of the places visited there looked suitable, but I should have turned the butterfly up at a couple of places. All the time the cloudy periods were lengthening and the sunny intervals dwindling. I found some highly promising-looking habitat, near Pontrilas, but lost the sun altogether. Then the rain began, and became relentless. When glimmers of watery sun appeared the midges and mosquitoes descended, and behaved like entomological Furies.

It is probable that the High Brown had either been recently lost or was in the latter stages of dying out from most of the places visited – steep south-facing Bracken hillsides along the Welsh border. All told, I found two new High Brown localities, both of which were poised to lose the butterfly. Eventually the sun reappeared: it was time for a stock take, which revealed that the butterfly was only present in pitiful numbers at its strongholds at Eastnor and Swinyard Hill in the southern Malverns, and at Bircher Common north of Leominster. If the butterfly was that scarce in its core sites there was little point in carrying on searching for it in poor habitat elsewhere. July 1988 was duly excommunicated and the expedition abandoned. The High Brown Fritillary owed me big time – or perhaps the Purple Emperor was wanting to reel me back in?

The butterfly season was running late after a rotten July, with the year's brood of Brimstones and Peacocks only starting to emerge in early August, along with a new, home-grown generation of Painted Ladies. August was a veritable Wendy house, in one day, out the next; or, for people on holiday, beach one day, historic mansion the next. The coppiced buckthorns in Cheriton Wood produced a superb hatch of Brimstones, which then fed avidly on Burdock flowers. An excursion to Hilliers Arboretum near Winchester revealed that the butterfly was breeding merrily there on two non-native buckthorns – *Rhamnus rupestris* from Eastern Europe and *R. globosa* from China. As is their habit during poor summers, the two cabbage whites, the Large White and Small White, appeared in unusually high numbers, making up for a general paucity of butterflies in gardens.

September began with a fully fledged autumn gale, but then settled down for a couple of weeks, perhaps seeking to redeem a wasted summer – before suddenly giving up and ushering in the autumn rains early. During the fine spell I saw my eighth and ninth (and final) Holly Blues of the year, a lousy annual tally for a supposedly 'common' insect, and all the more remarkable given that the butterfly became numerous the following spring. In September the damage caused by the poor summer sequence, now in its fourth year, became clear: despite excellent habitat conditions and exemplary habitat management the introduced colony of the Adonis Blue at Old Winchester Hill NNR, in Hampshire's lovely Meon valley, became extinct. The problem was that for several consecutive generations (the butterfly has two broods a year) the wretched weather did its worst at the worst possible time, just when the broods were emerging.

A scatter of freshly emerged Painted Ladies, home-grown individuals, appeared whenever the autumn produced a pleasant day. It could have won my Butterfly of the Year award, but merely came a good second. For, on a ridiculously mild day in mid-December a Brimstone was seen wandering around the Top Pit at Noar Hill. He may have been lured out of hibernation in a bramble patch by the warmth of a bonfire lit by Hampshire Conservation Volunteers nearby, but he became fully active, before settling down to hibernate in a tussock of Tufted Hair-grass. Brimstones were seen elsewhere that day. So, for lessons rendered in the odious conifer plantations of Cheriton Wood, and at Hilliers Arboretum, the Brimstone won Butterfly of the Year – though in all honesty the standard was decidedly low. We were due a good summer, and a decent butterfly season.

16 *Paradise regained:*
the great summer of 1989

Once in a lifetime a year actually gets it right. That year was 1989. It was an even better summer than that of 1976, offering more hot sunny days and fewer poor days. However, butterfly populations were by and large not a patch on those of 1976, for 1989 came in after a run of dismal summers during which butterfly populations had dwindled, whereas butterflies entered 1976 on a population high after two good summers. There was a fly in the ointment, too, for an underrated Australian side humiliated England in the summer's Ashes series.

The winter was ridiculously mild, and remarkably dry – as if the rain had exhausted itself during 1988. In Hampshire, Hawthorn leaves unfurled before Christmas on the early roadside tree near Jane Austen's house at Chawton, and Song Thrushes were piping away before New Year. The New Year itself was seen in by the Edward Thomas Memorial Stone on Shoulder of Mutton Hill above Steep, looking down on a spectacular firework display issuing from the vicinity of Bedales School. At the start of the year, then, the mood was celebratory.

January was so mild that Rooks were building their nests at Calne, in north Wiltshire, on the 22nd. Oddly, I did not see the first butterfly before February 21st, when a few Small Tortoiseshells came out to play. That tore it of course, a record deep depression, of 952 millibars, promptly deposited cold rain, and some snow, in a gale that lasted three days.

A major winter job was to search for Brown Hairstreak eggs in the Botley Wood area, north of Fareham in south Hampshire, which was threatened by major industrial development. The butterfly had been numerous there well into the 1970s, but had not been recorded since 1979. I drew a blank and concluded that the butterfly had died out due to a combination of factors. Within Botley Wood itself, the young plantations in which it had bred were maturing fast, and had choked out the young Blackthorn growth favoured by the butterfly. So the butterfly had become dependent on Blackthorn stands outside the forest fence, on farmland. There, before selling out to the developers, farmers had been busy grubbing out wood-edge Blackthorn stands and flail-cutting the thorn hedges mercilessly, whilst the few surviving Blackthorn stands were neglected and became too old and tall for this butterfly. It was a sad and sorry tale, of a butterfly caught between the hammer and anvil of intensification and neglect. There was hope, though: a walk through Hambledon Hanger, above the birthplace of cricket, revealed a huge and wonderfully healthy Wych Elm, complete with White-letter Hairstreak eggs. This leviathan of a tree had survived the ravages of Dutch elm disease.

March huffed and puffed, then dribbled and drabbled, before ending strongly. Easter arrived at the end of March. Early Easters always seem to bring dreadful weather, but 1989 had different ambitions, and the race was on for a March Orange-tip. Day after day I haunted the Gault Clay woods of the East Hampshire Hangers, where the butterfly's beloved Lady's Smock abounds, in an effort to beat the record for Hampshire's earliest ever Orange-tip – seen near Alton on March 31st 1920 by grammar school master and entomologist E A C Stowell. Eventually I had to admit defeat – only to see one on the outskirts of Pamber Forest, north of Basingstoke, on, you've guessed it, March 31st. So the record was merely equalled. Since 1989 butterfly seasons have advanced, and Orange-tips regularly appear in late March. In many ways, then, 1989 was a gateway year.

A cold and wet spell developed in mid-April, on a northerly airstream, to slow spring down. It was caterpillar-hunting weather, and the Pearl-bordered Fritillary obliged by providing some memorable hours in Parkhurst Forest on the Isle of Wight, just up from the prison. There, larvae were basking on dead oak leaves, warming up before crawling off at speed to feed briefly but frenetically on fresh violet leaves and flowers. Inspired, I looked again the following day in Alice Holt Forest, but found only a Large Skipper caterpillar feeding happily on Wood Sedge. The larvae of several of our so-called grass-feeding butterflies also eat sedges.

On May 2nd the wonderful summer of 1989 finally broke through. From then on it was glory all the way, beginning with the driest May for some 300 years, and the second sunniest (after 1909). London recorded 0.9 millimetres of rain all month. That day I was surveying insects at The Moors, a calcareous fen and carr system near Bishop's Waltham in south Hampshire. The rushy meadows were alive with Orange-tips, feeding joyously and laying eggs on Lady's Smock flowers. A week later they had been replaced by an even greater profusion of Green-veined Whites. There were strings of these gentle white butterflies bobbing about over the Lady's Smock stands, whilst numerous females were fluttering low to lay their eggs on the basal leaves. Orange-tip eggs are easy to find, below Lady's Smock flowers, but Green-veined White eggs are found on the underside of the basal rosette of leaves, right down at the base of the plant.

At the end of the first week of May, on the back of a strong anticyclone, the Pearl-bordered Fritillaries began to emerge. My first was ushered in by a Nightingale, hidden away in leafing trees. Once again they had timed their flight season with the flowering of their beloved Bugle. The Pearl-bordered was in goodly numbers that May, making the most of prolonged sunshine and the absence of any cold, wet or windy weather. New colonies were discovered in Harewood Forest, just west of Andover, and in a wood on the National Trust's estate at Mottisfont in west Hampshire. There, two dozen or so of these incessant wanderers of vernal woods were skimming about over a 1-hectare clearing in Drove Copse, on a calm sunny day when an azure sky was populated by tiny cotton-wool clouds. Parkhurst Forest was also revisited, and several strong colonies were found in young conifer plantations.

The Pearl-bordered Fritillary claimed a perfect May as its own, though many other species also fared well. On Noar Hill His Grace the Duke of Burgundy emerged in excellent numbers, for the weather and habitat conditions there were just about spot on for it. For once, its numbers were not depleted by a sudden deterioration in the weather. The first was seen on May 2nd, numbers peaked on the traditional National Duke of Burgundy Day of May 19th, and by the end of the month the butterfly was all but gone, having laid a great many eggs, and also having wandered off to establish new colonies. All that spells success for a butterfly. Remarkably, there were no butterfly losers during the spring of 1989.

Another great success story was the Glanville Fritillary on the Isle of Wight. A visit to Compton Chine, for daughter Lucy's birthday treat, found the butterfly abundant over the entire lower cliff slope system, and along the cliff top. They had even over-spilled onto the beach and into the National Trust car park. Ken Willmott, who had been monitoring that colony closely since 1973, was nonplussed. The diary ponders: *I wonder when*

I'll see cinxia *in such brilliant numbers again – if ever?* I am still waiting. On a return visit on August 20th I found the larval webs so prolific that I wondered whether the larvae were going to eat themselves out of house and home. Sure enough, the following season the population crashed, though several other factors may have contributed – notably the impact of drought, parasites, and erosion caused by the storms of January 1990.

The early morning of Wednesday May 24th saw a belt of thundery showers move up from the south, with a day of humid azure haze following. In the wake of the thunderstorms I arrived on the Stroud commons, in the Cotswolds, to survey the National Trust holdings of Minchinhampton and Rodborough commons. The lane surfaces were steaming after rain, with miniature rainbows shining through. It was a world of intense, other-worldly beauty, and a homecoming. It was Rodborough Common that really stole my heart. Little did I know that within three years I would be living nearby, having swapped it for Noar Hill. I found several Duke of Burgundy colonies, and numerous Brown Argus, Dingy Skippers, Green Hairstreaks and especially Small Blues on virtually all the slopes. Chalkhill Blue larvae were readily found hiding in the Horseshoe Vetch clumps. Iridescent green Cistus Forester moths danced everywhere, ethereal and fairy-like. I felt I had entered the state of mind so rapturously described in what must be Laurie Lee's greatest poem, 'April Rise', which captures the essence of spring in the Cotswolds.

Rain fell at the end of the first week of June, the first of any significance since April 24th (bar localised thunderstorms). A couple of frosts also occurred, which burnt off young Ash leaves and Bracken fronds. But then the fine weather built again, and butterfly populations with it. Large Skippers abounded on the grasslands. There was almost a plague of them at Keyhaven Marshes on the west Hampshire coast. Butterflies specialise in laying on localised population explosions, and this was one of them. On the downs, Meadow Brown, Marbled White and Ringlet all appeared unusually early, and in great numbers. Tuesday June 20th was stupefyingly hot – 30 degrees Celsius with an intense white light. I knew that light. I had last seen it during the high summer of 1976. There was only one place to be, an oak forest. Beneath the ancient oaks of Pamber Forest in north Hampshire I found my way back into that long hot summer. The first White Admiral and Silver-washed Fritillary males were emerging, and the weather was so hot and dry that some were drinking from the bed of the Bowmont Brook, which winds its way below tall oaks and Hazel coppice. The stream itself had retreated into a series of puddles. I sat down in the shade of an oak, and placed in my hat a Jay's feather found lying in the dust.

The Purple Emperor erupted into that summer in the most sudden and unexpected manner.

Diary, June 23rd 1989: *At 1.26 I was standing on the summit of the high Bracken-dominated promontory of Woolbeding Common, outside Midhurst in West Sussex, gazing into the Wealden landscape, when I was attacked by a freshly emerged male* iris. *He flew round me, settled on a little birch, bowled me a bouncer which nearly took my sunhat off, then shot off eastwards – doubtless ending up in Dragons Green some 20 miles distant. He was hill-topping, having flown up the wooded scarp slope. One of the most memorable Emperors of my life, though he actually looked slate grey rather than purple. This I thought could well be the UK's earliest Purple Emperor since the incredible summer of 1893, and travelled home in appropriate mood. Ken Willmott then informed me that he had seen one at Bookham Common, Surrey, yesterday. K J Willmott has therefore been declared apostate.*

After a couple of rather necessary rainy days June ended strongly, with an impressive hatch of Silver-washed Fritillaries in Harewood Forest, especially in the area known as Deadman's Plack, immortalised by W H Hudson in *Hampshire Days*. Over a hundred were seen, including a pristine female of the *valezina* colour form. Gatekeepers were emerging there, already, my first ever June Gatekeepers, along with the summer brood of the Green-veined White, again remarkably early. Above all, June had set July up superbly. It was time to leave a pregnant wife alone with a three-year-old child, and disappear off for three weeks in pursuit of the High Brown Fritillary in the West Country – I had a contract to survey High Browns there with the Nature Conservancy Council. To make the money run further and to get closer to Nature, I camped rather than bed and breakfasted, utilising some superb low-facility camp sites. For a briefing, I was handed the Biological Records Centre print-out of High Brown Fritillary records for Devon and Somerset, and was told to make contact with the key butterfly recorders there, and boldly go where no man had been before, boldly. I was the venturer into *terra nova*. This was a journey, if not into another world, then into another dimension of the one we think we know.

The journey started on the East Devon Pebblebed Heaths, an undulating expanse of ungrazed dry and humid heaths inland of the retirement haven of Budleigh Salterton. The first butterfly seen here was what proved to be the summer's only Clouded Yellow, which sped past on East Budleigh Common. Oddly, the great summer of 1989 proved to be a poor one for our migrant butterflies, as was the hot summer of 1984, with only the Red Admiral showing up in any numbers. I failed to find the High Brown Fritillary on those heaths, and suspect that the rotten summers of 1987 and 1988 had proved too much for the butterfly in what seemed to be marginally suitable habitat. The moister areas of the heaths were alive with Small Pearl-bordered Fritillaries, a few Dark Green Fritillaries hurtled past, and I found some strong colonies of the Silver-studded Blue dotted about. I had not seen butterflies so numerous and diverse on a heath before; in comparison, populations on the heavily grazed New Forest heaths paled into insignificance.

Next up, the assault on Dartmoor – not the brooding high moor, Baskerville country, but the warm southern flanks and the valleys of the tumbling rivers Bovey, Dart and Teign. Despite the moor's reputation, south-east Dartmoor enjoys a distinctly rosy climate. First off was a visit to the lower moorland edge above

Buckfastleigh, by way of a moment of quiet contemplation in Buckfast Abbey. One site on the To Visit list proved to be the infamous Site X, the last place to support the English race of the Large Blue and the first to receive the experimental introduction of the Swedish race, from the island of Öland. The locality was a closely guarded secret, so much so that I was blissfully unaware of where I was treading, net in hand. What mattered was that High Browns were known from the area, and I had a set of grid references to check out. At 12.30 on July 3rd I broke the Wildlife & Countryside Act rather spectacularly: I caught a Large Blue. It was a dwarf specimen which I mistook for a male Holly Blue. I casually swished a net at it, and discovered my mistake, though ignorance is no defence in law. It was actually the first Large Blue seen on Site Y, the rough heathy slope adjoining Site X. Then I bumped into Dave Simcox, the Large Blue Project Officer who was staying in an unholy caravan on Site X. He had seen two High Browns over the last few days. We saw none but were privileged to see four Large Blues, including a couple of females laying their eggs on the opening buds of Wild Thyme. Graylings abounded, breeding strongly there on tussocks of Bristle Bent Grass. But, as the day's final entry in the diary records: *Four days in and I have yet to see a High Brown Fritillary on this trip.* The weather, at least, was set fair.

The following day the High Brown Fritillary was at last encountered. First, half a dozen brassy males patrolling at pace above the stream that plunges from pool to pool in Trendlebere Combe, a steeply incised heathy combe dropping into the River Bovey a mile upstream of Bovey Tracey. The butterfly was breeding on violets under narrow ribbons of Bracken on the foot of the south-facing slope. Then a long arduous climb took me up along the steep west-facing slope of Lustleigh Cleave, with the River Bovey dancing away in the treed shadows below. Lustleigh is common land, but cattle were no longer depastured there and the slope was deteriorating into dense Bracken and invading oak woodland. Ten or so High Browns were seen swooping over the tall Bracken, including three in a vista, but it was obvious that the butterfly was doomed. Indeed, these were the last High Browns seen at Lustleigh Cleave.

One falls in love with the Teign valley instantly, most easily on a hot and cloudless day with an oven-blast wind issuing from the south-east. Two days were spent visiting often precipitous Bracken slopes along this valley and its many side combes. This was hard work, breast-stroking up pathless slopes of rank Bracken with bramble under foot. Every now and then a fritillary would speed past. My task was to identify and map it, without falling over. The sweat was profuse, the language at times coarse. At night, I was asleep by 9.30, scratched, bruised and satisfyingly exhausted. Happy campers returning from the pub failed to wake me up. The river sang sweet lullabies. Small colonies of High Brown Fritillaries were dotted about along the valley. Some of these were known sites, like Dunsford Meadow; some were rediscoveries, as on Piddledown Common, next to the imposing Castle Drogo, and some were new discoveries. Downstream of Chagford there was a matrix of small colonies dotted all along the slopes of the Teign valley and its side combes. Sadly, the butterfly was never seen again in some of the sites I visited that year, often because nobody looked subsequently! A few years later the High Brown Fritillary collapsed in the Teign valley.

I was burning out, and needed time on less taxing terrain. Under a cloudless sky I drove over Dartmoor, past the prison, to the extensive Bracken-filled commons south and west of Tavistock. West Down, above the River Walkham near Grenofen, was a well-known site, where the High Brown Fritillary occurred in goodly numbers, and still does. A couple of new sites, on Roborough Common near Horrabridge, were discovered. There the habitat was in much better condition, grazed extensively by ponies and sheep, with the animals pushing into the Bracken stands to break down the dead fronds and encourage violets through. Then the weather broke down. Stygian gloom and thundery rain descended. By then I was out of it anyway, bent double by food poisoning contracted from an errant pub meal in my ancestral Cornwall. The rain saved David Gower's England from ignominious defeat in the second Test, and allowed me to recover.

The weather recovered too, but it was time to move moors, to Exmoor. I had been asked to look in the Barle and Exe valleys upstream of Dulverton. If anything, the Barle valley was even more magical than the Teign valley, and much lonelier. The river here, too, was unduly low. Sunlight danced myriad patterns upon it, and warmed its ever-slippery pebbles. I walked the Barle from Mounsey up to Withypool and back, and ventured up Pennycombe Water valley above Withypool. There were small colonies of High Browns in Bracken patches all along this valley system. Two or three butterflies here, half a dozen there, intermingled with similar-looking Dark Green Fritillaries, ageing Small Pearl-bordered Fritillaries and freshly emerged Silver-washed Fritillaries. At one point, high up in the secluded Pennycombe valley, a battling pair of White-letter Hairstreak males took off from a lone stunted Wych Elm, spitting fire and brimstone at each other. This butterfly was unknown from the district, but butterflies here were seriously under-recorded. Where the Bracken stands were grazed, the High Brown colonies looked healthy, but where the Bracken was neglected the butterflies looked doomed. Shortly after my survey grazing either ceased or intensified in this valley system, and the butterfly disappeared. But in 1989 this survey work seemed far from futile, and I was absorbed, not by loneliness but by oneness.

Three new colonies were discovered in the upper Exe valley, downstream of Exford. One of these was remarkably uphill for the High Brown, being well above the 200-metre contour, its normal altitude limit, but this was a hot summer and the butterfly was expanding its range. Again, all colonies were based on south-facing stands of Bracken that were still grazed by cattle or sheep. Time was also spent searching the steep Bracken slopes between Porlock and Minehead. Eventually, the butterfly's headquarters here were identified – the lower slopes of Bossington Hill, above Porlock Vale. Finally, combes in the northern Quantocks were searched.

Here, the Bracken stands looked ideal in terms of structure and litter breakdown, but were lacking in one essential detail – the soils were largely too acidic for violets, and acid-loving Sheep Sorrel grew prolifically instead. The 1989 High Brown Fritillary Roadshow had suddenly run its course. The journey finished by a waterfall in the Quantocks beloved by Dorothy Wordsworth. Here in the northern Quantocks she had run amok by day and night with her beloved brother and with their soul mate and William's muse, Samuel Coleridge, during their golden era in the late 1790s.

That evening I had to travel to Stroud in the Cotswolds, to assist with a training course for National Trust wardens on limestone grassland ecology. The course was based at Hawkwood College, a Georgian mansion at the head of a valley which offers spectacular sunsets. The college had been established by the Steiner movement in 1948, and it has a unique feel. It was an excellent halfway house after three weeks in the wilds. Strangely, though, I could not get used to sleeping in a bed again, missing my tent and the murmurings of the river close by. My shins bore the scratches of innumerable brambles and I was blistered by mosquito and horsefly bites, but I was completely unscathed by ticks – indeed, I never saw a tick until the hot summers of the mid-1990s, despite spending copious amounts of high summer time in tick-infested Bracken beds. More importantly, on this trip I encountered a depth of experience, belonging and wonderment few can claim today. The following day the slopes of Rodborough Common, one of the limestone hills above Stroud, were alive with Chalkhill Blues but my soul was still on the moors, dancing with the High Browns over shining Bracken fronds. It was inevitable that the High Brown would make off with the title of Butterfly of the Year 1989.

But the summer was far from over. In early July second-brood Holly Blues began to appear, and by mid-July they were everywhere. In some places they emerged in remarkable numbers. I counted over 50 on Yateley Common, a scrubby heath in north-east Hampshire, including seven feeding together on a bramble patch. To put that into perspective, that was the most of this often quite common butterfly I had seen since finding it commonplace on Guernsey in August 1970. All told, I saw about 130 second-brood individuals that high summer, compared to seventeen first-brood specimens – and seventeen itself was a reasonable tally. The Holly Blue vanishes for years before suddenly coming from nowhere and becoming relatively numerous for three or four broods, during a good summer sequence, before fading again. These boom and bust cycles are supposed to be driven by the abundance of a tiny yellow and black wasp, *Listrodomus nycthemerus*, which parasitises the larvae in a classic host–parasite relationship: host numbers build up, the parasite increases, the host declines, the parasite then crashes, the gap between host and parasite widens, and the host increases again. Something like that. Doubtless other factors are at play too, besides the weather. With Holly Blues, enjoy them when you have them, for there are more lean times than bountiful years. In 1989, the second brood had virtually fizzled out by mid-August, but a small and highly localised third generation occurred during September and early October. Above all, the Holly Blue had set itself up well for 1990.

The humble Green-veined White, so often overlooked and lost amongst the ubiquitous 'cabbage whites', also produced a bumper second brood. Back at The Moors, near Bishop's Waltham, the summer brood was even more prolific than the spring brood had been. In searing heat on July 23rd the butterfly was probably twice as numerous as in early May. Again, the females were seeking out the basal rosette leaves of Lady's Smock, now hidden amongst lush meadowland grasses. I could see up to a dozen rising and falling over the fen meadow, seeking to lay their eggs. Also, females were watched freely laying eggs on Fools Watercress growing midstream in one of the chalky watercourses there. *So we have an aquatic butterfly*, the diary states enthusiastically.

In late July, the heaths started to frazzle, cracks appeared in exposed clay, trees dropped leaves and the downs turned a Mediterranean grey. A trip to the western Isle of Wight downs found the Chalkhill Blue in super-abundance, but they were having to disperse away from the downs to find nectar, for the downland flowers were in desperate need of rain. The Chalkhills wandered downslope into fields which had been cut for silage in June, and where plants were consequently re-flowering. They were also imbibing moisture from cattle dung, deposited by the Galloway cattle that have grazed the length of Brook and Compton downs since the herd was established there just after the Second World War. The drought was alleviated by showers and patchy drizzle in mid-August.

In early August I revisited one of my old heartlands, Watlington Hill on the scarp slope of the Chilterns, a couple of kilometres south of the M40. I had known it well during the late 1960s and early 1970s, visited again in 1976 and then briefly in 1981. I was surprised how much it had changed. The Rabbit population had increased massively. The areas of rough grass so prominent during the late 1960s were all gone, replaced by short billiard-table turf ideal for the Silver-spotted Skipper. Twenty years previously, the skipper had been restricted to a few acres of north-facing and south-facing slope at the east end of the National Trust holding, whilst rough-grassland butterflies like the Marbled White abounded elsewhere. Now the Silver-spotted Skipper had all the open grassland for its own, and the Marbled White & Co. were restricted to deeper soil pockets along the slope bottoms. I had never seen so many Silver-spotted Skippers, counting 350 at a rate of 1.96 per minute during a zigzag count across the main short-turf areas. Few butterflies are harder to count than this minuscule, hyperactive jet fighter of a butterfly that relishes hot sunshine.

The heat intensified, and brought out second broods of butterfly species which in normal summers are single-brooded. On the downs, and even on Yateley Common, quite a number of second-brood Dingy Skippers were seen. These were novel, for they were feeding on August flowers, not their usual spring flowers. The Small Blue produced quite a sizeable second generation at many sites, and in Alice Holt Forest the Small Pearl-bordered Fritillary was double-brooded. I counted over a dozen there on August 12th, though all were dwarf in size, mostly about the size of a Chalkhill Blue; one was tiny, the size of a Small Copper. Another feature of great butterfly summers is the way normally sedentary species turn up in strange places, miles from their normal habitat. Some Chalkhill Blue males become wanderers during prolonged hot weather, and in 1989 several turned up in the New Forest. I also rescued a stray Small Blue from Pamber Forest, and released it 25 kilometres away at the nearest known locality.

The hot summer weather finally broke on September 14th, when a vigorous depression came over from the west. I watched it advance, and the sun vanish, whilst having lunch by the Albert Memorial in London, my favourite piece of architecture. The best aspect of it is Asia's right breast, which was blasted into the Royal Albert Hall by a Nazi bomb – you can see the join line where they glued it back on.

Nonetheless, 1989 had one magical trick left up its sleeve. On a visit to Pamber Forest back on July 25th I had noted that White Admiral larvae were entering their third instar, whereas normally they bed down for their winter hibernation as second-instar larvae. Perhaps they were going to produce a second brood, for the first time in Hampshire since 1947? Then, during late September and early October a few second-brood butterflies were indeed seen in Hampshire and Sussex, including one in Pamber Forest. This inspired Mrs O and me to name our second daughter, born on October 10th, Camilla, after the White Admiral (*Limenitis camilla*), the most graceful of all our butterflies. The name could readily be shortened to Millie. In due course, it was.

Gradually summer sank into autumn. Then the long-awaited rains arrived with Valkyrien vengeance in mid-December. But I was oblivious to them, for much of that winter was spent in the sanctuary of the most wonderful building in London, the Natural History Museum. There, in a world far removed from the bustling public galleries, reside many of the museum's butterfly collections (many more are in an outpost at Tring) and an oasis of sublime tranquillity, the museum's reading room. There one can while away the winter months researching the fascinating history of butterflying in the British Isles, oblivious to the darkness and dismal weather outside. It was the easiest winter I ever passed. I have every intention of spending another winter there sometime. It is a place of deep belonging for every natural historian.

The Gift

Psyche, silent
as a butterfly,
glided softly down
to bask beside me,
within the stillness
of ethereal time,

And gild a primrose bank
with gold on darkling moss:

A gift from a forest to
a wanderer of woods.

In that ecstatic moment
Spring herself lay down
before me, and told me
how much I loved her,
that I might love her
more.

Spring

Now I know that Spring will come again,
Perhaps tomorrow ...

Edward Thomas, opening of 'March'

Spring always comes, yet there is an intense push-and-pull relationship between it and winter. One day, or week, is spring-like, and the birds sing; then winter pushes back, the land is silenced, and clouds billow. Consequently, spring has no true beginning, and of course it has no clear ending. It is, at least for much of its journey, intermittent and episodic, occurring in ecstatic pulses that are punctuated by periods of often bitter retreat. Always, winter is loath to lie down and die; as Edward Thomas claims at the end of his pastoral journey *In Pursuit of Spring* (1914), winter must be entombed, alive.

We yearn for spring, and watch out for its signs ardently. These occur in a sequence that may begin in late December, when the first Hazel catkins and Honeysuckle leaves can appear. The butterflies are most eagerly awaited. The first of the year – effectively one of five species, Brimstone, Comma, Peacock, Red Admiral and Small Tortoiseshell – may have much significance. There is folklore in several European cultures, especially in Scandinavia, which holds that if the first butterfly of the year is yellow you will have a happy summer (see Chapter 8). The odds for us in the British Isles, though,

are not good, with everything depending on the male Brimstone. Certainly, if I open my butterfly year with a Peacock or a Red Admiral a dire summer ensues – so much so that I actually fear encountering those two species in late winter, until the season has been opened by a Brimstone, a Comma, or a Small Tortoiseshell.

Each early spring, usually at the beginning of March, there is a day when the Brimstones take to the air – National Brimstone Lift-off Day, the first truly warm day of the year. At that time of year they fly only for a couple of hours or so, before bedding down again amongst the brambles or ivy growths. Those hours are deeply magical. Later, the first Orange-tip of the year is a celestial moment within Spring's dynasty; though it is wise not to seek it, but to let it find you – it is better that way, and it will seek and find you.

Being a springtime butterfly is risky. If they have high breeding success one year in three then they are doing well. In such years of plenty they can wander far and wide, to form new colonies, seizing the moment admirably. On calm days of azure haze in late April or early May they wander, seemingly into eternity. Follow the Orange-tips on such days. Frequently, though, entire spring broods are quickly blasted away. Yet somehow the butterflies return the following year, sometimes booming the year after busting. It is their ability to cope with the vagaries of spring weather that perhaps best demonstrates their true powers of resilience. Butterflies never surrender, they come back. The secret lies in staggering their emergence, over a period of two or three weeks, so that at least some part of the brood experiences reasonable weather, at least for a precious while.

But, above all, spring is about promise, the promise of summer's fulfilment; and release, release from winter's endlessness and vice-like grip. But promises are fickle things, easily misidentified, denied or lost in translation. And our weather too is at its most fickle in spring, often dashing from one extreme to the other, and seldom stable. It feels as if legion spirits up there in the sky are battling for control of the kingdom of Nature, grabbing the crown for a while, before being usurped. Somehow our wildlife has to adapt to this, even creatures as delicate as butterflies. Spring's eventual coming is one of joyous chaos, as if masterminded by Bacchus and his wild Maenads.

There are great springs, and poor springs, but surely there is no such thing as a bad spring – unless it is one you have wasted. Above all, spring is a riotous ministry, that rushes in delight, transforming the world with a rapid and dramatic metamorphosis that must make any butterfly green with envy. Butterflies transform themselves, spring transforms our whole world.

Some years, spring rushes ahead of itself, having got over-excited, and is gone all too soon. Blink, and you might miss it. Suddenly it is mid-May, or even late May, and spring has effectively passed: the countryside wears the colours of early summer; the Dog-roses and early brambles are in bloom, the Ash leaf canopy has closed over, and the barley ears are silvering. Blink, and you might miss it. Do not ever blink during spring, it offers too much vibrant wonder, and each drop must be drunk. Spring is the ultimate medicine, the ultimate metamorphosis. Throw yourself into it, utterly. It will cast you up on summer's shore.

Your heart dreams of spring. Trust the dreams.

Kahlil Gibran

17 *Spring perfected*

Diary, January 1st 1990: *New Year was seen in by the Edward Thomas Memorial Stone on Shoulder of Mutton Hill, above Steep, where I saw in the 1989 new year. I've never known such an intensely dark New Year. A completely black cat joined me, appearing out of nowhere and purring ecstatically round me before melting back into the darkness, nonplussed when I purred back at her – obviously, she hadn't met a human who could purr before.*

Years later, I began to ponder on what or even who that cat actually was.

The 1989/90 winter was ridiculously mild, bar a cold spell at the turn of November. It was also violent and extremely wet, memorable for the great 'Burns Night Storm' of January 25th when over fifty people lost their lives. Unlike the Great Storm of October 1987 this occurred during the day, when people were out and about. The anger – or was it hatred? – in the sky that day filled me, not so much with awe, but with fear. Having seen that apocalyptic sky it was no longer possible to deny climate change as a reality. Another legion of trees was felled, both forestry plantations of untended firs and ancient woodland. The skyline of the chalk hangers south of Selborne became even more broken. Selborne Common lost several veteran Beech and, worst of all, the ancient Yew in Selborne churchyard, mentioned by Gilbert White and reputed to be 1400 years old, was uprooted. I had courted on the iron bench that ran round its circumference, and later played there with my first-born. Selborne changed with the loss of that tree. The storm was followed by floods, notably in the Severn valley. One week a storm, the next floods.

Then the Rooks began to build and the immortal spring of 1990 began. It broke through wondrously on February 22nd: the first butterfly of the year was a Brimstone, seen by the Black Dam roundabout on the edge of Basingstoke, flying over dandelion-studded grassland – I had failed to get out on site before butterflies took to the air. By the end of the afternoon I had seen four species, Brimstone, Comma, Peacock and Small Tortoiseshell. By early March Primroses were fully out down south, sallows were in full bloom and the Hawthorn hedges were flushed with vibrant green. Winter had failed to show up.

The spring of 1990 was sublime. The first Holly Blues appeared in mid-March, telling of what was to come. One sauntered through our little town garden in Alton on March 10th. Early Red Admirals were seen, most likely having successfully overwintered. The race was then on for the first Orange-tip of the year. I managed my first on March 30th, dancing over sunlit daffodils beneath Sweet Chestnut trees at bud-break, in the gardens of Wyck Place, outside Alton, near The Lodge. Half a dozen were seen there that day, and an early Speckled Wood. That visit was so profound, with such deep pathos, that I knew I would never return there – Charlotte Bonham-Carter, its owner and my patron, had died; this was her farewell. The following day the first Painted Lady of the year appeared, whilst I was looking optimistically for a mad March Duke of Burgundy at Noar Hill.

Spring was in danger of overheating. April slowed it down, just a little, producing a cold third week. Then, from St George's Day there was no holding it back, with the first Duke of Burgundies appearing at Noar Hill, along with a significant hatch of Dingy Skippers and Holly Blues. Diary: *This has the makings of an excellent butterfly year...* At the end of the month the Pearl-bordered Fritillaries began to emerge, down in the New Forest, and I even saw an absurdly early Small Blue at Noar Hill, where the Duke of Burgundy was having a bumper year.

The spring of 1990 belonged to Harewood Forest, the ancient forest that straddles the A303 just east of Andover in north-west Hampshire. I had surveyed the insect fauna of the northern sector for the Nature Conservancy Council in 1989, and now had to investigate the southern third. Much of this southern block was old oak woodland, either high forest or derelict oak coppice with a heathy ground flora where the Clay-with-Flints cap had leached. Best of all was a shallow valley where the chalk came to the surface. I called it Happy Valley, for I was immensely happy there. Here, in an area where outgrown oak coppice had recently been thinned, was a magnificent colony of the Pearl-bordered Fritillary, visiting their beloved Bugle and Bluebell flowers and skimming low beneath the myriad yellow-greens of young oak leaves. The colours here – sapphire sky, yellow-green oak leaves, deep blue flowers, golden butterflies – formed the perfect combination that is forever spring. A Cuckoo called, perhaps eternally. A relic area of chalk grassland on the forest edge contained a few Dingy and Grizzled skippers, and several Duke of Burgundies, all tussling together. By May 25th the Pearl-bordereds were on the wane but a surprisingly large hatch of Duke of Burgundies had occurred: I counted 90 spread out along Happy Valley, fighting with each other and their arch enemy, the Dingy Skipper, launching themselves at passing Pearl-bordered Fritillaries and visiting Bugle flowers. True woodland Burgundies they were too, small and dark, breeding on Primrose, and flying much later in the spring than their downland counterparts. Holly Blues were present in high numbers too. Drought was kicking in, and many insects were seen imbibing the last of the moisture remaining along the woodland rides, including at the vestiges of the last puddle, two Burgundies, two Holly Blues, a Peacock, and a Pearl-bordered Fritillary. It was a time of kicking dust and cracks appearing in the rides, and Harewood revelled in it. Beneath the oak canopy Britain's dullest moth abounded, the aptly named Drab Looper, along with its foodplant, Wood Spurge.

Noar Hill produced an exceptional emergence of its star butterfly, the Duke of Burgundy. Habitat and weather conditions were, for once, spot on. On Monday May 7th, under an azure haze, I counted 96 of them along the butterfly transect route, which takes just over an hour to walk. This remains a transect record, anywhere. I failed to attain the century because a lone butterfly photographer had ensconced himself in the Top Pit, the butterfly's favoured area up against the Beech hanger, and had displaced most of the resident males from there. Many butterfly photographers do not know how to move amongst butterflies without disturbing them. By the end of a perfect May the Dukes were almost finished for the year, having laid a remarkable number of eggs – by mid-June virtually every suitable Cowslip plant on the reserve was peppered with holes left by Burgundy larvae.

In mid-May, Ivinghoe Beacon in the north Chilterns challenged Noar Hill for the right to be lauded as Britain's premier Duke of Burgundy locality. The way to sort this out was to conduct timed counts during the peak season period over the main flight areas of both sites, in good weather conditions – which for this butterfly means calm hazy sun. Luckily May 1990 produced many such days. At Noar Hill, 198 were counted in ideal weather on May 5th, and at Ivinghoe 207 in three hours of eye-straining concentration. Noar Hill won on a faster scoring rate (determined by cricket's Duckworth–Lewis method), averaging 1.32 individuals per minute as opposed to Ivinghoe's 1.18. It was a close-run thing.

The Holly Blue was ubiquitous that spring, in town and country. Normally the spring brood lays its eggs almost exclusively on Holly buds, favouring female trees – for the larvae feed on and even in the developing berries. But in 1990 they were also laying eggs commonly on the flowers of Dogwood, which was strongly favoured at Noar Hill, Purging Buckthorn on the west Hampshire downs, Alder Buckthorn on damp heaths, and elsewhere on Privet and Spindle. A number of berry-bearing garden shrubs were also selected, notably Portuguese Laurel and Snowberry. Like the Burgundies, though, the brood was all but finished by the end of May.

By then the season was so advanced that many spring butterflies were nearly over for the year, including Dingy Skipper, Duke of Burgundy, Glanville Fritillary, Pearl-bordered Fritillary and Orange-tip. Also, some of the summer species were remarkably advanced: summer-brood Small Tortoiseshells started to appear in Hampshire in late May, whilst in the woods White Admiral larvae were pupating. The downs had turned grey as drought conditions stealthily developed. The five months from January to May had been the warmest for at least 300 years. Then the weather broke, slowly and subtly, from June 1st. Gloom descended, accompanied by heavy showers or drizzle, giving day after day of lost time. The 1990 butterfly season stalled as, yet again, June proved to be a neurotic month.

The hot weather returned with a vengeance on July 11th, but by then much damage had been done. The most obvious casualty was the Large Skipper, whose flight season coincided with six cool and cloudy weeks, but some other butterflies suffered from becoming trapped in the vulnerable pupal stage for too long. The White Admiral appeared in very low numbers, probably for this reason. Had the fine weather held it would have come out at the start of June, if not earlier, as I had found a near-full-grown larva in Harewood Forest on May 3rd. As it was, the first Hampshire individuals were seen on June 19th. Then, and perhaps equally significant, the butterflies that did emerge had to contend with much bad weather, including a tremendous gale on July 4th. The Purple Emperor suffered similarly. Ken Willmott, whose heart is eternally Purple, reckons it was the poorest Emperor season he had known. I struggled to see a pair, close by in Harewood Forest. First, a male flew low and slow past me, with scarcely a wingbeat, and glided off under the oak canopy in search of a sap run on which to feed; then the Empress herself appeared around a group of shady sallow trees, where she was going about her business. This was quality, not quantity.

A week was spent surveying for High Brown Fritillaries on Exmoor, but little progress was made owing to poor weather. The weather allowed me one good day, during which I discovered a series of small colonies on south-facing Bracken slopes above the East Lyn River downstream of Robbers Bridge, in Lorna Doone country. Sadly, the butterfly was never recorded again in those rough paddocks. Also, a delightful little combe just north-west of Exford produced small colonies of High Brown Fritillary and Marsh Fritillary, as well as a lone Heath Fritillary, plus the more standard fare of Dark Green Fritillary and Small Pearl-bordered Fritillary – five species of fritillary. Within a decade the combe had been taken over for horsy culture and all its fritillary butterflies had gone.

In early July the second brood of the Holly Blue began to emerge, seeking world domination. This azure butterfly was even more profuse than in the spring, and easily won Butterfly of the Year. The brood peaked at the turn of July and remained prominent until a wet and windy third week of August, which relieved the developing drought conditions. As is their habit, most summer-brood individuals were seen on or around flowering bramble patches, with females also visiting flowering Ivy growths on which to lay their eggs. Later, a scatter of rare third-brood specimens was seen during September and October.

Two days of intense heat were spent up on the Morecambe Bay limestone hills with Martin Warren, looking closely at where High Brown Fritillaries were breeding, and also assessing the strength of Duke of Burgundy colonies by looking for the distinctive larval feeding marks on *Primula* leaves. We spent an oven-like day on Whitbarrow, north of the Kent estuary, where the High Brown was at peak season, and wonderfully numerous, and an even hotter day on Gait Barrows NNR down near Silverdale. Here, the butterfly flies and finishes earlier in the season than on the high hills, and was starting to look tired and ragged. It was wet-hat weather – take a white sunhat, soak it in water and put it on your head, and top it up regularly. That stops the brain from frazzling, though it produces a sticky damp patch at the base of the neck. I learnt it from an Australian who captained me at cricket. Without a wet hat the intense heat off the grey limestone rocks on Gait Barrows would have generated hallucinations, or even dried up the blood. High Browns, of course, loved it, and were darting about frenetically, and all was well with the world. The Burgundy had already had a good time, judging by the abundance of Cowslips and Primrose leaves bearing the tell-tale eating marks. Up on Arnside Knott, the Scotch Argus was just beginning to emerge – we saw the first two males.

The heat intensified. A massive anticyclone came over for the start of August, in time for a field-course weekend I was running on insect ecology at the newly opened Kingcombe Centre in west Dorset, just a few miles from my birthplace. It was to be a memorable weekend. The Kingcombe Centre came into being after one of the many celebrated conservation crises of the 1980s. In 1985 old Arthur Wallbridge died aged 94, blind and intestate, having farmed 600 acres of low-grade agricultural land in a west Dorset valley in the old-fashioned way. He avoided chemical sprays and fertilisers, and did not drain the marshy meadows. The outgrown hedges were managed by hand. Time stood still here, surrounded by a world of agricultural intensification and habitat loss. This was the Dorset Thomas Hardy knew and loved. After the National Trust failed to purchase the farm, Lower Kingcombe was acquired by a property developer for half a million pounds and split into fifteen lots for resale. The Dorset Wildlife Trust met the challenge of raising £150,000 in a month to purchase the SSSI meadows. The remainder was sold off in plots associated with rundown buildings, which were prime candidates for conversion to weekend homes for wealthy Londoners. The yuppification of the countryside was well under way.

One such plot, a few acres of tumbledown and a couple of derelict barns, was purchased by a young biology teacher from Blandford Forum, Nigel Spring. A man of vision and immense energy, Spring tamed the jungle and rebuilt the barns as an environmental studies centre, which opened in 1988, offering short courses for adults and children. Spring and Oates first met at a Jimi Hendrix concert in 1970, and were destined to meet again. Over the years I ran a number of long-weekend butterfly events, the odd course on other insects, and contributed to a long-running course on managing grazing animals for conservation. But it all began on one of the hottest weekends in the history of the British Isles, when the temperature reached a staggering 37.1 degrees Celsius in Cheltenham and 37 degrees in Leicester. My course participants rebelled en masse, and threw themselves into the sea at Ringstead Bay, where we had gone to see Lulworth Skippers and other insects – all except for one who was wearing a wet hat, and a lady from Madras who was not in the least bothered. Earlier I had taken them to a bog on Purbeck where they had been eaten alive by a rare species of horse fly, *Chrysops sepulcralis*, a Purbeck speciality, and been treated to a good flight of Graylings and the last Silver-studded Blues of the year.

August was heating up, and drought was returning. A visit to Alice Holt Forest on August 5th found Hazel leaves yellowing and curling, Honeysuckle leaves turning brown, the grasses in the rides droughting off, and deep cracks and fissures appearing in the clay. A second brood of the Small Pearl-bordered Fritillary was emerging. This occurred in central southern England only in the hottest of summers.

A visit to Watlington Hill in the Chilterns on August 7th found the drought conditions badly compounded by heavy Rabbit grazing. Diary: *Today the turf was ludicrously and dangerously short, sun-scorched and void of flowers. There's few things worse than a droughted Rabbit desert. The bunnies had even nibbled off the Ground Thistle buds and were starting on Hawthorn bark* (which they strip during severe winter weather). Silver-spotted Skipper numbers were well down, probably in part owing to poor weather during June, though doubtless in the main because of excessive Rabbit grazing. The heat was getting to me, despite the wet hat. The violence of the heat here scarred the earth, whilst the sun struck from above and also from sideways and below, reflecting off the arid turf. Worrying signs of drought were also noted at

Coombe Hill, further north in the Chilterns, where (diary) *a tiny and unhappy colony of Duke of Burgundy based on exposed and droughted Cowslips at the foot of the slope (was) threatened by Rabbit pressure.* Shortly afterwards that colony died out.

In early August I carried out an approved reintroduction of the Silver-spotted Skipper to two large areas of suitable habitat on the downland massif of Butser Hill, south of Petersfield in East Hampshire, by transferring butterflies from Broughton Down in the west of the county. At the time scientific thinking held this to be a highly sedentary butterfly, incapable of colonising far-flung habitat patches. Twenty females and nine males were released on Oxenbourne Down, and eighteen females and ten males in a deep combe called Grandfather's Bottom. The release was sanctioned by the Nature Conservancy Council, Hampshire Wildlife Trust and Hampshire County Council. Unfortunately, a spell of cool and wet weather set in almost immediately, which relieved the burgeoning drought conditions but was not good for the skippers. The long and short of it was that the butterfly definitely took to Oxenbourne Down but was not adequately searched for on the precipitous slopes of Grandfather's Bottom. Then, the butterfly went into a major expansion phase and colonised the area naturally, probably from populations in the Meon valley a few miles to the west. One of the main conclusions from a review of butterfly introductions in Britain which Martin Warren and I published in 1990 was that, historically, a great many introductions had taken place just in advance of, or even at the same time as, periods of natural spread. Here, I was hoist with my own petard, so to speak, though this particular release was based on the scientific evidence that existed at the time; it is just that the skippers, taking advantage of climate change and the resurgence of grazing on the downs, suddenly moved the goalposts. These changes have been well documented by Professor Chris Thomas.

Late in the second week of August the Clouded Yellows came in, accompanied by a fair few Painted Ladies. As a birthday treat I was offered the choice of having a party or going to the seaside.

Given the weather, it was a no-brainer, so off we went to Compton Bay on the Isle of Wight for the day. The first butterfly seen on the cliffs was a Clouded Yellow. Shortly afterwards another came in low over the sea, and hurtled up the cliffs at great speed. By mid-afternoon at least ten were present on the cliffs, feeding avidly on Fleabane flowers. There is little I would like more for a birthday present than a Clouded Yellow immigration. Strangely, though, the females did not seem to be interested in laying eggs, in contrast to the influx witnessed at the same place in June 1983. Painted Ladies and a couple of Red Admirals were also seen flying in low over the sea. 'Welcome to Britain!' I said to each and every one in my best Margaret Thatcher voice, stamping their passports and sending them on their way.

On August 15th the weather broke, though only for five days, producing the first effective rain in the south since July 6th. By the end of the day the lawns had visibly greened up, for brown lawns and fields almost instantly flush green again after a drop of rain. But by late August the drought had reasserted itself, especially on the thin chalk-soil slopes of the North Downs in Surrey. A visit to the Reigate downs with Gail Jeffcoate revealed desert-like conditions.

> Diary, August 28th 1990: *Juniper Hill is quite the worst Rabbit drought-scape I've yet encountered. Incredibly hard-grazed and droughted. Some 40–50 per cent of the slope is bare, with a stunted flora just managing to survive – bald-toothbrush tussocks of Sheep's Fescue Grass, tiny hard-grazed Tor-grass tussocks, and a prostrate carpet of Common Rockrose. Upright Brome Grass has been grazed out.*

A little further east the slope had been grazed hard by sheep during the winter, for conservation, and the Rabbits had moved straight in and turned it into another 'Rabbit drought-scape'. Similar problems were seen at Denbies Hillside, the scarp slope across the Mole Gap from Box Hill. Again, well-intentioned conservation grazing had been grossly exploited by Rabbits. In effect, conservationists were wanting to 'coppice' the grassland – graze it down and let it grow up again more modestly – only the combination of drought and Rabbits was preventing any regrowth and generating visions of desertification. Of course, after a couple of strong grass growth seasons the turf recovered well. We had seen drought impacting on the downs before, notably in 1976, only then Rabbits were still at a low ebb. During the 1980s Rabbits recovered in many places, just as sheep and cattle grazing was being restored to many nature conservation sites. The irony was considerable.

Overall, 1990 saw the hottest August in Britain since records began in 1659, and the summer period (June, July and August) was the ninth warmest of the century. Gradually, summer eased away during September as cloud and showers took over, the cracks and fissures disappeared and the fields and lawns turned green again. On many of the thin-soil chalk downs in the South-east, though, the Rabbits had taken over, and their vision was to restore the downs to pre-myxomatosis conditions. There were unexpected challenges for conservation here.

18 *Moving on*

New Year is often a time of illusion, or even self-delusion. Caught up on a wave of optimism we misread the signs, assuming they were signs in the first place. The truth is that New Year is in the wrong place: it should either be the day after the winter solstice or when the Rooks start building, though the latter is a variable feast. No wonder signs are misread and resolutions quickly abandoned.

The first words written in the 1991 diary were, *Destined to be the greatest summer of my life*. Needless to say, I had misread the signs (if signs they were), for the year brought a dreadful summer. Some butterflies, of course, did well, notably some of the species whose larvae feed on grasses, for the grasses grew spectacularly well after two drought summers, and the associated larvae benefited. Moreover, my life was in inner turmoil, torn between being hefted to Selborne and the desire to explore wider afield, to develop new heartlands; torn between fighting for nature conservation locally or nationally; torn between different options for developing a career and supporting a family. Above all, I was torn between heart and head. There was little hope there, for as Dylan Thomas deftly argues in his poem 'Should lanterns shine', heart and head both lead helplessly. Time creates these issues (whether they are problems or opportunities is secondary), and time alone will solve them.

Winter was dire. It included a twelve-day sunless period of hateable gloom in late January. Seasonal affective disorder (SAD), from which many British lovers of Nature suffer to a greater or even greater extent, was just being discovered. Then it snowed – 10 centimetres of the stuff in Hampshire, offering excellent tobogganing for a week. Eventually, winter ended, only for spring to relapse after a promising beginning. Brimstones opened the butterfly season, taking to the air en masse on March 7th. My first danced over gravestones at St Lawrence's Church in Alton, symbolising what?

All four of the butterfly species that hibernate annually appeared in good numbers, hardly surprising as they had been numerous the previous late summer and autumn. Then, an unusually prolific hatch of Holly Blue and Orange-tip commenced in mid-April. I watched a spectacular emergence of male Holly Blues on April 13th, from profuse Ivy growths on tall Ash trunks at Blacknest at the northern end of the East Hampshire Hangers, just west of Alice Holt Forest. One by one they began to search the self-same Ivy patches for emerging females. Now that's decisiveness and clarity of purpose for you! But spring was late, with April failing to produce either a Cuckoo or a Swallow, for migrant birds were held up by a cold northerly airflow which persisted well into May. Holly Blues defied the weather and continued to appear in even better numbers than they had during the great spring of 1990, but gradually the adverse weather conquered them, for May was dull and chilly, though dry. Slowly but surely the promise was squeezed out of the spring of 1991, and the Holly Blues and all they stood for succumbed.

There were some memorable days, of course, and adventures into new heartlands. At the end of May I explored, for the first time, the sea combe and undercliff system around the exquisite village of Branscombe on the south coast of Devon, close to the Dorset border. Now this is Wood White country, but with a difference. In England this most fragile-looking of our butterflies is strongly associated with grassy woodland rides and other sheltered grassland habitats. Here it occurs along a crumbling sandstone cliff system, and on the adjoining chalk slopes. Even the coast of the English Riviera seems too exposed for this butterfly, but there is shelter for it here and there, along the paths, in combes and in the slumps and hollows of old landslips. There were also abandoned potato fields studded along the slumped cliff system, for Branscombe was once famous for its new potatoes. Those fields, allotments effectively, are now reverting to scrubland. The butterfly breeds in all these situations, and along the margins of rough hillside fields, where Bracken and brambles encroach over sagging barbed wire. The best breeding grounds I found were where Bird's-foot Trefoil was growing through low Privet scrub in an area where a minor landslip had occurred a few years previously. There the females were busily laying their eggs, on foodplants straggling through developing scrub. Soon, of course, the scrub would win through and the butterfly would have to breed elsewhere. Best of all, Wood Whites were feeding hungrily on Purple Gromwell flowers, a rare and most lovely plant that grows along the coastal paths. And there were colonies of Pearl-bordered Fritillaries in Bracken stands along the rough field edges, and Small Pearl-bordered Fritillaries in a damp hollow full of Marsh Violets. With butterflying, there are many days, many excursions one would love to relive, and this was one.

If May was dull, June was duller. It made its way into the history books for being the cloudiest June in England and Wales since 1929. Butterflies tried to sit it out, but one by one they failed. There were a few good days. One, in early June, was memorable for a survey expedition to woodland on the Beaulieu River, close to the New Forest coast. Here were vistas into the New Forest of old, before mass coniferisation. Historic places possess cracks in time which allow us to peep into their past. The broad Bracken-filled rides amongst oak forest planted to provide timber for the Navy offered up colonies of Pearl-bordered Fritillaries and even a relic colony of the Duke of Burgundy, based on Primrose. The latter was especially important, for the Duke was on the point of extinction in the Forest, and was feared lost from the Crown lands. These were indeed the last Burgundies I saw in the New Forest – small and dark they were, true forest dwellers. I returned in high summer, hoping beyond hope to turn up the High Brown Fritillary there, but found only a few pockets of suitable-looking breeding habitat, though a worn Painted Lady female was seen laying her eggs on Marsh Cudweed along a bare track, an unusual foodplant for this butterfly.

There was a journey back into places buried in my personal past, Lambert's Castle and Pilsdon Pen near Crewkerne. I discovered a thriving colony of Small Pearl-bordered Fritillary in the bog below the Castle. Then a few years later the Marsh Fritillary colonised, providing a welcome example of a rare butterfly colonising somewhere new. My last visit to Pilsdon Pen, a brooding hill fort straight out of the darkest moments of a Thomas Hardy novel, had been on the day of my father's cremation (which I was deemed too young to attend). I was in safe hands on this return, being accompanied by William Keighley, the kindest of all National Trust wardens, a mild man whose relationship with the places in his care was based on love and understanding. Eggardon Hill, another of the west Dorset hill forts, this time on the Chalk, was discovered, and known for the first time. We also visited Bind Barrow, a low hill of Tor-grass on the coast near Burton Bradstock, and the westernmost site for the Lulworth Skipper. William and I found several larvae there, within loosely spun 'tents' on broad leaf blades in tall prominent tussocks of Tor-grass. These are quite easy to find if you spy out vigorous, semi-isolated tussocks and then look for the distinctive larval feeding marks either side of the larval 'tent'.

Up on the Bristol Channel coast, I checked out the colony of Glanville Fritillary at Sand Point, above Weston Super Mud. The butterfly had been kindly but unofficially introduced to the south-facing slope of this Carboniferous Limestone promontory in 1983 and had persisted, somehow. It had become quite a dilemma for the National Trust, for butterfly enthusiasts wanted the butterfly to flourish there, despite the limited size and varying quality of the habitat. The practice of moving butterflies around, to unoccupied suitable-looking habitat, is one of the many manifestations of people's love for butterflies, and an understandable reaction to their decline.

June worsened, eventually despairing of itself and giving up the ghost. One of its victims was the small colony of the Small Blue on Noar Hill, which all but failed in 1991, simply on account of the weather. Habitat conditions for it there were good, I had made sure of that. The cold dull June also meant that the midsummer butterflies emerged late – a trip down to Dartmoor in early July found that the High Brown Fritillary had scarcely started to emerge there, and also that many of the butterfly's Bracken stands had become too grassy, unsuitable for breeding. Elsewhere in Devon, I saw the last High Brown Fritillary ever seen on the National Trust's Arlington estate in west Exmoor, a victim of agricultural intensification. Eventually I discovered, or rather rediscovered, a large population on the Bracken-infested slopes above New Bridge in the Dart valley, running upstream to Aish Tor. Incredibly, there was only one previous record for the butterfly here – it seemed that no one had actually explored the area for butterflies, despite the presence of a large riverside car park and tourist information centre below at New Bridge. This turned out to be one of the strongest High Brown Fritillary populations in the UK.

July wobbled, alternating between weather moods. The Purple Emperor season came, stuttered and went. The best I saw of it was in Hartley Wood, near Oakhanger in East Hampshire, where several males were flying over thicket-stage conifer plantations choked with sallows. The same plantations had held Pearl-bordered Fritillaries and huge colonies of Small Pearl-bordered Fritillaries in the mid- to late 1970s. A few years later the woods changed hands; the new owners slaughtered the sallows and proceeded to run the woods for an intensive commercial pheasant shoot, and tolerated no visitors. At that point my relationship with Hartley Wood ended. It had fallen into darkness.

August proved to be the best of the summer months, though not without spells of adverse weather. The second brood of the Holly Blue appeared in fair numbers, though way down on the spring showing. The butterfly was now spiralling into decline. A few days on the south Devon coast in early August picked up a sizeable immigration of Small White on Bolt Head, west of the Kingsbridge estuary, and a similar influx of Large White around Prawle Point, a little way to the east. Oddly, the two species had come in separately.

The most wonderful place discovered during 1991 was the steep east-facing downland slopes of High and Over, above the Cuckmere valley south of Alfriston in East Sussex. This was part of a new National Trust acquisition that year, the gloriously named Frog Firle Farm, purchased under Enterprise Neptune funding. We did not realise just how rich it was for wildlife until after it had been acquired, so the discovery of thriving colonies of Silver-spotted Skipper, Grayling, Adonis Blue and Chalkhill Blue on the downland, and important Diptera and dragonfly populations in the river valley, came as a most pleasant surprise. At the time, Silver-spotted Skipper was only known from a single site in East Sussex, Deepdene, diagonally across the Cuckmere from High and Over. Presumably the butterfly had colonised from there during the hot summers of 1989 or 1990. Frog Firle also produced a Painted Lady invasion, on August 29th. They were taking nectar from, and depositing eggs on, Red Star-thistle, a rare non-native annual that looks like a cross between a thistle and a knapweed and which is reputed to have been accidentally imported in mud on the boots of Napoleonic prisoners. It is known only from that part of the East Sussex downs.

All summer I had been delaying a monumental decision, whether to stay in Hampshire and carry on as a self-employed ecologist, as economic recession loomed, or to take up the offer of a full-time post with the National Trust, with the glorious title of Advisor on Nature Conservation. Heart said the former, head said the latter. One choice offered freedom in Nature coupled with the insecurity that accompanies it, the other the potential to get to the roots of some nature conservation issues, be part of a movement, and something approximating to security for the family. The job offer was dependent on moving house to be based from an office in Cirencester. For the first and only time in my life head won over heart. The wrench was horrific, particularly from Noar Hill. I have missed Noar Hill every day of my life since leaving Hampshire in March 1992, for my relationship with the place then slowly broke; the deep *cynefin* I had developed for the Selborne area shattered into a myriad fragments, each one piercing deeply.

A job is, of course, largely what you make it, and this was definitely a job of a lifetime, which meant it had to be for a lifetime too. The opportunities to help butterflies, their habitats and wildlife in general were enormous, and irresistible. But it was the impact on my personal relationship with Nature which mattered most, and that was exchanged for a relationship with nature conservation – and there is a difference. Crucially, most people seeking to work in nature conservation do so in order to develop their personal relationships with Nature. However, today's nature conservation profession scarcely enables that, with its obsession with money, politics, targets and systems – not to mention business meetings.

Once the decision had been made the agony intensified, for now there was no going back. Gradually I said farewell to each dear place around Selborne, each vista, each gap between trees, each sunken lane where Robins nest in twisted tree roots, each mossy tree stump, each sunset. It was as if I was going off to war. Worse, it felt as though the place was pushing me out. Places do that: they can suddenly boot you out – though perhaps other places, as unheard voices, are calling?

The year started well, with the driest January since 1837 and then a mild, racy February. My first butterflies of 1992 – Comma, Brimstone and Peacock, all within a whirligig minute on March 4th – were seen in a meadow destined to go under the A34 Newbury bypass. It was an apt experience for a nature conservationist. So 1992 was only the second butterfly season to open with a Comma, after 1975 – which had also been a year of monumental personal change. Then, forty years after my father's death, the family moved to Gloucestershire, where he had grown up. In a way we had come back. The first lesson, though, was how much cloudier the climate is in Gloucestershire, especially in spring.

The Janus-eyed Peacock was the butterfly of the spring of 1992. Males established territories in every sheltered sunny spot. A return visit to Noar Hill at the start of May, as the Duke of Burgundies were beginning to emerge, produced the highest count of spring Peacocks recorded there. Then, during June, Peacock larvae abounded in many of the nation's sunnier nettle patches. The Peacock went on to become Butterfly of the Year, for a huge summer brood materialised, assisted by warm June weather and a glorious July.

A wave of new places was encountered, near and far. In the Cotswolds, effort concentrated on assessing the status of the Duke of Burgundy, stimulated by a few fascinating days back in 1985. During the 1970s and 1980s the butterfly had enjoyed a boom era in the Cotswolds. I arrived there at the end of that era, when neglected grasslands were becoming too rough even for this long-grass specialist, and as the conservation backlash against this neglect was gaining momentum. There were still some good colonies, notably on the National Trust's Rodborough Common near Stroud, and at Cranham Common, Edge Common and Juniper Hill near Painswick. But everywhere the writing was on the wall for this little butterfly. One terribly isolated colony on the Trust's Sherborne estate near Northleach said it all. The colony was found in a pocket of limestone grassland where planted trees had failed, and was surrounded by miles and miles of intensive arable farmland. Keeping small, isolated fragments in suitable condition for a demanding butterfly is a massive challenge. We managed it, only to lose the colony during a series of rotten springs. Pearl-bordered Fritillaries were discovered in Cirencester Park Woods, and also on several of the limestone grassland commons around Stroud. The places were new, but the players familiar.

Further afield, each trip to somewhere new produced a revelation. A visit to Lewesdon Hill, the highest point in west Dorset, in mid-May coincided with the arrival of immigrant Red Admirals and Painted Ladies. The males set up territories in glades in the woodland there, perched appealingly on Bluebell flowers, and behaved despicably towards each other. The scarp slope of the Mendips between Crook Peak and Cheddar revealed sizeable colonies of Small Pearl-bordered Fritillary and Grizzled Skipper, and some large Bracken stands which appeared to be in ideal condition for High Brown Fritillary. I could not wait to return during the High Brown season. The downs above Wrotham in north-west Kent, above the noisy M20, produced one of the best flights of Common Blue I have ever seen – seemingly because the foodplant, Bird's-foot Trefoil, had grown exceptionally well where arable fields had been sown with a conservation seed mix in an effort to restore chalk downland. A series of near-derelict orchards in a valley at Brockhampton in north Herefordshire revealed a colony of Wood Whites. The farm tenant here was elderly, merely tending a few beef cattle and sheep and leaning gently on the land. A little while later his son took over and the Wood Whites vanished. Such can be the difference between an old man's hand on the land, and that of a young man.

The inevitable burn-out occurred in early June. We were going to run an ecology training course in a hotel at Newby Bridge, at the southern end of Windermere, assembling on Sunday evening. Early that morning I set out for a day's butterflying in south Lakeland, visiting several of the limestone hills, where Pearl-bordered Fritillaries abounded and Small Pearl-bordered Fritillary and Northern Brown Argus were beginning their flight seasons. The day ended with a superb evening flight of Green Hairstreak on Meathop Moss, by Witherslack, where groups of up to eight were seen spiralling together over birch scrub. Later, they ascended into Scots Pine trees to roost. The first Large Heaths of the year were emerging, and all was well with the world. The following day, which was dull and lifeless, we had to climb up one of the Coniston fells, leaden-footed in my case. Not even the discovery of a little colony of Small Pearl-bordered Fritillaries in a boggy flush 220 metres up managed to raise my energy levels. That evening there was a lecture on multivariate analysis, and sleep blissfully descended.

June steadily bettered itself. At midsummer the Lakeland high fells called, and they meant business. The National Trust owns or leases most of the mountain tops haunted by the Mountain Ringlet. At the time next to nothing was known about this lovely dark butterfly – where it occurred, how it was doing, what made it tick – that sort of thing – on my patch, on my watch; it was time for action. Most butterfly enthusiasts make the effort to see the Mountain Ringlet maybe two or three times in a lifetime, visiting a couple of renowned localities where access is relatively easy, but in the early 1990s the species began to generate some interest. Amongst that disparate but coalescing body of people was John Hooson, the National Trust's ecologist for the Lake District. Hooson should have been born a mountain goat, for he will seize any excuse to ascend any mountain, preferably at speed. The secret of working with such people is to insist on leading the way, so that they move at your (much slower and more rational) pace. Hooson and I spent two glorious days up on the Langdale Pikes,

seeking the butterfly and asking questions of it. I wanted to follow the females, and discover where they lay their eggs, as an entry point towards understanding the insect's ecology. Hooson, an ace botanist, wanted to look closely at the vegetation characteristics of breeding areas. We covered a vast area, from Blea Rigg to Sargeant Man on the first day, and on the second day up the Mickleham Beck valley, up Stake Gill, over boggy Langdale Combe, up Mansey Pike, Buck Pike and Rosset Pike to Angle Tarn, and then to Tongue Head and Ore Gap, and to the summit of Bow Fell, before descending past Three Tarns and White Stones, down The Band and out through Stool End Farm. Those names rightly imply exhaustion. The Langdale Pikes are not for the fainthearted.

We found Mountain Ringlet colonies scattered seemingly at random over the vast expanses of Mat-grass grassland that characterise the less boggy or stony ground of the high fells. It seemed to occur in highly localised colonies separated by large areas of unoccupied terrain that appeared to be suitable. Now that's not logical, butterflies are not randomly distributed. The few eggs we saw being laid were placed in dry warm spots where there was an underlay of Sheep's Fescue grass amongst myriad tussocks of Mat-grass. Hypothesis: Does this butterfly require a mixed grass sward, do the larvae start feeding on the finer Sheep's Fescue before moving on to tough old Mat-grass? Butterflies are forever inspiring hypotheses, but are loath to reveal answers.

Two days later, twitching with anticipation, I was on the Bracken slopes of the Mendip escarpment at Cross Plain, south of Winscombe. There, notably above Kingswood, was some of the best-looking High Brown Fritillary habitat I had seen in years. I was going to rediscover Britain's fastest-declining butterfly in the Mendips, in my native Somerset! The butterfly was out in numbers in the West Country, my timing was perfect. Sure enough, as I came out from the trees innumerable large golden fritillaries were skimming fast over the Bracken, and visiting thistle flowers. There were hundreds of them. One by one they revealed themselves to be freshly emerged Dark Green Fritillaries.

In disbelief I returned two weeks later, with the same devastating result. Even a pristine Clouded Yellow failed to lift the depression. Worse, in the intervening period I saw what proved to be the last of the New Forest High Browns, and was worried by what little I saw of the butterfly in the Teign valley, near Castle Drogo on Dartmoor. Suffice to say that the highs and lows of butterflying are considerable, as is the vulnerability of butterflies.

But the High Brown Fritillary would not be put down. A long weekend was spent surveying the cluster of colonies in the enchanting Heddon valley on the Exmoor coast, the only known West Country locality for this butterfly not covered by my surveys of 1989 and 1990. The High Brown Fritillary is one of our least child-friendly butterflies, being largely a denizen of steep slopes thickly afforested with dense brambly Bracken, but the family came too, and played on the beach at Woolacombe when not delighting along Heddon's rushing, gushing stream. The High Brown population here was clearly large, one of the strongest in the country. Three tiny colonies were found on the National Trust's Watersmeet estate, upstream of Lynton and Lynmouth, though these were in a parlous state and destined not to persist. Heddon was the place to concentrate conservation effort. We did, and it worked.

The Purple Emperor shone brilliantly from late June through to late July. Impressive flights were seen in Alice Holt Forest and in the woods to the south-west, near Oakhanger. In the Oakhanger woods I also saw my first 'Black Admiral' since 1983. These dark White Admirals are very intermittent and localised in appearance. Then, on July 27th, a male Emperor was seen flying over the downland summit of Beeding Hill on the West Sussex downs. What on earth was this forest insect doing flying over open downland on the crest of the South Downs, some way from any wood? Where had he come from – over barren cereal fields above Shoreham? And where was he heading? I knew the answer to that – Dragons Green, and it meant I was being called.

The Clouded Yellows had come in, and in a big way. More than 50 were seen over fields on the South Devon coast between

Brixham and Kingswear, favouring south-facing slopes seeded with Rye Grass and White Clover, and grazed by cattle or sheep. The females were laying eggs on this agricultural White Clover, mainly on tiny isolated plants growing where the grasses were turning brown under advancing drought – in the hottest possible places. The same slopes were alive with Common Blues, also breeding on White Clover. Previously I had rather ignored these agricultural grasslands, but here in the South Hams they were clearly a useful butterfly habitat. Even more Clouded Yellows were seen on the Isle of Wight downs during early August. There, a constant stream of swift-flying males patrolled the lower south-facing slopes of the downs, squabbling terribly when two met.

But July belonged to the Peacock. The new brood began to appear in mid-July, and then fed up rapidly during a minor heatwave, such that most had entered hibernation by the end of the first week of August. They were wise, for the bulk of August was exceptionally poor – cool, sunless and wet, with just the odd reasonable day. The wonderful butterfly summer of 1992 was effectively cut off in its prime. In fairness, though, we were due a poor August.

The 1992 butterfly season had one last trick up its sleeve, before it was ended by an excessively wet November. On September 20th, during what the diary describes as a family *blackberrying and beach cricket expedition* to Middle Hope, just north of Weston-super-Mare on the Bristol Channel coast, a Monarch butterfly floated around us in Woodspring Priory car park, before batting off in a huff. And it was the size of a bat too, though faded and battered. The children were unimpressed, even by the likelihood that this giant of a butterfly had crossed the Atlantic in the wake of a mid-September gale. They wanted blackberries. The odd thing was that 1992 was not a known Monarch autumn; none had been recorded before this particular sighting, and very few subsequently. But butterflies specialise in the sudden and unexpected, so much so that it is wise to expect the unexpected.

Yet another mild winter ushered in the 1993 butterfly season. A visit to Devon on February 24th found hedges flushed with bright green Hawthorn leaves and starred with white Blackthorn and golden sallow blossom. The first butterflies took to the air on March 8th. Mine was a Peacock, which was hardly surprising, as this butterfly had been numerous in 1992.

March was dry and mild, April all over the place. One of the few reasonable days in April was the 24th, when I found myself on Meathop Moss in south Cumbria. The lady who walks the butterfly transect there was leaving as I arrived. She had just counted 38 Green Hairstreaks along the transect route. I ended up feeling that she should have been sent back to do it properly, for I counted 100 in eleven minutes around young birch bushes along the southern edge of the nature reserve, and went on to count 213 in 25 cloudy minutes in a walk across the edge of the open moss. That was the best Green Hairstreak display I had ever seen, and the butterfly was clearly not fully out. The diary remarks: *They were all so beautifully fresh, emerald green and dark. Several were seen taking nectar from Cranberry flowers, no other plant being in flower.* Shortly afterwards the Green Hairstreak emerged in unusually good numbers back in the Cotswolds, and elsewhere. Why, we know not, but it was definitely the butterfly of the spring – and of the year.

On one of the few pleasant days that May produced, I visited Halse Combe on the National Trust's vast Holnicote estate, near Porlock in Somerset, for the first time. I knew the landscape, for my Uncle Percy, the children's author J P Martin, had lived nearby, at Timberscombe. Heath Fritillaries were fluttering everywhere, the males roaming in loose packs through unfurling Bracken fronds in search of freshly emerged females. Groups of these exquisite black and amber butterflies were feeding greedily on Common Tormentil and Lesser Stitchwort flowers. When an afternoon breeze sprang up, they drifted down the slope to congregate for an evening bask in a rush-filled hollow along a stream that murmurs sweet nothings down the valley bottom. They looked in flight like a dark version of the Small Pearl-bordered Fritillary, though more graceful, with a gentle skimming flight. Along the gorse-lined path that runs along a mid-slope contour in this hot, steamy moorland-edge combe, male Green Hairstreaks were tussling with each other.

In early June I was back up in south Lakeland, to help with another nature conservation training course at Newby Bridge. Again, the course assembled on a Sunday evening, allowing a full day's butterflying around Morecambe Bay. This time I was wiser, pacing myself better, though I still visited Warton Crag, Beetham Fell, Yewbarrow, Latterbarrow and Meathop Moss. I had visited most of these sites on the corresponding Sunday the previous year, but the butterfly season was running later this time. In contrast to 1992, Pearl-bordered Fritillary was still at peak season, whilst its cousin the Small Pearl-bordered Fritillary was only just beginning to emerge that day; on Meathop Moss, the Large Heath had not started, though the Green Hairstreaks were still numerous, if terribly old, faded and grey. Two females were watched laying their eggs on Cranberry. Two days later, over on Arnside Knott Rabbit pressure had increased alarmingly during the 1992 drought and was now threatening the future of the Duke of Burgundy colony on the low hill to the west of the Knott, known as Heathwaite. Indeed, what had been quite a strong colony eight years ago was in the process of dying out, owing to a dramatic increase in the Rabbit population. There was little that could be done.

In mid-June, a visit to one of the top butterfly sites in the UK, the MOD's vast holding of chalk grassland and scrub at Porton Down, north-east of Salisbury, found butterfly populations at a very low ebb. A wet week had knocked out the spring butterflies, and the high-summer species were waiting for the weather to improve. We saw about 20 per cent of the expected butterflies, and were reduced to searching for Dark Green Fritillary larvae hiding under Hairy Violet clumps – their larval feeding marks are salient and fairly diagnostic.

The weather improved at the very end of June, producing three hot summer days. Drop everything and go up north, for the Mountain Ringlet! Unfortunately, the weather did the dirty on us, or rather the forecast did – the forecast mini-heatwave confined itself to southern Britain, while the north descended into fog and bog. A few miserable-looking Mountain Ringlets were walked up during a long wander over Wrynose Breast to Cold Pike and Pike o'Blisco and back. Then a chilly mountain wind sprang up. It was time to abandon the Lakes, albeit after kicking up a few chilled Large Heaths on Meathop Moss. The truth is that Lakeland offers the best butterflying in Britain when midsummer is kind, and the worst when it isn't.

In early July, down at Site X, the Large Blue reintroduction site, two of us bumped into old Arthur Brown, tenant farmer. A Dartmoor man born and bred, he leant over a rickety gate one evening, spat once or twice, and offered his perspective on the Large Blue's fortunes there over the years.

'It wur all right back-along,' he related in slow drawl, 'so long as we wur burning the gorze and doing everything that comes natural to a varmin' man, if you know what I mean like.'

I didn't, and neither did colleague Nigel Adams.

'The best year it evurr 'ad was after we'd spread basic slag [a cheap fertiliser] over the whole [adjective deleted] place!'

This was actually true, though only because that incident coincided with ideal spring and summer weather for the butterfly and its fastidious caterpillars – the fertiliser went on to cause significant damage.

Old Arthur continued, with a twinkle in his eye: 'We had butturrflies coming out of my backside!'

Then he paused, whilst our tongues recovered from a severe biting, before continuing: 'Then there was a lot of thissing and thatting, if you know what I mean like.'

We didn't, and inquired, so he continued: 'Well, they asked us to do this, so we did that for 'em but it wurrn't no good. No, they says, it's this we wants not that, so we did that for 'em but they didn't like that, they wanted this. And we went on and on thissing and thatting till the cows came home and [adverb deleted] milked themselves. Then they stopped us burning the furze, [noun deleted] knows why!'

There was a lengthy pause before he reached his climax, 'and the bugger went and died out!'

Reading between the lines, Nigel, a wise countryman from farming stock himself, and I both rather suspected that the thissing and thatting might have not involved doing what was actually being asked. Tentatively, one of us suggested it, and were promptly treated to a long shaggy dog story about how one of his sons, 'boys' he called them, lost a leg in an accident involving a tractor, a Fordson Major or a Davey Brown 910 – Arthur couldn't remember which.

The interview culminated with the threat of a major revelation: "Ere, let me tell 'ee about the time I sent the vicar's daughter home with 'er knickers in 'er handbag.'

At that point, Nigel and I exited hurriedly.

This may or may not be a fair account of how, and indeed why, the original UK race of the Large Blue died out at Site X back in 1979. Shortly after this most memorable of meetings old Arthur took to his bed with a bottle of Scotch and announced that he was buggered. All of Dartmoor attended his funeral. We shall not see his likes again. Professor Jeremy Thomas, whose life has been devoted to the conservation of the Large Blue, may be able to tell this tale with a finer degree of resolution.

By the end of a July which the weathermen irritatingly termed 'changeable' I had managed to see 51 species of butterfly. The diary states: *Sounds impressive, but isn't, as I've only walked up Lulworth Skipper and Large Heath, seen 30 seconds' worth of Wood White, seven Mountain Ringlets, one Adonis Blue (in rain), etc. I've hardly seen any females laying eggs.* Never substitute quality for quantity.

August tried hard, but butterfly populations were badly reduced by a gale mid-month. Before that, I spent three days surveying the National Trust chalk grasslands on the North Downs escarpment between Shere, east of Guildford, and Reigate. Many of these slopes had been severely damaged by excessive Rabbit grazing during the drought summers of 1989, 1990 and 1992. On the thin soil slopes the grasses had been grazed out, so that the only vegetation cover that remained consisted of the aromatic herbs that Rabbits avoid and the more prickly or toxic varieties of scrub. Of course, in the absence of a tight grass cover, the chalky soil became a perfect seedbed for scrub seedlings. This explained how the downs scrubbed up so badly after Rabbit populations were lost to myxomatosis during the 1950s. Worse, we were wanting to graze these slopes with stock, though they essentially needed browsing (to control scrub) rather than grazing (to regulate coarse grasses). Eventually we learnt that time creates these problems, and that time alone solves them. Moreover, farm animals only effectively browse bushes after they have consumed the grasses; and even then they avoid some scrub species, notably Hawthorn, together with toxic seedlings.

Down at Dover, in mid-August, an immigration of Large Whites was taking place – loose groups of them were seen flopping low over the Channel and ascending the white cliffs, where the females immediately began to lay their eggs on the abundant Sea Cabbage that grows there, favouring the smaller, younger plants. The Dover area is a superb locality for the two cabbage whites, especially for the Large White. Advice to gardeners in the Dover district: net your brassicas, carefully. In those days, Langdon Hole, a chalk combe on the cliff above Dover harbour, was dominated by impenetrable Tor-grass, tall, dense and full of the dead blades of years gone by. The Lulworth Skipper would have loved it, but was not known to cross the Channel from the distant Calais downs and occurred in England no nearer than Swanage. Moreover, we knew from historic records that this had been a rich site for short-turf butterflies and orchids. No farmer was interested in running stock there, not least because this was cereal country. We decided to fence the cliff tops and introduce our own grazing animals, native-breed ponies, which thrive on Tor-grass. The practical work was done by

Jimmy Green, a big-hearted cockney bruiser who had become the National Trust's first warden there, probably as a calling. There was nothing Jimmy would not do for his patch. Gradually he tamed Langdon with his bare hands, including its vertiginous Tor-grass. Jimmy, who struggled to tell a buttercup from a daisy, is one of the many unsung heroes of nature conservation.

Steadily, a combination of cold nights and pulses of heavy rains brought the 1993 butterfly season to a premature end, though the odd Red Admiral persisted until around Bonfire Night, the traditional end of the butterfly season. The year ended with something approximating to a white Christmas, though the light dusting had melted by the time the turkey came out of the oven.

19 *High adventures in the mid-1990s*

The 1994 butterflying season was launched by a Small Tortoiseshell at Chartwell, Sir Winston Churchill's former residence west of Sevenoaks in Kent, with shimmering views over the High Weald. There are many hidden aspects of Churchill, such as his ability as an artist, his passion for bricklaying, his love of cats and, most notably for us, his interest in butterflies. He began collecting butterflies at prep school, on the Sussex downs, then maintained his interest abroad as a young man, collecting in India, South Africa and the West Indies. It was, of course, a common hobby at the time. His collections, sadly, have not survived. Indeed, one was eaten by a rat. A letter home recalls that he then caught the rat, and had it dispatched by his pet dog, which happened to be called Winston. After the Second World War Churchill's passion was revived, partly through the energies of L Hugh Newman, who ran a butterfly farm at nearby Westerham, selling livestock and specimens from home and abroad. The farm had been started by Newman's father, Leonard, a deeply respected lepidopterist, in a back garden in Bexley in 1894. Hugh Newman persuaded Churchill to breed and release butterflies at Chartwell, and advised on how to develop a butterfly garden in the grounds, elements of which still survive. Churchill knew his butterflies, and not merely by their English names. In correspondence with Newman he freely uses the scientific names.

When it came to butterflies and moths, Hugh Newman epitomised over-enthusiasm. He got carried away with himself at

Chartwell, making naive attempts to establish the Black-veined White and the continental subspecies of the Swallowtail there. These attempts ended farcically, when the gardeners burnt the muslin sleeves containing the Black-veined White caterpillars and cut down the Swallowtail's Fennel plants. Churchill wanted the garden full of butterflies for his famous summer parties, but quickly realised that butterflies have a strong dispersal instinct, a fact that Newman had curiously overlooked. Churchill therefore tactfully dispensed with Newman's services. Nonetheless, Newman went on to other great things, becoming a regular contributor to *Nature Parliament* on BBC Radio's Children's Hour and appearing on *Desert Island Discs*.

On the positive side, Newman converted a summerhouse, originally built as a game larder, into an insectorium. Here Churchill used to watch caterpillars feeding, and would release freshly emerged butterflies into the gardens. In effect, the butterfly borders at Chartwell are probably the oldest surviving butterfly garden in the country. Moreover, we can regard Churchill as a pioneer of wildlife gardening. The National Trust, which runs Chartwell, restored Churchill's butterfly house and breeds a small number of common butterflies for release into the garden.

Winter sogged on, enlightened by a few periods when the rain turned briefly to snow, only to melt as the temperature rose fractionally and the rains returned. Churchill would have loathed it. March dripped and dripped, before eventually producing a few reasonable days. One pleasant day in early March was spent looking for Heath Fritillary larvae at Halse Combe, with naturalist colleague Nigel Hester. We found 20 of these tiny dark creatures, fresh out of hibernation, basking in loose groups of two or three amongst Bracken litter where their foodplant, Common Cow-wheat, was germinating. The plant is hard to spot, consisting of a pair of tiny leaves which can be mistaken for baby gorse seedlings. It was interesting to find that the caterpillars appeared from hibernation just as their foodplant, an annual, was germinating.

April roared in, with a gale which uprooted a large number of
trees. It then became cold and wet, ensuring a terrible lambing
season. Marsh Fritillary larvae, though, were numerous at
Strawberry Banks, a magical Cotswold combe near Stroud. The
Orange-tip started late, kicking off on St George's day. May began
well, producing an abundance of Green Hairstreaks on the lower
slopes of Rodborough Common, and the first Duke of Burgundies
of the year. Things were looking up, not least when a scatter of
Painted Ladies and Red Admirals turned up during a visit to the
south Devon coast. The first Marsh and Pearl-bordered fritillaries
appeared in the Cotswolds on May 15th. Then the weather fell
apart, spectacularly, and spring butterflies suffered terribly. The
year went into free fall, producing a wet end to May and a truly
vile first three weeks of June. A spectacular emergence of Marsh
Fritillary at Strawberry Banks was blasted away by foul weather. It
was money-back time.

Suddenly, and dramatically, the year turned itself round, on
June 23rd, as the first proper anticyclone of the season developed.
I was surveying Heath Fritillaries in Bin Combe, the deep heathy
combe running eastwards off Dunkery Beacon, on Exmoor. It
seemed that the fritillaries had all hatched at once. At one point
I counted 225 in 20 minutes, which by modern butterflying
standards is top notch. A few fresh Small Pearl-bordered Fritillaries
were skimming low over the rushy streamside in the combe bottom
and, surprise surprise, a stray female Pearl-bordered Fritillary. The
latter proved to be both historic and melancholic, for it was the last
Pearl-bordered Fritillary ever recorded on Exmoor.

A week-long trip to Northern Ireland followed. By Northern
Ireland standards the weather was reasonable, but the butterfly
season was struggling. High-summer species like the Dark
Green Fritillary and Large Heath had not started to emerge, in
fact Primroses and Bluebells were still in flower along the North
Antrim cliffs. It was on this trip that I discovered, and fell deeply
in love with, Murlough Dunes NNR, a wild land of mobile and
fixed acidic sand dunes and heathland on the County Down coast,

in the shadow of the Mountains of Mourne. It is one of Northern Ireland's top butterfly sites, with fifteen species breeding annually including Marsh Fritillary, Dark Green Fritillary, Grayling and what in those days was simply regarded as the Wood White. The Marsh Fritillary first appeared at Murlough in 1978, colonising one or two of the more inland dune slacks (hollows). Then, it expanded considerably during the great Marsh Fritillary years of 1982–1985, in keeping with its performance on the mainland. Since then its fortunes at Murlough have ebbed and flowed, but as in the Cotswolds it had emerged in good numbers in 1994. During damp drizzly weather the males were at roost, but the females were crawling around, seeking to lay their eggs. Butterflies cannot hang about waiting for perfect weather in Northern Ireland. The Wood White colonised Murlough in 1981, breeding on Bird's-foot Trefoil growing amongst loose Burnet Rose scrub on the inland dune slopes. Since then it has steadily expanded, to colonise the fore dunes. My diary entry for June 30th 1994 is almost visionary: *It's a very different butterfly in NI to how it is in England; much more widespread, less woodland associated, different habits, and a different colour.* In little over a decade the Northern Ireland Wood Whites had been proven to be a different species, the Cryptic Wood White.

The weather had sorted itself – either that or I had dumped the lousy weather in Northern Ireland. An excellent July and a reasonable August materialised. The high-summer butterflies emerged and made the most of the sunshine. Marbled Whites, Ringlets and Small Blues abounded on the Cotswold limestone grasslands, and White Admirals, Silver-washed Fritillaries and even the elusive Purple Emperor impressed in the woods. It was an unusually good year for White Admiral and Purple Emperor, two species that normally appear in low numbers after a miserable June. They broke their own rules in 1994, but that's butterflies all over. I saw impressive flights of both species in the Straits Inclosure in Alice Holt Forest, Hampshire, and went on to find a goodly number of Purple Emperor eggs on shaded sallow leaves. However, back near Porlock, in north-west Somerset, the High Brown Fritillary appeared in rather disappointing numbers, presumably the victim of poor spring and early summer weather. July butterflies hurried over in the heat – a matter of short, sharp and sweet flight seasons. By the end of the month patches of drought were showing on some downland slopes.

As July ended a host of immigrant butterflies, moths and hoverflies suddenly appeared, crossing the English Channel in the wake of a series of thunderstorms. During five hours on Ballard Down, the towering chalk down above Swanage, I saw six golden Clouded Yellows, twenty or so Painted Ladies, a dozen or more Red Admirals and innumerable Small Whites. They eclipsed an excellent flight of Dark Green Fritillaries. The Ladies and Admirals had reached Arnside and Silverdale, on the Cumbria/Lancashire border, by the time I got there a few days later. The Scotch Argus was at its peak on Arnside Knott but its numbers were unimpressive. The Knott had been grazed during the late winter period by Shetland ponies, who took a strong liking to the Blue Moor-grass, and hammered it. We had grazed the Knott too hard, to the detriment of the Scotch Argus. The eggs I saw being laid were all placed in the few remaining ranker areas of Blue Moor-grass grassland. There was a need to follow the egg-laying females and discover precisely where they laid, and also to search for the larvae in early summer.

Two important discoveries were made during that trip, both involving my children. They now numbered four, but only my two elder daughters had accompanied me on this occasion. Firstly, I discovered that children fall instantly in love with limestone pavement, that other-worldly terrain of bare Carboniferous Limestone rock, clints and grykes, of ferns and stunted trees. Secondly, Miss Camilla 'Millie' Oates picked a bunch of Common Knapweed flowers from the lane below the Knott, and stuck them in a grass tussock in the main Scotch Argus area, where few plants were in flower. A procession of hungry Scotch Argus butterflies visited that bunch of flowers, as many as three at a time, and an

Clockwise from top: Starting out, Easter 1964. At Timberscombe, north-west Somerset, with Great Uncle Percy, the children's author J. P. Martin; Small Pearl-bordered Fritillary on Foxglove, Exmoor; BB (Denys Watkins-Pitchford) out Emperoring (© the BB Society); the Adonis Blue, back home in the Cotswolds after a 40-year absence; a Green Hairstreak on Rodborough Common.

Top: Silver-washed Fritillary, a woodland butterfly now on the increase.
Left: Marlpost Wood, West Sussex, July 2012. Duke of Burgundy and Pearl-bordered Fritillaries flew along this ride in the late 1960s, breeding in the young oak plantation on the left, which is now a breeding locality for Silver-washed Fritillary and White Admiral.
Bottom: A female Purple Hairstreak, a tree-top species that pupates on the ground.

Top: Edward Thomas country; the little-known paradise that is the East Hampshire Hangers. Looking north towards Noar Hill and Selborne from Wheatham Hill, near Petersfield.

Left: Straits Inclosure, Alice Holt Forest, Hampshire, July 1980. Each mid-summer morning numerous Silver-washed Fritillaries and White Admirals would breakfast on the profuse bramble blossom.

Bottom: A freshly emerged White Admiral on bramble flowers.

Clockwise from top: Noar Hill, Selborne, May 1986, when Cowslips and Duke of Burgundies abounded, the air pulsated with the songs of Willow Warblers, and all was right with the world dissecting the experimental cage built to determine where Duke of Burgundy larvae pupate, 'HM Prison Wyck', Hampshire, August 1984; a rare second-brood Duke of Burgundy from Rodborough Common; looking back at Noar Hill – Thomas Mouse, who conducted frequent small mammal surveys there, and daughter Lucina (Lucy), who didn't; a sylph-like and remarkably hirsute author marking Duke of Burgundies for ecological research work on Noar Hill, May 1984.

Above: Camilla (Millie) Oates in July 1996 at Meathop Moss, south Cumbria, the haunt of the Large Heath. In the distance lies the limestone massif of Whitbarrow Scar.

Left: A Large Heath at Meathop Moss in July.

Below right: A Brown Argus, a common butterfly on the Cotswold grasslands.

Below left: A Long-tailed Blue from the famous 2013 influx of this exceedingly scarce migrant. This female was photographed at Kingsdown Leas in Kent, in September.

Above: Arnside Knott, south Cumbria, July 2013. A place of pilgrimage, and probably the UK's best-loved butterfly site. Below: Dark Green Fritillary is locally common on the Morecambe Bay hills.

Top: the kingdom of the Mountain Ringlet. Near Stickle Tarn and Pavey Ark in the Langdale Pikes, Lake District, June 1995. Below left: the lady of the high fells, the Mountain Ringlet. A female basking on discarded sheep wool, Grey Knotts, Cumbria, July. Below right: Thunacar Knott, Langdale Pikes, June 1995. Analysing vegetation structure where a Mountain Ringlet egg has been laid.

Top left: the Malvern Hills, looking north from the British Camp (© National Trust Images/Joe Cornish). Right: male High Brown Fritillary from Heddon Valley, north Devon. Below: four High Brown Fritillaries drinking by a puddle. Eleven were clustered there one hot day in July 1986 – then a jogger ran through as I was lining up the photograph. Just four returned. Forgiveness, like many other things, can take time.

Above: Glanville Fritillary at Compton Bay. Below: The ever-changing shoreline of Compton Bay on the Isle of Wight – the 'island home' of the Glanville Fritillary. June 1996.

Above: male Heath Fritillary displaying in Halse Combe, near Porlock on east Exmoor. Below: large-scale experimental plots in Halse Combe, set up to determine how to manage Bracken habitats for this rare butterfly. June, 2004. Inset: Heath Fritillary underwing, at Halse Combe.

Clockwise from top: a male Large Blue at Collard Hill in June; a female Large Blue laying eggs on Wild Thyme in June; early days at Collard Hill, the National Trust's open-access site for the Large Blue in the Polden Hills, Somerset, in June 2002. From left to right, Nigel Bourn, David Simcox, Martin Warren and Jeremy Thomas; a female Large Blue at Collard Hill, showing the upperwing.

Above: His Grace the Duke of Burgundy, on Rodborough Common. Left: Burgundy country; the steep slopes of Rodborough Common, in the heart of the Cotswolds, June 2013. Below: Purple Haze! Strawberry Banks, alive with Devil's-bit Scabious flowers and an assortment of random small children. September 1996.

Above: Pearl-bordered Fritillary at Cwm Soden on the Ceredigion coast. Middle: freshly emerged Pearl-bordered Fritillary in Cirencester Park Woods. Bottom: two Pearl-bordered Fritillary larvae feeding on a violet clump amongst a tangle of dead bramble leaves, a classic breeding location. Cirencester Park Woods, Gloucestershire, April 1998.

Above: a pristine male Purple Emperor, feeding on Fox scat. Fermyn Woods, Northamptonshire, June 2014. Below: a posse of four Purple Emperors feeding on Fox scat. Fermyn Woods, July 2013.

Above: Purple Emperor larva named 'Keats' at dinner, Savernake Forest, early June 2010.

Left: male Purple Emperor of the rare colour form ab. *lugenda*, Fermyn Woods, July.

And that dark prince, the oakwood haunting thing/ Dyed with blue burnish like the mallard's wing (John Masefield, 'King Cole').

Below: autumn in Savernake Forest, 2010. *Our life is no dream, but it may and perhaps will become one* (Novalis).

Clockwise from top: Painted Lady time: a cluster of Painted Ladies feeding on Saw-wort Lydlinch Common, August 1996; Orange-tip from Culkerton, May; rare ab. *suffusa* form of the Comma, Fermyn Woods, July; the author in a shepherd's hut at Knepp Wildlands, West Sussex, July 2014 (© Neil Hulme).

old High Brown Fritillary. In those days very few plants flowered on the Knott in early August.

Kingcombe called, for a weekend 'butterfly course' in mid-August, down in Dorset. The weather was set fair, and the butterflies fairer. Hod Hill, a historic butterfly collecting ground on a steep chalk dome outside Blandford Forum, laid on a stunning Clouded Yellow show. Half a dozen or so were parading over a field of Lucerne growing on the slope below the hill fort, and others were flying at pace over the sunny rampart slopes. One was the pale white female, form *helice*, which the diary recalls was caught with a reverse sweep (a legitimate butterfly-catching stroke long before Sir Ian Botham pioneered it in cricket – one of the glories of running a butterfly course is that one can carry and even use a butterfly net without causing offence). We saw 24 species of butterfly that afternoon, and found well over a hundred gregarious 'webs' of tiny Marsh Fritillary larvae. Fuelled by Kingcombe's homemade cake and serenity we saw 30 species of butterfly on the wing that weekend, and found the immature stages of six more. That's quality for you.

Butterflies are essential to childhood, and to any seaside holiday; and there are few better venues for butterflies and seaside than Compton Bay on the south-west coast of the Isle of Wight. This is truest in mid-August when the weather is set fair and Clouded Yellows are in. Furthermore, there are few better campsites anywhere in Britain than the site run by the Phillips family at Compton Farm on the island. In the mid-1990s, when old Denny Phillips was still alive, the farm was a glorious adventure playground for children, for Denny collected old tractors and other ancient farm equipment. The deader it was, the more he liked it. Children could play on the rusting Fordson Majors, watch the cows being milked in an old herringbone milking parlour, and help with some farm jobs. It was a return to my own childhood days. To young Arion Oates, aged four, it was Paradise. Health and Safety thinking had scarcely penetrated the farm. Instead, the place was run by common sense, a love of life, and rural contentment.

Butterflying had to take second place on this trip, but that was no problem, for Clouded Yellows patrolled the camp site and Adonis and Chalkhill Blues descended from the downland slopes to visit clover flowers. Also, Compton Beach is not just a superb sandy beach, for those who do not require 'facilities', but is backed by sandy slumped cliffs alive with Common Blues, Wall Browns and, in early summer, Glanville Fritillaries. Larval webs of the latter were frequent on the cliffs that August, suggesting that Compton would host a massive flight of the butterfly the following June (it did). Here a father can relax, and listen to England's fast bowlers blasting South Africa away on the radio (Devon Malcolm, nine for 57), whilst the children play in the sea. Our first and last butterflies of the trip were Clouded Yellows. It was the sort of holiday after which one needs a couple of days off, to recover.

Unfortunately, September was dire, the poorest since 1983, and early October brought some sharp frosts. This terminated the 1994 butterfly season prematurely, though the odd Clouded Yellow was seen on the Isle of Wight when I returned there on a work visit in October. But the 1994 butterfly season had set its successor up very well.

The new year was seen in on a clear, black night, with England under-performing in a Test match Down Under. Winter was wet and mild, and London experienced its wettest January. The first butterfly of 1995 did not appear until March 10th, late, when a golden Brimstone was seen dancing through sunlight that slanted its way past Beech trunks on the slopes of Three Groves Wood, by Strawberry Banks in the Frome valley east of Stroud. Such sightings can only portend a good summer. Every winter Brimstones hibernate on the south-facing slope of the sheltered combe at the mouth of that wood. They seem to have habitual wintering quarters.

The National Trust had just acquired Collard Hill in mid-Somerset, a stretch of steep downland on the south-facing escarpment of the Polden Hills, the calcareous clay ridge that runs east from Bridgwater to Street before turning south towards Somerton. Collard Hill offered spectacular views over the Somerset Levels and along the flanks of the Poldens. Moreover, the hillside, which had been heavily grazed by sheep, shouted two words at me: Large Blue. It would need to be assessed by the Large Blue experts, Jeremy Thomas and Dave Simcox. The butterfly was thriving at Green Down, a Somerset Wildlife Trust reserve a few kilometres away, and there were aspirations to restore it to other sites in the Poldens. Little is known about the history of Collard Hill, though for years the word FISONS was embossed on its steep slope, as a novel advertisement aimed at travellers on the Somerton-to-Street road below – and perhaps as a statement of the power of agriculture in Somerset. In 1995 the gentler slopes consisted of fertilised rye grass, cut annually for silage. These areas have since reverted splendidly to calcareous grassland and have become heavily studded with ant hills. The place was obviously keen on butterflies, offering up the first Small Tortoiseshell of the year and a few Brown Hairstreak eggs on young Blackthorn shoots. There was history in the making here.

In early April the first migrant butterflies showed up, testosterone-loaded male Red Admirals and a Painted Lady, battling for possession of a sheltered hilltop glade high up in the Blackdown Hills, south of Taunton. It seemed a long way to travel, just to squabble, but these boys knew where females in need of their services would appear, and were up for it. Spring was breaking through nicely, only for a cloudy northerly airflow to develop, which dominated for the rest of the month. May then got off to a flyer, bringing out the first Pearl-bordered Fritillaries in Cirencester Park Woods and on Daneway Banks, at the head of the Frome valley in the Cotswolds. But once again, spring capitulated, after having all but broken through. The weather collapse commenced on May 8th, Victory in Europe Day, fifty years on. Butterflying stalled, then the butterflies themselves stalled as quotidian gloom descended, alleviated only by a couple of bright days in late May.

Gradually the spring butterflies gave up the ghost, exasperated. Like us, they can take only so much.

There was only one thing to do, work caterpillars – and there was an urgent need to look closely at Scotch Argus larvae on Arnside Knott, which had been too heavily grazed. Scotch Argus larvae, like most other members of the Brown family, Satyridae, are night feeders. That meant there was time for short visits to Meathop Moss and Yewbarrow, two of my heartlands at Witherslack in south Cumbria, before ascending the Knott at dusk. At Meathop Moss, a raised bog, Green Hairstreak females were observed laying eggs on the buds and terminal leaves of Cranberry. The young larvae would then feed on, and even in, the developing fruits. In the secret glades surrounded by ancient Yew trees on lonely Yewbarrow, Pearl-bordered Fritillaries were numerous, feeding on Bird's-foot Trefoil flowers, and fresh males of its close cousin the Small Pearl-bordered Fritillary were also emerging. Then, in the midst of them all was an extremely pale, almost white specimen. But was it a Pearl-bordered or a Small Pearl-bordered, *euphrosyne* or *selene*? This proved to be one of the hardest pieces of butterfly identification I have ever attempted. It was a male, that much could be determined by its behaviour, and it was obviously freshly emerged. Of course I had no net, and the beast proved distinctly camera-shy. The underside, which should have revealed all, proved to be decidedly unhelpful. Before it flew tantalisingly away over a belt of Hazel bushes, it visited a few flowers for nectar – Cat's-ears – and it completely ignored the Bird's-foot Trefoil flowers that the Pearl-bordered Fritillaries were favouring. This pushed it towards Small Pearl-bordered Fritillary. My guess is that it was *Boloria selene* ab. *pallida*, but the truth is that these things are sent to try us – and they do.

At dusk, naturalist colleague John Hooson, MSc student Steve Beaumont and I ascended the Knott, to search for Scotch Argus larvae. Our aim was to set Steve up to conduct an ecological study of the larvae. A Little Owl repeatedly mocked us from the bushes, so much so that a ten-minute bombardment of scree and clitter was necessary to move the irritating thing on. The literature on finding Scotch Argus larvae proved misleading, not least a 1895 claim by a Mr Haggart of Galashiels that, 'no artificial light can be used as the larvae immediately drop down.' In three heady hours we struggled to find six larvae between us, finding none until it was pitch black. Part of the problem was that under lamplight they mimic the dead flower heads of Blue Moor-grass, in size, shape and colour. Interestingly, the two smallest larvae were both feeding on Sheep's Fescue, the larger ones on Blue Moor-grass. We returned the following night, which was warmer; so much warmer that I stumbled upon an active pairing of *Homo sapiens*: 'I hope you have twins, dear!' I muttered as a blessing on their union, and scuttled off. We found seven larvae, all in the final instar and feeding on Blue Moor-grass, all in turf about 10 centimetres tall. Steve went on to spend several more nights looking for Scotch Argus larvae on the Knott, though he was hampered by a lengthy spell of utterly vile weather in mid-June. His conclusion was that, on Arnside Knott, the butterfly requires turf that is at least 8 centimetres tall during May and June. Had he been able to start earlier in the year he could have investigated whether the very small larvae prefer Sheep's Fescue, then grade on to the broader-leaved Blue Moor-grass as they develop. Years later, Paul Kirkland from Butterfly Conservation published an excellent study on the ecology of Scotch Argus larvae, indicating that grasslands can be grazed too tight for this lovely butterfly.

Diary, June 12th 1995: *Vile. Uniform leaden grey skies, slow moving on a northerly airstream. Again cold, only 14°C max. Identical weather to what we had late last May. All because for the last three weeks a big anticyclone has been stuck in the Atlantic. Had it become stuck a few hundred miles further east we would be having a heatwave. As it is we've got the central heating on and the chickens have gone off lay.*

Eventually the grot cleared away, and the high pressure moved in. I was in Cornwall on the first sunny day, June 21st, close to where my paternal grandfather grew up, a blacksmith's son in Holywell, near Newquay. On Holywell Dunes the Silver-studded Blue was emerging in numbers. This was subspecies *cretaceus*, which breeds on Bird's-foot Trefoil. And they were unusually large, almost the size of a Common Blue. Fortunately the first brood of the Common Blue had finished, for separating the two species out on the wing might have proved difficult. The females were laying their eggs close to small clumps of Bird's-foot Trefoil amongst open sand, placing the tiny white discs on the undersides of leaves and on moss fronds. The incredible thing is that Holywell Dunes did not exist in grandfather's day, being less than a century old. Grandfather caught Methodism, Strict Methodism at that, and 'went abroad' as the Cornish say, settling near Gloucester.

The last few days had been set aside, optimistically, for the Mountain Ringlet on the Lake District high fells. John Hooson and I had found a student, Sarah Shannon from Leicester University, who was keen to do some research on the butterfly for an MSc thesis. Get her to follow the egg-laying females, we thought, and do detailed vegetation quadrats where eggs are laid. Incredibly, the weather came good, and remained so for the rest of the summer: 1995 had broken through. The Mountain Ringlets were only just starting to emerge when I arrived up on Wrynose Pass on June 26th. England was beating the West Indies at Lords, with Dominic Cork taking seven wickets. The world was righting itself.

So was the weather. In fact, from the point of view of studying the Mountain Ringlet the weather righted itself rather too well, for it quickly became too hot for a dark butterfly whose body is covered in black hairs designed to absorb and retain heat in a cool montane environment. In hot weather this butterfly, the females especially, resort to hiding, wings closed, in Mat-grass tussocks – for ages. Hooson, Shannon and Oates stormed the Langdale Pikes, where my rucksack thermometer soared to 26 degrees Celsius. We managed to spot one egg-laying female, who laid two eggs on horizontal blades of Sheep's Fescue grass at lunchtime. Then the ringlets effectively went into a siesta. Eventually the three of us staggered down to the Stickle Tarn Inn to rehydrate. The following day was even hotter, with the Lakeland valley roads melting. We took a more gentle route, up to the saddle between Fleetwith Pike and Grey Knotts, above the Honister Pass youth hostel. There, the Mountain Ringlet was emerging in numbers, Big Bang day, but again most females were shading in grass tussocks. Only two egg-laying females were seen, again laying on horizontal blades of Sheep's Fescue amongst Mat-grass tussocks. I watched one shading female for an hour and a half, before she eventually sprang into action and laid a couple of eggs. At one point a fell runner sped past us, in training for a 72-hour, fourteen-peak marathon to be staged in mid-July, and for which Hooson was also training. There was madness on the high fells that day. Day three was hotter and madder still: the ringlets had retreated to the tussocks before we ascended, and were not in the egg-laying vein at all. Instead, I came upon an elderly couple, National Trust members it later transpired, standing stark naked beneath a minor waterfall: 'Come on in!' they shouted, 'it's fantastic!' History does not record whether their invitation was accepted or not. Sarah remained up on the fells for several more sweltering days, but only saw a few more Mountain Ringlet eggs laid. The experience probably put her off butterflies for life.

The High Fells had not experienced anything as mad as the 1995 Mountain Ringlet Expedition since Samuel Taylor Coleridge's great 'Circumcision of the Lakes' in August 1802. Then, Coleridge set off for a two-week feral jaunt, taking the house broom handle as a staff, and leaving the besom twigs scattered on the kitchen floor. That angered Mrs C considerably, for the marriage was already in free fall. He lost the broom handle during a lunatic descent of Skiddaw. We know all this because he sent a detailed account of the expedition to the woman of his insatiable dreams – who was not Mrs C but one Sara Hutchinson, Wordsworth's sister-in-law. Coleridge effectively invented fell walking, and probably fell running. He would have been an excellent partner on the 1995 Mountain Ringlet expedition.

July dragged on in stupefying heat. The Purple Emperor emerged only in low numbers, and went over rapidly in the heat. White Admiral numbers, however, were impressive. Several days were spent searching for High Brown Fritillaries in the New Forest. But I was too late, the butterfly had almost certainly died out. It turned out that the female I had seen in Matley Passage, south-east of Lyndhurst, back in early July 1992 was the last High Brown Fritillary recorded in the New Forest, formerly one of its national headquarters. Radical changes in the Forest had led to the collapse of the metapopulation structure so vital to the butterfly. The High Brown had been booted out of the inclosures (the woods) by twentieth-century forestry and had become restricted to the open heaths, where the bracken stands it could breed in jumped in and out of suitability. We must stand in silence for the New Forest *adippe*.

My sojourn in the Forest had one memorable moment of gross eccentricity. Late on in a sweltering day, of intense heat and high humidity, I wandered off the beaten track in one of the less well-frequented inclosures and followed the course of a gravel-bottomed stream in search of a pool in which to bathe. This was a tradition amongst the old New Forest butterfly collectors; Sydney Castle Russell himself was a keen exponent. Within seconds of immersing myself in a cool shaded pool a swarm of teenage girls burst through the bracken. Worse, they were French, and though hopelessly lost, ooh-la-laad me mercilessly. Unfortunately, I could understand them. There is only one thing a gentleman can do in such a situation.

There was some good news on the High Brown Fritillary front that summer. The butterfly resurged well on the steep Bracken slopes of Bossington Hill, near Porlock on the edge of Exmoor. Surveying for them here, however, necessitated swimming, breast stroke, through head high Bracken, with bramble and rubble underfoot. Up at Bircher Common, in north Herefordshire, the High Brown positively abounded, at least over the core 10-hectare area of Bracken. Best of all, the southern end of the Malvern Hills revealed a respectable flight of this magnificent golden insect for the first time in years, on the slope below the obelisk in Eastnor Park and on the east-facing slope of Swinyard Hill. Numbers seemed to be back to their 1988 levels, though way below the abundance of 1986. Sadly, though, the High Brown Fritillary collapsed horrifically throughout the Malverns after the summer of 1995, and now appears to be lost from those loveliest of hills, from Edward Elgar's heartland. I saw my last of the Malvern High Browns that summer. It hurts now to return, not least because I believe conservation effort could have been more successful there.

Thursday July 20th dawned cloudless and calm – the sort of weather in which *The Sun* newspaper runs its 'Phew What a Scorcher!' headline. Indeed, the temperature went on to reach 32 degrees in central London. It was the National Trust's centenary year, and staff were invited to a Royal Garden Party at Buckingham Palace, attended by Her Majesty, a small prim figure beneath a pale green parasol, held perpendicularly without a single waver. She was, as ever, Duty personified. I had butterflyed before in St James's Park and knew there was a strong colony of Holly Blue there. Indeed, a dozen freshly emerged males were present, buzzing around bushes. Then, about twenty were seen in the Palace grounds. This was of significance, as nationally the butterfly was at a low ebb at the time: I saw but a singleton in 1994, and had not seen any in 1995 before this day. The Palace gardens also revealed a small colony of Essex Skipper along the lake margins, and a large colony of the rare mining bee *Macropis europaea*. It was well worth having to wear a suit and tie.

August began with a heatwave, and carried on regardless. It was the hottest August since records began in the seventeenth century, and almost the hottest month ever. It was also the sunniest August, and the fourth driest. August 1st was staggeringly hot, and was spent unwisely trying to count hyperactive Silver-spotted Skippers whizzing over the short turf of Watlington Hill, my old butterflying heartland on the Chilterns escarpment. It was the best flight of this challenging little butterfly I had ever encountered, certainly in terms of density of butterflies, though the population at the MOD's Porton Down in Wiltshire ranges over a far greater area. The skippers were omnipresent. At one stage a dozen or so males shot off together in pursuit of a virgin female. God knows what happened when they forced the poor girl to the ground – I had had enough by then and left Nature to sort itself out. The weather had got into a strange phase: day after cloudless day thunder clouds developed in late afternoon, offering a few rumbles, bad-light-stop-play conditions for cricketers, and one or two large drops of rain – before dissipating, to clear into a sultry evening. A hot weekend followed at Kingcombe, in west Dorset, running another butterfly course, only the Clouded Yellows were not in. Indeed, I did not see a Clouded Yellow all year. They tend to take a season off after a bumper year.

A new anticyclone moved in, this time over northern England. I followed it, with the family, to study the Scotch Argus on Arnside Knott further. We camped at a low-facility camp site on the south-west flank of Arnside Knott. In contrast to the drought conditions down south, the Morecambe Bay limestone hills looked positively verdant, though here too the grasses were destined to brown off as the heat intensified. The Graylings and High Brown Fritillaries were going over fast, but the Scotch Argus was just a little past peak season. My timing was perfect, the females would be laying the bulk of their eggs. Hooson appeared, bronzed, to assist me. We were armed with colour-coded plant support stakes, to insert close to each egg as it was laid, carefully keeping watch on the female. We would return to analyse the vegetation structure at the egg site later. A familiar problem befell us, though: it was so hot that the females were sitting around, wings closed, shading, for ages, comatose.

Diary, August 9th 1995: *I followed one from 12.30 until I lost her amongst a sudden bevy of other females at 1.50. She sat still, wings closed, until 1.02 when she literally jumped 30 cm and quickly laid one egg, 6 cm up on dead Blue Moor-grass in a dense, 8 cm tall tussock. After a short bask she jumped again, at 1.07, to lay another egg on a live Sheep's Fescue grass 4 cm up in 7 cm turf, before flying 2 m to settle, wings closed, shading again. At 1.30 she again jumped 30 cm and, after a short crawl, laid 6 cm up on the underside of a Common Tormentil leaf amongst 8 cm tall Blue Moor-grass turf. Then she returned to shading before, suddenly, she joined a loose pack of similar-looking females that arrived in the glade.*

The diary continues:

We then spent ages watching inactive females shading before two females suddenly crash-landed at my feet, at 3.06. One of them quickly laid an egg, in a similar situation.

And that was it for the day: four eggs, hours and hours of inaction, and a lot of sunburn. The family had gone off to visit Beatrix Potter, wisely.

A change in tactic was required, so the following day we visited Smardale, a Cumbria Wildlife Trust reserve on the edge of the Yorkshire Dales, vaguely near Kirkby Stephen but actually near Nowhere, deep in the heart of tranquillity itself. It is one of the most idyllic, if lonely, places I have ever visited, with an intense spirit of place. The reserve consists of some 2 kilometres of disused railway line (one of dear Dr Beeching's, probably), with steep grassy cuttings and embankments, and a spectacular viaduct over a river valley. Smardale is an essential pilgrimage site for anyone with an interest in our butterflies, and is the only other site in England where the Scotch Argus occurs, after Arnside Knott. Here the butterfly was in stupendous abundance, in a series of colonies strung out along the old railway. It is very much a morning butterfly here, as the afternoon sun leaves many of the colonies in shade. Of course, in the intense heat of August 1995 the females shut up shop for the day at lunchtime, and not a single egg was seen being laid. One of the difficulties was that the butterfly was in such profusion here that males were forever encountering the females, and pestering them, such that egg laying became extremely difficult. The children loved this place deeply, not least the viaduct (by Thomas Bouch). Also, they found Otter spraints along the river and, best of all, piles of White-clawed Crayfish shells left over from Otter meals. On this day the Scotch Argus claimed the crown of Butterfly of the Year 1995.

The summer had another trick up its sleeve. The Brown Hairstreak put on an *annus mirabilis* show on Noar Hill, back in Hampshire. The emergence began there in late July – the first time I had recorded the butterfly in July at Noar Hill, as traditionally it started there around August 7th. A visit on August 14th produced a tally of 41 in two hours, 25 of them feeding on Hemp Agrimony flowers. This Hairstreak had been relatively numerous on the reserve back in September 1977, but this was significantly better. Perhaps the butterflies were more keen than usual in seeking nectar in the sustained and intense heat? I can offer another theory. Throughout the 1980s and into the nineties Noar Hill was frequented each September by the West Sussex naturalist Doris Ashby. This was her butterfly, and she loved it dearly. Doris was Midhurst born and bred, and spoke with a strong Sussex accent – such that many people found her unintelligible. She was one of the best all-round naturalists I have had the privilege to meet, and entirely self-taught. Her relationship with Nature was deep and honest, and was shared with her beloved dog Cathy, an adorable Battersea dog. She abhorred blood sports, was secretary to the Midhurst branch of the Labour Party, and had worked as a gardener on various big estates. Doris had a dodgy heart and had been instructed to slow down, but being Doris, and it being early spring she did the opposite – and suffered a massive heart attack after a morning watching Adders on a local common. What I witnessed at Noar Hill on August 14th 1995 was the Doris Ashby Memorial Flight.

A long lazy week was spent camping on Compton Farm on the Isle of Wight again, only this year there were no Clouded Yellows. Instead, the Camberwell Beauty had showed up. Some 350 were seen nationally, mainly in eastern counties, having migrated across the North Sea from Scandinavia on easterly winds. They frequented the shady side of Buddleia bushes – apparently, for I never saw one. The downs above Compton had turned grey with drought but were alive with Adonis and Chalkhill Blues. The diary recalls that I spent much time *floating on an air bed in Compton Bay contemplating Tennyson's poetical works. After a lengthy debate I decided not to open Tennyson's poetical works but to find out whether they floated or not. They did.*

But the great summer of 1995 descended suddenly into the wettest September since 1976. The fine weather returned for October and early November, enabling the Red Admiral to appear in immense numbers, and Small Coppers and Wall Browns to put on a good third brood. Some butterflies lingered on during a decidedly mild November, before a cold December ended what had been the warmest year on record for the UK.

The New Forest

Culturally and historically, the New Forest is the spiritual homeland of butterflying in Britain. For well over a century it was the epicentre of butterfly collecting, being revered by collectors as a place of pilgrimage, a promised land, a place of deep belonging. Throughout these decades the Forest hosted annual influxes of collectors, many of them from London. Collectors came as individuals, as groups of friends, or as families, often for short collecting holidays. During the main season, in July, they occupied most of the inns and boarding houses in Brockenhurst, Lyndhurst and Ringwood, small towns which were endeavouring to become holiday venues. There was also a minor season in late spring. Collectors came from many walks of life, but particularly from the professional and upper classes. A number participated in the often lucrative trade of dealing in specimens and livestock, for one unusual specimen could pay for an entire collecting holiday, or more. Snobbery, competitiveness and downright skulduggery were rampant, along with gross eccentricity.

Collecting, not just of butterflies but also of moths, beetles and bird eggs, and some other taxa, was almost a mania during the Victorian era. The Forest, as it was and is still known, gained a reputation for being a great collecting venue as rail links with

London became established, primarily during the 1860s. The Forest, being Crown land, was effectively open-access land at a time when most countryside was distinctly private – and butterflies and moths abounded there. During the heyday of butterfly and moth collecting, from the late 1880s through to the First World War, the pastime generated a massive seasonal industry in the Forest – providing accommodation, food and drink, transport hire (pony and traps and the like) and forest guides. Some of the Forest keepers (crown foresters) ran rather lucrative side-line businesses selling insects and acting as guides, notably the Gulliver family. Livestock and specimens were traded by dealers in hostelries on Saturday nights, particularly in *The Rose & Crown* in Brockenhurst. The pioneer conservationist W H Hudson (1841–1922) thought very little of it all, describing Lyndhurst in *Hampshire Days* (1903) as being the place where:

> London vomits out its annual crowd of collectors, who fill its numerous and ever-increasing brand-new red-brick lodging houses, and who swarm through all the adjacent woods and heaths, men, women and children (hateful little prigs!) with their vasculums [plants], beer and treacle pots [moth bait], green and blue butterfly nets, killing bottles, and all the detestable paraphernalia of what they would probably call 'Nature Study'.

Hudson was not normally so vitriolic.

The more experienced collectors were after unusually marked specimens – aberrations or variations – such as the White Admiral with the distinctive white bands completely absent (ab. *nigrina*) or reduced (ab. *semi-nigrina,* now called ab. *obliterae*). Such specimens are symptomatic of strong populations. The collectors particularly prized the greenish colour form of the female Silver-washed Fritillary, form *valezina*, which at the time was regarded as being a New Forest speciality. They would go to great lengths to procure desired specimens. For example, one account in *The Entomologist* magazine reads:

> In August, 1887, whilst driving in a dog-cart from Christchurch, I saw *Apatura iris* [Purple Emperor] flying along the hedge of a bare roadside. I immediately gave the reins to a friend who was in the cart with me and pursued it with the dog-cart whip, and through a piece of luck I managed to disable it enough to capture it. It was a fine male specimen and not in the least damaged.

It was to the enclosed, ungrazed woods on the more clayey soils that the collectors flocked, though they also made sorties out onto the open heaths. The woods, or inclosures as they are known, had been created under various Acts of Parliament. Some had been established by sowing acorns. Perhaps the most significant of these Acts was that of 1851, known as the New Forest Deer Removal Act, which effectively transferred the Forest from being a royal hunting forest to being a centre for producing oak timber, primarily for the Royal Navy. This act brought about the slaughter of almost the entire deer population – the animals took decades to return. The removal of deer (mainly Fallow Deer) must have led to massive regeneration of brambles and scrub, to the benefit of many butterflies and moths. Many of the descriptions in entomological literature tell of broad rides fringed with luxurious growths of bramble and shrubs such as sallows.

It is difficult for the modern naturalist to imagine the super-abundance of butterflies in the New Forest inclosures of old. Sydney Castle Russell (1866–1955) describes a visit during the hot summer of 1892:

> As I slowly walked along, butterflies alarmed by my approach arose in immense numbers to take refuge in the trees above. They were so thick that I could hardly see ahead and indeed resembled a fall of brown leaves.

The summer of 1893 was probably the greatest summer in the history of butterflying in Britain, completely outgunning the likes of 1976. One experienced collector had a remarkable experience in one of the inclosures near Ringwood:

> I followed the bed of one of the streams in search of water to drink, and was disappointed in not finding sufficient to quench my thirst, not a pool being left, but I was repaid by the sighting I witnessed; the said bed of the stream for more than a mile was literally crowded with butterflies, the bulk of them being *adippe* [High Brown Fritillary], *paphia* [Silver-washed Fritillary] and *sibylla* [White Admiral].

The great lepidopterist and wildlife artist F W Frohawk (1861–1946) made almost annual pilgrimages to the Forest, and became known by fellow enthusiasts as The Old Man of the Forest. A ride in Parkhill Inclosure, south-east of Lyndhurst, is dedicated to him. He recalls his first visit to the Forest, entering the woods just after a thunderstorm in July 1888:

> I shall never forget the impression it made upon my friend and self. Insects of various kinds literally swarmed. Butterflies were in profusion. *A. paphia* [Silver-washed Fritillary] were in hordes, the var. *valezina* was met every few yards, as were *A. aglaia* [Dark Green Fritillary] and *A. adippe* [High Brown Fritillary]. *L. camilla* [White Admiral] were sailing about everywhere. On a bank under a sallow in the sunshine a large female *A. iris* [Purple Emperor] with wings expanded, evidently washed out of the sallow by heavy rain. *N. polychloros* [Large Tortoiseshell] was of frequent occurrence.

Other, less desirable insects also abounded. Castle Russell recalls: 'A fly resembling the common house fly [the muscid *Hydrotaea irritans*] was in clouds and followed one in a dense stream. Immediately you stopped ... they settled on you in a mass.' He covered his exposed skin with nicotine juice obtained from his pipe, as did other collectors. Some wore beekeeping veils.

Perhaps the most eccentric collector was Sir Vauncey Harpur Crewe, of Calke Abbey (now National Trust) in Derbyshire. A second-generation collector, Sir Vauncey was a recluse who surely suffered from what is now recognised as obsessive–compulsive disorder (OCD). He specialised in Lepidoptera and taxidermy (mainly birds), and amassed perhaps the greatest collection of British butterflies ever assembled, collecting in the field with his trusty head gamekeeper Agathus Pegg, and by means of his chequebook at sales at Stevens Auction Rooms in The Strand and privately. Sir Vauncey had the habit of issuing forth from the Crown Hotel in Lyndhurst and bagging an inclosure, for a day, or two, or three. He would station flunkies at the entrances to keep out the riff-raff. This led to a series of rumpuses, for he was deemed to be denying rights of access. He banned his four daughters from marrying, communicated with them mainly by means of notes conveyed by footmen, and banished one of them altogether for smoking. Perhaps predictably, he outlived his son and heir. When Sir Vauncey died, in 1924, the bulk of his vast Lepidoptera collection was sold in lots to meet death duties. Many entomological store boxes remain at Calke, containing uncatalogued specimens. This residue includes several boxes of *valezina* Silver-washed Fritillary females from the Forest, making one wonder just how many *valezina* females a man actually needs.

All this troubled the Hon. Gerald Lascelles, Deputy Surveyor (senior Crown officer), who published his memoirs in a book entitled *Thirty Years in the New Forest*. But Lascelles was heavily outnumbered, and effectively powerless. Even his keepers ignored his instructions.

Of course this Elysium could not last. A generation of collectors was lost to the First World War, along with cohorts of Forest trees. Then, the sleepy old Office of Woods, which had administered the Forest for the Crown, was replaced by the Forestry Commission, a new organisation geared to economic forestry using fast-growing and largely non-native conifers. The war fellings were accepted by the collectors as a necessary evil, not least because several of the fritillary butterflies thrived in the resultant clearings and young plantations, but the Forestry Commission changed the feel of the place greatly and became instantly disliked by collectors and naturalists alike. One collector bemoaned, 'The Forest generally appears to be well on the way to becoming a second Black Forest of pines.' The Second World War changed the character of the Forest woods further, and indeed of the open Forest. The writing was on the wall – a silvicultural revolution was in full swing.

Matters steadily worsened during the decades after the war. Coniferisation became rampant, the ride-edge shrub zone – so crucial to butterflies – was systematically obliterated, and after 1965 commoners' ponies and cattle were finally allowed into most inclosures, to the great detriment of the ground flora. In many parts of the Forest deer numbers rose astronomically, which led to Fallow Deer browsing out the White Admiral's Honeysuckle. By 1970 more than 60 per cent of the inclosures were under conifers. It then became apparent that the Commission planned to reduce broad-leaved woodland to mere cosmetic fringes around pure conifer plantations. In the ensuing row the Minister of Agriculture issued a moratorium prohibiting further fellings of broad-leaved woodland. That moratorium, known as the Minister's Mandate, is still in place today. Ironically, it led to the decline of the 'spring fritillaries' – by cutting off the supply of clearings from broad-leaved woodland on which they had become strongly dependent.

Today, many of the New Forest inclosures consist of anodyne plantations of non-native conifers, through which the wind soughs vacantly. We are told that William the Conqueror, who founded the New Forest, would recognise today's Forest. He would not, and neither would the old butterfly collectors, due to the gross intrusions of the twentieth-century silvicultural revolution, of which the Forest's woodland butterflies were unscheduled victims. In places there are narrow vistas back into history. Pondhead

Inclosure, to the immediate south-east of Lyndhurst, is perhaps the best relic of the New Forest inclosures of old. Outside the silvicultural inclosures – which were admittedly started for silviculture – elements of the old Forest are still recognisable, notably the ancient pasture-woodlands such as those at Mark Ash and Pinnick Wood, and vistas across the ancient heathland, both dry and wet. But it is hard to wander anywhere in today's New Forest without hearing the sound of traffic, at least distantly, especially when the leaves are off. And everywhere, against the skyline, near and far, stand sullied ranks of sombre, brooding alien conifers. On the eastern skyline glows the towering beacon of the Fawley oil refinery.

Much laudable heathland restoration work has been carried out by the Forestry Commission over the last two decades – restoring bogs that had been partly drained in order to provide better grazing land, removing invasive Rhododendron and, at places such as Highland Water, removing some of the more modern conifer plantations to restore open heathland. Better still, from the narrow point of view of the woodland butterflies, since the mid-1990s commoners' stock (ponies and cattle) have again been excluded from most of the enclosed woods and the fences reinstated. Habitat conditions have improved dramatically for some butterflies following the removal of commoners' stock, notably for long-grass species such as the Ringlet which had become a rarity, but in many of the woods flowering bramble patches are scarce and few Honeysuckle tangles exist for the White Admiral. The latter, for so long one of the Forest's most ubiquitous butterflies, is now decidedly scarce here in its former national stronghold, on account of deer browsing and because forestry thinning works have acted heavily against it. Mercifully, the Silver-washed Fritillary, with which it flew in close companionship, remains reasonably well established in many inclosures, though nowhere is it remotely as profuse as it once was. Var. *valezina*, as the old collectors knew the beautiful fulvous-green colour form of the female, still occurs – sparingly.

Recently, the fortunes of the Pearl-bordered Fritillary have turned round wondrously in its traditional heartland north-east of Brockenhurst, where it became very scarce during the 1980s. There, this nationally rare springtime butterfly has resurged spectacularly as a result of ride widening work and the felling of some large blocks of conifers. Its congener, the Small Pearl-bordered Fritillary, which was always a butterfly of damp hollows in the New Forest, is still hanging on, mainly in the Forest's south-west sector, both inside some of the inclosures there and along stream sides in the open heath. Formerly, though, it was far more widespread. The third of the 'spring fritillaries', the Duke of Burgundy, appears to be extinct in the Forest – the intrusion of ponies into its favoured inclosures probably proved too much for it – but it is a tenacious little butterfly, capable of pulling off surprises. The Dark Green Fritillary has increased somewhat of late, at least on the open heaths and in some of the inclosures between Brockenhurst and Beaulieu. Best of all, the Purple Emperor has made a most welcome return to the fringes of the Forest, albeit at low population density. The golden High Brown Fritillary, sadly, is almost certainly extinct. I have the melancholy privilege of having seen the last of the New Forest High Browns, back in 1992. Outside the woods, the drier heaths are currently just a little too heavily grazed for most butterfly species, though Grayling and Silver-studded Blue colonies are plentiful enough.

But forests can restore themselves, though they function over longer timescales than we do, and butterflies are tougher than we sometimes think. Despite everything, the New Forest inclosures remain of realisable potential for many of our butterfly species, whilst the open heaths and pasture-woodlands merely require a drop in grazing pressure for butterfly populations to increase spectacularly. This will occur in time. Time creates difficulties, and time alone will solve them; it is merely a matter of how we work with time. In time, lovers of our butterflies may return to their New Forest heartland.

20 *Summer of the Painted Lady*

Freezing rain is a rare phenomenon, and at New Year it is both rare and inauspicious. Nonetheless, that is how 1996 began. December had been cold and, after a brief mild and wet spell, January and then February followed suit. Cold easterly winds dominated, bringing snowfalls to the north and east, a few of which crept towards the west. The first reasonable day of the year, at least in the Cotswolds, was February 27th, which brought out the first bumblebees and Marsh Fritillary larvae at Strawberry Banks, near Stroud. The following day the first butterfly appeared, a Small Tortoiseshell basking upside down on a wall in Cirencester, though the temperature did not feel quite warm enough. Butterflies often appear earlier in the year in towns than in the countryside, simply because of the extra warmth issuing from heated buildings.

The year's first proper butterfly was a male Red Admiral, patrolling a hilltop territory at the old Large Blue site near Buckfastleigh in south Devon, the infamous Site X. It was flying in the glade that contained the Large Blue warden's dilapidated caravan and may even have overwintered therein, alongside various Field Mice, beetles, spiders, slime moulds and other esoteric biodiversity – and the previous August's washing-up. Think of the most disgusting domestic mess you have ever encountered, double it, multiply that by pi *r* squared, stick it in a white caravan turned green with age and algae and you've got the Large Blue warden's caravan. But that splendid and deeply memorable Red Admiral was a foretaste of what was to come. Oh, and by the way, the Large Blue site had been seriously over-grazed by Farmer Brown's cattle, again.

Thereafter March was cold and sunless, but reasonably dry. Hardly a butterfly showed. Winter would not let go. Chiffchaffs were only just starting to arrive on the south Devon coast at the end of March. April did not burst through, offering only a handful of warm days. It was not until almost the end of the month that the first Orange-tip was seen, a fresh male dancing over a roadside patch of Lady's Smock on the edge of Meathop Moss, in south Cumbria. On the moss itself the Green Hairstreak was only just starting, in contrast to the abundance noted there on April 24th 1993. Up on the nearby limestone hills the Blue Moor-grass had been severely scorched by frost and lying snow, and was straw-coloured, whereas this is normally one of the earliest of our native grasses to flush green. The north had clearly had it tough. A group of us up there for a Butterfly Conservation seminar thought about going out to look for the nocturnal larvae of the Scotch Argus, then realised the idea was daft and retreated to the pub instead.

It would be pleasing to say that May redeemed the situation, but it was the second coldest May of the century, after 1902. Frosts were a prominent feature well into the month. It was, though, like the preceding months, distinctly dry. Pearl-bordered Fritillaries, somehow, emerged with a bang mid-month in Ashclyst Forest, north-east of Exeter, and over Bracken stands in the steep gorge-like valley by Castle Drogo, on the north edge of Dartmoor. The late May period, normally a peak time of year for our early-season butterflies, then became stuck in a rut.

Unexpectedly, one of the most memorable dates in twentieth-century butterflying folklore dawned, Thursday May 30th 1996. It started grey, but a pale sun appeared, which burnt away the clouds of morning, and a clear afternoon materialised. Moreover, the wind was in the south, the deep south, and increased steadily, depositing a film of Sahara dust on parked cars. At Strawberry Banks the first Marsh Fritillaries appeared, along with my first Common Blue of the year – very late. At Rodborough Common the butterfly transect route was walked in full sun, for the first time that year. Nothing special was flying there but it was good to note that the Duke of Burgundy had not been entirely written off by the poor May, and that the Brown Argus was out in good numbers. Then, I retreated to the north end of Cirencester Park Woods where the Pearl-bordered Fritillaries were at last emerging, some forty of them, resplendent over Bluebell carpets which were just starting to flower properly. At 3.15 precisely, a Painted Lady appeared; it dropped out of the sky to feed on Bluebell flowers in one of the clearings. One Painted Lady does not make a summer, but sixteen do! By the end of the day I had counted that many, almost all of them dropping into the Pearl-bordered Fritillary clearings to feed on Bluebell flowers, which traced the afternoon with heady fragrance. The following day I surveyed other parts of the woods and saw another eighteen, again all looking pristine, complete with the iridescent sheen they bear when freshly emerged, and again feasting avidly on Bluebells. These were not home-grown butterflies but immigrants from way across the Channel, and they were accompanied by myriad Silver Y moths. Within the space of two days the 1996 butterfly season had metamorphosed into a veritable paradise. The Painted Lady had blasted all the doom and gloom away. Thank God I had booked those two days off!

There was no stopping 1996 now. Thirty-six Painted Ladies were seen on June 1st, mostly on Bluebells, in Cirencester Park

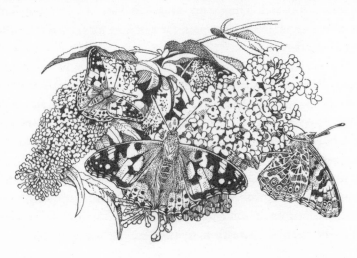

Woods, where they outshone the Pearl-bordered Fritillaries. Some were also seen basking in late evening light along the lanes as I took a daughter for a pony ride. They had already reached the north of Scotland. By happy chance I had a work trip to the Isle of Wight booked, to advise on conservation grazing regimes. A fresh wave of Painted Ladies hit the Island on June 5th. I saw over a hundred feasting on, and laying eggs on, thistles along the cliff top at Compton Chine. They completely outstaged and outnumbered the Glanville Fritillaries. On the way home I called in at Pondhead Inclosure, south-east of Lyndhurst in the New Forest – Lyndhurst was traffic-jammed and the Forest was calling. There again were Painted Ladies feasting on Bluebells. Other Ladies were seen along the road home, active during a warm evening. The diary recalls: *The first thing I saw on crossing into Gloucestershire was a Painted Lady. That was at 8.45 pm.* It had been a twelve-hour day. Diary again: *Arrived home to find an empty house and a note reading 'Millie Hospital Cirencester'.* It turned out that she had broken an arm whilst being chased in the garden by an errant brother.

During the emotional days that followed, butterflying had to be rationalised. The odd cloudy, even drizzly day was actually welcome. Mercifully the Painted Ladies quickly found our garden. There was a constant stream of them heading through, northbound, on June 6th and 7th. An expedition to Bircher Common, north of Leominster in Herefordshire, on June 13th, to advise a new warden on management for the High Brown Fritillary, was memorable for the car journey: I passed 50 Painted Ladies, all heading west into Wales. They were active long into the evenings. Regular evening pony rides, with an able daughter, produced counts of up to 45 along a 5-kilometre route of quiet rural lanes. Many were basking on a hillock I christened Painted Lady Rise, which attracted them in subsequent years.

Eventually I was able to get out properly again. A trip to Cheddar Gorge, primarily to assess the ecological impact of free-ranging Soay Sheep, turned into a memorable butterflying trip. Above the gorge, on its western side, Painted Lady males had set up territories along the cliff tops, particularly at a dizzy spot called Hart's Leap. They were accompanied by a scatter of Red Admirals, newly arrived too, and a dozen or more immigrant Hummingbird Hawkmoths. Best of all, the first Clouded Yellow of the year flew past us, on Heidi Hill. We cheered like football supporters. There was even a thriving colony of Small Pearl-bordered Fritillary, breeding on violets amongst coppiced gorse scrub. It was so magical that I returned there at the weekend with a car full of children, for a picnic, then took them strawberry picking. Summertime had broken through.

It was Midsummer Day and the Painted Lady swarm was weakening. In Cirencester Park Woods the Pearl-bordered Fritillaries suddenly shot over. Down near Porlock, the High Brown Fritillaries were starting on Bossington Hill, and Heath Fritillaries were in fairly impressive numbers at Bin Combe, on the east side of Dunkery Beacon. They were emerging late, as larval development had been held up by the cold, slow spring.

The Fates, being kindly disposed, had arranged for me to travel to North Wales to help with a training course. We were to meet at the Great Orme headland, just outside Llandudno. Here, I visited the richest area of limestone grassland I have ever seen – adrift with Bloody Crane's-bill, Dropwort, Nottingham Catchfly and mega rarities like Hoary Rock-rose and Spiked Speedwell, not to mention the commonalities like Bird's-foot Trefoil. There were also problems, in the form of invasive Cotoneaster, Strawberry Tree and Turkey Oak. The local subspecies of the Silver-studded Blue was more abundant, nay profuse, than I had ever seen a butterfly, with the possible exception of the Meadow Brown in an East Hampshire wood on Midsummer Day 1976. We were only there for a short while, but I left my heart behind and swore to return for a proper exploration. That evening I had to do something absurd – give a lecture during an England *v* Germany football match. As this was in Wales, and North Wales to boot, there was no escape. Now, had this been rugby, or rather *rygbi* …

The journey home involved a stop at a Carboniferous Limestone promontory called Graig Fawr near Prestatyn. Here, an erstwhile National Trust tenant farmer had abused much of the SSSI with chicken manure, slurry and Rye Grass, before going bust and surrendering the tenancy. The steeper land was beyond his reach and still supports a very rich limestone flora. It is in effect an outpost of the Great Orme in miniature. In 1983 Professor Chris Thomas released thirty female and ten male Silver-studded Blues, from the Great Orme, as part of his PhD research. A thriving colony resulted: I saw over 500 during my visit. Of course, the first and last butterflies seen in Wales that trip were Painted Ladies, though they were ageing.

July came in promisingly. In the Cotswolds, grassland butterflies were appearing late, but in pleasing numbers. The transect route on Rodborough Common abounded with Marbled Whites, Meadow Browns and Small Heaths, though Ringlet numbers were down – it does not enjoy hot summers. Even nearer to home, White-letter Hairstreaks were in goodly numbers, with most local clumps of mature Wych Elm holding a colony. Some appeared in our garden, even drinking by the side of the children's paddling pool one hot afternoon. A new generation of elms, mainly Wych Elm, had reached maturity and had become suitable for this beleaguered butterfly.

In the woods, White Admirals were emerging late. A short visit to Ashclyst Forest on July 10th was memorable for the sight of males searching Honeysuckle tangles, repeatedly pecking at certain spots. Close inspection revealed that they had located female pupae that were about to emerge. This was an old New Forest collectors' trick, used as a way to acquire perfect specimens. The other admiral, the Red Admiral, was prominent that day. A mass arrival had recently hit Devon.

By happy chance a mid-July trip up to the Lake District had been arranged with Martin Warren of Butterfly Conservation. Millie, recovering from her broken arm, came too. First stop, Meathop Moss, at Witherslack. It was calm, hot and sunny, with an anticyclone stationed over the Lakes. Large Heath was fully out and truly abundant, clearly having a good year. It was not possible to count them, though, as I had left my watch in the car – never make that mistake, as timed counts produce invaluable data. The butterflies would disappear when a cloud came over, reappearing wondrously with the sun. One such revelation offered a vista of sixteen Large Heaths close by as the sun reappeared. It was too hot for the females, though, for they had taken to shading in cottongrass tussocks. Up on Yewbarrow, the Yew-haunted hill above Witherslack church, High Brown Fritillary and Dark Green Fritillary males were emerging nicely, whilst June's Small Pearl-bordered Fritillaries were still flying in numbers. I needed a photograph of a Northern Brown Argus with the white forewing spots, only most of them lacked these spots. Indeed, during the years I have known the Morecambe Bay limestone hills the Northern Brown Argus seems to have all but lost its white spots, and now looks very much like an ordinary Brown Argus.

It was time for the Mountain Ringlet. All good Mountain Ringlet expeditions begin with a visit to Wordsworth country at Grasmere, in this instance because a young lady needed to visit the facilities. I also showed her Wordsworth's grave. That did the trick. She progressed to become an English scholar. Martin decided to visit the Mountain Ringlet colony at Fleetwith and Grey Knotts, south of the Honister Pass youth hostel. Millie and I took the more arduous side, the north side, ascending Seatoller Fell and Dale Head. The lower south-facing slopes of Seatoller Fell drew a blank, probably because the butterfly had finished for the year there, but higher up below Yew Crag we found a colony still going, though the males were all but spent. Millie spotted a female Mountain Ringlet drowning in a shallow pool, and promptly rescued it. After drying its wings for a couple of minutes it embarked on a crawl through the short grasses, laying two eggs on dead horizontal Sheep's Fescue blades before fluttering off, crash-landing as Mountain Ringlets do, crawling again, and laying two more eggs, again on horizontal blades of Sheep's Fescue close to Mat-grass tussocks. Four eggs in five minutes! By Mountain Ringlet productivity standards that was amazing. And Millie found a Wheatear's nest, with young, amongst rocky rubble. On descending we found a note from Martin, who had departed for the south, on our car windscreen. It read: 'The MR roadshow hits big! I saw 158 in 60 mins, a staggering 128 in 30 mins in the best bit. Mega. I failed on egg laying, they all just sat there. Thanks for the trip – another to remember. Safe journey. Pip, pip.'

Millie and I stayed on an extra day. It was obvious where we would go, Fleetwith. Only by the time we had ascended, 11 am, it was already hot and cloudless, and Mountain Ringlet females were shading in grass tussocks. The mountains became obscured in a heat haze. My timed count outscored Martin's of the previous day – totalling 211 in 50 minutes, including 137 in the core area. The vegetation structure in this favoured area, where females had gathered en masse, consisted of a carpet of dense Sheep's Fescue with frequent tussocks of Mat-grass. That seems to be what Mountain Ringlets like best, but butterflies eternally encourage theorisation and hypotheses, which they then shoot down in flames. Meanwhile, young Millie made a delightful rock garden of lichens and mosses over a flat rock, and found a Ring Ouzel nest amongst the rocks, only the young were just leaving the nest. The journey home was arrested by an excellent evening flight of Purple Hairstreaks at the Hilton Park Service Station on the M6.

Down south, the Purple Emperor seemed to be having a poor season, especially in Alice Holt Forest where Forestry Commission thinning works were decimating its habitat. Nationally, it was first noted on July 13th, at Bookham Common in Surrey, by Ken Willmott. I searched for it vainly in woods in south Gloucestershire and north Wiltshire, feeling that it was calling for me. The White Admiral was shooting over quickly in the heat, as is its habit in hot summers. On the East Hampshire heaths the Silver-studded Blues were long gone, after a short, sharp and sweet flight season.

Then, at the end of July, the home-grown brood of Painted Ladies started to emerge – and threatened to obscure the entire UK, town and country, under a cloud of butterflies. There was some evidence to suggest that this might happen:

Diary, July 24th 1996: *Babbacombe, north Devon. Amazing abundance of Painted Lady larvae. The immigration here must have been incredible. In the thistle-infested field in front of the house I estimated that 60 per cent of all the Creeping Thistle plants held at least one larva, most had more – and there were literally hundreds of Creeping Thistle plants. In another field I found a single 1-metre tall Spear Thistle which had over 50 larval tents on it, and other Spear Thistles there were skeletonised. I even found larval tents on 30-centimetre tall nettles and tiny isolated thistle plants among a maize crop. Very few on Marsh Thistle, and then only on well-leaved plants. Most of the larvae were full grown, many had already pupated.*

There was no need for farmers to mow thistles in north Devon – the caterpillars had done it for them. The previous day I had found numerous full-grown larvae on nettles along a lane in the Heddon valley, on the Exmoor coast. There was going to be an eruption, even an eructation.

There was only one place for the Painted Lady show to kick off, the Kingcombe Centre in West Dorset, just down the road from where I was born. In 1996 my Kingcombe butterfly course (only it was never a course, more of an experience) ran over the weekend of August 2nd to 4th. We were in luck, an anticyclone was building. We started with a visit to see the Lulworth Skipper in its most westerly locality, Bind Barrow near Burton Bradstock, in near-calm conditions. The skipper was abundant: I counted 138 during my standard fifteen-minute walk around this small clifftop site. Impressive. There was also an impressive evening flight of Purple Hairstreak in the Kingcombe meadows that evening, plus a scatter of freshly emerged and rather crepuscular Painted Ladies. As in north Devon, Painted Lady larvae were almost profuse on Creeping and Spear thistles in the Kingcombe meadows.

The following day I saw well over a thousand pristine Painted Ladies. At one point I had to stop the Kingcombe Centre's minibus and remonstrate with the driver, Nigel Spring, who was squashing

Ladies willy-nilly along a hilltop lane. 'You can get out and walk!' he replied. I did, and found that a minor cloud of Painted Ladies was feasting in the adjoining Red Clover field. At Lydlinch Common, near Sturminster Newton, groups of 20–30 Ladies were feasting on small patches of Saw-wort. Then, in a fifteen-minute spell of bliss, I counted 334 on Hemp Agrimony patches along the western ramparts at Hod Hill, near Blandford Forum. The Red Admiral was almost as profuse, with a massive appearance of fresh specimens. They had crept up on us unnoticed, amongst the blizzard of Painted Ladies. Best of all, the Clouded Yellows were in properly at last. We saw nine on Hod Hill, and would have seen more had we investigated the large field of Lucerne on the southern slope below the hill fort – there is nothing Clouded Yellows like better than a Lucerne field. The following day Powerstock Common, near Maiden Newton, gave a count of 352 Painted Lady in two hours, plus over a hundred pristine Red Admirals. Kingcombe had put the world to rights.

It was my birthday. Where did we want to go? 'Slimbridge!' the children all shouted. It was a wise choice, as it produced 400 Painted Ladies, including 100 on old Buddleia bushes by the Wild Goose Observatory. Those bushes had been planted by butterfly lover Sir Peter Scott. Sir Peter was not just a birder, and was for some time President of the British Butterfly Conservation Society, now Butterfly Conservation. More Ladies were feasting on Common Fleabane, Hemp Agrimony and Purple Loosestrife in tall fen vegetation. On the way back I was permitted to walk the week's butterfly transect at Rodborough Common, near Stroud, whilst the children visited the ice-cream emporium on the top of the common. The transect count produced 74 Painted Ladies, and a Clouded Yellow. Quality.

A week later I visited Noar Hill, to walk the week's butterfly transect there, as Tony James, the recorder, was on holiday. Our youngest daughter, Rosie (full name Euphrosyne), aged nearly four, accompanied me. She often did that summer, simply because she liked to sing in the car, without risk of being teased by her siblings. She sang her own songs: 'Naughty, Naughty Dumper Truck', 'Horsy Wants to Eat the Jam' and, best of all, 'Dinosaur Goes Crunch! Crunch! Crunch!' The latter was too much: I swerved into a lay-by, helpless – and discovered a White-letter Hairstreak colony, based on a mature Wych Elm. 'Dad,' she asked, when we were halfway to Selborne, 'where are we going?' 'Home,' I replied. 'Oh,' she said, and fell asleep. At Noar Hill, Painted Lady numbers were down from 145 the previous week to a mere 46, but Red Admirals were profuse and I counted nine Clouded Yellows. The Brown Hairstreak was just getting going, with a scatter of fresh males, though it was apparent that there was not going to be a repeat of the previous year's abundance.

It was time for a short seaside camping holiday, taken at the National Trust's low-facility camp site at St Gabriel's Mouth on the Golden Cap estate, on the West Dorset coast. No caravans with loud TVs, no families rioting past the midnight hour, no live entertainment every Saturday night, and no rip-off shop selling UHT milk – i.e. a proper camp site, and in SSSI meadows. It was populated by National Trust countryside supporters, folk who seldom if ever visit NT mansions. Round a camp fire at St Gabriel's one evening, it became clear that several of them had visited far more National Trust countryside than I had. They lived and breathed it. On the way to Dorset, we broke our journey at Barrington Court garden, near Ilminster. Painted Ladies, Red Admirals and Peacocks were numerous there, and I utterly disgraced myself. In the Jekyll-designed white garden, flitting jerkily round clumps of Broad-leaved Everlasting-pea (perennial sweet pea), was a strange blue butterfly, behaving rather like a hairstreak. It was a Long-tailed Blue, one of our rarest migrants, only it quickly shot off, claiming another engagement. One can behave as I did during that minute at a football match when one's team scores, and be considered perfectly normal; in a National Trust garden, though, such behaviour is deemed inappropriate, and a gross embarrassment to children.

Painted Ladies and Red Admirals were congregating along the Dorset coast. At St Gabriel's Mouth, they clustered on the clifftop flowers; then, each afternoon, many would set out south-westwards across Lyme Bay, perhaps heading towards Prawle Point, the southernmost tip of Devon, prior to proper emigration. On August 17th they were setting out to sea at the rate of one per minute. All told, over a period of three days about 500 individuals of each species were seen flying out to sea, following the same course, low over the wavelets. Back home, the Painted Ladies had virtually all gone. None of the prolific home-grown brood had shown any interest in establishing territories, courtship, mating or laying eggs.

After the first week of September the Ladies literally disappeared. I saw just three after September 8th. It seems that they emigrated during late August and early September. South-coast birders watched them go, low over the waves. The Red Admirals and Clouded Yellows remained, though their numbers steadily dwindled. The great butterfly summer of 1996 gradually waned, then slid into the past – to take its rightful place on the high table of great butterfly summers.

21 *Leaving the nineties*

The summer of 1996 had set up its successor nicely. The new year started amidst a prolonged period of cold coming from the east. I welcomed it in whilst taking my cats for a midnight walk across snowy fields. Earth stood hard as iron. It took five days for the temperature to rise above freezing. Then, a dry January developed, which of course gave way to a mild, wet and windy February, which predictably led into a dry, warm and sunny March. I got through the winter on a diet of Brown, Purple and White-letter Hairstreak eggs, searching for them on Blackthorn stems and around oak and elm buds respectively. All three seemed to be in unusually good numbers, presumably as a result of the hot summer sequence. Then, at the end of January, Marsh Fritillary larvae started to emerge out of hibernation at Strawberry Banks, near Stroud.

The butterfly season began impressively, on March 2nd, with first a Brimstone and then a Peacock followed by a Comma, all in Three Groves Wood, a classic Cotswold Beech wood by Strawberry Banks; all within a whirligig five-minute spell as spring magically burst through. The year was off to a flyer, and we were seriously overdue a good spring. We got it, almost.

Hours were spent studying Pearl-bordered Fritillary larvae in Cirencester Park Woods, mainly in lunchtime visits from our office in Cirencester. They have the habit of basking on dead leaves whilst the day is warming up, favouring oak and bramble leaves, close to the violets on which they feed. When populations are high, as they were in early 1997, they are relatively easy to find – in the right weather conditions. One magical visit produced 20 in an hour.

Once the day has warmed up properly, and the leaf litter has dried out, though, they go into feed-and-retreat mode, in which they hide under dead leaves for long periods, only emerging for brief frenetic feeding spells, consuming fresh violet leaves, buds and flowers. The amount of feeding damage on the violets in one of the Cirencester Park Woods clearings, a spot known as Botany Bay, was enormous, suggesting a massive emergence to come. This was a clearing of some 2.5 hectares where mature broad-leaved trees and Scots Pines had been felled the previous winter, and promptly planted up with Corsican Pines. Colonisation took place on Day One of the 1996 flight season for, apart from rows of young pines and a scatter of retained young oaks, the clearing consisted mainly of myriad bramble seedlings and clumps of Common Dog-violet amongst tree leaf litter – and little else. Patches of Bugle and Primrose grew along the adjoining rides. This was paradise for the Pearl-bordered Fritillary. They don't actually need anything else, just scattered violets amongst leaf litter, and as little green grass as possible – for green grass cools the microclimate down, and the caterpillars need heat.

Butterflies were emerging unusually early: Orange-tip, Green-veined White and Small White on the last day of March, Holly Blue on April 1st and Green Hairstreak as early as April 8th in the Cotswolds. Duke of Burgundy appeared at Noar Hill on the 10th, though much later at Rodborough Common. Grizzled Skippers were out in early April in amazing numbers. I saw impressive flights of them on the North Downs near Dorking, on the East Sussex downs either side of Lewes, and on Hod Hill in north-east Dorset. It was definitely the butterfly of the month throughout southern England. All told, I saw nineteen species by the end of April, a third of our fauna, and could have managed one or two more.

The weather wobbled late in the month, which meant that the Cirencester Park Woods Pearl-bordered Fritillaries did not start to emerge until early May. Then the woods erupted with them. In Botany Bay clearing I counted 100 in 23 heady minutes on

May 3rd. I would have been able to count far more than that later, but something despicable happened: the weather collapsed, horribly, on May 5th. First it rained, hard and near-continuously, then it became cold, with frequent heavy showers. Ash leaves and Bracken fronds were frosted off. The Pearl-bordered Fritillaries made the most of whatever sunny spells came their way, roosting during inclement weather on bramble stems, Bluebell heads and dead Bracken fronds, often for a day or two at a time. Somehow a great many of them managed to sit out the mid-May deluges, whilst others held back from emerging from their pupae until the weather improved. Spring butterflies have to be tough and able to leap into action the moment the sun comes out. This one is Tough, and springs instantly into the air as the sun appears. All butterflies need to be able to stagger their emergence, usually over a period of 10–20 days, so that an entire brood does not get written off by a single bad-weather event.

In good weather at the end of May I carried out mark-and-recapture work on Pearl-bordered Fritillaries in clearings at the north end of Cirencester Park Woods. These young plantations were separated by blocks of mature trees but linked by a mix of open and overhung rides. It was hard work, for the butterfly is difficult to catch, especially in flight. In these woods, there is too much snaring bramble for net swishing, so one has to drop down on one knee and quickly drop the net over a basking or feeding butterfly. Knee pads are essential, to prevent impalement on bramble thorns. The work determined that Pearl-bordered Fritillaries move quite freely between clearings during good weather. One female travelled as far as 4.5 kilometres, over arable fields, being accidentally found in the upper Frome valley. Some individuals lived for as long as three weeks.

The family wanted to go somewhere nice for half term. The weather said Go East, so we drove to the Norfolk Broads, a journey of some five hours. Except by boat, public access to the Broads is poor, due to intensely private large estates and a paucity of rights of way. Families in search of wildlife experiences are effectively restricted to pay-for-entry nature reserves. The children loved the place, its Swallowtails, and above all the constant bird song all around them. Millie, a budding naturalist if ever there was one, found several Willow Warblers' nests. Cuckoos called all through the mornings, and Marsh Harriers hung meditatively in azure skies. Our first Swallowtail flew over us as we were picnicking, fifteen minutes after we had arrived. But they were in aloof mood, flying across the lodes (ditches) and scarcely visiting flowers. We had one good session with three males visiting Yellow Iris and Red Campion flowers at Hickling Broad, in a sheltered area along the boardwalk called Derrys, a renowned spot for close encounters with the Lord of the Broads. But after two glorious days a strong east wind sprang up. Swallowtails detest wind, retreating to sheltered areas in the lee of trees and perching interminably on reed heads there.

June became the wettest of the century in England and Wales. The weather was particularly savage during the Wimbledon fortnight. June butterflies, such as the Large Blue, suffered accordingly. Yet the midsummer butterflies were emerging earlier than normal, having got ahead of themselves as their larvae had grown rapidly during the fine spring. Marbled White, for example, made its appearance on June 9th at Rodborough Common, and a visit to Meathop Moss in south Cumbria on Midsummer Day found Large Heath fully out, and High Brown Fritillaries emerging in numbers on the nearby hills. At Meathop, Swallows were swooping low over the bog, picking off Large Heaths as they bobbed about above the cottongrass. Then the weather worsened as a front became stuck over England, and June ended rottenly. The White Admiral, a butterfly highly prone to being knocked out by poor midsummer weather, suffered badly. It had an especially difficult time in Alice Holt Forest, down in Hampshire, where contractors working under the antagonistic name of Euroforest were harvesting trees, and pulverising the butterfly's breeding grounds with considerable insensitivity.

We were due a poor July. Rather incredibly, we got a reasonable one. There was even the opportunity for a three-day Mountain Ringlet expedition to the Lakeland fells, primarily to follow the egg-laying females. With this butterfly it is imperative to pick the right weather – and an anticyclone was stationed over western Britain. Go! The valley farmers were busy making hay and the rivers were quietening down. Mountain Ringlet numbers were, though, disappointing on the slopes of Grey Knotts, above the Honister Pass youth hostel, but increased the higher we ascended. Perhaps the butterfly was starting to go over at the lower levels? The following day, July 9th, a more ambitious route was taken, over the Langdale Pikes. That is as demanding a day's butterflying as any on offer in the British Isles. The weather was cloudless, with the temperature reaching 23 degrees on the mountains. From Dungeon Ghyll we took the arduous route up Mark Gate to Thorn Crag and towards the summit of Pavey Ark, then over to the flanks of Thunacar Knott. Mountain Ringlets were in goodly numbers over an extensive area of west-facing slopes above Thorn Crag and in pockets around Thunacar Knott. But it was too hot for them, and the females had taken up shading in the Mat-grass tussocks. Thunder was brewing there, unforecast; it did not materialise but we took no chances, and got down quickly, to swim in a deep sun-drenched pool. The following day the females were shading by 11 am, on the slopes of Cold Pike and Wrynose Breast, above Wrynose Pass. The journey home from this trip was difficult – my companion, my eldest daughter, insisted on playing a Spice Girls CD for the entire journey. In desperation I started translating 'Spice Up Your Life' into Latin (*Populus mundi condi vester vita! Hic quassate ad sinistrum*, etc.).

It was Emperor time, only there were precious few of them about. But it was worse than that: I had spent so little time working them over the previous ten years that I had all but lost the ability to find them, especially as the population in my beloved Alice Holt Forest was at a low ebb, due to Euroforest's merciless activities. A diary entry for a visit to Alice Holt's Straits Inclosure on July 19th recalls: *Nightmare visit to the sound of chain-saws ripping through oak. Horrific dearth of butterflies – even the common Browns were scarce. No White Admiral, which is unthinkable.* I had struggled to glimpse one Emperor in the woods west of Mottisfont in west Hampshire and failed altogether in West Sussex. Then, accompanied by Dr Chris Luckens, an entomological GP, I saw a splendid female in Abbots Wood Inclosure in Alice Holt. It was no good, my relationship with the one butterfly that mattered most to me had all but dwindled away. I had been hijacked by nature conservation.

August started and ended wet but was otherwise superb. It began at Kingcombe in west Dorset, with my annual butterfly-course weekend. Brown Hairstreaks were emerging on Lydlinch Common, outside Sturminster Newton. We found a fresh female and two males settled in – and I mean in – an Ash tree. They were busy probing the following spring's tiny black buds for some sugary sustenance. Then something Ghastly and unprecedented happened on my Kingcombe course – it rained. Death By PowerPoint? No! Never! We looked at the centre's butterfly collection, donated by Bill Shreeves, who had collected butterflies as a boy at Christ's Hospital school a decade before me. There were stories in each of those specimens. There were specimens there from the woods in which Bill and I had gone under the spell of butterflying – Pearl-bordered and Small Pearl-bordered fritillaries, and some Duke of Burgundies too, all from Marlpost Wood, near Southwater. And some old specimens from the New Forest, bought or handed down, collected by ace Edwardian collector and dealer A B Farn. Then the rain eased, so we went out, finding Grizzled Skipper larvae in rolled-up Wild Strawberry leaves over bare clinkers in the old railway cutting at Powerstock Common, a sizeable web of Marsh Fritillary larvae and, surprisingly, some freshly laid Dingy Skipper eggs, indicating that rare second-brood adults were out and about.

The Isle of Wight called, hosting a short camping holiday at Compton Farm. The National Trust warden, Paul Davies, informed me that there had not been any Clouded Yellows on the island all summer – so we immediately saw a large male patrolling the lower slopes of Brook Down. Don't blame the warden, butterflies do things like that on purpose. That trip also brought my ninth and tenth Painted Ladies of the year; they had been conspicuous by their absence, in stark contrast to the previous summer. The diary recalls a plethora of Large White pupae in the Compton Farm campsite washrooms: *Counted thirteen in the Gents. Apparently there were even more in the Ladies. Quite a few on the outside walls too. There was a particularly silly one on a loo-roll holder and another on a light switch.* Later, at home, I found one in the attic light switch. Beat that! It needed rescuing, of course. Caterpillars can wander far and wide prior to pupating, and find their way into the most incredible places. The following spring a Small White was spotted emerging from a pupa in the redundant keyhole of our front door!

August belonged to the Small Tortoiseshells. They seized the month, outscoring the Peacock and even the cabbage whites. In our garden, counts of over a hundred were made on several occasions. They lasted unusually long into a fair September. They saved their best show for a visit to Hod Hill in early September, the famous old collecting ground above Blandford Forum in Dorset. Hundreds were feeding on Devil's-bit Scabious flowers there, having bred profusely on nettle patches growing in the rampart ditch bottoms.

Gradually, the Small Tortoiseshells went into hibernation, and a pleasant autumn was lorded over by the Red Admiral. There is always one butterfly that claims the autumn for its own. This was a Red Admiral autumn. The weather was ridiculously mild, such that Common Wasp workers persisted almost into the New Year – I suffered the indignity of being stung by one on December 9th.

❧

A severe storm brought 1998 roaring in. It was the fiercest in southern Britain since January 1990, but, flooding apart, it did not do much damage. After nine horrendously wet days January took the pledge and dried out.

February became the warmest on record, both by day and by night. Friday February 13th was remarkable, achieving a maximum of 20 degrees Celsius in Herefordshire. Several Butterfly Conservation volunteers managed to walk Week Minus 6 of their butterfly transect route – the butterfly monitoring season is not scheduled to start before April 1st, when Week 1 commences, but it regularly jumps the gun, notably so in 1998. Butterflies took to the air that day, but so did Hazel pollen, generating one of the worst hay-fever days I have suffered. For the record, I developed the condition aged four, inherited from my mother, and have had it ever since. My allergies have changed over time, moving from grass, sedge and rush pollens to tree pollens. Medication has proved at best mildly effective, and, during my teens, counter-productive – the school doctor put me on sedatives during my O-level summer. None of this has stopped me butterflying, though it can be used as an excuse to avoid paltry corporate events and the like.

March was mild, though dull. Pearl-bordered Fritillary larvae were even more profuse in Botany Bay clearing in Cirencester Park Woods than they had been in 1997. Twenty-five were found there in two hours on March 23rd, many of them nearly full grown. The system needed slowing down. Sure enough, April 1998 was the wettest in England and Wales since 1818. It was also dominated by cold northerly winds. That slowed things down, such that Pearl-bordered Fritillary larvae were still around on May 9th. I searched hard for their pupae then, and later, when the adults were emerging, by looking for freshly emerged butterflies drying their wings, in order to home in on the vacated pupal case. However, the mysteries of where this butterfly pupates have evaded me: I have never found one. The larvae definitely move away from the violets on which they have been feeding, and I suspect the freshly emerged adults crawl some way before expanding their wings. Someone else can crack the mysteries of where the Pearl-bordered Fritillary pupates. I have failed.

The first of Cirencester Park Woods Pearl-bordered Fritillaries appeared on May 15th. This year they were in luck, for the weather was terrific between the 12th and the 22nd – which is enough for a spring butterfly to do its thing. June, though, was extremely cloudy, and wet, and Pearl-bordered Fritillaries were rapidly eroded away. February had actually been better! It was a struggle merely to carry out the weekly butterfly monitoring transect at Rodborough Common.

July was little better. It was not especially wet, just sunless, and went down as the dullest since 1934. We were worried about the Heath Fritillary on Exmoor and the High Brown Fritillary on Exmoor and in Herefordshire and the Malverns. The Heath Fritillary was collapsing on Exmoor, and not simply because of poor weather – if it lives on Exmoor it has to cope with Extreme Weather, full stop. One of the best colonies, in Halse Combe on the edge of Porlock, had all but died out. There the butterfly had gone from abundant to rare within five years – on my watch, and on my patch. Halse Combe was almost bereft of the butterfly's foodplant, Common Cow-wheat. The combe had become dominated by tall dense Bracken, and European Gorse was spreading rampantly. Similar problems were developing in other Heath Fritillary combes. Stock grazing had collapsed, largely at the instigation of the government's new Environmentally Sensitive Area (ESA) scheme which was (rightly) concerned about the over-grazing that was taking place in other parts of the moor.

Across Porlock Vale, the High Brown Fritillary was found in modest numbers on the lower slopes of Bossington Hill, but again Bracken and gorse were intensifying, and habitat conditions were deteriorating. Up on Bircher Common, in north Herefordshire, the High Brown Fritillary colony seemed to be thriving, though only in a relatively small area of the common. The butterfly, though, was declining rapidly in the Malverns, where a visit by the 1986 Malverns High Brown Fritillary survey gang of Oates and Grove struggled to see three individuals, only.

An expedition was launched to rediscover Purple Emperor in Ashclyst Forest in east Devon, where the butterfly had occurred until about 1990, and following reports of a 'probable' sighting. One should always be a trifle sceptical about 'probable' Emperors, for 99 per cent of the time this butterfly leaves you in no doubt. With Emperor sightings, 'if in doubt chuck it out' is a good maxim. We failed to turn him up, but I made good by seeing an impressive flight at Bookham Common in Surrey. Better still, a splendid female was seen laying eggs at the far end of my beloved Straits Inclosure in Alice Holt Forest, the first Emperor recorded in the wood since 1996. Euroforest's contractors were leaving the wood alone that summer, and its butterflies were returning.

A weekend running a butterflying course at Kingcombe ushered in what proved to be a fair August in the south, though the north had a rotten month. A Clouded Yellow kicked off the weekend – my second of the year. The Brown Hairstreak was starting at Lydlinch Common. However, an early evening walk around Kingcombe meadows found that Purple Hairstreaks were in decidedly low numbers, and down on the coast at Burton Bradstock the small and isolated colony of Lulworth Skipper (which I studied for some years) was having a miserable season. The windblown state of its beloved Tor-grass patches suggested that pulses of severe weather were responsible.

Kingcombe did what it does best and restored the fortunes of the summer. Then, Graylings appeared in stunning numbers on the scarp slope of Selsley Common, just south of Stroud in the Cotswolds. I counted 325 there in a 55-minute amble. I wanted to observe egg laying but it was hot and the females were shading in grass tussocks. The Grayling also impressed during a short holiday in Pembrokeshire, walking sections of the coastal path around St David's with four children, rock pooling, and playing on sandy beaches bedecked with washed-up jellyfish – jellyfish are essential to a good seaside holiday, but so are butterflies. Wall Browns were also impressive, in sheltered places on cliff slopes, rocky outcrops and cliff paths.

Back home, the Chalkhill Blue had erupted at Rodborough Common. Its foodplant, Horseshoe Vetch, had grown unusually lush during the spring, seemingly due to weather conditions. Back at my other home, Selborne, the Brown Hairstreak was out and about in good numbers, for once. And for once they actually outnumbered photographers wanting to photograph them. Perhaps the butterfly had benefited from the late spring, with eggs hatching in early May, so that the larvae avoided the bad April and were then able to feed up fast in reasonable weather during May? The truth is that we have little idea as to what really makes most of these butterflies tick, which means that we can speculate and theorise like mad. That is really what makes butterflying so fascinating.

Yet another mild winter, snow-less down south, introduced the 1999 butterfly season. The children's childhood was passing, and they had scarcely played in snow, let alone gone tobogganing – and this was in the Cotswolds to boot, with a reputation for winter snow. Clouded Yellow larvae successfully got through the winter on the Bournemouth cliff system, monitored by retired biologist Michael Skelton. Home-grown adults began to appear there in March. This was radical stuff, the first evidence of the butterfly surviving the British winter, fuelling the growing conviction amongst British ecologists that climate change was indeed a reality.

But the legacy of the disappointing season of 1998 was already becoming apparent. Pearl-bordered Fritillary larvae were hard to find anywhere in Cirencester Park Woods, and there was such concern over the status of the Marsh Fritillary at Hod Hill, in Dorset, that I hastily organised a gang of four to search for larval webs there in mid-March. We found sixteen larval webs. By Hod Hill's high standards that is poor, but it exceeded expectations and represented a viable population.

April was all over the place: good one week, lousy the next. The first Orange-tip of the year was a gem, a male flying in the garden of the National Trust's moated medieval manor house at Brockhampton in north Herefordshire on April 9th. He fed on Honesty flowers along the moat edge before sauntering off through sunlit damson orchards in full bloom. Such butterflies fly on in the mind. They do, after all, seek eternity.

In early May I was invited back to Noar Hill, to explain why the Duke of Burgundy population was in decline. The place had changed radically since I left in 1992, and from a Burgundy perspective it had not changed for the better. Cowslips had declined considerably in areas which had been major breeding grounds during the 1980s – I had good data to prove it. The sward in these areas had tightened up, choking Cowslips out. Also, the chalk-pit banks, habitually used by the butterfly for breeding, had become far more dominated by scrub. These would not have constituted a problem if other areas had improved in suitability, but none had. In effect, the reserve had declined in suitability significantly. The good news, though, was that Rabbit numbers were low, for high Rabbit populations are anathema to His Grace, shortening the turf height too much and rendering the Cowslips unsuitable for breeding.

Back in the Cotswolds, Green Hairstreak and Dingy Skipper were the two immediate beneficiaries of conservation grazing by the National Trust's new small herd of Belted Galloway cattle at Rodborough Common. Both appeared in pleasing numbers in what was a disappointing May. The grazing, carried out during the winter, had reinvigorated their foodplants, Common Rockrose and Bird's-foot Trefoil respectively. Elsewhere, Pearl-bordered and Marsh Fritillaries both began to emerge on May 15th. They experienced mixed fortunes during an indifferent May: Pearl-bordered Fritillary appeared in at best modest numbers in Cirencester Park Woods, whilst the Marsh Fritillary emerged in bumper numbers on Strawberry Banks – I counted 287 there in an hour on May 27th, regularly counting three or four at a time. Sadly, however, a four-day spell of heavy rains at the start of June decimated these and all other spring species.

June was plagued by stagnant cloud, and was also cool and, in the south-east, unusually wet. Butterflies suffered further. There was a scatter of decent days, or rather decent half-days. One such afternoon produced a delightful flight of the dainty Wood White at Butterfly Conservation's woodland reserve at Monkwood in Worcestershire, visited en route from running a training course on conservation grazing at Plas Tan y Bwlch in Snowdonia. Monkwood had supplied handles for the Harris paint-brush manufacturers, before plastic intervened, so it had a long history of active coppice management. Then the wood became redundant and was put up for sale: Butterfly Conservation came to the rescue, in partnership with the Worcestershire Wildlife Trust. In the late 1990s the Wood White was quite numerous along the narrow, flowery rides, but then the butterfly suddenly nose-dived there and is now almost extinct. There are not many modern-day examples of rare butterflies dying out on nature reserves managed specifically for them, and it is hard to envisage what, if anything, went wrong here. The truth is that despite the best of endeavours conservation effort does not always work.

Neither does parenting. All parents fail every now and then, but the following is an example of extreme failure. After several days of intensive work surveying Heath and High Brown fritillaries on east Exmoor, then High Brown Fritillaries in Herefordshire, and seeing Purple Emperors in Surrey on my 'day off', I deemed it sensible to shoot up to the Lake District early one Sunday morning in pursuit of the Mountain Ringlet. It was a spur-of-the-moment decision. To compound that, as I was leaving I inquired whether any of the family wished to come. Two girls, aged nine and six, immediately volunteered, including Millie who was a veteran of the Great 1996 Mountain Ringlet expedition and knew what she was letting herself in for. The weather was set fair, very fair. The girls bundled themselves into the car, followed by camping equipment, books, CDs, cuddly toys etc., and off we went. I wanted to check out the Blea Rigg colony on the Langdale Pikes, last visited in 1992. The M6 was bloody, but we eventually squeezed into the last parking space in the Dungeon Ghyll car park and, rather in the manner of Abraham and Isaac, started up the mountain. The girls skipped on ahead, their doting father lagging behind, carrying Everything. Lunch was taken by Stickle Tarn, and toes were dipped in the crystal water whilst cotton-wool clouds scudded past the sublime landform of Harrison Stickle. The girls were in paradise, and knew it. Up on Blea Rigg, I set them up making fairies out of cast-off pieces of Herdwick sheep wool and floating them down a little waterfall, and sauntered off to find the ringlets. Unfortunately, the butterfly proved hard to find, having moved location.

At that point I somehow forgot that I had taken two children up the mountain with me. It took a while to find them, one weeping helplessly, the other hands-on-hips in fury and indignation. Despite frequent and copious expressions of eternal remorse the tender hand of forgiveness has still not been offered, even sixteen years later. I spent the rest of the summer contemplating giving up butterflying in order to concentrate on parenthood, then thought better of it and carried on regardless.

22 *Time out of time*

Thank God we've got rid of the twentieth century, were the first words consigned to the diary. There was a chance of a new beginning, a better world. The new millennium had come in on a mild but dark and drizzly night, during a damp yet mild winter. But New Year's Day was cloudless, mild and totally calm. It was perfect cycling weather, and the children were keen. After three or four kilometres Millie shouted, 'Daddy, there's a butterfly!' She had spotted the first British butterfly of the century, a female Brimstone fluttering round a clump of Ivy along a south-facing wood edge. Presumably it had been hibernating in the Ivy. A scatter of other butterfly sightings were made that day nationally, and butterflying for the year, century and millennium was up and away. Shortly afterwards, on January 9th, the first Marsh Fritillary larvae emerged from hibernation at Strawberry Banks, near Stroud – ridiculously early.

March was kind. Two days were spent surveying for Heath Fritillary caterpillars on Exmoor, with National Trust and Butterfly Conservation staff, trying to determine why the butterfly was in steep decline there. The butterfly was thriving in places that were still being periodically burnt, or grazed by numbers of deer or farm stock. Elsewhere, colonies were vanishing fast. The problem was that the pastoral system under which the butterfly had thrived had suddenly ceased, so something had to be done. We found thirty or so larvae, basking in hot dappled sunshine beneath Bilberry plants. Their foodplant, Common Cow-wheat, a decidedly uncommon annual, had germinated and was showing a tiny pair of fresh leaves.

Soon the caterpillars would begin to feed, but April was foul – unrelentingly wet, and with two snowfalls. Early-spring Cotswold butterflies, like the Duke of Burgundy and Green Hairstreak, appeared right at the end of the month, shivering.

May started well, allowing them a narrow window of opportunity before it capitulated, yet again. Mid-month I saw one of the best flights of Duke of Burgundy I have ever seen, on a privately owned downland slope in Hampshire's Meon valley. The slope had been grazed by cattle into the early 1980s, then abandoned. Cowslips abounded, and the site was in perfect condition for the butterfly – but it would not remain so indefinitely, for coarse grasses and then scrub would gradually take over and the Cowslips would vanish. Doing nothing was not an option, but what and when, and would the owner be willing and able?

The day May 2000 capitulated I was in Northern Ireland, on the Divis Mountain, the vast dome of moorland blanket bog that overshadows Belfast. Little of the mountain was visible as cloud and heavy rain swirled, first, around us, then within us. We were, of course, standing round in a circle, discussing conservation. Worse, we took that wretched weather back to England with us. Somehow, I had found a few miserable Green-veined Whites and Orange-tips roosting on Lady's Smock heads on the lower Divis slopes, and even a scatter of their eggs.

Back on the mainland, Orange-tips had been blasted away. I saw one on May 20th, then no more until a late one on June 6th. That proved to be the year's last. Pearl-bordered Fritillaries had had a miserable time and the Marsh Fritillary, which had emerged in great numbers, got knocked out worryingly early. Had they laid sufficient eggs to sustain the population? On June 7th I saw the last of the Sand Point, Weston-super-Mare, Glanville Fritillaries, a lone male. The rampant grass and bramble growth associated with a series of wet summers had proved too much for this small and highly isolated colony, and there was nowhere new to which they could spread. The colony had, after all, resulted from a clandestine introduction, and to keep it the poor National Trust rangers and volunteers would have had to garden the slope unrealistically. Too much was being asked here.

But butterfly introductions can work, when properly conducted, and where suitable habitat conditions can be maintained. On June 23rd Dave Simcox, the Large Blue project officer, transferred a dozen female Large Blues from a sizeable colony in the southern Polden Hills to the National Trust's Collard Hill just south of Street. These girls were undoubtedly mated, for virginity lasts minutes with most female butterflies, but Simcox took along three males as well, just in case. We had agonised over whether Collard Hill was suitable for the butterfly or not. Perhaps the slope was too exposed and would at best support a token population? It was worth a trial, not least because of the urgent need for an open-access site, which people could freely visit to see this royal blue butterfly. The Trust had moved heaven and earth to get the slope into suitable condition by carefully grazing down the dominant coarse grasses. Despite some wobbles, due to challenging weather conditions and difficulties in ensuring the necessary grazing, the Large Blue has since thrived at Collard Hill, exceeding all expectations. Within a decade it had become the second-strongest colony in the country and one of the largest known colonies in Europe. Better still, some 10,000 visitors have seen the butterfly there over the years. Butterflies, especially rare ones, need friends.

In mid-June I visited the Norfolk Broads to study Swallowtails and their habitats, notably the impact of cattle and ponies on the butterfly's foodplant, Milk-parsley. The good news was that these animals do not eat Milk-parsley. Better still, their grazing checks the surrounding vegetation which otherwise covers the plant, and their hooves create bare ground pockets in which the plant can propagate – so, a triple tick there. The problem the Swallowtail has is that the females preferentially lay their eggs on plants that are standing proud of the surrounding reeds and sedges, but these tend to grow taller than the Milk-parsley itself. Achieving the right height differential can be crucial. At Irstead Street Marsh, across the River Ant from How Hill Nature Reserve, the Broads Authority had achieved this differential by cutting reed and sedge beds with a giant fen harvester machine during spring and early summer. This work was not without controversy, as it had taken place during the nesting season, but it produced the highest density of Milk-parsley I have encountered and the best flight of Swallowtails. Here, I saw up to 24 Swallowtails in 30 minutes in the core area. Several courting pairs were seen: mated females dropped to the ground on being accosted by an amorous male, in the manner of the Purple Emperor. One receptive female, though, flew off and away with her suitor in tow. Mated females were seen laying their eggs, hurriedly, whilst hovering over the foodplant. Late in the day the butterflies took to basking on the ground, prior to roosting in the reeds. The Swallowtail was also on top form at Butterfly Conservation's exquisite reserve at Catfield Fen, with up to four being seen in a vista.

The Swallowtail was an obvious candidate for Butterfly of the Year, though a casual inspection of Greater Bird's-foot Trefoil plants growing on dry peaty mounds in the cut fen areas at Irstead revealed that the Clouded Yellow was in – three eggs were found – I thought I had seen a female at a great distance. They had started to come in on a deep south wind on June 8th, along with a scatter of Painted Lady and Red Admiral. Summer was heating up. June had been reasonable – not great, but certainly not poor.

On the National Trust's adorable Holnicote estate on east Exmoor the Heath Fritillary required much survey attention. Populations were weakening, even disappearing, apart from a thriving new colony in a young forestry plantation where Bracken had been sprayed off to encourage the new trees. Forty or so were skimming low over the Bilberry carpet here, including three acute, almost black aberrations – ab. *corythalia* and ab. *cymothoe*, the latter like a resplendent Scotch Argus. These are the only Heath Fritillary aberrations I have seen on Exmoor. That colony, though, boomed for two years then died out, as the young trees grew rapidly. However, it taught us that spraying off Bracken could assist this vulnerable butterfly. Would that we could have done more for the High Brown Fritillary on Holnicote, when it was disappearing from the hill flanks above the villages of Bossington, Allerford and Selworthy. But the truth is that we lacked the resources to manage for both the Heath Fritillary on the Dunkery slopes and the High Brown across the Porlock Vale. The latter was probably a lost cause anyway, though recognising lost causes in nature conservation is extremely difficult. Later that summer, I saw the last of the Bossington Hill High Brown Fritillaries. Habitat conditions there were deteriorating acutely, and the higher priorities were the Heath Fritillary around Dunkery Beacon and the High Brown Fritillary further west, in Heddon valley. In nature conservation we cannot fight every battle, let alone win. With today's enhanced resources, though, we would have made more effort for the High Brown at Bossington.

July started poorly, though with a scatter of reasonable days. Something strange, distant and diffuse was calling, as in the 'Piper at the Gates of Dawn' chapter of *The Wind in the Willows*. I had been away from the Purple Emperor for way too long, away from my heartland in the Wealden woods. It was Bookham Common, on the outskirts at Leatherhead, which taught me this. Bookham is Ken Willmott's heartland. He is part of the place, belonging there, especially during the Emperor season. Following the Emperor there is his life's work. Back in the mid-1970s he discovered, by happy chance, two places on the densely wooded common where Emperor males gather each afternoon. Both were sheltered groves on high points, with distinct topographical and arboreal characteristics. Because Ken is hefted to Bookham he had scarcely been able to look for comparable places elsewhere. I studied Bookham, and realised it illustrated a perfectly good way of surveying for this most elusive and evasive of butterflies. Above all, that July Bookham offered me a depth of personal experience in butterflying which I had not felt for years – for, oddly, being immersed in nature conservation had deprived me of it.

The Emperor put on a mighty performance that dismal July. Yet whilst he was battling with the mighty Swallowtail over the destiny of Butterfly of the Year, the Clouded Yellow sneaked off with the trophy. Clouded Yellows had started coming across the

Channel in early June. Subsequent waves occurred, augmented by the emergence of a home-grown brood. I must have seen at least 60 individuals that August, and went on to see well over a hundred during a wet September. Over 50 were seen skimming over the steep slopes of Fontmell and Melbury downs, south of Shaftesbury in north-east Dorset, on September 3rd, and a similar number on the downs between Folkestone and Dover mid-month. At the end of September I spotted that most magnetic of attractions for the Clouded Yellow – a Lucerne field in full bloom. Better still, it was on Prince Charles's organic farmland near Tetbury, a mile from home. It was in this field that my butterfly year ended, for the males gathered there in some numbers. But September was wet and gale-ridden, ending in a vicious storm on the 30th. The autumn rains blasted the 2000 butterfly season away.

Most of us have a year taken out of our lives at some point. For butterflyers in the UK, 2001 was such a year. To naturalists, including those with a love of butterflies, spring means Everything. They yearn for it, physically, mentally and spiritually and welcome it religiously. It fills them. But we did not have a spring in 2001: the weather was foul, and the countryside was closed due to a massive outbreak of foot & mouth disease. The outbreak started at a pig farm in Northumberland on February 21st and spread rapidly, largely due to livestock dealers, as at the time cattle and sheep were being treated widely as trading commodities and were moved from market to market as prices fluctuated. Dealers used their farms purely as holding places until market prices increased somewhere else. So the disease was spread primarily via the livestock market system, with contiguous spread occurring once animals arrived at their new destination. The main epicentres were in north Cumbria and the Borders, north Devon, and Herefordshire. The hearts of many true farmers were broken. The government panicked, a form of national hysteria broke out, and MAFF – the omnipotent Ministry of Agriculture, Fisheries and Food – seized control.

In early March the footpath network was closed down almost UK-wide and the National Parks were shut, then the Prime Minister assured us that 'The countryside is open for business.' It was not. The impact on the tourism and recreation industries was acute. Had the Government Chief Scientist's late March prognostication come true – namely that the disease would necessitate the slaughtering of half the UK's livestock and months of countryside closure – even wealthy organisations like the National Trust and RSPB would have been at risk, and much of the UK rural tourism and recreation industry would have collapsed. All the while the hope was that the virus would vanish naturally in sustained warm weather. A warm spring was essential.

April, however, was cold and grey. May offered two brief warm spells but much grot, and June was cloudy, though with a good spell late on. The only good news was that the introduced Large Blue population at Collard Hill had come through well.

Spring butterflying was restricted largely to rural lanes and National Trust gardens. These are alive with butterflies during good summers, but there were few of the insects around in early 2001. The lanes were full of displaced walkers. I managed to get smuggled in to Strawberry Banks, via a sympathetic owner's land, to keep up my studies of Marsh Fritillary larvae. No grazing animals were present, or likely to be, so there was no possibility of spreading the dreaded virus. Shorn of its dog walkers the Banks was a different place, full of Adders, birds, deer and Foxes. On one occasion a family of Stoats gambolled around me, showing no fear of a human being prepared to be still in nature. I was lucky, for much countryside in northern England remained closed until the end of the summer, including many of the Lake District fells. Nonetheless, the whole experience was severely traumatising, because of the denial of access to the countryside and the sheer lunacy of the situation – but at least I was not a livestock farmer.

Above all, the foot & mouth saga illustrated the firm grip agriculture has over rural Britain. Agriculture is our default setting for both the countryside and for Nature, and as it intensifies, through technological development, so each generation settles for a more homogeneous countryside and less and less Nature. The main challenge for nature conservation is to reverse that downward spiral.

Gradually, some worthwhile days came around. An expedition to the Portland quarries on June 17th found that the local race of the Silver-studded Blue had not yet started to emerge. However, the pupae can be found in the galleries of ant nests under flat stones. We found thirteen, in a small area of scree with isolated clumps of the larval foodplant, Bird's-foot Trefoil, and little else. Most were in the galleries of the common black ant *Lasius niger*, with which the butterfly seems to have a symbiotic relationship. We also found a Chalkhill Blue pupa under a stone. I took it home, but it proved to be parasitised – only, foolishly, I lost the parasite, a tiny wasp, before it could be identified. That's bad natural history.

Inspired by Ken Willmott's Purple Emperor assembly points on Bookham Common the previous year, I went in search of comparable sheltered high-point territories in Alice Holt Forest, and almost immediately struck gold, or rather Purple. I explored upslope of the huge sallow jungle in Abbots Wood Inclosure, to the crest of the forest. Here, across a lane, stood a small copse of mature oaks, sheltered from westerly winds by tall pines. Nothing. Then a Nuthatch shot out at speed, petrified by something – a male Emperor, in hot pursuit. Seconds later a pair of battling males erupted high above me. I had discovered a male territory every bit as good as those at Bookham. Call it Seven Ways Copse. At least half a dozen males were active in the copse that afternoon. A week later a dozen were flying there, though by then they were ageing, torn and battered. They were fighting to the last, even evicting the resident Spotted Flycatchers. Best of all, I met the owners: 'Come on in,' they said, delighted by the prospect of a rare butterfly doing something esoteric on their land. A difficult July was ending.

August was disappointing, with a scatter of warm days punctuated by spells of heavy rain. In such conditions butterflies do not live long, and whole populations can be blasted away. Somehow that miserable summer managed to generate a plague of Small and Essex skippers on Salisbury Plain, that vast expanse of rough rolling downland preserved as a military training ground. The security men at the check-in point to the MOD's West Down Camp were besieged by these small orange butterflies. It meant nothing to them that there were two highly similar species encrusting the walls of their hut and invading their kitchenette. The things were a darned nuisance. Along the nearby arable field margins every flower head held half a dozen or more, and in areas of tall False Oat-grass and Yorkshire-fog grass on the Plain proper these butterflies truly abounded.

The initial impact of foot & mouth on our butterflies was that some places became heavily over-grazed and others scarcely grazed or not grazed at all, due to the necessary restrictions on livestock movement. Part of Rodborough Common, called Swellshill Bank, lost its Cowslips when the National Trust's conservation herd of Belted Galloway cattle became impounded there, and heavily over-grazed the slope. The Cowslips have yet to reappear. Swellshill's Duke of Burgundy colony has been a shadow of its former self ever since. For the opposite reason, a large Grayling colony on Selsley Common, across the valley from Rodborough, collapsed in 2001, and never recovered, dying out a few years later. The butterfly had been breeding on small tussocks of fine-leaved grasses along the cattle walkways there. Annual grazing was essential, to maintain these precise breeding conditions, but cattle came on late in the summer of 2001, after foot & mouth restrictions had been lifted, and then made little impact. Grasses grew tall and thick there, accentuated by another wet summer. A disastrous break in continuity of habitat conditions had occurred. This pattern was replicated throughout the countryside.

The last item to be cast upon the funeral pyres that characterised the landscape of 2001 was MAFF itself. But Phoenix-like, Defra arose from the political flames. Within a decade it had absorbed nature conservation, at least outside of forests. Gradually, I ceased to be a nature conservationist.

❧

We desperately needed a great summer in 2002 to assuage the traumas of 2001. The year's first butterflying expedition was to a bat hibernation tunnel, where a few Peacocks and Small Tortoiseshells were hanging upside down, like bats, and Herald moths were also hibernating. The year's first butterfly seen on the wing was a Crow Swallowtail (*Papilio bianor*), flapping haphazardly on a grey late January day below Richmond Hill in south-west London. This dark giant of a butterfly is a common habitué of butterfly houses, and this one must have been an escapee from the nearby butterfly house at Syon Park. With butterflying, always expect the unexpected.

Winter was mild and wet, and March indifferent, but April was fair and turned things round. Spring butterflies, though, were emerging on the late side. The good April led to a sizeable emergence of Pearl-bordered Fritillaries. Impressive flights of this spirit of the spring were witnessed at Pignal, Ramnor and New Copse inclosures in the central New Forest, in Ashclyst Forest and at Hembury Rough Pastures in Devon, and in the Wyre Forest in the West Midlands. Earlier, I had cycled round large tracts of the New Forest looking for potential habitat, visiting parts of the Forest which had not been assessed for butterflies for many years, though in the past they had been great. Little of potential was found – just pockets of suitable habitat here and there, telling of the glories of yesterday. However, it was good to see the butterfly increasing and expanding in its traditional stronghold to the north-east of Brockenhurst.

The Pearl-bordered Fritillary's survival at Ashclyst Forest, on the National Trust's Killerton estate just north-east of Exeter, can be attributed to sustained conservation effort. The butterfly had become dependent on a 300-metre-long way-leave carved through broad-leaved woodland to supply electricity to a couple of chocolate box thatched cottages in the forest's centre. Keeping the way-leave Bracken stands in suitable condition for the butterfly has been a major challenge over the years, as not everything that has been done has actually worked. But in 2002, after much encouragement, the butterfly spread out from the way-leave rather spectacularly, to colonise newly opened rides elsewhere in the forest. We had turned the corner. At present, the Pearl-bordered Fritillary is doing well in Ashclyst, though the old way-leave has slowly declined in suitability. The truth is that it is all but impossible to hold vegetation change in check indefinitely and to keep even small, simple sites like the Ashclyst way-leave unchanged. All conservation effort can do in such situations is slow down the rate of change and buy a little precious time, and help butterflies to colonise elsewhere.

As an add-on to a work-related trip to the Dover cliffs in mid-June, I sneaked a couple of hours in East Blean Woods, near Herne. The Kent Wildlife Trust interpretation board there informed me that these Sweet Chestnut coppice woods hold the largest population of Heath Fritillary in the UK. As founder of the Friends of Bin Combe, the inhospitable combe on the east slope of Dunkery Beacon that holds the strongest of the Exmoor Heath Fritillary colonies, I was deeply affronted by this statement, especially as it was probably true. I walked straight into a thriving colony, in an area where chestnut coppice had recently been cut. Then, after walking down a dark tunnel of tall, overhanging chestnuts, the blinding light of another clearing revealed a second, larger colony. Here, a freshly emerged male was drying his wings, having just emerged from a pupa deep within a tussock of Creeping Soft-grass. A week later I was up on Exmoor, where haughty Bin Combe put on an even more edifying display – even if I did get eaten alive by horse flies and ticks in the process. Some places require you to be faithful to them, none more so than Bin Combe.

At last we were able to open Collard Hill as an open-access site for the Large Blue. The slope had been grazed to perfection and a seasonal warden was in place, to facilitate visits rather than to police anything – the challenge was to ensure that every visitor saw at least one Large Blue. This was radical, as hitherto the butterfly had, somewhat of necessity, been the domain of a rather private gentlemen's club. Initial visitors to Collard Hill included one determined old boy who had earnestly but fruitlessly sought this butterfly as a young man, and who was about to go into hospital for a double hip replacement. Getting him down the slope, and then back up again, proved decidedly troublesome, but he was a gentleman of considerable determination. It turned out that he had flown fifty bombing missions over Nazi Germany. You don't mess with folk like that. A Large Blue settled to bask right beside him, and in that moment he fulfilled his lifelong ambition to see every species of British butterfly.

On the last day of June the first Purple Emperor of the year appeared, beating the living daylights out of a Black Hairstreak at the wondrously named Drunkard's Corner, an ancient Blackthorn-lined lane that curls its way round the edge of Bernwood Forest, north-east of Oxford. The Emperor went on to make a disappointing July his own. He was not out in good numbers, in fact this was a decidedly poor year for this and the other high-summer forest species. By mid-July the White Admirals, for example, had been blasted away by foul weather. Only the Ringlet was in good numbers in the woods. But there was a determination about the Emperor's manner that year. An impressive number of male territories were found, in Alice Holt Forest in Hampshire, at Ashtead Common in Surrey, in my old woods back in West Sussex – Southwater Forest – and in Savernake Forest in Wiltshire. An incredibly useful survey technique had been discovered, and not merely by myself and my companion Ashley Whitlock, for Liz Goodyear and Andrew Middleton were making similar discoveries by searching for male territories in Hertfordshire. The one place that refused to reveal its secrets was Bentley Wood in south Wiltshire. This was I R P Heslop's heartland, where he collected most of the 196 Emperors in his collection. Despite having written an appreciative biography of the man whose writings inspired me as a teenager, I struggled to see Emperors in his old woods, and felt that I was intruding and unwelcome there – even when accompanied by his youngest daughter, Jane Murray. My diary for July 11th includes the curious comment: *I got the feeling that even now IRPH resents people Emperoring in his woods.* Somehow, people's experiences, memories and values become part of places with which they are intimately entwined – I am struggling to comprehend this, the collective memory of place.

Purple Emperor numbers in the little copse I had discovered on the edge of Alice Holt Forest the previous season, Seven Ways Copse, were at best half what they had been in 2001. One afternoon was particularly quiet: a female had appeared and a whole bevy of males had shot off after her. One by one they returned. One ragged male, with a badly pecked left forewing, perched high up on a partially shaded Beech branch, intermittently launching himself against passing birds and insects. The diary recalls that *Pecked Left Forewing was taken by a Spotted Flycatcher over the Beech. They ganged up on him: he attacked one but was taken by its partner from behind.* A couple of shredded wings softly spiralled through dappled sunlight to the ground. The 2002 Purple Emperor season had ended.

August was quite a reasonable month. At last butterflies started to appear on garden Buddleias. The two cabbage whites, in particular, were in goodly numbers, as they tend to be after a couple of poor summers. The month even brought an influx of Clouded Yellows. Within a couple of weeks they were widespread in southern Britain, and made the most of the sunniest September since 1991. It was as if the year was trying to turn things round, and to set up its successor as a proper butterfly season.

Drunkard's Corner

Here is a place outside of ordered time,
Where the same cows graze the clay mead,
And light spindles soft along a stippled lane
As if, perhaps, it has always rested so,
Filtered by ever-ancient blackthorn boughs
That tunnel haphazard over age itself,
Through summer, once more, and on again.

I cannot say how this lonely place
Took its name, a name of man,
For no man comes here, drunk or not,
No singer staggers along the ruts,
In time of slipping mud or kicking dust,
On Midsummer or on any other eve.

One act, or one man, long ago aroused this name,
And so it has ever rested so, and ever always will.
But here, still now, amongst the brambled tangles
A whitethroat scratches out his rusty song,
While an ancient peeling notice reads and pleads:
'Please close the gate', the gate that leads to time.

23 The Emperor's return

The next year, 2003, did not start well, with widespread flooding followed by lengthy cold spells that brought the first snow in southern England for a couple of winters. February stabilised things, steadily drying out the land. The first butterflies of the year took to the air on February 23rd, when my family and I were attending an anti-war demonstration at Fairford, Gloucestershire, in my case under the metaphysical banner of Butterflies for Peace. The diary records that *Rooks were building, cock Greenfinches displaying and buds swelling. Best of all, a gloriously eccentric middle-aged lady, dressed in a bright pink nylon fairy outfit, complete with wings and wand, was arrested by a butch-looking police lady for attempting to scale the airbase fence.* Parliament had spent seven hours debating whether to go to war in Iraq, compared to 700 debating the future of hunting.

March was sublime, dominated by anticyclones stationed over Scandinavia. It was the sunniest March since 1907. However, as so often happens in early spring, a chilly east wind developed, which kept day temperatures a little too cool for butterfly activity. It was, though, ideal caterpillar-hunting weather. At Strawberry Banks, 27 larval webs of Marsh Fritillary were closely studied (containing some 1500 larvae). These began to change their skins mid-month, a week earlier than in 2002. Thirteen of these webs proved to be free of parasitic wasps, and only six seemed to hold significant parasite numbers. A reasonable emergence of Marsh Fritillary butterflies was on the cards, weather permitting.

But the month belonged to Pearl-bordered Fritillary larvae. The first was found on March 2nd, in Cirencester Park Woods, basking in gentle sunshine on a dead bramble leaf. Later, on March 29th, one of my more bizarre butterflying experiences (or rather caterpillaring experiences) occurred, again in Cirencester Park Woods. Just after I had located three Pearl-bordered Fritillary larvae in a pocket of tree leaf litter and violets, the Vale of the White Horse Hunt appeared and utterly surrounded me. Diary: *This I chose to ignore, and they obliged me by returning the compliment. I had nothing polite to say to them.* The message is simple: Carry on caterpillaring.

Expeditions in search of Pearl-bordered Fritillary larvae also took place in Wyre Forest on the Shropshire/Worcestershire border, in Bentley Wood in south Wiltshire, in worked Hazel coppice woods near Stockbridge in Hampshire, and in the heartland of all butterflying, the New Forest. The Wyre was particularly exciting. There the mission was to determine where the butterfly was actually breeding – no easy task in a vast forest. Butterfly breeding grounds can be decidedly small, localised, discrete and short-lived, and do not necessarily correlate with where the adult butterflies are seen. Breeding can be restricted to tiny pockets scattered amongst an ocean of unsuitable terrain. That is very much the case in the Wyre, where Pearl-bordered Fritillary butterflies are seen in numbers in several places where they cannot possibly be breeding. The narrow linear meadows bordering the delightful Dowles Brook in Wyre are great for the adults, being sunny, sheltered, and rich in nectar-bearing flowers – only the violets on which this butterfly breeds are all but absent. Much of the Wyre is too acidic for the violets, though suitable violet habitat occurs in minute pockets. Somehow, the canny females find those isolated hot spots. Worse, the females have to find spots that are going to be suitable for the tiny baby larvae in early summer *and* the following spring, after hibernation.

In early April the Pearl-bordered Fritillary larvae wandered off to pupate. In Cirencester Park Woods, the adults started to emerge on April 22nd, with a bang. There was clearly going to be a mighty emergence. The Duke of Burgundy and his arch enemy the Dingy Skipper appeared early at Rodborough Common near Stroud, on April 15th, and immediately began squabbling. Grizzled Skipper was out nearby even earlier, on April 7th. More significantly, an influx of Painted Ladies took place on March 12th. A good butterfly season was developing, but would the weather hold?

April ended poorly, and then:

Diary, monthly summary: *May was a disgrace and undid the good work done by March and April. Eight days were spitefully vile. There was a spell of fine weather from the 4th to the 9th inclusive, when it seemed a fine month was developing, especially as the Painted Lady appeared in good numbers. [I saw 34 in Ashclyst Forest, East Devon, on the 6th, and 28 in the New Forest on the 7th.] However, it then lapsed into the odious pattern of clearing for the night and clouding up for the day. A horrid wet seven days developed, which effectively blasted the spring butterflies away, Pearl-bordered Fritillary included. The month ended well in the east of England.*

It did indeed, for I was in Norfolk. There, the Wall Brown was numerous: fifteen were seen basking in evening sunlight along a 50-metre section of flint wall near Burnham Overy. Painted Ladies were here too, worn males hurtling northwards, accompanied by a few Red Admirals. White Admiral larvae were full-grown, on Honeysuckle tangles in the woods around Sheringham Park and on West Runton Heath, a ridge-top heath which had become a wood in the absence of grazing. The trip was blessed with the first Swallowtail of the season too, just.

Diary, May 29th 2003: *Things had got pretty desperate on the Swallowtail front. Then, whilst driving along the road from Horsey to Somerton a resplendent Swallowtail flew across the road right in front of my car, heading seawards. In a truly memorable moment the car veered ditchwards in reverence to the Lord of the Broads, then miraculously righted itself when all seemed lost, perhaps through Divine intervention.*

Later that day a freshly emerged male was seen feeding on Red Campion at Hickling Broad. The sunshine accompanied me home to Gloucestershire.

June righted things, not least because it ended a run of six poor Junes. It was benign, without heavy or prolonged rain, gales and cold spells. The month began with a Spanish Plume wind, which brought in more Painted Ladies and a scatter of Red Admirals. Despite the poor May the butterfly season was running a week or so early: Marbled Whites and Ringlets were emerging well in the Cotswolds on June 13th, and White Admirals were out – very early – in Bernwood Forest, near Oxford, on the 15th.

One of the best butterfly shows in the British Isles is to be experienced around Midsummer Day at the Great Orme (or Great Orme's Head), by Llandudno in North Wales. The Great Orme is a massif of Carboniferous Limestone jutting out into the Irish Sea. It looks more Continental than British – French or Yugoslavian Dolomite, perhaps. It is grazed by wandering sheep and Kashmir goats whose ancestors were given to Queen Victoria by the Shah of Persia. I was there on June 24th in 2003, in sublime weather – cloudless and calm. Llandudno itself was hosting the Methodist Conference and also boasted a remarkable array of loose drain covers – every street went clang, ting, ping! The Great Orme was hosting spectacular emergences of its two specialist butterflies, the local races of the Silver-studded Blue and the Grayling. Both look unique, and truly abound on the Great Orme. The Silver-studded Blue here is minuscule and dark, with deep-blue females fringed by orange beading, subspecies *caernensis*. It breeds on Bird's-foot Trefoil in short turf. Many of the colonies here are vast – in fact it is hard to find a butterfly in greater abundance anywhere in the British Isles. In one spot, Happy Valley, or Wyddfid in Welsh, I counted 273 in fifteen minutes along 300 metres of path. In the evenings they gather in pockets of rough grass or on low bushes in sunny, sheltered hollows to bask communally before closing their wings and roosting head-down. These communal roosts provide some of the best wildlife photography opportunities on offer in our islands.

The Orme's race of the Grayling is small and pale. It flies earlier in the year than other Graylings, but otherwise behaves exactly like its cousins. On the Great Orme it is very much a butterfly of the crag and scar system, where the males battle amongst themselves and with the wind. I photographed one perched on the horn of a sleeping goat.

June ended strongly. On the 28th the first Purple Emperors appeared, four of them battling away over the line of tall poplars that fringes the western edge of Oakley Wood, in the heart of Bernwood Forest. They meant business, for testosterone levels were high. Nearby I released a captive-bred male, 'Percy', on the sallow bush on which I had found him as a tiny caterpillar the previous August. It was not possible to put him on the exact bough on which he had been found, as that had been wantonly lopped off during the winter. Obviously, I was meant to find, remove and rear him. The following day the Emperors were starting in Alice Holt Forest, down in Hampshire.

But before one could become absorbed by the Emperor there was unfinished business. A visit to Bircher Common, the Bracken-filled common north of Leominster in Herefordshire, found the High Brown Fritillary in the process of dying out. Conservation effort here had not sufficed, probably because too small an area had been maintained in suitable condition and, more crucially, because other Bracken slopes in the vicinity, under private ownership, had all become unsuitable. The matrix of habitat patches that this large and highly mobile butterfly requires had collapsed. This species can perhaps only be conserved at landscape (or metapopulation) level. Eight hectares (20 acres) of carefully maintained habitat will not suffice. I saw the last of Bircher's lovely High Browns that summer, a lone male on a tall Marsh Thistle. Down in Devon, though, the butterfly was thriving. A visit to Heddon valley on the Exmoor coast on July 1st found the butterfly in good numbers in several distinct areas, an intact metapopulation within the valley system. There was even a black one, an acute aberration. The diary relates: *I got over-excited, lost my balance and fell backwards down the steep slope into a gorse bush.* The black High Brown was not seen again. *Sic transit gloria mundi.*

I had been invited to stay at Seven Ways, on the edge of Alice Holt Forest, for my annual adventure into the Purple world. 'Come on in, Man,' they said, so I did. The window of the tiny mezzanine room they gave me overlooked the copse in which male Emperors were assembling, and offered wondrous views of the Purple Hairstreak's evening flight. Seven Ways was the UK centre of a movement called Sufi Way. Please do not think this is a religious sect, weird, wacky or otherwise. Sufism is really a framework for understanding and handling religion, and wider spirituality. Seven Ways advocated a highly westernised form of Sufism developed by Hazrat Inayat Khan (1882–1927), a sitar player and poet who brought the Sufi message to the West during the First World War. Of course, the denizens of Seven Ways understood my fixation with the Purple Emperor and, more importantly, what I was seeking, far better than I. They understood callings.

Sufi Way had been based there for decades, the house having been built by some of Inayat Khan's pioneer converts, from theosophy probably, and bequeathed to the movement. The house itself was not ancient, rather it was timeless. It had its own idiosyncrasies. A strange humming noise reverberated on still nights. Was it the electrics, they wondered? – for the wiring was decidedly dodgy. I knew that sound, it was a Nightjar churring away in a Bracken-filled clearing up the lane. Indeed, Henry the Nightjar, as he became known, was part of the place, sitting for hours on end on a high horizontal branch of a deformed Christmas tree. He made those hot July nights his own, even as the Emperor made Seven Ways Copse his own by day. One afternoon, when the air was loaded with Emperors, I found a blue Jay's feather lying in the dust, and placed it in my hatband. The Emperor of the Woods had claimed me back.

Based here, I could track the daily movements of male Purple Emperors. Few if any were truly resident in the copse, though the odd male would spend the night there if a bank of cloud curtailed the day. Most would depart the copse around 5 pm, dropping westwards down to the wooded slopes of the main body of Alice Holt. I followed them down in the evening, and them or others back up each midday. They were spending the mornings searching the sallow jungles a few hundred metres away westwards, down slope, in Abbots Wood Inclosure. Presumably they were searching for emerging females, then tiring of that they would ascend to the sheltered high point of Seven Ways Copse, and behave despicably. Most days there were at least half a dozen males present in or around the copse. Tussles of three or four males were regularly seen. At one point a male Painted Lady attempted to take over the favoured male territory. All hell broke loose, before the Lady was successfully removed. I would like to say that I regularly saw courtship flights and even witnessed pairings here, but the females generally avoided the place like the plague. Perhaps, like many a pub and club, it was full of males unsuccessful at the mating game.

A small gang of us systematically searched for male territories along the ridge that runs along the eastern edge of Alice Holt before it turns into the forest itself, and runs through its northern half. All told we found nine territories that were in regular use, the best of which were Seven Ways Copse itself, and scattered oaks and Sweet Chestnuts in a disused Forestry Commission car park at the northern end of Goose Green Inclosure by the village of Bucks Horn Oak. The latter was an embarrassment: I had discovered it back in 1983, but in a year when Emperors seemed to be everywhere, so I subsequently overlooked it, only realising its true significance late in the 2002 season. Half a dozen or more Emperors take up afternoon residency there.

At the end of the Purple Emperor season, safely back at work, I had to visit Wicken Fen, north-east of Cambridge. Wicken hurts me, for it has lost its soul, the majestic Swallowtail butterfly. After the New Forest, Wicken must be the most renowned historical locality for the collecting of Lepidoptera in Britain. Sadly, the Swallowtail died out there during the 1950s, due to massive habitat changes associated with the drainage of the surrounding land.

The surviving fen then vanished under a forest of Grey Willow and other scrub as the peat steadily dried out, and as the essential harvesting of reed and sedge ceased. Various attempts to re-establish the Swallowtail failed, before a lost cause was recognised. Although much of the scrub has now been cleared, re-establishing the Swallowtail is currently some way down the agenda, for the fen must first be made wetter for the butterfly's foodplant, Milk-parsley, and larger for this huge and highly mobile butterfly. Guilt wells up within me every time I visit Wicken, for I should be championing the return of *machaon*, but realistically I know that this is some way off. In late July 2003 the droves, or broad paths, were alive with nymphalid butterflies. The home-grown brood of Painted Ladies was hatching. I counted 95 in an hour and a half, feeding on Hemp Agrimony, thistles and, by the intriguingly named Cock-up Bridge, on Burdock. Red Admiral was even more numerous, as was the Small Tortoiseshell, but I had chosen not to count these. The Peacock, however, was even more profuse. It had become a great butterfly year.

On the way home I stopped off in BB's old woods, Fermyn Woods near Brigstock in east Northamptonshire. I had heard reports of goodly numbers of Purple Emperors in these woods but had not previously visited. No less a being than Robin Page had seen seven flying together – as many as I have ever seen together – and had eulogised the woods in a newspaper article. Within an hour I knew I was in the best Purple Emperor wood I had visited, and that I had found a new heartland. Never before had I seen such abundance of sallows over such a large area of woodland. BB would have been ecstatic. The Emperor season was ending that day: I saw just two, but this was their true empire.

Back home, our garden was alive with butterflies, particularly Small Tortoiseshells, with counts of this species ranging from 63 to 80 on the Buddleias. August burnt on in heat and drought, as the Azores High expressed itself wondrously over the British Isles. The average daily maximum temperature at Heathrow Airport was an impressive 26.4 degrees. Painted Ladies, Small Tortoiseshells and

Peacocks abounded. A visit to Watlington Hill in the Chilterns on August 4th, under a burning sun, found Silver-spotted Skippers zigzagging at breakneck speed low over their beloved short turf, and impossible to follow. Indeed, this small, fast-flying butterfly excels in heatwave conditions, and the temperature that day reached 30 degrees.

A long weekend on the Gower coast was necessary, primarily to celebrate a fiftieth birthday and to touch base with the man from Cwmdonkin Drive, Swansea, Dylan Thomas. The weather was cloudless, with searing heat by day and sweltering nights. We were staying in a hobbit-hole sunk into the dunes at Whiteford Burrows, a tin shack of green corrugated iron built in the 1920s as a shooting lodge, and sinking slowly into the sand, and into time itself. Dylan would have adored it. Painted Ladies abounded, feeding on Sea Rocket and Sea-holly in the fore dunes. Grayling colonies were scattered along the limestone crags and, more locally, in the sand dunes, where the butterfly seemed to be breeding on Sand Sedge. A strong second brood of Small Blues was showing, in the dune slacks. The final diary entry for the month reads: *The month ended with Mars prominent in the south-eastern sky, the closest it's been to earth for 6000 years. It looked like stationary aeroplane headlights.* And then, more lucidly: *August 2003 will live forever in entomological history.*

At the end of August the phone rang. It was Gail Jeffcoate from Dorking: the Long-tailed Blue had appeared along the old coach road at Denbies Hillside, the scarp slope of the North Downs to the west of the Mole Gap – on NT land. This is one of the rarest of our migrant, or vagrant, butterflies, a once-in-a-lifetime butterflying experience. It was the sort of situation in which everything has to be dropped, excuses made and apologies delivered later. Serendipitously, I was due to head past anyway, en route to Dover. But the morning of September 1st was dominated by stagnant cloud. Would it clear? At 2 pm a large hole suddenly appeared in the cloud cover, and a worn male Long-tailed Blue instantly appeared, flitting about jerkily, like a Hairstreak, over clumps of Broad-leaved Everlasting-pea (perennial sweet pea) which grew along the old coach road banks. A group of us watched him for nearly an hour, feeding on the pea flowers. Then he was off and away at speed, and was not seen again. But a female was present, and had been busy, laying eggs on virtually all the pea clumps along a kilometre of south-facing bank. The plant was not supposed to be there at all, being a garden escapee, but that afternoon it justified its existence. Gail, Ken Willmott and I found over 100 eggs, on the sepals of the pea flowers. Some of these eggs had already hatched, and the tiny larvae had burrowed into the developing pods, for Long-tailed Blue larvae feed within the pods of the pea family.

Inspired, the following day I searched Kingsdown Leas cliff on the coast near Dover. Here Broad-leaved Everlasting-pea abounds, but there was no sign of the Long-tailed Blue, adults or eggs. I was ten years early, for the butterfly colonised Kingsdown Leas spectacularly in 2013. Back at Denbies, the eggs were vanishing. Was it the dreaded butterfly collectors, snipping off the flower heads? Anger rose, then it became apparent that deer were browsing the pea flowers avidly – though even without the unwelcome attentions of the deer the heavy frosts of mid-October would most likely have put paid to what could have been a sizeable brood that autumn. In the event the butterfly fizzled out at Denbies in early September. Curiously, one of the first records of the Long-tailed Blue breeding in the UK was from close by, for in 1952 it was discovered to be breeding outside Ranmore post office at the top of the Denbies Hillside escarpment – on Broad-leaved Everlasting-pea. In 2003, then, the butterfly came back home.

The autumn of 2003 was deeply memorable. It gave us the September and October we should have had at the end of the long hot summer of 1976. The Clouded Yellows were in, and in goodly numbers too. September was remarkable, especially in the South-east where grass remained brown all month, cattle were being fed hay and straw, trees went into senescence early, Ash trees aborted their keys and Elder bushes their berries. By the end of October the trees wore their late-November colours. Some unduly stressed trees died. The autumn rains held off until the end of the month, then they rather made up for lost time. Before then, the Indian summer enabled many butterflies to fit in extra broods. Second-generation White Admirals appeared in several southern woods. I even searched, over-optimistically, for second-brood Purple Emperors. In butterflying, always push limits. It is what the butterflies themselves do.

24 *Hairstreaks to the fore*

It was obvious that 2004 was going to be difficult: the Hogmanay celebrations in Edinburgh were cancelled, though the forecast storm never actually materialised. At the start of the year I visited a new site, West Woods near Marlborough in Wiltshire. Here the boys of Marlborough College and members of the town's natural history society had collected butterflies in abundance – modern rarities like the High Brown and Marsh fritillaries and the Duke of Burgundy. That was way back in the Victorian and Edwardian eras, but like so many of our glorious woods West Woods was sacrificed on the altar of twentieth-century forestry, mainly in the form of monotonous Beech plantations. The sad thing was that I could feel its rich entomological history; there were fragments, tiny vistas into what had been – secret glades, bramble bushes, sallow trees, a Blackthorn patch. Peacocks were hibernating on the ceiling of a derelict woodman's shed. Such sheds used to be commonplace when forests were regularly worked, but nowadays forestry contractors periodically arrive, as mechanised as modern farm contractors, blitzkrieg huge areas, and disappear. The impact on butterfly populations is usually negative. Many woodland butterflies seek to follow the woodcutter, in succession, and need continuity of habitat supply within a woodland system – a little-and-often approach.

Things did improve. The first butterfly of the year was, incredibly, a Painted Lady, seen from the Isle of Wight ferry on February 4th. Another was seen at Yarmouth, fresh-looking too, and others were reported from Portland Bill bird observatory. This species is forever testing the limits of existence, pressing against its range edges. Winter immigrations are not that unusual, at least in the climate-change era. I had gone over to the island to look at the feral goat grazing regime on Bonchurch Down, Ventnor, where goats were doing a splendid job at browsing out Holm Oak and Elder invading the chalk grassland slopes. We saw a kid being born. Sadly though, the Painted Lady flattered to deceive, for 2004 became only a modest year for it.

Spring produced just the odd fine day. Orange-tips appeared late, and were then forced to sit out some lousy weather. On May 2nd, a pair of Orange-tips that had sat for five consecutive wet days in our garden, on Tulip and Garlic Mustard heads respectively, became active as soon as the sun reappeared. They mated almost immediately. That's spring butterflies for you, great survivors, but six or seven consecutive wet days might have proven too much for them; they can take so much, but not too much, and the vagaries of spring are often too much.

Miraculously, after eight rotten days May materialised into the best since 1992, as high-pressure systems bubbled up nicely. Pearl-bordered Fritillaries made the most of it. Their numbers were not high, as their larvae had endured a difficult March and April, but at least eight colonies were present in Cirencester Park Woods and good flights were witnessed at Hembury on south Dartmoor, Ashclyst Forest in east Devon, Cwm Soden near New Quay on the Ceredigion coast and in Parkhill and Pignall inclosures in the New Forest near Brockenhurst. May 2004 belonged essentially to this fritillary. With butterflying, it often happens that a single species lays claim to a particular month.

June actually behaved itself, providing a number of fine sunny days without ever developing into a great summer month. It started on the Isle of Wight, where the Glanville Fritillary was having a bumper year, not least at Compton Chine, where 266 were counted in a 20-minute circuit of the main flight area, at the foot of the flight of wooden steps which have to be repaired at the end of each winter. The old butterfly collectors would have liked this emergence, for several aberrations were noted, mainly with reduced black vein markings on the wing uppersides, and a blurring of markings on the undersides (probably ab. *uhryki*). The butterflies had spread well the previous May, to form or strengthen colonies all along the nearby downs, breeding in areas where gorse had been either mown or burnt. The flora, and its associated insects, relishes the windows of opportunities these actions provide.

Not too many British butterfly enthusiasts have seen Large Blue, Black Hairstreak and Swallowtail on three successive days, plus Wood White, Duke of Burgundy, Small Blue and the first Meadow Brown of the year. But the Large Blue began to emerge at Daneway Banks in the Cotswolds on June 5th, along with the first Meadow Brown; Black Hairstreaks and Wood Whites were flying at Whitecross Green Wood in Buckinghamshire on the 6th, and on the 7th I found myself in the Norfolk Broads, where Swallowtails were emerging strongly. Catfield Fen put on a terrific show of magnificent Swallowtails – 34 sightings in a couple of hours along the path bordering the Butterfly Conservation reserve, mainly of males feeding on early bramble flowers. But the following day I encountered the dark side of the Swallowtail. After a meeting in an anaerobic office in Norwich, I escaped to a site on the edge of Hickling Broad that had been highly recommended. The diary account explains all:

> Diary, June 8th 2004: *The site was thickly fringed by dense, dangerously wet carr with the highest density of mosquitoes I've ever encountered. They attacked me viciously as soon as I hopped over the gate. After failing to get to the recommended open area, as the ground was too wet and clearly too dangerous for lone working, I retreated to an open glade. Here Milk-parsley abounded, amongst low reed and sedge, but I failed to see a single Swallowtail or find any eggs.*

Worse:

> *I ended up in an oxygen-free room in a rotten B&B next to an all-night-lorry road. Some of the mosquito bites became infected and remained troublesome until mid-July, and I swear they attracted more mosquitoes.*

This was one of only two occasions when I felt in danger whilst butterflying in this country, and dipped out on health and safety grounds. The other was a manic attempt to flush up Large Heaths on Rannoch Moor in the Highlands, in precipitous rain.

Precipitous rain dominated July 2004 as well, a month that commenced with a gale and deteriorated from there. The Purple Emperor and White Admiral were effectively written off, though Silver-washed Fritillary flourished, as it seems better equipped to cope with bad weather. The Emperor season had started ominously, on Midsummer Day. I was attending a meeting, deep underground in Defra HQ, Horseferry Road, in Westminster. The diary relates: *I was captive in another world, and all the time the iris were calling for me, I could feel them emerging.* They were too – the text message came in as I was travelling home. Fred and George, the two Purple Emperors that I had found as larvae the previous late summer, were dutifully returned to their place of origin, only they had transmogrified into Frederica and Georgina, big girls too. They may not have fared at all well, for deluge after deluge fell in the hours and days after their release. At one point I walked out of the Purple Emperor season and returned back to work. Things were that desperate. Curiously, though, the Holly Blue made one of its periodic bids for freedom, appearing in surprisingly good numbers, only to be blasted to kingdom come. The diary concludes: *This goes down as The Lost July.*

August had to save the show, and some butterfly had to redeem the year, by claiming it as its own. The answer came on August 1st, a wonderful hot sunny day after a clear night with a harvest moon. I arrived at Whitecross Green Wood, in the old Bernwood Forest woodland complex near Oxford, at 10.30, later than intended, and saw 20 Brown Hairstreaks, without making much effort. Sixteen of them were on, or even in, the Ash trees that are scattered throughout this nature reserve, which the Forestry Commission started to coniferise before selling it off to the county wildlife trust. Sixteen represented a good start to the Brown Hairstreak season. Despite a dismally wet August, memorable for the Boscastle floods

in which TV news showed four-wheel-drive vehicles being washed out to sea, the Brown Hairstreak did well. The eggs had hatched late, so young larvae had been spared the worst of the spring weather; then larval development was blessed by fine weather during May and June, and the insects were safely inside their pupal cases by the time the July monsoons arrived. This elusive butterfly was equally impressive in north Wiltshire, at Noar Hill in Hampshire, and near Tidworth on the Hampshire/Wiltshire border. There, in early September I counted 36 apparent individuals in a day, the second highest day tally I have ever made – and I would have seen more had I started earlier, before 9 am.

The Brown Hairstreak has much in common with the Purple Emperor, occurring at low population density and being a canopy-dwelling butterfly which is active only intermittently. Above all, it is both elusive and evasive, and can be downright infuriating, not least because it takes days off. Unlike His Imperial Majesty it does visit flowers – mainly brambles, but also Angelica, Hemp Agrimony and ragworts, and the males are only modestly belligerent, and then only during a happy hour of indulgence in the early morning, as the day warms up. Butterfly people who work Purple Emperors tend to gravitate to Brown Hairstreaks as the Emperor season ends, perhaps because Brown Hairstreaking actually generates worse eye strain and neck ache, and because the Hairstreak is almost as enigmatic. After having been grossly neglected throughout the long and glorious history of entomology in this country the Brown Hairstreak suddenly became popular during the early noughties – and in 2013 it became only the second butterfly to gain its own website and blog, after the Purple Emperor. The season ended with a late flush of Clouded Yellows and a modest show of Holly Blues, including a partial third brood that lasted into mid-November.

My last butterflying expedition of 2004 was opportunistic and spontaneous. In early December, whilst standing around in a circle with thirty colleagues, discussing a coastal retreat scheme on the Essex marshes, I started looking for the opaque lozenge-shaped eggs of the Essex Skipper in grass tussocks. No one noticed, for nature conservationists enter some bizarre Buddhist state whilst standing around in circles in the rain, so I carried on, and became absorbed. A good two dozen of these overwintering eggs were found, in strings of three, four or five, several centimetres above ground level in the sheaths of old Cock's-foot and Sea Couch flower stalks. Always go butterflying, it helps. Perhaps the collective noun for an encirclement of nature conservationists should be 'a waffle'?

Winter had to make up for the lack of a proper summer. It seemed that the seasons were merging into one. The winter of 2004/05 was devoted to searching for Brown Hairstreak eggs in the hedges and thickets of the Oxford Clay vale north-west of Swindon. A small group of us systematically surveyed a large chunk of what was formerly known as the Forest of Braydon. Time ago, Braydon consisted of rough boggy pastures belonging to small dairy and stock farms, interspersed by woods and copses of oak and Hazel. Edward Thomas knew it well as a youth, having relatives in Swindon, but it is now scarcely recognisable as the rural idyll he describes in the second chapter of his first piece of rural prose, *The Woodland Life*. That chapter is entitled 'Lydiard Tregose', but the parish has largely been absorbed within the urban sprawl of Swindon. Through sheer tenacity the Brown Hairstreak has survived, mainly around a scatter of old ridge and furrow meadows.

The butterfly's distinctive white eggs are relatively easy to find during the winter, and can be easier to spot than the adult butterflies. Most are laid in forks on Blackthorn stems. But the females strongly favour young, dynamic growth, especially along advancing scrub edges. Also, as I had discovered in Hampshire in 1982, grey-stemmed growth is strongly preferred to the shiny red growth that occurs in many places, and browsed growth is largely avoided. The Brown Hairstreak should be a moderately common butterfly in landscapes where Blackthorn hedges abound, and has no business being a national rarity. However, scrub is deeply resented in today's countryside, particularly invading scrub edges, even on many nature reserves, and the vast majority of eggs laid on hedges are destroyed by hedge cutting. The potential for bringing this butterfly back is enormous, given more sympathetic hedge management and a more positive attitude to scrub as a habitat, not least because the butterfly appears to be a great wanderer.

Today, groups of devotees survey and monitor Brown Hairstreak eggs virtually throughout the butterfly's range. It is the staple winter activity of several of the Butterfly Conservation regional and county branches. Participants are known to carry on, regardless, in heavy rain, or when the Blackthorn is white with hoar frost, or even when snow is falling. On occasions some have been known to carry on after dark, to finish a length of hedge by torchlight or even by car headlights. Many a dog walker has been alarmed by this activity. One group of egg hunters was accused of setting snares, another of stealing fairies.

Early in January 2005 Butterfly Conservation HQ arranged a mini conference on the ecology and conservation of the Brown Hairstreak at Brinkworth, a hilltop settlement village in the Forest of Braydon. This was the society at its very best, with fifty or so friends of the Brown Hairstreak meeting to share experiences, knowledge and ideas. People had travelled from as far away as Pembrokeshire and Lincolnshire. The amount of effort being put into unravelling the mysteries of this enigmatic butterfly, and determining its conservation needs, was hugely impressive. Despite the fact that Professor Jeremy Thomas had conducted invaluable research into this insect, as part of his PhD, a vast amount of new knowledge had been determined. The butterfly has become far better known, both within and outside conservation circles. It now features intermittently as a local speciality in *The Archers* on Radio 4.

During my perambulations in the Forest of Braydon early in 2005 I discovered something quite remarkable, a derelict farm, of some 80 ha (200 acres). Rundown farms were moderately commonplace in the nether regions of Somerset during my childhood, but I had not encountered one for decades. This example was all the more remarkable because the fields were unimproved ridge-and-furrow meadows, which had been spared modern fertilisers and sprays. The holding had been a small stock farm, where a few beef cattle were raised. Early in 2005 the fields consisted of dense mats of grasses, with huge tussocks of Cock's-foot and Tufted Hair-grass and a thick layer of dead litter. They were so difficult to walk through that the village dog walkers had kept away. It was forsaken, apart from by Nature. The smaller herbs were of course heavily suppressed, though taller herbs such as Common Sorrel, Betony, Devil's-bit Scabious, Marsh Thistle and Saw-wort were prominent enough. Now that's Marsh Fritillary country. Sure enough, larval searches in late winter revealed a couple of sizeable colonies – just as the butterfly was feared to have died out in the Forest of Braydon. A few years later, the farm was sold and brought back into productive agriculture.

The spring of 2005 came and went. I rather missed it, as my mother died in late March. She had supported me through thick and thin. A male Brimstone flew along over her coffin as it was being carried up to the church. So that was *her butterfly*! Butterflies have the remarkable habit of appearing at times of bereavement.

May started and ended well, but sandwiched in between were three dire weeks – especially in Gloucestershire, which seems to suffer the worst of any adverse spring weather. In Cirencester Park Woods, Pearl-bordered Fritillary colonies at the northern, higher end of the woods emerge a week later than those at the southern, lower end. In 2005 the southern colonies were blasted away by lousy weather but those in the north emerged as the weather improved, and fared well. Never put your eggs in one basket, particularly if you're a butterfly.

June was also a major disappointment. The first six days were despicable, and effectively wrote off the spring-flying butterflies, again. Some short spells of hot sunny weather followed, though they were ended by pulses of bad weather. Violent thunderstorms on Midsummer Day caused a vast amount of damage, and not merely to butterfly populations: the first day of the Glastonbury Festival was wakened at dawn by a deluge that deposited 5 centimetres of rain there, and washed tents away. Somehow, I managed a sublime three-day expedition to the Norfolk Broads, where the Swallowtail was at peak season, seemingly in good numbers. The highlight was the discovery of a colony on the eastern edge of Duck Broad, on the western edge of the National Trust's Heigham Holmes holding. From the raised bank here one could watch eight or more males patrolling over the reed beds that fringe the open water. They were, of course, utterly inapproachable, without a boat.

The diary states that July started with *A thoroughly depressing day, of endless drizzle, spent vacating our beloved office in happy Cirencester.* We were being moved to a new open-plan office in Swindon. The damage this did to my personal relationship with Nature was immense, and not simply because my job changed and I became more office-bound – crucially, lunch-hour butterflying ceased, as there was nowhere nearby worth visiting. The diary entry concludes: *This whole year is in free-fall. Only one thing can save it, the* iris…

The Emperor season started promisingly. On Saturday July 2nd, as I entered the Straits Inclosure in Alice Holt Forest, the

Aussie skipper was out to the first ball bowled. Another Australian wicket fell as I entered Goose Green Inclosure, where the Emperor season exploded with a trio of battling males. This promising start, however, heralded only a modest Emperor season. Seven Ways again provided a few days' shelter from the storm, and Alice Holt some rewarding days surveying for male territories along the ridge that runs lengthways through the forest, but Seven Ways had been put up for sale and was emptying itself, with a view to relocating to California. The message I was handed by the Sufi community was clear, and hugely challenging: Develop the spiritual side of butterflying. This message was not enthusiastically received. 'Not me,' I thought, 'I'm irresponsible.' As I was leaving I picked a pristine Jay's feather out of a flowerbed.

As the door to Seven Ways Copse was closing, another door was opening elsewhere.

Diary, July 16th 2005: *Fermyn Woods, Northamptonshire. Previously visited briefly late in the great 2003 Emperor season. Today I saw one of the best flights of Purple Emperor I've ever seen – and the locals (Doug Goddard & Co.) say that this is very much an average* iris *season here! I was absolutely right in 2003: this is the best* iris *wood I've seen since Straits Inclosure in the mid-1970s. It must support the largest population in the country, by a long way. The reason is obvious: the quality and quantity of sallow is greater than elsewhere, seemingly as a standard feature of clearings and rides on Boulder Clay. Even fellings from conifer plantations here are choked with sallows. All told, I saw about 32 males and 10 distinct females.*

Another heartland had been established.

But then July ended in another wet spell. The roof of our wonderful new office leaked spectacularly. Buckets and mops were everywhere. Men with giant sealant guns gradually filled the cracks. Incredibly, August was genuinely good, though the few poor days that occurred tended to coincide with weekends. The month commenced at the Kingcombe Centre in west Dorset, where Oates's butterfly weekend was running again, after a five-year break. The month then belonged to the Brown Hairstreak. The first was seen at Lydlinch Common, near Sturminster Newton, on August 2nd, in the same Ash tree which the insect had been using in 1997. The Kingcombe group also visited the new Butterfly Conservation reserve at nearby Alners Gorse, where three species of Hairstreak were seen – Brown, Purple and White-letter. Things were looking up. A patch of grassy rubble in Swindon (now the site of a Tesco Express store) even revealed a small colony of Essex Skippers.

Brown Hairstreaks were emerging well, but on Sunday August 7th, my birthday, butterflying was affected by a tumultuous end to the second Test match, at Edgbaston. Australia began the day needing 107 to win with just two wickets left, and nearly got them. Gloom and despondency descended on all loyal Brits, despite the sunshine – only for England to win by two runs. Millie and I were out Brown Hairstreaking in the Forest of Braydon meadows; or rather one of us was butterflying, whilst listening ardently to the cricket on the radio, the other was reading Chaucer under an oak tree. The diary recalls that *A fresh male flew joyously round us in celebration of England's great victory.*

August was devoted to studying Brown Hairstreaks in the Forest of Braydon, whilst listening to England regaining the Ashes. The object was to gain some understanding of the insect's population structure in the district. In other words, discover where they were, when, and in what numbers; where the males were assembling, which Ash trees they were favouring; and above all, try to work out what they were doing, and why. Although I had seen Brown Hairstreak annually since 1969, and had spent countless hours looking either at it or for it at Noar Hill, I scarcely knew it. In Braydon, in 2005, they were found to be occurring in low numbers locally throughout the Blackthorn hedge system, though favouring certain spots, usually the more sheltered pockets. A number of favoured Ash trees were found, most of which are still in use today.

IN PURSUIT OF BUTTERFLIES

But after the males start to die off, usually in late August, the females seem to disperse away from these activity centres, at least in favourable weather, as was the case in September 2005. The last of the year was seen on October 9th, so worn, battered and scaleless that it took me several minutes to identify it.

Some Cotswold places

And butterflies in their disorder ...

Laurie Lee

The Cotswold Hills lie on Jurassic Limestone and run north-east from Jane Austen's Bath up towards Shakespeare's Stratford-on-Avon. They consist of a steep west-facing escarpment, and a broad gentle dip slope that runs away eastwards towards Oxford and is dissected by a series of minor river valleys. Today, away from the steeper slopes the Cotswolds are dominated by arable farming, but long ago this was the centre of the medieval wool trade. The legacy of wool, and its associated wealth, is illustrated by the spires of churches, built ostentatiously from honeyed Cotswold stone. The slopes are either wooded, mainly with Ash or Beech, or covered in limestone grassland. After Rabbits were killed off by myxomatosis most of the grasslands, or 'banks' to use the local name, became dominated by coarse grasses and scrub. Many slopes reverted to Ash woodland.

One of the largest and richest areas of limestone grassland is Rodborough Common, a 100-hectare (250-acre) promontory that towers above the suburbanised Stroud valleys and which adjoins the flatter, archaeologically rich Minchinhampton Common and its small satellite commons. These commons are owned by the National Trust and are designated as SSSI. Rodborough is also a Special Area for Conservation, the only limestone grassland SAC in the Cotswolds. The commons are grazed by cattle run by local commoners, between early May and the autumn. Although Minchinhampton Common is quite heavily grazed, certainly from a butterfly perspective, the steep flanks of Rodborough are decidedly under-grazed, as stock only venture off the flat top during summer droughts. To counter this, in 1999 the Trust developed a conservation herd of Belted Galloway cattle which grazed the slopes inside temporary electric fencing pennings. The commoners have now taken over the running of this essential herd.

Rodborough was given to the National Trust in 1937 by Thomas Bainbrigge Fletcher (1878–1950), former Naval Paymaster and, later, Imperial Entomologist in India – surely the most glorious title the Empire and the Raj ever combined to produce. Bainbrigge Fletcher was a well-respected figure in entomology and a specialist in micro-moths. Consequently, he persuaded many of the leading entomologists of the interwar years to survey his land. Today, Rodborough seems hugely proud of its entomological heritage and makes visiting entomologists welcome.

As is the case in most of the Cotswolds, Rodborough's steep slopes are dominated by Tor-grass and Upright Brome grass (CG5 in the language of the National Vegetation Classification), though prevalent thin soil conditions mean that these thuggish grasses only become genuinely rank where deeper soil has collected along the old cattle-walk terraces that traverse the slope contours. Amongst these rough grasses exists a rich flora: Common Rock-rose occurs extensively as an underlying carpet, and there are drifts of Horseshoe Vetch, Chalk Milkwort, Cowslip and, less prominently, Bird's-foot Trefoil and Wild Thyme. Kidney Vetch occurs in gaps in the sward, becoming numerous in places after a hot summer in which grass growth has been checked. Buried in the grass litter is much Hairy Violet. All these, bar the Milkwort, are butterfly larval foodplants. There are also many butterfly nectar plants, particularly scabiouses and knapweeds, though Marjoram, a favourite nectar source on southern chalk downs, is scarce here and in the Cotswolds generally. The slopes of Rodborough turn yellow with Cowslip, vetch and rock-rose flowers in May, then pink with thyme and orchids in June, before the fading grasses take over in late summer, and the flanks take on a straw-like hue.

This flora enables a wide range of downland butterflies to occur. In early spring Green Hairstreaks are numerous, appearing sometimes as early as late March. The Duke of Burgundy has several colonies along the foot of Rodborough's steep east- and west-facing flanks – usually three sizeable colonies and three or four tiny, satellite colonies, but much depends on the vagaries of spring weather. His Grace moves around a fair bit on Rodborough, for butterflies can freely wander there. Dingy Skippers are numerous, but the Grizzled Skipper is all but absent, as is its main foodplant, Wild Strawberry. Brown Argus and Small Blue are ubiquitous both here and elsewhere on the Cotswold grasslands. Marbled Whites and Ringlets abound from mid-June through to late July, when they suddenly finish. The Dark Green Fritillary has occasional years of plenty, but is sometimes seen only singly. Several spots along the slopes support colonies of the Chalkhill Blue, which usually appear around July 25th and linger on into September. These colonies ebb and flow acutely, for no obvious reason. The sward is too dense and coarse for Grayling and Silver-spotted Skipper, though both occurred in the not-distant past, when the slopes were well grazed by Rabbits. In the early 2000s the Adonis Blue mysteriously, perhaps miraculously, reappeared, after an absence of some fifty years, and has established some impressive colonies along the slopes. Bainbrigge Fletcher's records indicate that the Large Blue occurred on Rodborough Common during the 1890s.

The commons are used extensively for recreation, being the green lung of the ribbon-like development in the Stroud valleys, though there are many secret, unfrequented spots, mainly at the foot of precipitous slopes. Rodborough Common boasts its own ice-cream factory, Winstones of Rodborough, which was established there in 1925 and is open almost every day of the year.

On hot summer days it attracts, rightly, a veritable multitude, and also sends ice-cream vans onto various other parts of the commons. Winstones is a glorious ice-cream empire, and a fundamental part of the spirit of the Stroud commons. Kite flying is prominent on windy days on the commons, and Minchinhampton Common boasts the country's first organic golf course. Of course, dog walking is now pre-emptory, especially on Rodborough where it is a 24/7/365 activity. Dog walkers almost exclusively confine themselves to the slope tops there, not least for the panoramic views – across the Severn to the Forest of Dean and the Welsh hills blueing in the distance. Occasionally a ball bounces down towards a lone naturalist out butterflying on the lower slopes, followed by a panting dog. The slope bottoms are littered with lost balls, Frisbees and the like. Each Christmas, a group of dog walkers decorates a prominent Hawthorn tree on the slope top, with tinsel and baubles and Christmas cards from their dogs – to the place. This act exemplifies the extent to which the commons are deeply loved and revered. The commons also host an interesting night life, but that may best be left to the imagination. At midnight on New Year's Eve, however, one can look down from the heights of Rodborough onto spectacular firework displays erupting from the surrounding valleys. Without doubt, Rodborough, with its Skylarks and Meadow Pipits, offers interesting and unique experiences. It is a quintessential part of the Cotswold experience, as integral as the poet Laurie Lee's heartland, which lies a few kilometres to the north at Slad.

Some 5 kilometres eastwards up the Frome valley from Rodborough nestles a hidden side combe, known locally as Strawberry Banks, below the perched village of Oakridge. Surrounded by dense and ancient Beech woodland, the Banks consist of a few acres of SSSI limestone grassland on a west-facing slope. This is a world apart, a place of pensive mood unpenetrated by traffic noise, where a rushing stream hidden in the combe bottom murmurs melodically to all who would listen, where bird song resonates wondrously, and where meditative Buzzards drift slowly overhead. The Banks are in the stewardship of the Short family, who understand the place profoundly, truly belonging there, and run the 4 hectares (10 acres) as a nature reserve in partnership with the Gloucestershire Wildlife Trust. In consequence, Strawberry Banks is a most contented place. The flora is rich, containing Lesser Butterfly-orchids, much Dyer's Greenweed and drifts of Kidney Vetch, though some classic downland plants are absent, notably Common Rock-rose and Horseshoe Vetch – together with their associated butterflies. The deeper soils, on the lower reaches of what by Cotswold standard is only a modest slope, support swathes of Devil's-bit Scabious. In September, these lower slopes haze over with the purple flowers of this plant. The butterflies of early autumn home in here, to feed up prior to hibernation. Brimstones then overwinter in Ivy tangles on the nearby Beech trunks, Peacocks in hollow trees, and Commas amongst the Beech leaf litter.

This is the heartland of the Marsh Fritillary, the only place in the Cotswolds where this rare butterfly maintains a permanent – or rather, long-term – population. During sequences of poor springs and wet summers the population plunges – as low as 52 individual larvae recently. Occasionally, when Gloucestershire's neurotic spring climate actually allows a series of clement springs, the butterfly sallies forth to colonise other slopes in the vicinity, sometimes reaching as far as Rodborough Common. During the remarkable Marsh Fritillary expansion phase of 1982–1985 the butterfly colonised much of the southern Cotswolds, reaching as far as Painswick and the southern flanks of Cheltenham, to the north-west and north. Dingy Skipper and Small Blue also occur in good numbers on Strawberry Banks, Green Hairstreak breeds merrily on Dyer's Greenweed and hangs about on Hawthorn and Crab Apple blossom, and during high summer Marbled White and Ringlet abound, along with modest numbers of Dark Green Fritillary. Formerly, a tiny colony of the Duke of Burgundy existed, but it was lost when the all-important Cowslips succumbed to drought during hot summers in the mid-1990s. The Banks are grazed in autumn, usually by ponies but occasionally by cattle. Here, at last, is a place at peace with itself.

Head eastwards, up and out of the Frome valley, through sleepy Sapperton, and just before Cirencester (Roman Corinium) stands the dark mass of Cirencester Park Woods, some 805 hectares (2000 acres) of silvicultural woodland on terrain that has been wooded for centuries. The woods lie on land that rises gently from Hailey Wood, by the village of Coates in the south, through Oakley Wood in the centre, to Overley Wood at the north end. The woods are part of a vast estate that has been in the ownership of the Bathurst family since 1715. They have a varied history. The old medieval coppices are no longer traceable but the embankments of a medieval deer park are still prominent, as are the broad straight rides and intersections of a designed landscape laid out in 1718 under the direction of the poet Alexander Pope. There is a long tradition of silviculture here, for the woods are renowned for having hosted early experiments with continental varieties of Beech. Consequently, the woods are not SSSI. The late Earl Bathurst was a champion of twentieth-century silviculture, and introduced a number of conifer species to the estate – the usual motley crew of Corsican Pine, hybrid larch, Norway Spruce and Western Red Cedar. Until he died, in 2011, the woods were intensively managed: almost every year two or three blocks of mature trees, 1–3 hectares in size, were felled, and the land replanted with a mix of trees – conifers or conifer and broad-leaved mixes in the main, though fellings of old Beech and Pedunculate Oak were by and large replanted with those species. Young plantations were assiduously weeded, and herbicide was often sprayed between rows of young trees to control brambles and coarse grasses. The estate is not without its idiosyncrasies: public access is permitted on foot and horseback, from 8 am to 5 pm, but cycles and dogs are prohibited. Dog walkers are, of course, steadily penetrating the woods. The woods are not shot but are hunted, vigorously, often by Royalty, who also frequent the polo grounds that lie to the immediate east of Oakley Wood.

Cirencester Park Woods are the last stronghold of the Pearl-bordered Fritillary in Gloucestershire – for the butterfly is deemed extinct in the vast Forest of Dean, across the River Severn. Here the butterfly has survived, and at times thrived, utilising the uninterrupted supply of clearings and young plantations produced by forestry operations. It has followed the commercial woodcutter from place to place, as always was its wont in woods. Some fifty colonies have been formed since an in-depth study began in 1992. However, by no means all felling operations have produced suitable Pearl-bordered Fritillary habitat; indeed, only about a third have. Sometimes the butterfly moved straight in, but quite often it waited until a secondary forestry operation took place – such as cutting or spraying brambles. The activities of a large Fallow Deer population extended the longevity of several colonies, by slowing down or even destroying saplings – until a vigorous deer culling programme commenced during the late 1990s. Many clearings failed to come good and produce the necessary violets, because felling and extraction took place during wet weather, or simply because the ground got covered by coarse grasses in wet springs and strong grass growth seasons. By far the best habitat appeared during dry springs, in which violets were not out-competed by rampant Wood False Brome or Tufted Hair-grass.

Following the Pearl-bordered Fritillary in these woods is not easy, partly on account of the sheer scale of the woods, but also because colonies continually shift, appearing and disappearing with surprising alacrity. Many colonies persist only for a year or two, the longest for thirteen. Often, a clearing was occupied initially, for a short while, before the colony died out, only for the butterfly to reappear there a few years later, after a secondary phase of management. The butterfly is very much under the thumb of spring weather in these woods (the district is plagued by convective cloud during spring and, being on the western side of Britain, is prone to lingering weather fronts). Curiously, the climate at the lower, southern end of the wood is sunnier and drier: consequently the butterfly often appears there a good week earlier than at the higher, cloudier northern end. In flight seasons dominated by poor weather, the butterflies are loath to cross from an ageing habitat patch on one side of the ride to new habitat on the other side, yet in hot weather they become highly mobile and wander throughout the woods, and even beyond.

The soils in Cirencester Park Woods are probably too fast-draining for the Small Pearl-bordered Fritillary, which was never a Cotswold butterfly anyway, though colonies of Dark Green Fritillary form periodically in some of the larger clearings. Silver-washed Fritillary occurs in modest numbers around the surviving areas of mature broad-leaved woodland, though much of its former breeding areas have been felled – and have become, at least *pro tempore*, Pearl-bordered Fritillary habitat. The White Admiral is all but absent – as its larval foodplant, Honeysuckle, is rare due to browsing by Fallow Deer. In spring, colonies of Grizzled Skipper occur in some of the young plantations, notably where its favoured foodplant, Wild Strawberry, grows. The Duke of Burgundy has the vaguest of presences in the woods, breeding apparently on Primrose, but disappearing for years before suddenly reappearing. The broad grassy rides support good populations of the commoner grass-feeding butterflies, though they have been mown every late summer and are often heavily poached by horses.

Above all, Cirencester Park Woods have a unique feel about them. Overley is far and distant, Oakley is haughty and aristocratic, and Hailey is ethereal and poetic. The woods are not remotely like Forestry Commission woods, despite the presence of acres and acres of ranks of sombre conifers. For a start, the conifers are well maintained, as the estate foresters regularly thin out the timber stands. The main difficulty here is that the forestry that has been practised here for the last few decades is not sustainable, let alone cost-effective. Furthermore, the supply of mature broad-leaved woodland for felling is dwindling, and the estate is moving over from plantation forestry to what is called continuous-cover forestry. In butterfly terms, that is good news for the Silver-washed Fritillary but bad news for the Pearl-bordered Fritillary. To date, the latter has survived, and often thrived, on the back of commercial forestry; but from now on it will require positive conservation measures if it is to remain not just in Cirencester Park Woods but in the entire county of Gloucestershire.

Of course, there are many other rich butterfly localities in the southern Cotswolds, but the above are the ones to which I became hefted, and where I carried out long-term studies. But please do not think that the Cotswolds are a butterfly paradise. Several species have become extinct there, though the Large Blue is being reintroduced and the Adonis Blue successfully reintroduced itself. Moreover, butterflies and butterflying are somewhat handicapped by the region's climate, which is cooler, cloudier and wetter than much of the rest of southern England, especially in spring and early summer. There are, though, elements of the rural idyll so brilliantly eulogised by Laurie Lee in *Cider with Rosie*, and in his poetry.

All are but parts of one stupendous whole,
Whose body Nature is, and God the soul.

Alexander Pope, 1734

25 *Of Iris and Adonis*

In a dataset that goes back to the 1650s, 2006 went down in history as England's warmest year on record. It brought the warmest June since the long hot summer of 1976, the hottest and sunniest July and the mildest autumn on record. Climate-change thinking was to the fore, for this was the year when so-called 'global warming' hit the UK, at least as a mindset. Yet despite widespread hose-pipe bans it was not an especially dry year, but one that began with groundwater levels very low after a dry winter. A wet second half of May restored river levels, there were frequent if localised thunderstorms during the summer, August was indifferent, and the autumn eventually became extremely wet.

Good summers quite often come in on the back of a late spring. March 2006 was cold and at times bitter, with a wet ending. There were few opportunities for butterflies to fly. April dried things up, but was dominated by northerly airstreams, which brought cold nights. At the end of April the dandelions were only just at peak and the oaks merely starting to leaf. In effect, this was a slow, late spring – the sort good summers prefer. The Duke of Burgundy only started to emerge at the turn of April – I saw Noar Hill's first of the year on the 30th, and the first at Rodborough Common the following day, May Day. Pearl-bordered Fritillary was even later, only beginning its flight season on May 4th near Buckfastleigh on the southern slopes of Dartmoor, where it usually starts to emerge about April 20th. The first individuals were seen in Cirencester Park Woods on May 11th, but the butterfly invariably appears a good week later in Gloucestershire than in warm south Devon.

Yet May came good, at least initially. A modest influx of Painted Ladies and Red Admirals occurred, following a deposit of Sahara dust on parked vehicles overnight on May 5th. Sahara dust is a good omen. Duke of Burgundies and Green Hairstreaks abounded – but then the fine weather dramatically ended. Somehow, the bulk of the Cirencester Pearl-bordered Fritillaries and Marsh Fritillaries almost nationally managed to delay emerging from their pupae until the fine weather returned at the start of June. It seems that these creatures can hold back from emerging for a week, or perhaps two, though they cannot delay indefinitely.

Butterflies were becoming popular, receiving media attention. The Fates drew me in to television that year, an area in which I harboured no ambition, though I had some previous experience. Lion TV approached me out of the blue, wanting a 'butterfly man' for a major series on the summer of 2006, to be screened in the Sunday evening BBC primetime 9 pm slot during the autumn. Never mind a butterfly man, the series represented a great opportunity to take British butterflies into six million or so homes. It was interesting that butterflies were deemed integral to the great British summertime experience. The crew were a delight to work with, even if much of the footage they filmed did not make the final cut. Thus, some superb footage of Duke of Burgundies at Rodborough Common, filmed on a sublime May morning straight out of *Cider With Rosie*, got the chop – not because there was anything wrong with it. Filming started at the dawn of May at the Cerne Abbas Giant. Marsh Fritillary caterpillars were crawling off to pupate. For some inexplicable reason several of them were heading towards the Giant's willy, maybe to pupate en masse there? We returned to Giant Hill at the end of May to film the only placid male Green Hairstreak I have ever encountered, and a superb flight of Marsh Fritillaries. The eventual transmission included a clip of a freshly emerged Marsh Fritillary female being – courted is the wrong word – by half a dozen over-amorous males. Whatever you think about butterflies, please do not consider them artisans of the gentle art of courtship – smash and grab is more their style. There

is no way that that clip could have been broadcast before the 9 pm watershed. I returned to Giant Hill on August 1st with a group from the Kingcombe Centre, and wrote: *Some poor soul will have the rotten job of counting or estimating Marsh Fritillary larval webs here – the scale of abundance is such that this task should be handed out as a punishment.*

June became a belter. The Clouded Yellow appeared, which is nearly always a sign that the weather is set fair. The butterfly season, which had been running late, gradually switched over, so that the high-summer species began to emerge early. At the start of the month, Swallowtails were only just starting to appear in the Norfolk Broads. I saw the first proper emergence of the year at How Hill Nature Reserve, near Ludham, on June 6th, en route to Blakeney Point on the north Norfolk coast.

By the end of the month, the high-summer butterfly species were well out and the Purple Emperor was imminent. The Large Blue was successfully filmed at Collard Hill in Somerset, on what was just about the only cloudy day of the month. It was out-staged, however, by the Heath Fritillary, which declared itself to be the easiest butterfly on the British list to film. At Bin Combe, one of the deep combes radiating off Dunkery Beacon, they flopped wantonly in front of the camera, feeding from Heath

Bedstraw and Common Tormentil flowers, true media tarts. The storyline needed to be kept simple: this butterfly had been on the point of extinction nationally when stonking great colonies were discovered on east Exmoor, only for agricultural changes to take place and numbers to plummet; enter the National Trust and Butterfly Conservation to rescue the situation. Something like that.

The Lake District called at the end of the month. Meathop Moss was so dry that sandals could have been worn, albeit at the expense of prickled toes. This was ironic, as a board walk had recently been installed. Impressive amounts of Scots Pine and birch had been cleared. Large Heath was emerging well, but only males were seen, bumbling about over the peat bog. We were staying at the Red Lion in Grasmere, in Wordsworth's heartland. I sprinkled rose petals on William and Dorothy's graves, whilst reciting some lines from Coleridge. Ennerdale, a lost and much-abused valley in north-west Lakeland, is in the process of being 're-wilded' by a partnership led by the Forestry Commission, which had planted much of it up with highly invasive Sitka Spruce, the water board and the National Trust, which owns the valley mouth. The diary was succinct: *Moving on from the mistakes of twentieth-century forestry – Death By Sitka. The process of debuggerisation.* But the only thing genuinely wild about the valley was the naturally functioning river, the only one in the Lakes allowed to express itself freely as a mountain river. On the south side of the river, in an area where tall Sitka had been cleared, was a majestic colony of Small Pearl-bordered Fritillary and a lone Dark Green Fritillary. Butterflies are essential to any re-wilding scheme. These particular guys were pioneer colonisers.

All day the mountain tops had been calling; my heart had scarcely been in Ennerdale at all. So the following day, June 29th, the old Mountain Ringlet partnership of Hooson and Oates re-formed. We took the easy route, from Honister youth hostel up to Fleetwith and then on to Brandreth, and in passing looked down into Ennerdale and the braided streams of its river, bright with boulders and pebbles, for water levels were low. Mountain cloud was loath to clear, so the ringlets needed to be walked up.

Diary, June 29th 2006: *As fragments of brightness increased, more and more ringlets became apparent, and a few tentative flights ensued – especially when the breeze sprang up. Then I found a freshly emerged male drying his wings, and quickly located the vacated pupal case – attached by a couple of silk strands rather randomly on the side of a small Mat-grass tussock. We were surprised by its open situation: I had expected to find it inside a tussock.*

That generated a frenetic search for Mountain Ringlet pupae, with some success. The significance here is not the eccentricity of the venture, but the likelihood that no one had found Mountain Ringlet pupae in the wild before, or indeed the larvae. Of course, scientific endeavour quickly lost out to aesthetics, as more and more ringlets took to the air, or basked on the sides of tussocks, displaying Starling-like iridescence. I had first visited the Honister fells thirty years and a day ago, and had returned home.

Home also lay to the south, on the lonely limestone hills surrounding the Kent estuary. There, the powerful Dark Green Fritillary had erupted on Helsington Barrows, part of the National Trust's Sizergh estate. Two hundred were counted in an hour. After decades of damaging summer sheep grazing the Barrows had come under the custodianship of a small herd of Galloway cattle, ranging there all year long. The changes were impressive, with the flora recovering spectacularly and the butterflies tracking these beneficial changes. High Brown Fritillary was starting to emerge in fair numbers, having been a rarity there during the sheep-grazing era. Grassland butterfly habitats tend to recover more quickly after spells of so-called over-grazing than following periods of neglect.

It was July 1st, and White-letter Hairstreaks were emerging in impressive numbers at the western end of Westonbirt Arboretum back in Gloucestershire. A sizeable population was based on a large stand of the Himalayan elm *Ulmus villosa* planted in an early attempt to find a type of elm resistant to Dutch elm disease. The males were busily sparring with each other, engaging in spiral combats high over rather randomly selected elms and Ash trees.

Emperor time began explosively. I nearly trod on the first Emperor of the year – never answer the mobile phone as you walk into an Emperor wood, you will fail to spot the distinctive shark's-fin shape of his closed wings on the ride. Diary: *This male didn't mind, he flew round me several times and almost landed on me, before wandering off low into the wood, big and dark.* That was in the Straits Inclosure of Alice Holt Forest. Later, ten or twelve males were battling away in the favoured territory up at Goose Green Inclosure, by the village of Bucks Horn Oak. Things were looking good, very good. The Emperor had to be filmed, his appearance would be the pinnacle of the TV programme. The date was set, Thursday July 6th.

Diary, July 6th 2006: *Massive thunderstorms and flooding in central southern England. In Alice Holt, dull and damp till 12.30, then brightening nicely. Quite sunny from 1.15. Light south-westerly breeze. 22°C max.*

The entry continues:

An eventful and memorable day, starting with a nightmare journey (Swindon was seriously flooded). Arrived in damp gloom at the Forestry Commission visitor centre in Alice Holt. A long period of indecision there, hoping that it would clear (as forecast) and dithering over whether to cancel the cherry-picker and abandon the day. I turned things round by visiting the Gents: some bright spark had left the lights on overnight and the doors and windows open, the result being that the Gents had miraculously turned into a walk-in moth trap. We filmed a ridiculously silly piece, with me showing off the night's catch above the urinals to a dead-pan sound technician playing the innocent visitor.

And that, Dear Reader, is how the rare Waved Black moth was discovered in Alice Holt Forest.

The difficult start to the day mattered little. A hugely successful Emperor filming session ensued, using a cherry-picker with a 22-metre reach parked slap bang in the middle of the prime male territory near Bucks Horn Oak.

Diary, July 6th 2006: *His Imperial Majesty allowed us to film him with the greatest of ease. We were able to manoeuvre the cradle, containing three men, to within a metre of perched males ... but we had a problem with hoverflies regularly trying to land on basking males, mainly* Xylota segnis, *which was common high up.*

The diary entry reaches a climax:

It was edifying in the extreme to watch iris *in flight from above and, especially, to look down on chasing males. Until you've seen HIM in flight from above you have no idea how purple he is, and how much the purple iridescence flashes and changes, from Adonis blue, through royal and dark blues, through deep purple to almost violet, and back. Indeed, until you have been Up There with HIM you have not experienced The Purple Emperor at all.*

Let it be freely known that I will do anything – repeat, anything – to spend time in a cherry-picker up in the Emperor's trees. By happy chance, just two weeks later the BBC Natural History Unit needed a guide to help obtain footage of males for its *Nature of Britain* series. Consequently, two more days were spent up there, in the real world, guiding a wildlife cameraman and making detailed notes of what was going on. In the heat of one of those July days, things did not run entirely to plan:

Diary, July 20th 2006: *The cherry-picker succumbed to the heat and jammed 20 metres up in the air, with us in it. This precipitated a ridiculous rescue saga. First, the Forestry Commission sent out one of their engineers, who took the piss out of us mercilessly but was otherwise ineffective. Then the rescue engineer from Cherry-Picker HQ at Heathrow grabbed his shades and a can of Red Bull, revved up his white van and shot out onto the M25 to encounter, predictably, gridlock. We were 'rescued' after some four hours, re-ascended only for the thing to jam again half an hour later, necessitating White Van Rescue Man to extricate himself from a traffic jam on the Farnham bypass.*

The Natural History Unit had wanted to obtain footage of Emperors feasting on honey dew, the supposedly sweet secretion of aphids on tree leaves. Here it must be stated that, all told, I have spent nine afternoons admiring Emperors from cherry-pickers and have yet to see one imbibing honey dew. It may be myth, derived from the Emperor's habit of periodically cleaning his proboscis, the butterfly equivalent of beak wiping in birds.

In July 2006, Seven Ways was no more, but instead I was able to stay in an old caravan in my friend Lynn Fomison's wildlife orchard down at Ropley, in Edward Thomas country. The caravan had been white, but had painted itself green with algae. Wood Pigeons copulated at dawn on the roof. It was all rather reminiscent of The Lodge.

In stultifying heat on July 12th, Mr Yasutaka Murata, a leading Japanese businessman, gentleman butterfly photographer

and devotee of *Apatura* butterflies, descended on the Straits Inclosure. He was driven there by his UK managing director, who was introduced to me as Mr Decorum, but was probably called Dick Oram. At the far end of the main ride Mr Murata placed a tablespoon of Malaysian curried shrimp paste on a tree stump. Within fifteen minutes this bait had attracted a male Emperor, which he duly admired and photographed. That heady day Mr Murata unwittingly introduced a craze, for today no Emperoring expedition is complete without a supply of shrimp paste, or belachan as it is commonly known. Various different types of shrimp paste have been trialled, and most Emperorphiles have determined their own favourite. The bait only works, however, in warm, dry weather early in the Emperor season – and it is actually bettered by fresh Fox scat and fermenting oak sap. The Emperor, like many tropical butterflies, seldom if ever visits flowers.

The culmination of the magnificent 2006 Purple Emperor season took place in heatwave conditions on July 18th and 19th, just before my two days in the cherry-picker with the Natural History Unit wildlife cameraman. The 19th was the hottest July day on record, with 36.5 degrees registered at Wisley. The males were faded and in decline, yet in the heat of the afternoon ageing females were coming up to the Bucks Horn Oak territories in need of male services, presumably in the form of second matings. Normally, they only mate the once, we think. The diary for the 18th states: *I had sightings of several courting pairs between 4.15 and 6.16 and nearly witnessed an actual pairing. At 5.06 a female led a string of six males off into the bushes.* The following afternoon several more 'second honeymoon' courtship flights were witnessed. In fact there seemed to be so much female pheromone floating around that males were accidentally courting each other, and telling the sexes apart became near-impossible. At 5.35 a female was seen being followed by a train of four males. A few minutes later she returned, having shed one male, and met up with another female being pursued by two males. The significance of this is simple: with Purple Emperors, second matings only seem to occur late on in flight seasons dominated by hot weather, and are decidedly unusual. Moreover, seven is the maximum number of Purple Emperors I have ever seen in vista; I have managed it several times, but never bettered it.

July had expressed itself fully, and Alice Holt had been memorable. Only the White Admiral had been difficult, for it is not an easy butterfly to film and seems to resent TV cameras. In the early evening, though, they congregate around bramble patches that catch late shafts of forest sunshine, feeding and intermittently basking, often in loose groups of half a dozen or more. One cross-rides in Alice Holt's Straits Inclosure is the perfect place to witness this exquisite high-summer activity, and there we dutifully filmed *Camilla* of the Brambles. Not for nothing is that cross-rides known as Camilla Corner. But the White Admiral was to feature again in 2006.

August was memorable for the wondrous spread of the Adonis Blue in the Cotswolds. Twenty-three colonies were found in the southern Cotswolds, as far north as Cranham and Northleach. Most were on short-turf slopes around Stroud, including a sizeable colony on one of the Rodborough Common slopes where I counted an impressive 228 in a 40-minute timed zigzag count. To put this into context, historically the butterfly had at best been a rarity in the Cotswolds and had only ever been recorded from 27 sites, from Bristol northwards. The Adonis died out within a decade of myxomatosis arriving, and was last seen in the Cotswolds in 1962, just a century after it was first recorded. Coombe Hill, by Wotton-under-Edge, proved to be both its first and last locality. Its reappearance in the Cotswolds during the early noughties is the most impressive colonisation by a butterfly I have experienced in half a century of butterflying. Above all, it offers visceral Hope.

The first modern-era Cotswold colony was found at Stinchcombe Hill, near Dursley, in 2001, and was immediately dismissed as a clandestine release – with some justification, as Glanville Fritillary has intermittently appeared there, certainly not of its own accord. But then it became known that the Adonis Blue had maintained a population in the extreme south-east of the Jurassic Limestone Cotswold range, near Castle Combe, north-east of Bath, since at least 1976. Perhaps the butterfly had spread from there during good summers, and had taken advantage of improved habitat conditions produced by conservation grazing? Maybe it had even spread from burgeoning populations near Calne on the north Wiltshire downs? Certainly, there are records of odd individuals appearing in the southern Cotswolds during hot summers from 1976 into the new century. For what it is worth, my opinion is that the butterfly recolonised the Cotswolds all but wholly naturally, and that any introduction that may have taken place was an irrelevance – the butterfly would have got there anyway. The appearance of the Adonis Blue in the Cotswolds coincided with the appearance of a rare bee fly, the Downland Bee Fly (*Villa cingulata*), a short-turf species which had not previously been known from the Cotswolds and had not been seen since the 1930s, anywhere. But if that shadowy band of men, the butterfly breeders, are truly responsible for the reappearance of one of Britain's most splendid butterflies in the Cotswolds, then my message to them is one of admiration and gratitude.

The summer of 2006 evolved into a wonderful autumn, providing the warmest September and October on record. Drought cracks appeared in the clay, and many a day of Keatsian 'season of mists and mellow fruitfulness' weather occurred. Butterflies responded, admirably in fact. One in particular seized the moment, and one you would not expect – the White Admiral. There now follows a moment of humble pride, for on August 1st my diary stated: *Good to find a couple of White Admiral larvae on semi-shaded Honeysuckle just off the edge of the glade. I was surprised how well developed they were – a second brood could well be on the cards.* Second broods of the White Admiral are decidedly rare in the UK, though probably under-recorded. They may occur more frequently with climate change, as they are quite normal further south in Europe. Although the main brood did not appear unusually early in 2006, generally around June 21st, eggs were then laid quickly, hatched rapidly, and larvae developed apace during the hot July – despite the fact that the Honeysuckle leaves wilted in the drought. How this butterfly copes with its precious Honeysuckle droughting off is as yet unknown, but it does. Perhaps the larvae sense what is happening and feed up apace, before the leaves prematurely wither? Sure enough, second-brood White Admirals began to appear in woods in central southern England in mid-September. A visit to my beloved Straits Inclosure in Alice Holt on the 21st revealed no fewer than six, including a female laying eggs on Honeysuckle straggling along ditch banks. I saw another second-generation specimen there on October 15th, and two at Somerford Common in north Wiltshire on September 23rd, the first ever recorded in that county. All told, second-generation specimens were recorded in ten counties, from Norfolk across to the West Midlands, and south-east to Kent.

The Red Admiral was also deeply memorable that autumn, occurring in profusion in gardens and on Ivy tangles everywhere. 2006 had battled its way to glory. The Purple Emperor, of course, comfortably won Butterfly of the Year.

26 *A fall from grace*

Years can fall from grace, like fallen angels, and 2007 did just that. A mild winter and an early spring is always a high-risk strategy: the earlier spring comes, the easier it falls apart. The marvellous benefit of hindsight indicates that the severe gale that rampaged across southern Britain in mid-January 2007 was a portent of things to come. Gusts of up to 125 kilometres an hour (78 mph) were recorded at Heathrow, eleven lives were lost, high-sided lorries were blown over, and the roof of the Tavern Stand at Lords was damaged. January was, though, the second mildest recorded in England, after that of 1916, apparently. February was also mild, but decidedly wet. All this meant that Red Admirals survived the winter in perhaps unprecedented numbers. I saw my first of the year on February 1st and had seen ten by the end of March, in town and country, probably each one of them UK-born butterflies which had successfully overwintered. However, if my first butterfly of the year is a Peacock or a Red Admiral a poor summer ensues – and 2007 was a double Red Admiral Year …

The year careered away, producing a definitive April, the warmest and sunniest on record in England and Wales. By the end of the month I had seen 23 species of butterfly, comfortably surpassing my previous end-of-April record of seventeen, reached in both 1990 and 1997. Pearl-bordered Fritillaries started to emerge in numbers in Cirencester Park Woods on April 18th, a remarkably early appearance for the frozen wastes of Gloucestershire. On the Isle of Wight, the Glanville Fritillary excelled itself, appearing at Ventnor on April 18th, taking eleven days off its previous record there. The migrants were in, too: Clouded Yellows along the south coast, Large Tortoiseshells on Portland and the Isle of Wight, and even the odd Camberwell Beauty, a few Long-tailed Blues and a Queen of Spain Fritillary on the South Downs. Strangely, though, April 2007 did not remain definitive for long, for it was eclipsed four years later. My lasting memory of that April is of the Orange-tips over the valley meadows at Kingcombe in west Dorset. I had gone to Kingcombe, with my mentor David Russell, to run a philosophical workshop, or waffle, called 'Nature Beyond Science', discussing people's relationships with Nature. The Orange-tips taught us much that weekend, being closer to Nature than mere humans could ever hope to be. The diary describes them, *moving without pressure over marshy meadows bedecked with Lady's Smock. Spirits of the April air.* One flew over my car as I was driving away at the end of the weekend. Such events do not seem stochastic.

We are supposed to remember where we were during key moments in world history. Let it be known, then, that I was in Bin Combe, on east Exmoor, with Nigel Bourn from Butterfly Conservation, when the sublime spring of 2007 collapsed. It happened on May 10th, as we were discussing conservation management for the Heath Fritillary. By evening the rain had become torrential. Three days later the Ten Tors Challenge on Dartmoor had to be abandoned in mid-competition and 2500 teenagers air-lifted to safety.

On May 17th, when conglomerate cloud peeled back along the coastal fringe, I was at Sand Point just to the north of Weston-super-Mare. The Glanville Fritillary was back. The first incarnation of the Glanville Fritillary at Sand Point lasted from 1983, when the butterfly was unofficially released there, to 2000. I saw the last of that population, on June 7th 2000, as poor flight-season weather and oscillating habitat suitability finally brought a weak colony to its knees. Then, early in 2006 I was approached by the late Roger Sutton, a founder member of the British Butterfly Conservation Society, to ask whether the National Trust would like to have the butterfly back. He was acting on behalf of others, who had a surfeit of captive-bred Glanvilles. Thank you so much for asking, but no thanks because there's no way we could maintain the butterfly on such a small and isolated site which continually dips in and out of suitability, and where we could not guarantee the necessary habitat management for it, was the gist of my reply. The real problem for the Glanville on Sand Point was that its foodplant, Ribwort Plantain, was dependent there on regular drought, which burnt off competing grasses, but was swamped by rampant grass growth in wet summers. The butterfly requires exposed Ribwort Plantain plants growing in bare ground pockets and does not use plants covered in long grass. Moreover, the south-facing slope favoured by the butterfly was suffering from vigorous bramble invasion. Despite these remonstrations, the butterfly reappeared there in 2006, blossomed a while, and then faded out in the face of bramble and coarse grass growth. The butterfly was finally doomed once the Rabbit population died out, due to myxomatosis, during 2011 and 2012, for lush grass growth promptly suppressed the plantain. I saw the last of Sand Point's second Glanville Fritillary incarnation in June 2013. The colony, though, attracted butterfly enthusiasts from far and wide, saving them the expensive but joyous pilgrimage to the Glanville's heartland on the Isle of Wight.

May 2007 became wetter and wetter, and was duly excommunicated. June started promisingly, but then changed its mind and degenerated into a month of summer floods. The diary summary of May's weather states:

> Six people have died, 600 injured and 3500 rescued in floods that start at Gloucester, go up the Severn valley, turn north-east and run through the East Midlands before fully expressing themselves in Lincolnshire and Yorkshire. This is June, not November.

Incredibly, the weather was dry in Northern Ireland for a visit to County Down in early June. Each day, after a grey start the clouds would dissipate. The lovely Marsh Fritillary was having one of its periodic bumper years at Murlough Dunes NNR, close to where the Mountains of Mourne run down to the sea. Some 450 larval webs had been counted there in March. The butterflies then appeared in such high numbers that they had spilled out from their dune-slack haunts and invaded the fore dunes. Marsh Fritillaries, like so many other butterflies, are fervent opportunists.

Since my last early-summer visit to Murlough, in 1994, one species of butterfly had disappeared and a new one had appeared, disappeared, and been replaced by another. These changes were not ecological but due to the wonders of taxonomy: the Wood White had been split into two near-identical species, the ordinary Wood White and Réal's Wood White, after examination of male gonads had determined that one set of willies was longer than the other. Then, DNA analysis determined that Réal's Wood White is absent from the British Isles. Instead, we have the ordinary Wood White, which occurs very locally in southern England and in Ireland flies only in the Burren, and the Cryptic Wood White, which is reasonably widespread in Northern Ireland but absent from England. Back in 1994 I had sensed something different about the Northern Ireland Wood Whites, so it came as no major surprise to find that the so-called Wood Whites of Northern Ireland were actually Cryptic Wood Whites. On this particular trip, Cryptic males were bumbling about over the heathy inland dunes and slacks whilst the females were skulking around in the fore dunes, where the breeding grounds are. There I watched females laying eggs, low down on Bird's-foot Trefoil plants growing over bare sand on the south-facing edges of Marram Grass tussocks high up on the fore dunes – i.e. in hot spots.

A week later I was hitting the high road to Scotland, or rather the airlines, with naturalist friend and colleague Mike Ingram. Luck had it that I was one of the organisers of a conference at Stirling University, which was to commence on a Tuesday. Better still, Mike's brother owned a bothy in the woods near Kingussie. It was expedient to go up in advance, in pursuit of the Chequered Skipper and other Highland wildlife. We arrived to find a Grey Partridge brooding her chicks in the porch, and a Red Squirrel scurrying across the lawn. The weather was cloudless and hot, in southern England. In the Highlands, cloud streamed across from the east, and the rivers were running high. I had not visited Loch Arkaig for thirty years:

> Diary, June 10th 2007: *Changes included two fish farms, power boats on the loch, increases in caravans and cars, vast amounts of deer fencing, the abandonment of a croft (doubtless to be sold as a holiday home), the collapse of sheep grazing in the western half, a two-mile-long timber extraction road, and Butterfly Conservation acquiring as a nature reserve the young conifer plantation in which I saw Chequered Skippers back in 1974.*

Another change was the colonisation of the Speckled Wood, a new arrival to the district.

Incredibly, I saw a couple of Chequered Skippers in the very spot where I saw my first, back in 1974, a sheltered Bracken-filled stream gully on the western edge of Allt Cheanna Mhuir, at the far end of Butterfly Conservation's Allt Mhuic reserve. Here the butterflies appeared and disappeared at will within the Bracken glades, occasionally visiting Bugle flowers, but that's typical of Chequered Skippers – a matter of small colonies here and there, with the butterflies appearing and vanishing with the sun, masters of dematerialisation.

The best Chequered Skipper colonies were found towards the western end of the loch's northern shore, west of Caonich. I had only once wandered that far west before, in 1975, and had failed to find the butterfly there. Perhaps it had spread westwards in the intervening years? But the Small Pearl-bordered Fritillary steals the show along the West Highland loch sides in early June. Its cousin *euphrosyne*, the Pearl-bordered Fritillary, was sadly finished for the year, but *selene* abounded, at least towards the western end. Eighteen were feeding on a metre-square patch of early-flowering bramble. Two males lacked the prominent black veining on the wing uppersides, ab. *obsoleta* probably. The first Meadow Browns and Dark Green Fritillaries of the year were appearing. As the sun came out fully, revealing the true ethereal glory of the West Highlands, Mike and I were faced with a difficult choice: carry on westwards, on what had become a pilgrimage into Nature, and disappear into the alluring paradise that is Knoydart, never to be heard of again; or retreat and go to the conference in Stirling. We made the wrong decision. When next I tread the shores of Loch Arkaig I will go the whole way, deep into Knoydart; I might be there some time.

As in politics, a week in butterflying is a long time, and the following week I was in North Wales. Between downpours I spotted the first Silver-studded Blues of 2007 in the wet heath colony at Hafod Garregog NNR, inland from Porthmadog. Here, the conservation issue was over whether the cattle, brought in to counter Purple Moor-grass growth, were trampling out the butterfly's preferred breeding habitat, a series of old peat mounds rising above the wet heath. Cattle had the habit of standing on these mounds, to avoid wet ground and escape from flies. I was on their side and felt that they were doing more good than harm on the mounds, producing the sort of young heather growths favoured by the caterpillars. The problem is that this is a single isolated colony, perhaps of a unique subspecies (the necessary DNA work has not been done), and recolonisation would not occur if the site deteriorated. It is the most interesting Silver-studded Blue population I know, perhaps similar to the extinct race that formerly occurred on the mosses around Witherslack in south Cumbria, known as ssp. *masseyi*.

Having failed to see Large Heath out in Scotland, during a visit to Flanders Moss, near Stirling, it was necessary to call in at Whixall Moss on the Welsh border. Here, the grey wanderer of peat bogs was only just beginning to emerge, rather late considering that butterflies were still emerging earlier than normal – not that butterflies ever do anything that is remotely normal. I expected to see a hundred, but struggled to see a dozen males, the first of the year's emergence. I left pondering whether the butterfly was emerging later here after the water levels had been raised in order to restore the bog's all-important hydrology.

The following day, for time was running ahead of itself, the Purple Emperor season commenced, in the form of a male seeing off a Great Spotted Woodpecker in Alice Holt Forest. The Emperor also started that day (June 20th) at Bookham Common in Surrey, Ken Willmott seeing the first of the year there, albeit after a week-long vigil. However, the weather then deteriorated, considerably, with low-pressure systems becoming stuck over the UK. The Glastonbury Festival turned into the biggest mud bath since the Battle of Passchendaele, the county cricket ground at Worcester vanished beneath several feet of water, and Sheffield suffered its wettest day on record. June joined May in excommunication and the entire summer of 2007 was declared apostate. July then started despicably.

Between the periodic aspersions, deluges, drenches, immersions, pluviosities, saturations and swampings, butterflies put on a brave face. They had to: each minute of fitful sunshine meant life or death, not so much to them as individuals but to the future of their colonies – and they knew it, and seized the day, or rather the moment. Butterflies are particularly good at the latter, as they live in the moment, the moment of being.

I had seen my first White Admirals in Marlpost Wood, West Sussex, in 1968, and now I faithfully returned there, albeit in a howling gale. In early July 1968 these butterflies were just starting to emerge. Now, on the very same date four decades later, they were finishing for the season, having emerged ridiculously early because the fine spring had advanced larval development. The visit produced two 'Black Admirals', old specimens of ab. *obliterae* (or *semi-nigrina*) and a pristine Comma female ab. *suffusa*. The latter was incredibly wary and inapproachable, but my companion, West Sussex nationalist Neil Hulme, returned the following day and, in his words, nailed the witch (i.e. photographed her).

It was time to visit Fermyn Woods, up in Rockingham Forest, in east Northamptonshire. Here, Oliver Bancroft, a hairy giant of a man carving out a career as a cinematographic artist, had been commissioned by Fermyn Woods Contemporary Art to make a film about the Purple Emperor. He needed help, not least because he had decided to haul a 7-kilogram salmon 11 metres up into the oak canopy, as a sacrificial offering to the Emperor of all the Butterflies. The salmon was duly hoisted (I conducted the hoisting), to dangle from a prominent oak branch above the ride at the entrance to Cherry Lap, where its pointless oscillations in July's gentle zephyrs bemused innumerable butterfly photographers who had not read their Heslop, and thoroughly confused various dog walkers, who did what dog walkers do with the unfamiliar – ignored it. The Emperor also ignored the fish, which was steadily devoured by Hornets.

At 11.35 on the morning of July 10th a male Purple Emperor flushed out a lovely fresh female from the sallows, lucky boy. A one-minute follow-my-leader courtship flight ensued before she settled 10 metres up in the crown of a Corsican Pine tree on the ride edge, and was instantly joined by the male, literally. They remained there, *in copula* for 3 hours 40 minutes, moving only to flick away the attentions of an irritating wasp. This was only the second time I had seen Purple Emperors mating, after a pairing on July 11th 1976 which lasted for 3 hours 30 minutes.

Diary, July 10th 2007: *We did not have a good enough zoom lens to film them, so we requisitioned a 6-metre scaffold tower off another of the Fermyn artists, and raised Oliver, all 16 stone of him, + camera + tripod. This mating pair generated a spectacular display of bizarre human behaviour which wondrously befuddled a succession of butterfly photographers.*

Fermyn's tradition of bizarre eccentricity during the Purple Emperor season was born this day. The following day I witnessed another courtship flight which also ended in a pairing, high up in a Turkey Oak. This pair stayed together all night, though only because it started to rain shortly after they had joined.

Exhausted by intensive butterflying, involving 47 species in six weeks, there was only one thing to do – return to work, in order to recover. This happened just in time for the apocalyptic rains of July 20th. Then, twelve hours of non-stop heavy rain led to widespread flooding, in what became known as the Tewkesbury Floods. Berkshire, Oxfordshire, Gloucestershire, Herefordshire and Worcestershire were worst affected. That day, 135 millimetres of rain fell at Pershore, Worcestershire. The journey home from the office in Swindon usually takes 45 minutes; that day it took five hours. Every dip in the road network around Swindon was flooded, and each flood contained at least one stranded vehicle. Gridlock developed into stasis. Ironically, my journey was softened by the dulcet tones of *Test Match Special* on the car radio, for the first Test at Lords enjoyed virtually a full day's play. I was fortunate, some of my colleagues failed to get home at all.

Incredibly, some butterflies actually survived this deluge, probably because there was no buffeting wind. As a generalisation, rain accompanied by wind destroys butterflies more, and they seem to be able to survive 24 hours of rain, providing it is not tumultuous. This rain was, of course, tumultuous, or to use the modern vernacular, stair rods. Much, though, must depend on where individual butterflies roost during extreme wet-weather events. The impact of heavy rain and accompanying floods may be more severe on butterfly immature stages, though we do know that some species, notably our wetland specialists the Large Heath and Swallowtail, regularly survive winter inundation, as larvae and pupae respectively.

August was welcomed in at Arnside and Silverdale, looking at the developing plight of the Duke of Burgundy in a district which had recently been a national stronghold. Surveys organised by Butterfly Conservation revealed that it was still relatively strong on Whitbarrow, north of the Kent estuary, and at Gait Barrows NNR south of the river, but in a parlous state elsewhere. The main problem was fairly obvious: despite good habitat connectivity within this relatively unspoilt landscape no new colonies had been formed, whilst habitat conditions at the long-established colonies inevitably deteriorated. This is one of many butterflies which mainly occupies successional (changing) habitats and so needs to move on periodically. Rabbit population increases play havoc with it on grasslands. Its demise should be measured by the paucity of new colonisations rather than by colony disappearance, for it cannot stay forever in any one place. The conundrum in the Morecambe Bay district is why it had not moved back into the woods, following the extensive reintroduction of coppicing there. Oddly, the essential primulas had simply not appeared in the reinvigorated woods, or had not been found by wandering females.

August provided little relief. It was a fairly average August down south, but very wet from the Midlands northwards. Incredibly, this wretched month produced a small second brood of Duke of Burgundy at Noar Hill in Hampshire. Second generations of this vernal butterfly have been extremely rare in this country, though normal in southern Europe. Second-brood specimens were seen on Noar Hill from August 3rd through to the 17th. I had assiduously searched for second-brood individuals there in hot summers during the 1980s, without success. Another partial second brood occurred in 2011, again at Noar Hill and also at Rodborough Common in the Cotswolds, where specimens were seen between July 26th and August 6th. It seems very much as though the second brood of the Duke of Burgundy occurs only after the spring brood has appeared very early, as happened in 2007 and 2011, and the resultant larvae have fed up and pupated unusually early. The 2011 second brood at Rodborough was almost inevitable, given that some larvae were full-grown there by the start of June. On June 9th I felt that some would have pupated, a month or more earlier than normal.

But August 2007 was most notable for the paucity of that most ubiquitous of garden butterflies, the Small Tortoiseshell. Being a nerd and a fanatical butterfly diarist, I note every individual butterfly of any interest. By August 19th I had seen a maximum of

45 Small Tortoiseshells during 2007 (counted as day individuals), 19 in the spring and 26 in the summer. The theory at the time was that the species was suffering from the impact of a new parasitic fly, *Sturmia bella*, which had recently colonised from the Continent and was heavily parasitising Small Tortoiseshell larvae. I must confess that I rather struggled to find *S. bella*, a distinctive tachinid fly, and I searched many a nettle patch for it, using a sweep-net. By the end of August 2007 I had added an extra three Small Tortoiseshells. Mercifully, they picked up a little in early September, as did the Red Admiral and the two cabbage whites, which had also been unusually scarce all summer. Then in mid-September I saw an impressive 53 Small Tortoiseshells – nearly doubling my year's tally – during a three-day visit to the North Antrim coast in Northern Ireland. I saw 23 around the Bishop's Palace (an eighteenth-century excrescence) near Downhill, feeding up on yellow composites and Escallonias, and 20 at White Park Bay. This was followed by a pleasing display the following April, of Small Tortoiseshells feeding on dandelions around Strangford

Lough and nearby in County Down. Normally, one takes such sights for granted. It was not until 2013 that Small Tortoiseshell numbers picked up again in mainland UK. Verdict: next time the Small Tortoiseshell nosedives, visit Northern Ireland; or visit Northern Ireland anyway, it is the most welcoming and hospitable of countries.

The Small Tortoiseshell was also prominent on the Isles of Scilly in the early autumn of 2007. It was, though, thoroughly outgunned by the Peacock. I saw about 150 freshly emerged Peacocks on Tresco on September 28th and similar numbers on Bryher and St Mary's. This abundance must have been the main emergence of a second generation, resultant from the main brood appearing ridiculously early due to the good spring. Presumably, butterflies exist in different dynamics on Scilly. One is not supposed to visit Scilly for common nymphalid butterflies, but the Peacock did rather steal the show during that trip, and there was not much competition from the birds. Bird-wise, the best on offer was a Buff-bellied Pipit – no match for a phalanx of Peacocks on Ivy blossom. I also saw a Comma in Old Town Churchyard on St Mary's, where Harold Wilson is buried. This butterfly first reached the islands in 1997 and was just starting to establish itself properly in 2007. I also saw a Clouded Yellow fly over Sir Cloudesley Shovell's grave at Porthellick Cove nearby. Sir Cloudesley was not actually there at the time, having been re-interred in Westminster Abbey by Queen Anne and a grateful nation. All trips to Scilly should include a pilgrimage to the (original) grave of Sir Cloudesley, naval hero, Admiral of the Fleet, MP and Commissioner of London Sewers, who perished along with 2000 other souls when the British fleet under him was wrecked off the Isles of Scilly in October 1707.

The final diary entry for 2007 reads: *Never before has a year promised so much and ascended to such great heights, only to flounder and then crash into a pitiless chasm.* Like Sir Cloudesley's fleet, it had floundered hopelessly on the rocks.

On Whixall Moss

Grey pilgrim of the peat hags, wandering the wind
That blows the waste of quivering cotton grass,
Stirring you to rise from nowhere, drift in time,
As midsummer too, arises, sinks and then is passed.
And we must squelch behind you, in hopeless pursuit
Of some perfect image, framed within eternity,
Captured breathless at some place, flowerless and destitute,
That shows you for what you cannot be, a humbled deity.
We were not born for this, you and I, for we were free
Upon the breeze that chimes the endless summer hours,
Above a wasted land of boggy pool and waving reed,
Beyond the pleasantries of budding heather flowers,
Into the passion of the scudding clouds themselves,
Bridging the interstices between two living souls.

It would be pleasant to record that 2008 redeemed the situation, but it did not. March was vile, April even worse. May was good in Scotland and Northern Ireland, though poor down south. June was utterly unmemorable. July started promisingly but fell away badly. August was the dullest and coldest on record, and also one of the wettest. Northern Ireland suffered its wettest August ever, and significant flooding. September started catastrophically wet, effectively ending the butterfly season early – only to come good too late, and a fairly pleasant autumn ensued. But even in the direst of butterfly summers there are highlights. Butterflies are irrepressible spirits, it takes a lot to put them down. That is one reason why they are loved so deeply.

Butterflies also look after those in need of being looked after by them. On St George's Day I was in Northern Ireland ...

Diary, April 23rd 2008: ... *and found myself in paradise – the gardens of Rowallane in County Down – where the butterflies looked after me well. Straight in on a male Holly Blue around a clump of hollies. This is a rare and protected species in Northern Ireland, and Rowallane is one of the best known sites for it. Another good sighting was of a Comma, a recent colonist of NI.*

There were even Small Tortoiseshells in County Down, feasting up on dandelion flowers.

Three weeks later I was on the Isle of Man, which like most islands has a decidedly odd butterfly fauna. Wall Browns and Dark Green Fritillaries abound along the coastal fringe, but several species regarded as standard on the British mainland are absent; not a single species of skipper occurs, and Green Hairstreak is also absent. But Holly Blues were here too, gathered around clumps of clifftop gorse on which they must have been breeding, given the absence of hollies. The real highlights were singletons of Speckled Wood and Comma, at Laxey, both recent colonists to Man.

The BBC chose the miserable summer of 2008 to film five pieces on butterflies for the popular *One Show*, with me as the contributor. This represented something of a breakthrough, as butterflies had been held too difficult, too fidgety to film. They wanted the rarest, biggest, most rapidly declining, zaniest, and commonest, and of course beauty, wonder and passion, and strong story lines. That meant Large Blue, Swallowtail, High Brown Fritillary, Purple Emperor and the ubiquitous cabbage whites – quite a tall order. Incredibly, the Large Blue behaved impeccably, so much so that the piece was wrapped in three hours, on the eastern bank of Collard Hill, Somerset. We even filmed a female laying her eggs amongst the Wild Thyme buds. Weather conditions were perfect though, with the butterflies basking as the cloud cover slowly broke, before becoming nicely active – perfect butterfly photography weather. One–nil!

But the Swallowtail is a haughty king and was not in the giving vein. The signs were ominous on a precursor expedition in mid-June, arranged to capture some close-up footage with ace wildlife cameraman Alastair MacEwen. This was not a good Swallowtail year, with only a modest show along the edge of Butterfly Conservation's reserve at Catfield Fen in the Broads. They were taking afternoon tea: two on early-flowering brambles and one on Ragged-Robin, the latter flapping whilst feeding, to prevent the weak stem from collapsing under the butterfly's weight. The following day something made the weather misbehave: the gorgeous day that was forecast was lost to unforecast cloud, and a completely unforecast west wind. Swallowtails hate wind, and are creatures of warm sunshine. But the sheltering scrub at Hickling Broad produced only nine brief sightings, of intermittently patrolling males, before gloom descended and all butterflies ceased flying. Another stab was made with another wildlife cameraman, the day before the piece was to be filmed. Once more the weather gods were in malevolent mood, as the forecast was wrong again. A scatter of largely distant sightings were made, 'largely distant' being the operative term as this giant of a butterfly can be seen by the naked eye at 250 metres distance, appearing coffee-coloured.

Finally the *dies irae* arrived, Friday June 27th, when the piece had to be filmed, with a film crew of six and presenter Miranda Krestovnikoff in attendance.

Diary, June 27th 2008: *Like the Battle of Waterloo it was a close-run thing. We were fortunate in that the weather relented, for a while, allowing three hours of sun during which the butterflies were fully active.*

But the beasts had retreated to their reed-bed bastions. A secret weapon was required, a Trojan horse: we borrowed the Norfolk Wildlife Trust's electric boat, and stormed the high citadels of proud *Machaon* and, metaphorically at least, put him to the sword, pillaged and plundered, and razed the place to the ground. We even got the all-essential two-shot, of a male flying around an overjoyed Miranda. There must have been twenty or thirty of the cowardly animals hiding in the reed beds, including a couple of courting pairs. The diary concludes:

Throughout the three days spent trying to film this blighter I felt I was up against a mastermind determined to thwart my every move. He had to be forced into submission, but submit he did.

Conversely, the High Brown Fritillary and the Purple Emperor behaved impeccably, being easily filmed at Heddon valley on the Exmoor coast and in Fermyn Woods, Northamptonshire, respectively. Heddon, my old High Brown heartland, was on stupendous form, welcoming us on a day of long sunny spells. Fermyn was short-changed by the weather, but the Emperor overrode that minor impediment and performed admirably. And as for cabbage whites, visit any National Trust mansion with a walled kitchen garden. We chose Barrington Court, a garden idyll near Ilminster in Somerset, where cabbages are grown along predominately organic lines, alongside drifts of Nasturtiums. The two cabbage whites consequently abounded; indeed 2008 was an extremely good year for the Large White in particular – perhaps because its larval parasites had been harder hit during the wet summer of 2007 than the host. It was the caterpillars that really stole the show, with young and full-grown individuals fully expressing themselves by perforating every Brassica leaf in the garden. Caterpillars are misunderstood. Like us, they are trying to become butterflies. They need friends.

August 2008 was written off early. The diary philosophised with paradoxes: *It deserves to burn in hell but cannot: it is too wet to burn, and it already is hell.* By mid-month I had seen a mere nineteen Small Tortoiseshells all year in England, plus a few in Northern Ireland. Somehow the tortoiseshell clawed its way back from beyond the gates of death during a modestly sunny spell in September. All told I saw a meagre 54 Small Tortoiseshells in England that year, which indicates what a lousy butterfly season it was, and the dire state into which this most ubiquitous of our garden butterflies had fallen. We were overdue a good butterfly summer.

Summer

The little darling, Spring,
Has run away;
The sunshine grew too hot for her to stay.

She kissed her sister, Summer,
And she said:
'When I am gone, you must be queen
Instead.'

Cicely Mary Barker,
Flower Fairies of the Summer

If we belong anywhere, it is within summer. It is perhaps the truest reality we can experience here, representing the Garden of Eden, perhaps. Yet, as with the other seasons, summer has no clear beginning, and just a gradual dwindling for an end. In summer, the green of the countryside, particularly of the trees, quite suddenly deepens: spring's yellow-greens are replaced first by darkening greens, and then by blue-greens – this is particularly noticeable in oak-dominated landscapes.

Above all, summer slows time down; gone is the reckless gushing of spring, to be replaced by more measured hours – as we reach the pinnacle of the year. We can actually relax. For at its zenith summer transcends time itself, offering some genuine lucidity. It is the stillness within the turning world. It is summer's

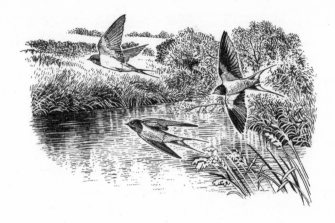

zenith that matters most, not its beginning, nor its ending. There, the memory of the year is created, and dyed fast.

We have some June specialist butterflies, notably the Heath Fritillary and Large Blue, but within the butterflying world the year reaches up towards the midsummer period. In the woods this begins with the first White Admirals and Silver-washed Fritillaries, which by tradition appear around Midsummer Day, but it then ascends higher – into the Purple Emperor season, when the butterflying year soars above the tree tops. On the downs, the Marbled Whites and Ringlets appear prodigiously in midsummer, on the heaths the Silver-studded Blues, and up north the Large Heath and the Mountain Ringlet, the king of the mountains. In days of yore the High Brown Fritillaries started to emerge at midsummer. They still do, in their remaining heartlands.

But after early or mid-July, and once the Purple Emperor is on the wane, very few butterflies are left to make their appearance for the year – effectively only the Brown Hairstreak, Chalkhill Blue, Silver-spotted Skipper and Scotch Argus. At last, butterfly enthusiasts stop assiduously seeking out the first this and that of the year, for the list is ending. Also, they may be seriously burnt out – certainly so if spring and early summer have been good. August is the ageing of summer, and of butterflying.

More of our species are on the wing in late July than at any other time of year: the midsummer species linger on, albeit in dwindling numbers, whilst their late-summer counterparts begin to appear, along with the second broods of several species. August is indeed a month of second broods – of Brown Argus, Common Blue, Small Heath, Small Tortoiseshell, Wall Brown, the whites, and others. It is also the month for garden butterflies. Until the third week of July our gardens are rather bereft of butterflies; then the cabbage whites – the Large White and Small White – appear, sometimes in great numbers, followed by the annual hatch of fresh Brimstones, Peacocks, a new, larger brood of Small Tortoiseshells, and Red Admirals and Painted Ladies of immigrant or home-grown provenance. Buddleias flower at precisely the right time for this pageant.

Yet, every summer, there is a day when the light suddenly changes – when the silver light of high summer is dramatically replaced by the golden light of September. This change is most noticeable in shafts of sunlight, which suddenly become golden, Septemberine. These shafts, which at times appear almost as angels, when glimpsed over our shoulders, have lost the dancing miasma of tiny flies they host in high summer; instead they contain harvest dust, the dust of the ageing year. Also, and crucially, the birds have ceased to sing. That day – which is quite noticeable – used to occur in late July, round about the 28th; but in poor summers it can occur as early as July's second week, and during my lifetime it has stealthily crept forward.

But summer is essentially about fulfilment, of spring's promise, and of the year itself. And it leaves something wonderful behind – memories. Like no other season, summer instils memories, deep and profound. Its journey is into memory, within us as individuals and collectively. And people collect memories, perhaps inadvertently but nonetheless, and are moulded by them. And butterflying is all about the collecting of memories in moments of time within idylls of place.

A butterfly alighted. From aloft
He took the heat of the sun, and from below,
On the hot stone he perched contented so,
As if never a cart would pass again
That way; as if I were the last of men
And he the first of insects to have earth
And sun together and to know their worth.
I was divided between him and the gleam,
The motion, and the voices, of the stream,
The waters running frizzled over gravel,
That never vanish and for ever travel.

From 'The Brook', by Edward Thomas
(Bramdean Common, Hampshire, July 10th 1915)

27 A tale of two butterflies

The summer of 2009 saw the clash of two mighty titans, the Painted Lady and the Purple Emperor. Between them they eclipsed all other butterflies, despite the fact that several other species put on hugely impressive performances, notably the Silver-washed Fritillary and the Comma. But the latter two picked the wrong year to bid for glory, coming a distant third and fourth respectively in my Butterfly of the Year stakes.

The new butterfly season came in on the back of a couple of dire butterfly years, a cold but relatively dry winter and a pleasant March. Spring then welled up nicely: an early and promising season was developing.

> Diary, April 22nd 2009: *Bookham Common, Surrey. Thirty magical minutes here en route to an indoor meeting, with the most magical combination of morning sunlight on unfurling leaves – then I got bounced by a wanton dog and the spell was broken.*

Springs, and summers, are like that – the spell can suddenly and unexpectedly be broken, most notably by changes in the weather. The entry for April 22nd concludes: *My life is primarily about the love of natural beauty, with butterflies providing a focus that may not always be necessary.* Two hours later I saw my first Holly Blues of the year, azure jewels over vernal shrubs in the gardens of Polesden Lacey house. They made me forget instantly what the meeting in the National Trust offices there had been about.

But spring fell apart in early May: the jet stream jumped south on the May Day bank holiday, the 4th, and trashed a most promising spring. Many of the early butterflies were then effectively written off by two hostile weeks. Being a spring butterfly is high-risk business – they are so often blasted away, yet they stagger back for more the following year. The Duke of Burgundy, which had started at Rodborough Common so wondrously on St George's Day, suffered particularly badly. Patrick Barkham visited Rodborough Common that day, to see the first Burgundies of the year, and his first ever. His eulogy on that memorable day, in his ground-breaking book *The Butterfly Isles*, rather pales in the knowledge that the 2009 Duke of Burgundy season fell spectacularly apart just after his visit.

The most significant day in the early spring of 2009 was April 11th, Holy Saturday, for a minor influx of Painted Lady took place. No one took much notice of it on the day, for small immigrations of Painted Ladies can occur at just about any time of year, and mostly come to nothing. Earlier, however, my friends Andy and Linda Barker of Hampshire had seen hundreds whilst holidaying in Mallorca, and the Reverend Prebendary John Woolmer had seen scores in the desert near Marrakesh. The entomological grapevine was buzzing with accounts of numbers in Spain, apparently all heading north. It seems that the population explosion had started in the Atlas Mountains, where good winter rains had led to massive germination of the butterfly's favourite foodplants, thistles.

These reports came sharply into focus whilst I was leading a Romantic Nature walk for the National Trust in the footsteps of Coleridge and the two Wordsworths in the Quantocks on April 19th. There, on the summit of Dowsborough Castle, where young Romantic poets were wont to frolic by moonlight, I came upon a trio of Painted Ladies – a female being courted by two males. On the metaphorical level they seemed to represent Samuel, William and Dorothy. Never before had I opened the Painted Lady season so spectacularly, especially in somewhere as special as the epicentre of the birthplace of Romanticism. But then all went quiet: I did not see any more until May 12th when I unexpectedly flushed up three grey pilgrims along a path through a clifftop field in a howling gale near Dover. *So something is happening*, I wrote. But the mid-May weather was most uncooperative.

Something had to be done, so on May 21st I bundled the foul and abusive weather into the boot of my car and deposited it in the Black Mountains, where it could not do much harm, en route to visiting the Ceredigion coast south of New Quay. That did the trick, and in the Elysian sea combe known as Cwm Soden (which is also known as Cwm Silio and Cwm Birlip) on the Ceredigion coast I saw another Painted Lady, an old grey male hurtling northwards over the Bracken slopes. The Pearl-bordered Fritillaries I had gone to see there had been knocked out by bad mid-May weather, but their eggs could freely be found on and around violets amongst the Bracken litter. Their cousin, the Small Pearl-bordered Fritillary, was emerging in numbers, so things were looking up, and the meeting determined a sound policy on Bracken management for the resident fritillary butterflies, whatever the cwm wished to call itself. But perhaps I was in the wrong place that day, for a swarm of Painted Ladies was sighted off Portland Bill, heading north.

Through a piece of supreme luck I had managed to wangle a three-month sabbatical, ostensibly in recognition of many years of unblemished service. That was a major piece of good fortune, as sabbaticals are not easy to wangle, dipping in and out of corporate fashion. The main objective was to get utterly lost in the real world, though the scoping document I was obliged to write stated that I was going off to study the ecology of the Purple Emperor and help people's engagement with this elusive butterfly. Funding was tight, so I had to stay in England – which was fine if the weather behaved. And the weather was clearly going to behave, for Painted Ladies had suddenly arrived in numbers – and they meant business. Also, the Australians had come over, ostensibly to regain the Ashes – and they meant business.

Business as usual for the Painted Lady means pushing limits – not so much their limits as our limits, and seeking to conquer the world. In late May 2009 our islands experienced an invasion which probably eclipsed that of 1996, and utterly eclipsed the Norman Conquest. Away from the coast, the invasion got going properly on May 23rd, when I managed to see seventeen whilst visiting the National Trust gardens at The Courts, near Bradford-on-Avon in Wiltshire.

The following day, Sunday the 24th, the floodgates opened and the Painted Ladies flocked north in stupendous numbers. I counted 241 whilst conducting the annual survey of Pearl-bordered Fritillaries in Cirencester Park Woods, but naturalists elsewhere saw many more. In Chiddingfold Forest on the Surrey/Sussex border, Ken Willmott counted 157 in an hour in mid-afternoon, Neil Hulme timed 133 jumping over a gate in an hour at Plashett Wood, near Lewes, and Bill Shreeves saw 128 in 90 minutes following an identical route across Melbury Down valley, near Shaftesbury. Back home, Mrs O timed them at the rate of one a minute passing through our garden, following the same route: hopping over the Beech hedge at the southern end, hurtling through without a cursory look, rising over the summerhouse and vanishing. Similar events were happening in gardens throughout southern England. Nearly all these were old males, grey with scale loss, heading north or north-west. Never mind the Day of the Triffids, this was the Day of the Painted Lady. A swarm of some 18,000 was seen off Scolt Head on the Norfolk coast.

A visit to the Isle of Wight on the 26th and 27th was aptly timed, to contribute to a TV piece about the subject matter of a new historical novel, *Lady of the Butterflies*, by Fiona Mountain. The lady in question here is one Eleanor Glanville, who was the first female naturalist, I think globally, and after whom is named the Glanville Fritillary, which she discovered in Lincolnshire in about the year 1700 whilst searching for an errant son. Her will was successfully overturned on the grounds of insanity, the proof of which was her keen interest in butterflies, other bugs, and thinges that creepe and crawle. In 2009, though, the Glanville was seriously upstaged by another Lady. We counted seventeen

Painted Ladies during the 40-minute crossing of the Solent from Lymington to Yarmouth, all northward-bound. The island was alive with them. Most were heading north, but new arrivals paused to refuel on thistles and other flowers on the southern cliff tops. At Wheelers Bay, Ventnor, several hundred were feeding on Red Valerian flowers, and many more were feeding on clifftop thistles at Compton Bay. We were conquered, and the poor Glanville Fritillary knew it – so much so that they were reduced to hiding in the grasses. But, in contrast to the great Painted Lady invasion of 1996, which was accompanied by numbers of other immigrant butterflies and insects, this invasion consisted almost entirely of Painted Ladies, plus a fair number of Silver-Y moths, only. At Compton Bay I managed a huge and regal Clouded Yellow and a splendid Red-veined Darter dragonfly, only.

The influx continued almost unabated throughout late May. On the 28th Neil Hulme counted a staggering 1590 during an hour's recording at Park Corner Heath, in East Sussex, including a peak of 42 per minute, all heading north-north-west. I wrote in the diary: *I can't compete with that, and neither I fear can His Imperial Majesty, the Purple Emperor.* Butterfly Conservation rose to the challenge, organising a national count for two hours on Saturday May 30th. Contributors were to count them passing within a 10-metre radius. Hundreds of people rallied to the call. My contribution was 270 counted passing through a broad cross-rides in Cirencester Park Woods. All told, that day I saw over a thousand.

The following day the sabbatical began. The diary mused: *The first concern of freedom is worrying about what to do*, before concluding, perhaps wisely, *Let Nature lead.* It led me east, to my old forest heartland in West Sussex, via a stop-off in Edward Thomas country above Petersfield. I spent the night in the old woods, hoping to be serenaded by Nightingales, only the males were ceasing singing for the year – and some fool had unleashed a Nightjar somewhere in the distance. It mattered not, for the Blackbirds and Song Thrushes ethereally sung out the last evening of May and rang in the dawn of June. They were stupendous. *This is what we've lost*, I wrote, *celestial choirs of Blackbirds*. The first butterfly of the month appeared at 7.40 am, a worn Painted Lady, but they were now very much on the wane; their invasion had ended, and another power was rising.

It was time to penetrate deep inside the Purple Empire. Three weeks were to be spent exploring previously unvisited Purple Emperor sites, in diverse counties, before the butterfly himself would appear. June wobbled, then righted itself on the longest day. Something mighty was brewing.

The Purple Emperor appears when the oak leaves suddenly turn deep green, and the reddish-tinged Lammas shoots appear. I looked for him in Alice Holt Forest on June 22nd, but knew instantly on arrival there that he would not be out – the oaks were still a tinge too light. But He was imminent, almost.

On June 23rd I was scheduled to visit the Wai Yee Hong oriental foodstore in Bristol to do a piece for camera for a BBC Natural History Unit film *Butterflies, a Very British Obsession*. It was inevitable that the first Purple Emperors of the year would appear whilst I was purchasing various Eastern culinary delights with which to tempt the monarch of all the butterflies – jellyfish slices, maimed octopus, giant prawns and three types of shrimp paste, including the much sought-after Big Cock brand. Sure enough, Neil Hulme texted to announce the first *iris* of the year, in Marlpost Wood, West Sussex, at 12.05. Shortly afterwards he saw another in nearby Dogbarking Wood, and Ken Willmott saw three at Bookham Common, Surrey, battling with ageing male Painted Ladies which had arrogantly invaded an Emperor territory. Suffice to say that my oriental shopping expedition was by far the best thing I ever did for television, only it was deemed too eccentric to make the final programme cut. The cameraman was ferried round the store behind me in a shopping trolley, much to the surprise of various shoppers.

In Stella Gibbons's classic *Cold Comfort Farm* (1932) the heady aroma of the Sukebind, a plant of unkempt South Downs hedgerows, sends people into the nether regions of insanity. It is also an aphrodisiac, but never mind that. Sadly, the Sukebind is entirely mythological, but the Purple Emperor does exist, and performs exactly what Miss Gibbons most feared – though seemingly without the amatorious effect (though as far as I know, and I would know, no one has ever tested this). In late June 2009 the Sukebind came spectacularly into bloom.

On Midsummer Day I was in Alice Holt Forest early. The colours of the oak leaves were right, and male White Admirals and Silver-washed Fritillaries were emerging strongly. But the Emperor was being recalcitrant. Surely he would appear? Then, sudden in the heat of a cloudless afternoon, the Rooks of Bentley Copse flew out into an azure sky to play, tumbling about in sullen air, before retreating back to the shade of their copse. Shortly afterwards I discovered what they were celebrating – the first Alice Holt Purple Emperor of the year, a freshly emerged male testing out his wings high on a Sweet Chestnut tree. Interestingly, the Painted Ladies had cleared out of the forest.

The following day my old hunting grounds in West Sussex revealed eight Purple Emperor males, including a trio sparring over their favoured oaks on the cross-ride high point in Dogbarking Wood. There, the day's only Painted Lady, a grey male, was duly but spectacularly obliterated, having had the effrontery to invade the Emperor's territory. It fled. And there were aberrations on the wing too: a 'Black Admiral' brambling in Madgeland Wood, a freshly emerged blackened Silver-washed Fritillary ab. *ocellata* in Marlpost Wood, and a dark Comma ab. *suffusa*. There was magic in the air.

On Sunday June 28th I walked into paradise. The old Straits Inclosure of Alice Holt Forest was calling me. Incredibly, nobody else was there – on a cloudless and hot Sunday morning early in the Purple Emperor season to boot. It was as if no one else had been invited. And there, a little way along the main ride, in a pool of dappled sunlight, was a pristine male Purple Emperor, feeding placidly on some sylvan excrescence – only there was scarcely a vestige of any of the standard white markings on his wings. This was what I knew as aberration *iole*. It was the fulfilment of a dream I had cherished since being transfixed by the specimen of ab. *iole* figured in South's *British Butterflies* back in the old school library during the autumn of 1967.

> Diary, June 28th 2009: *And there he was, on a perfect late June morning, basking and feeding quietly on the ride, with a Turtle Dove cooing distantly. The rest of the world cut out instantly, irrelevant ... In such situations there are two ways one can react: turn it into a Eureka moment and run through the woods stark bollock naked, in front of the dog walkers (well, the dogs would surely love it), or sink to one's knees in some form of poetic or religious trance.*

One of those options still needs doing.

After 25 minutes, into which was packed all the intensity of fifty years of butterflying, this immaculate visionary being floated effortlessly away eastwards, low over the ride, skimming over the forest gate, passing over (and beatifying) my parked car, crossing the Frith End lane, and rising over a bungalow called Oaklands and vanishing up and away into Goose Green Inclosure. I had seen many an Emperor take that precise route out of the Straits and into the main block of Alice Holt over the years, presumably en route to one of the distant hilltop territories, and now the one that mattered more than all the rest put together had followed suit. The diary entry concludes: *I then lost it – something blanked out in me. I've no idea what happened to me for an hour ... At last some depth of experience ... I was in a waking dream.* Finally, *The rest is silence.* Dear Reader, the truth is that for much of my life I had wanted, and had sought, precious little else. The day's magic, though, was not done. Another aberrant Purple Emperor male was watched searching the ride sallows, this time a mere ab. *iolata* or *semi-iole*, and a fully Black Admiral, ab. *nigrina*, also appeared. I also saw a Peacock of 2008 vintage, the latest and presumably oldest Peacock I have ever seen.

My come-down was provided by taxonomy, for it turned out that the goal posts had been moved by the taxonomists, and that my specimen was not the elusive and much-desired ab. *iole* but ab. *lugenda*, on account of the presence of a few tiny white spots in the forewings. Ab. *iole* is, nowadays, void of any white whatsoever. Either way, this remains the most beautiful butterfly I have ever seen. But my dream of encountering a genuine, full ab. *iole* is still on. Once I finally encounter this miraculous chimera I will give up butterflying, for the dream will then have been fulfilled.

July came in most memorably. Two hot sunny days were spent assisting top wildlife cameraman Mark Payne-Gill to film Purple Emperors, White Admirals and Silver-washed Fritillaries in Alice Holt Forest. Mornings were spent in the Straits Inclosure, primarily targeting male Emperors searching the ride-edge sallows for females, then at high noon we would move to the prime male Emperor territory at the top end of Goose Green Inclosure, and film the butterfly's activities from a cherry-picker there. Relatively little of the footage shot actually made the final programme cut, but other clips were used in subsequent BBC programmes. The truth is that we gained enough material for an hour-long programme purely on the Purple Emperor. In the can was footage of four males searching sallows simultaneously, a female laying eggs under the sallow canopy, males clashing and chasing, one particularly violent

male pursuing Blue Tit, Chaffinch, Collared Dove, Great Tit, Great Spotted (or rather, Splatted) Woodpecker and Wood Pigeon out of his treetop territory, and a line of five chasing males. Of course, ab. *lugenda*, or *iole*, or whatever the vision was, was never seen again.

The Sukebind was now fully in bloom, which meant it was time for something Extremely Silly. There is only one place for that, Fermyn Woods up in Northamptonshire. On Sunday July 5th *The Emperor's Breakfast* was staged there, as chronicled by Patrick Barkham in *The Butterfly Isles*. This gross eccentricity was hosted by Fermyn Woods Contemporary Art, as an Artistic event (my sole contribution to Art, contemporary or otherwise), and was filmed for the BBC East Midlands *Inside Out* series, with Mike Dilger presenting. The Breakfast consisted of 50 metres of trestle tables draped in virginal white table cloths. On these were set Waitrose disposable party plates bearing an assortment of offerings to the gods of the high-summer forest, in replicate plots, viz: rotten moist bananas, crushed grapes, Stinking Bishop cheese, horse manure (fresh), fox scats gathered from the rides that very morning, saturated salt, honeyed water, pickled mudfish, four types of shrimp paste (Jennies, Thai Boy Delight, Big Cock and something in Chinese), potted shrimps, giant prawns, Pimms No. 1, a wet bar of soap, the risk assessment for the day, the complete poems of M R Oates and, as a sop to Science, an empty plate as a control. The dress rehearsal the previous day had worked impressively well, with one male even perusing the poetical works, which were soaked in gin.

A group of twenty invited guests gathered around the table, then pulled back to await the arrival of His Imperial Majesty. One male instantly appeared, only to land on the table cloth. Then one of the most unwelcome banks of cloud ever to irritate the blessed realm of Albion appeared, and most butterflies stopped flying. In order to give the honoured guests something to do we picked the whole caboodle up, pickled mudfish and all, and carted it 300 metres up the ride. Eventually, the sun reappeared and some rather sulky Emperors deigned to visit the table, effectively for afternoon tea, along with a couple of Commas and a White Admiral, two other butterflies with appallingly bad taste. For the record, pickled mudfish and Big Cock shrimp paste were clear winners, and during the day I noted some fifty male Purple Emperors and a lone female. For much of the day Margaret Thatcher's voice had been echoing in my head, in speech-making mode, saying: 'When it comes to eccentricity Britain still has what it takes!'

The following day, the 2009 Ashes series began, with England reaching 335–7 at Cardiff. Consequently, the jet stream jumped south, and the weather collapsed. On Friday the 10th, two BBC film crews returned to finish off *The Emperor's Breakfast* and to film Hulme and Oates's annual contest to find out which one of them could bait the most Emperors down. The competition boiled down to Big Cock brand versus a particularly vile Vietnamese shrimp paste called Hau Loc, which was subsequently banned by the EU as being unfit for consumption, human or otherwise. The contest ended in a draw, largely because both participants lost count of how many Emperors had descended to their respective baits. Australia declared at 674–6 and reduced England to 20–2. More significantly, the first of the home-grown brood of Painted Ladies appeared, just overlapping with the last of their pilgrim fathers. Eventually the first Test ended in a remarkable draw, with a last-wicket stand saving England from ignominious defeat. This drama was dutifully followed in Savernake Forest, in deepest Wiltshire.

Then something terrible happened to the 2009 Purple Emperors: a vicious autumn gale came over during the night, when they were at roost high in the oak crowns. It was St Swithun's Day, of course, July 15th. Numbers in Alice Holt halved overnight. It was time to move on, to survey the developing Emperor grounds in the re-wilding lands of the Knepp Castle Estate in West Sussex, just south of my old heartland woods. Here, visionary landowner Charlie Burrell is 're-wilding' some 1300 hectares (3200 acres) of low-grade agricultural land on heavy Wealden Clay, inspired by the great Dutch ecologist Frans Vera's theory of naturalistic grazing systems. Many of the fields taken out of arable production some ten years previously and allowed to re-wild, under a low-density grazing regime, had sown themselves with myriad sallow saplings. In mid-July 2009 these fields held huge stands of young hybrid sallow whips, 2–3 metres tall. It soon became clear that the Emperor, supposedly the archetypal high-forest insect, had moved in to colonise. He had probably always had some exiguous form of existence there, perhaps moving in during fine summers and disappearing during sequences of poor summers, breeding intermittently on a scatter of old sallows growing in the green lanes and lags (a Sussex word for a shallow damp combe). Other butterflies abounded, meadowland species like Meadow Brown, Gatekeeper, Ringlet, Marbled White, Small and Essex skippers, and Common Blue. A mighty hatch of Small Tortoiseshell was taking place. Missing, though, were the anticipated hordes of freshly emerged, British-passport Painted Ladies, emerging off the extensive drifts of Creeping Thistles. Only two were seen.

I spent the night as a house guest at Knepp Castle, a crenellated castle designed by John Nash. From a sunken bath in a bathroom the size of a small universe I watched a cataclysmic thunderstorm raging over the park outside, as the summer of 2009 imploded. I had come a long way from a leaky tent in the nearby woods, yet my heart had not travelled far. Knepp Castle is lived in, as a family home, and consequently lives. It is the antithesis of a National Trust stately home. Inside the iron-studded oak front door lies a motley array of muddied Wellington boots, wet weather gear, sunhats, fishing rods, walking sticks and umbrellas – all the things house guests might need, for grand houses were built for hospitality. Inside, bath water reverberates along miles of ancient plumbing, footsteps run up and down stairs, doors slam, unseen things crepitate, laughter echoes down smiling corridors, and the entire establishment is run by an ancient basset hound called Spider – a canine version of Lord Emsworth's accommodating butler, Beach.

The Emperor was winding down, the Painted Lady was failing to wind up, the weather was at best indifferent, but it became clear that the Purple Emperor had laid an enormous number of eggs. I searched for eggs when the sun was not shining, which was most of the time. When they hatched the search continued, for the minute larvae hiding in curled leaf tips on shady sallow sprays. In all, still on sabbatical, I searched for Emperor eggs and larvae in ten counties. There was little else to do: July had fallen spectacularly from grace and had become very wet in most places. The last Emperor of the year was seen in Savernake Forest on August 7th, my birthday; a male so worn, torn and faded that I mistook him for an ancient Painted Lady up in the Beech canopy. He was fighting to the bitter end, but the lone Large White he rose to intercept chose to ignore him. In the evening I gave a poetry recital to the Malmesbury Festival – always do something new and different on your birthday. The only blemish on the day was the England captain winning the toss at Headingley in classic seam-bowling conditions, and unwisely deciding to bat. England were shot out for 102.

Eyestrain kicked in, as it will if you spend hour after hour hunting for butterfly eggs and tiny larvae on myriad leaves. It could not have been done without the accompaniment of a riveting Ashes series. One can do So Much under the influence of *Test Match Special*. Most of the time I was alone, but Dennis Dell, Ken Willmott and other like minds joined in periodically. Most notable here was an Abyssinian cat who spent a sultry afternoon helping to find larvae on Selborne Common, clowning about in sallow trees with me (much to the surprise of a passing dog walker, who had blundered into an anamorphic world) and at one point catching a Bank Vole. Saying farewell to her was difficult. Every now and then we fall in love – with individuals of a different species.

The Brown Hairstreak provided a welcome distraction, at least during the early mornings when this generally indolent butterfly is actually active. On the morning of August 9th I counted 44 in three heady hours and witnessed a pairing, on rough MOD land near Shipton Bellinger on the Hampshire/Wiltshire border. That tally remains the most of that elusive species I have seen in a day. They became active that morning at 8.45 and, as usual, were quiescent by high noon. Most were seen on or even within the scatter of Ash trees that protrude above the thickets that blanket much of the landscape there. Just before 10 am a female flew low across a field and rose up into a row of tall Ash trees occupied by half a dozen males. She was instantly accosted by a male. Within half a minute they were mating, motionless and wings closed, on the underside of an Ash leaf some 4 metres up. Their coitus lasted 40 minutes before, without any ceremony, they parted and flew their separate airways.

Another search of Knepp Castle Estate's re-wilding lands revealed a sizeable population of Brown Hairstreak, when the sun shone, and, when it didn't, Purple Emperor breeding at low density throughout the developing sallow jungles. And at last the long-awaited explosion of freshly emerged Painted Ladies took place, but this was way short of the billion predicted to emerge in early August, and it was now mid-August. Other people certainly witnessed some mass emergences, locally, including Neil Hulme on the South Downs a short flight away from Knepp, but my fate was not to see more than around fifty anywhere in a day. I should have visited the woods less and visited the downs more, perhaps, but my heart was in the woods; or rather, it was in the forest, for Savernake steadily absorbed me. Gradually, I retreated there, systematically surveying the entire 1000-hectare forest and many of its outliers for sallows, and for Emperor larvae. This work continued deep into the autumn. Even Neil Hulme's discovery of a breeding colony of the Queen of Spain Fritillary, one of the rarest of our vagrant butterflies, near Chichester in West Sussex, could not lure me away from Savernake's cathedral Beech trees, hidden Bracken glades and immense sense of history. It had become integral to my life, a deep heartland had been established.

The summer was ageing. Soon it would be time to end my sabbatical and return to normality, only normality had flown out of the window as the organisation was in the throes of another massive though well-intentioned restructuring programme. In big organisations restructuring can become endemic and cyclical, like myxomatosis in Rabbit populations. There seems to be some deep desire within some of us to seek perfection in systems. My last month of freedom passed in increasing dread – of having to retreat from the real world of Nature back into the world of business systems. The message from a sabbatical is simple: stay healthy, stay sane, retire at the earliest opportunity – and let your life's real ministry commence. We spend too much time in the unreal world of systems. As the American poet-ecologist Gary Snyder puts it, Nature is not a place to visit, it is home. I had just spent three months at home. We spend so little time there.

Somehow I was at last reaching a fair understanding of the sort of situations the Purple Emperor breeds in, and his breeding requirements are most exacting. It became clear that eggs are laid in quite heavy shade, because leaves in exposed situations grow coarse and thick, and are presumably unsuitable for tiny young larvae. In shade, sallow leaves that are mid-green in colour, soft in feel and dull in finish are selected. Find mid-green, soft, matt leaves and you will find the Emperor, at least after good egg-lay seasons. Old 'BB' knew this, and he called them 'apple leaves'. Those subjective characteristics are associated with leaf thickness, which can be measured. Sallow taxonomy proved to be a red herring, for the

vast majority of sallows assessed proved to be hybrids, and highly variable hybrids at that. Everything that could readily be measured was measured, though the Emperor does not really do Science; everything else was estimated, as consistently as possible. It felt that, after many years stuck in a Western Front-type situation, I had finally broken through with the Emperor. Time would tell, though, whether the breakthrough was actual, or a phantom.

All told, 181 eggs and larvae were found, 141 of them in Savernake. By Emperor standards, that is one heck of a sample size. Many in Savernake were marked out for following through the winter and into the following spring. Perhaps the highlight, though, was finding a larva at the Clacket Lane Service Station on the M25 (anticlockwise), in full view of a couple of lethargic police officers, sipping coffee in their vehicle. They had accrued a few years' service between them and had seen it all. 'Purple Emperor?' one of them inquired through a wound-down window. I nodded. Miraculously, that caterpillar survived to be photographed the following May.

One by one the surviving Savernake caterpillars entered hibernation, the first on October 23rd and the last on November 8th. All told, 38 were found in hibernation there, out of some 67 autumn larvae that had been followed closely. That is one mighty sample, and enabled close study of the previously unstudied five-month hibernation period. Thirty of the 38 were aligned on stems next to buds, five in damaged areas in bark and three in twig forks. All matched the colour of the substrate they were on. They had journeyed distances of up to 3.5 metres to find a suitable hibernation spot – not bad for an animal less than a centimetre long. Perhaps some of the lost legions had travelled up and away, out of searching range. Whatever mistakes you make in life, please do not underestimate a caterpillar.

And as for the Painted Ladies? They emerged in good numbers in some places, especially close to the south coast, but their aspirations were limited, as if some mysterious power had thwarted them. As in August 1996, this home-grown brood did not pair up and lay eggs. They hung around in gardens and other flowery places, sipping nectar and behaving like tame garden butterflies feeding up prior to hibernation or death. In late August and throughout September they were seen drifting out across the Channel, heading south, in ones and twos. Perhaps they had taken on and been bettered by a greater butterfly? Amazingly, though, by means of an entomological radar, scientists from the Rothamsted Research Institute proved that most journeyed south at incredibly high altitudes, taking advantage of high-level winds more than 350 metres up, the insect equivalent of the Mile High Club. Perhaps Psyche herself had dismissed them?

28 *Adventures with caterpillars*

Finally, I had broken winter's grip. By following Purple Emperor larvae in the wild on their journey from autumn into spring, I had at last made butterflying an all-year-round activity, and winter had become a mere phantom. Hairstreak eggs, the staple winter activity of many butterflyers, only take you so far. Marsh Fritillary larvae, which appear in late winter, had helped, by shortening the close season. But there was a need to venture deeper, and the Emperor does go deeper; indeed, it reaches the parts other butterflies cannot reach.

Down in Savernake Forest, hibernating Purple Emperor larvae were slowly disappearing. Three vanished without trace during December, presumably to avian predation. Interestingly, though, none disappeared during January 2010, which was cold and snowy with much lingering frost. There was a ten-day spell of lying snow, which may well have protected the hibernating larvae, and may also have driven hungry birds, such as tits, out of the forest, to bird feeders in the surrounding gardens. However, although February was also cold the precipitation that fell down south occurred mostly as rain, cold bitter winter rain. A little further north much of this fell as snow. During February, unprotected by snow or ice, nine more Purple Emperor larvae vanished to assumed or actual predation, a worrying number, as it meant that twelve of the original 38 had now vanished. Worse, a butterfly collector – for such people still exist – had followed me on my rounds and had callously snipped off five hibernating larvae. Doubtless he (it would not have been a she) had been following my postings on the Purple Emperor Blog.

The secateur cuts were all too obvious, as had been my location markers. Sadly, the Emperor remains highly collectable, and will remain so for so long as he is regarded, wrongly, as a great rarity.

A sequence of broadcasts on Radio 4's *On The Move* programme followed the fate of the monitored Emperor caterpillars. In the interests of storytelling, and against the strictures of science, the participant caterpillars had all been named after great poets of the English language. This proved unduly stressful, not least when the mighty T S Eliot vanished without trace, though the loss of a platoon of Great War poets was perhaps predictable. The real horror was when Coleridge himself was stolen, snipped off in his slumbers (I immediately upgraded a replacement caterpillar, originally named after his daughter, Sara, and can announce that Coleridge successfully pupated). The truth is that I had no idea what to expect in terms of winter mortality, as no comparable studies of similarly behaving larvae had been attempted in Britain. The Emperor was breaking new ground. At the end of a long winter only thirteen of the 33 followed larvae (excluding five which had been collected) survived into the spring, 20 having succumbed to probable predation, most likely by tits.

March began gloriously, luring out the first butterflies, then fell back into deep midwinter mode. The first fourteen nights brought heavy frosts, often as low as minus 7 degrees Celsius in central southern England. The month then ended cold and wet, with heavy snow up north. Winter would not let go. It became apparent, though, that Marsh Fritillary larvae were in excellent numbers at Strawberry Banks, near Stroud, doubtless owing to good weather when the females were laying eggs during the early summer of 2009, in Painted Lady time. Seventy-four webs of the gregarious larvae were found, containing in the region of 5600 caterpillars. Better still, the parasite load, as measured at the fourth skin change, appeared to be insignificant. If the weather was fine in early summer the Marsh Fritillary would abound here.

Our relationships with places are complex in the extreme. On March 14th I found myself travelling, unplanned, to Alice Holt Forest. The place seemed to be calling me. It felt as though something was wrong there. I arrived in the Straits Inclosure to find that most of the sallow trees growing along the main ride there had just been felled. Only 61 remained – out of the 510 I had counted, sexed and identified into taxa the previous June. I managed to rescue a lone Purple Emperor caterpillar found crawling over the felled corpses. The news got out amongst the butterflying fellowship and a mighty row ensued, which I ended up having to pacify. What the Forestry Commission had failed to comprehend is that to the hundreds of naturalists who visit the place during the high summer period, it is not a wood, let alone a standing cash crop, but a forest cathedral. A year later most of the complainers were up in arms defending the Forestry Commission against proposals made by Caroline Spellman, Minister of the Environment, to sell off the state forests. I was not amongst their number.

April came in on the back of a cold, late winter. Primroses and daffodils only got going properly at the start of the month, but after a poor and wet beginning April was dry and sunny, with a warm ending. Somehow, the spring butterflies were emerging on time or even a little early. My first Orange-tip was duly noted:

Diary, April 10th 2010: *He ascended from a patch of Wood Anemone, flew through a shaft of sunlight and bumbled happily past me. He then spent 10 minutes visiting Celandines and more Wood Anemones before I lost him.*

The world was slowly righting itself. On the 17th the first Gloucestershire Duke of Burgundy of the year appeared. Diary: *She flew up over me as I was kneeling down to admire her, and vanished – the minx.* The Painted Lady even put in an appearance, on the 24th. Apparently they had been massing again in Morocco and southern Spain. *Bring them on!* I wrote, but sensed that entomological lightning would not strike twice, at least not in consecutive years. Perhaps they were scared of the Emperors? At the end of the month the first Pearl-bordered Fritillaries appeared in Cirencester Park Woods, and the thirteen surviving Purple Emperor larvae in Savernake were at last feeding properly.

May behaved itself, for once. There were no frosts, gales, deluges, floodings or other ghastlinesses so characteristic of modern Mays. That meant that spring butterflies were not blasted away prematurely, for once. At the end of the month a hand-picked gang, organised by Dr Dan Hoare of Butterfly Conservation, spent two fine days surveying the northern half of the MOD's vast woodland and downland complex at Porton Down for the Duke of Burgundy. Over the two days 256 Burgundies were counted there, a huge tally by modern standards, indicative of a nationally important site. Unusually, many of them were seen well away from any visible Cowslips or Primroses, the larval foodplants. I myself found twelve male territories nowhere near any obvious *Primula* patches. Although our butterflies behave, and perform, differently in the few large sites which still offer them landscape-scale mobility, this was distinctly odd, and worrying. The diary concluded: *I'm not sure why the butterfly is still thriving at Porton and suspect it could suddenly crash.* A delightful colony of Pearl-bordered Fritillary was flying along the edge of Towerhill Plantation there, breeding in violet-filled glades where young Beech trees had died off prematurely, through what foresters call crop fail. Four Small Pearl-bordered Fritillaries were also seen, the first recorded at Porton for some twenty years. There are remarkably few records of this butterfly breeding on chalk downland, though it breeds freely on Carboniferous Limestone.

And the Marsh Fritillary exploded wondrously at Strawberry Banks, producing the best adult counts in twenty years of close monitoring. I counted 557 in 45 minutes over the 4-hectare site. The males were jostling for position on buttercup flowers and chasing each other about merrily all along the valley bottom. Some dispersed, and were seen as far away as Stroud. The females, though, had been driven away from the breeding grounds on the lower slopes by the over-amorous males and were sulking high up on the upper slopes, well away from their foodplants. At some point they would have to sneak back down slope to lay their eggs.

Then, over in Savernake Forest, at the end of the month, Keats ascended. He had been found as a caterpillar the previous September, when less than a centimetre long, and was now full-grown and turning pale at the feet – a sure sign of a Purple Emperor caterpillar ready to pupate. I watched him ascend from his feeding bough about 2.5 metres above ground to the top of the 10-metre sallow that had been his home for the last ten months. He disappeared into the upper canopy and was seen no more. The journey took all of seven minutes, during which time I recited Shelley's 'Adonais' for this most illustrious of caterpillars. It ends:

> The soul of Adonais, like a star
> Beacons from the abode where the Eternal are.

Keats was arguably the greatest caterpillar ever to walk this earth. Later, I searched in vain for his pupa, spending 45 minutes scanning every spray through binoculars, lying on the ground to obviate back and neck ache. A dog woman passed by, silently.

June produced its worst on its first day. Then, having got that over and done with, came good, delivering a superb second half. A very good butterfly year was steadily materialising, 2010 was battling its way to greatness. At Collard Hill, the Large Blue started to emerge on the 6th. Soon it became apparent that this royal-blue butterfly was set for a bumper year there. Habitat conditions were spot on, following precision grazing management, a goodly number of eggs had been laid the previous June, and the weather was set fair. The weather got a bit too fair, as the sward began to show signs of drought, which can be disastrous for the ants on which this most fastidious of butterflies depends. It was the visiting butterfly photographers who really suffered, though, for this steep slope reflects heat intensely. On hot midsummer days the males would become active after 8 am, to fly along the slope bottom for an hour or two in the hope that virgin females in need of their services would tumble down to seek them. Then, as the day heated up they would fly up to the upper slope, and patrol there, taking advantage of some vestige of a cooling breeze. When that got too hot, they would take an afternoon siesta, becoming active again as the day started to cool down.

Even the Black Hairstreak, one of my bogey butterflies, produced one of its occasional years of plenty. A visit to the meadows and hedges around Finemere Wood in north Buckinghamshire, with Dennis Dell, produced a tally of 46 individuals. That is as prolific as I have ever seen this butterfly. Luck was with us, as the day was dead calm, which meant that the butterfly could flit merrily along Blackthorn hedges that are too exposed in any noticeable breeze. It is perhaps its own worst enemy here, detesting wind but inhabiting exposed hedgerows – probably because it has largely been ousted from its preferred sheltered woodland haunts.

In some of the combes radiating off Dunkery Beacon, on Exmoor, the Heath Fritillary resurged wonderfully, due to a combination of good weather and successful habitat management work. The colony at Bin Combe put on a stunning show. Tick numbers seemed to be well down as a result of the cold winter – I found only five on me. At Halse Combe, on the edge of Porlock, experimental management enabled the butterfly to recolonise one of its strongholds. I even saw a female laying a batch of eggs, the first time I think anyone has seen this approachable and unwary butterfly laying eggs on Exmoor. Normally, the females must lay amongst the Bracken, out of sight. This particular female was spotted fluttering with dithering wings along Grannies' Ride, the bulldozed track that runs along a contour line halfway up the steep south-facing slope of Halse Combe. I knew that flight, it was of a female intent on laying eggs. She was spying out warm hollows in the bankside vegetation.

> Diary, June 15th 2010: *Eventually she settled in one such Aladdin's cave, overhung by gorse, Honeysuckle, low Bracken and Bell Heather, and was clearly laying, deep in amongst dead litter. It was hard to see what she was laying on but no Common Cow-wheat [the larval foodplant] was evident there.*

I returned at 6 pm to analyse the laying site and do a detailed vegetation quadrat, only to find that the footpaths gang had been along during the afternoon and strimmed the entire breeding area. Sometimes the Fates are cruel.

Late in the month the last of my Savernake Purple Emperor larvae, Ted Hughes, went off to pupate and in doing so revealed itself to be … female. Yes, Ted Hughes had transmogrified into Sylvia Plath. The folly of my naming caterpillars after great poets of the English language was finally rammed home.

In the Sussex woods, the White Admirals and Silver-washed Fritillaries were appearing in numbers, and were promising great things. I saw two totally black 'Black Admirals', the rare ab. *nigrina* form of the White Admiral, in Madgeland Wood. There followed an excellent night at Knepp Castle, where dinner consisted of eel cutlets, partridge and guinea-fowl breasts with asparagus, a definitive gooseberry tart, a serious cheese board and three different wines. Keats's 'endless fountain of immortal drink' was spouting rampantly.

Diary, June 24th 2010: *As a result I broke out of my garret bedroom, at 1.30 am, and rampaged on the castle battlements under a trenchant full moon, in the manner of Percy Bysshe Shelley and Lord Byron at the Villa Diodati. Too much coffee probably. Hornets were batting about. The only thing missing was a loose woman.*

The following day the eyesight was playing up and I misidentified a butterfly. The first Purple Emperor of the year was seen that day, at Bookham Common, Surrey, by Ken Willmott – after a vigil of three consecutive days. I may have seen one earlier that morning, at a distance, in Madgeland Wood, near Knepp, but for some reason the eyes were not focusing properly. The summer of 2010 was becoming glorious.

Fermyn Woods were calling, up in Northamptonshire. This is BB's heartland, and these are his Emperors – 'my Emperors,' he used to call them, believing he had re-established the species there through breeding Emperors in his garden. Certainly he helped them, but it is likely that the butterfly had never died out in Rockingham Forest. Whatever, it is vital to be in Fermyn for Big Bang day, which sees the main emergence of Purple Emperor males. Big Bang day actually lasts for two or three days. In 2010 it took place on July 3rd to 5th, after the butterfly had started to emerge there on June 30th. Staying in Sudborough Green Lodge cottages again, by courtesy of Fermyn Woods Contemporary Art, I knew there was deep magic in the air early on July 4th, the sort of magic in which BB believed. Sure enough:

Diary, July 4th 2010: *At 11.45 I spotted a pristine Purple Emperor male ab.* lugenda *flying low down the ride some 60 metres distant, in dappled shade. I recognised him as a dark variation instantly. Incredibly, I had the ride to myself at the time – for the Gods choose their moments carefully. This butterfly was one of the wariest Emperors I've encountered. He favoured dappled shade, as do 'Black Admirals' and* valezina *females of the Silver-washed Fritillary, as did last year's* lugenda *in Alice Holt. But he never settled for more than a minute, not finding much to his royal liking, and he led me a merry dance along half a mile of ride. I lost him at one point, but he returned three minutes later to the favoured stretch below the oaks just north of Neil's Corner. Eventually he flew off north, and I lost him as he flew away over dense sallow scrub. I lost a few pounds in weight in pursuit of this miraculous insect.*

He was very similar to last year's Straits lugenda, *though a little darker, with fractionally less white (two and a half white spots in the forewing only, and not a vestige of any other whiteness, at any angle). Until one has seen the true purple of* lugenda *(formerly* iole*) shimmering in low flight through the dappled shade of the July oaks One Has Not Lived. All told, I reckon I saw about forty male* iris *today, all pristine or nearly so. No females, again, though they must be starting to emerge.*

Entomological lightning can indeed strike twice in successive years, but only with the Purple Emperor.

But it was the White Admirals and Silver-washed Fritillaries that really stole the show in July 2010. The old collectors would have loved this year, for *camilla* and *paphia*, as they knew these two forest giants, varied strongly. My personal tally was ten 'Black Admirals', three or four of which were probably the rare all-black ab. *nigrina*, the others the less rare semi-black ab. *obliterae*. This haul took my lifetime's tally of 'Black Admirals' into three figures. *Paphia* also produced a scatter of black aberrations, called ab. *confluens* and ab. *ocellata*, and a fair few females of the *valezina* colour form. Both these two species emerged in excellent numbers in many southern woods, and Silver-washed Fritillary was seen in many new localities, outside its known range. Butterfly of the year was a toss-up between these two and the Purple Emperor, though the White-letter Hairstreak also needs mentioning in dispatches, for making one of its periodic come-back tours.

Lightning also struck twice in that St Swithun, for the second year running, brought an autumnal gale, a worse one which lasted for 48 hours. Again, Purple Emperors and the Purple and White-letter hairstreaks were decimated in the modern sense of the term, *in sensu hodie*. The day after the storm I visited Oversley Wood, a Forestry Commission wood near Alcester in Warwickshire. The Purple Emperor had been introduced here eight years previously, and was thriving. A spectacular emergence took place in 2010, with no fewer than eighteen individuals being seen at the start of the Oversley flight season on June 28th. I watched a courting pair.

Diary, July 16th 2010: *At 2.10 a nice-looking female flew high along the ride and was intercepted by the resident male. A promising courtship flight instantly commenced, lasting three minutes before they nearly joined on a high Scots Pine spray. However, the minx suddenly changed her mind and dropped to the ground, in rejection mode, before ascending to the sallows and vanishing, leaving the poor male chasing pheromone scent in the air. Ladies, you can behave better than that. During this courtship my colleagues were led astray by a loud shout of 'Camberwell Beauty!' from down the ride. This I chose to ignore, and rightly so, for it proved to be a phantom.*

The diary continues: *I must congratulate Derek Smith, who bred and released Purple Emperors here, on his fantastic judgement of habitat suitability and sallow quality.* Butterfly breeders are often castigated for their activities, and their expertise is seldom recognised or accepted, but Derek has done a superb job in establishing this lovely butterfly here, and in some other Warwickshire woods where it has thrived and spread.

Weather-wise, July 2010 saw a north-west/south-east split, with dry and sometimes hot weather dominating the south-east, whilst the north and west became increasingly cloudy and wet. Gradually the sun sank on the whole summer. August was decidedly poor, especially in the west where the holiday season was spoilt by rain. When the sun shone, butterflies were actually in good numbers, but their opportunities steadily diminished. On August 22nd I arrived at the entrance to Calstone Coombes, an unknown land of secret downland combes near Calne in north Wiltshire, and *was welcomed by a stunning display of Adonis Blue males seeking moisture from mud down-slope of an overflowing cattle trough. This was an amazing, tropical-like experience. A cloud of azure butterflies rose before me. It was not of this earth.* However, a wet end to August effectively wrote off the summer brood of the Adonis Blue. The late summer weather was so poor that the Clouded Yellow did not bother to cross the Channel. Maybe they sensed that September was going to be poor.

It was poor, and in consequence the butterfly season fizzled out early. I spent much of the autumn searching for Purple Emperor larvae in Savernake Forest, conducting standardised searches, repeating the previous autumn's work. The final tally was 66, down from 141. Presumably many females had been killed off by the St Swithun's night gale, resulting in a greatly reduced egg lay. The autumn was intermittently very wet, but with a scatter of glorious autumn days wherein Savernake shone. Then, quite suddenly, on November 19th conditions became intensely cold, with the leaves still on the Beech and oak trees. These leaves were bleached by the bitter weather; lifeless and colourless, they remained frozen to the trees, unable to drop. Snow fell at the end of November extensively in the north and east, and the coldest December on record in the UK ensued. Snowfalls occurred throughout much of the UK on the 1st and 2nd, the north and east became snowbound, the M25 gridlocked itself spectacularly and Gatwick airport closed down for three days. Starving birds flocked into gardens. A short mild spell provided some respite before a nationwide ten-day freeze-up commenced, which included a bitter White Christmas. The year ended spectacularly.

The new year was borne in on a calm, grey and mild night, with moths fluttering at the study window. Purple Hairstreak eggs were hard to find. The adults had been clobbered by the St Swithun's gale of 2010. Conversely, White-letter Hairstreak eggs were relatively plentiful, perhaps because this butterfly lays its eggs a little earlier in the year than its cousin and so had managed to lay the bulk of them before the gale hit. Down in Savernake, the snow and frost had protected hibernating Purple Emperor larvae, and not a single loss was incurred during December. Best of all, Mrs O found an Orange-tip pupa on a dead Garlic Mustard head. Orange-tip larvae almost invariably wander off their Garlic Mustard plants prior to pupating, so pupae are rarely found. This pupa was extra special in that it was completely black. Sadly, it vanished in late February.

Despite the cold December some Marsh Fritillary larvae emerged from hibernation at Strawberry Banks on January 19th, ten days earlier than normal. By early February they were coming out en masse. Soon it became apparent that a record number of larval webs were present. An absolute count of webs over the 4 hectares in mid-March reached a dizzy total of 340 webs, each containing an average of 75 larvae. That worked out at some 25,000 larvae in total, only a tiny percentage of which appeared to be parasitised. Numbers were also remarkably high at Hod Hill and on Fontmell Down in Dorset. It looked as if the Marsh Fritillary was going to take over the world, especially as winter petered out early and gave way to a sublime March, which in turn led into the warmest April on record, and one of the driest.

The only problem for the Marsh Fritillary was that its larval foodplant, Devil's-bit Scabious, had not grown at all in the early spring drought. Normally the emerging caterpillars make do with the previous year's leaves for a while before homing in on the fresh growth, but this time it was different: the bitter December had withered the previous year's leaves into the botanical equivalent of slivers of old leather, whilst the drought prevented fresh growth. The spiny black caterpillars carried on regardless. By early April they had eaten virtually all vestige of Devil's-bit Scabious on the Banks, old leather, stalks and all. Twenty-five thousand larvae over a maximum of 2 hectares of turf in which the foodplant grew proved to be an unrealistic stocking rate, especially in a drought. They ate themselves out of house and home, and then broke out. They invaded the adjoining Three Groves Wood, an ancient Beech wood, where they consumed Honeysuckle leaves, which Marsh Fritillary larvae will eat in captivity. They dispersed far and wide. I found one down the path 255 metres into the wood. Better still, they crossed the stream that gushes along the valley bottom, somehow. One was found up by Oakridge church, half a kilometre up a steep slope! Many died, either of starvation or from being trampled on whilst warming up along the footpaths. I found 22 squashed larvae along one 100-metre stretch of path, suggesting that far more were squashed by walkers than were parasitised.

Later, I found the pupae, the butterfly equivalent of a Yellowhammer's egg – pale, with curious and rather random black squiggles, and surprisingly cryptic amongst dead grass. They were not in grass tussocks, where I had expected them to be, but right out in the open, in sparse short turf. If the fine weather held the butterfly would abound, and take over the whole royal county of Gloucestershire. If ...

By the end of a remarkable April I had seen 27 species of butterfly, beating my previous personal end-of-April record of 23 in 2007. With a little more effort I could have seen 30 species, half the UK fauna. As it was, April 2011 produced my earliest ever Duke of Burgundy (on the 9th), Adonis Blue (30th), Brown Argus (24th), Common Blue (26th), Small Blue (24th), Marsh Fritillary (26th) and Small Pearl-bordered Fritillary (20th). More relevant, 2011 went on to claim the earliest UK sightings for a number of species, despite the fact that the fine weather ended during May.

In Cirencester Park Woods the Pearl-bordered Fritillary abounded from April 20th into mid-May, establishing over thirty colonies and wandering almost everywhere. Some of the colonies were genuinely large, where over a hundred individuals could be counted fluttering low over the clearings and young plantations, visiting Bugle and Bluebell flowers. Somehow, they out-performed the Strawberry Banks Marsh Fritillaries, who flattered to deceive.

Much to my surprise, Marsh Fritillary numbers there were almost identical to those of 2010, raising the question of what happened to all those caterpillars. To recap, there were some 5000 larvae in 2010 and 25,000 in 2011, only for both years to produce peak adult counts of around 550. Perhaps a large number of 2011's larvae starved, or were trodden on, predated or parasitised? The latter seems least likely – unless my careful and assiduous monitoring of the parasite load has been grossly inaccurate.

Then along came June. The diary summarises it thus:

> June 2011 was despicable, though we were due a poor one. It produced a good spell from the 2nd to the 4th, a reasonable day on the 6th, a lovely day on the 14th and short bursts of hot sun on the 26th and 27th. That apart it was Vile, with much heavy rain (especially during the second half), many clear cold nights, and many cloudy days. And it was even worse in northern Britain.

The latter remark is borne out by a weather-spoilt trip to the North York Moors and the Durham coast cliffs. Between squalls I managed to see the first Large Heaths of the year at Fen Bog, near lonely Goathland on the Moors, and visited the coastal cliffs at Easington, which are some of the loveliest, flower-rich cliffs I have seen. There, the Northern Brown Argus was just starting to emerge on cliff slopes jewelled with the flowers of Bird's-foot Trefoil, Bloody Crane's-bill, Common Rock-rose, Kidney Vetch, Northern Marsh-orchid, Common Spotted-orchid and, the best of the bunch, Burnet Rose. The adjoining beach had been used for dumping coal spoil, only for the light to be seen, the mess removed and the sea allowed to cleanse the beach. A visit there does much good to one's faith in our sensitivity to Nature, and in Nature's self-restorative powers.

The race was on for the earliest ever Purple Emperor. The records are vague, though, and emanate from the remarkable spring and summer of 1893, when March and April behaved as they did in 2011, but then led into the most glorious, if drought-struck, of summers. Certainly, *iris* was out in the New Forest 'by early June' that year and the boys of Marlborough College took a specimen in West Woods on June 10th. It is probable that the butterfly actually appeared in May that year. In 2013, after a lot of kerfuffle, the first was seen on June 13th, at Bookham Common, Surrey. It must be recorded, somewhat diplomatically, that Bookham's Emperor Watcher-in-Residence Ken Willmott was abroad at the time, and that this remarkable record was achieved by Rob Hill, his deputy. I was in Alice Holt that day, where *iris* was not out but White Admiral and Silver-washed Fritillary were starting. Then the weather worsened, and the emergence was held back. Purple Emperor probably started in Alice Holt Forest on the 21st, only I was in Heddon valley on the Exmoor coast that day, where High Brown Fritillary was emerging strongly (having initially appeared there as early as May 19th). The High Brown Fritillary was calling me back out on to active service, perhaps rightly so, as it is our most rapidly declining butterfly; also, I seem to have the knack of being able to separate it in flight from the highly similar Dark Green Fritillary.

Oates's grand entrance to Fermyn Woods took place on July 1st, at the start of a short spell of fine weather. I drove past, and disturbed, 21 butterfly photographers en route to the cottage I was staying in on the edge of the wood. Unfortunately there is no other way to the cottage, and at that time of year the rides are almost infested with butterfly photographers, after Emperors. I estimated that some 2000 butterfly photographers visited Fermyn Woods that season. That figure was included in a proof of evidence laid before a public inquiry that autumn into proposals for a wind farm on the edge of the wood. My argument was quite simple: this is the Emperor's heartland, this is BB's heartland, and four 125-metre giant wind turbines on the hill top would destroy the immense sense of spirit of place that exists there. Eventually common sense prevailed.

The first Emperor I saw in the woods that morning was an extreme aberration. It was a male, later identified as ab. *afflicta*.

He possessed more white spots than ab. *lugenda*, having three large white spots and half a dozen small and indistinct white speckles on the forewings, though lacking the normal white bands. He had been seen, and photographed, down on the ride two days previously by Neil Hulme and others, and here he was, basking in dappled shade in front of me, slightly less than pristine but still beautiful beyond words. Three years on the trot I had seen and photographed acute aberrations of the Purple Emperor. Either my luck was ridiculously in or some god was smiling down on me. I was the last person ever to see this specimen, for despite constant vigilance from many of the visiting photographers he did not reappear. He had moved into a different phase of life and had stopped visiting the ride surfaces for sustenance. That same day I saw and photographed a superb Comma aberration, a freshly emerged ab. *suffusa* male, whose wings were extensively suffused with dark markings. He too was not seen again, but that mattered little: my goal was a full *iole iris*, without a vestige of any white markings – that and only that.

It mattered not that the rest of July was poor, that August became cool, cloudy and often wet and windy, or that to add insult to an injured summer, the hottest weather of the year occurred at the end of September and the start of October, when the temperature almost reached 30 degrees. Only the pursuit of *iole* mattered, and that would have to wait for another year.

That early July night I wandered the woods, to celebrate, and also to give thanks. There was no moon, but a pall of cloud overhead, and the sky was immensely dark, but I took no torch, for that would have been a gross intrusion. The air was heavy, with a warm stillness. Wisps of wood smoke hung about in a wooded hollow, yet there was no obvious sign of fire, for no woodmen had been working there. Shapes of trees could just be made out, within a deepening shadow land where dark greeted darkness, but at best they flickered in and out of focus and were merely benign. In places glow worms wanly lit the way along the vagueness that was the edge of the riding, Grasshopper Warblers reeled away in a clearing amongst Wood Small-reed tussocks, and ghosting moths flew around haphazardly in a lightless world. I was in the Emperor's kingdom, within BB's heartland, and no harm could possibly come my way. It mattered not that I was walking blind. The forest had closed around me.

Green Man

If I could but more than sense you
sudden in a wisp of smoke-wood
rising from within a hidden glade
the invisible face of the greenwood
flitting between mind and focus
betwixt countless dancing leaves
foxglove bells or sweetbriar scent
carried on the vibrant hum of insects
hoverflies through evening sunlight
midges dancing joyously to death

In every one of these you might yet be
but only in the half-seen moment
when the last swallow passes high
or the first bat flickers stilling air
as a spark explodes in vibrant flame
your spirit so rampantly appears
then disappears outside wooded time
in and out of mind and leaf and fire
there and not there yet within us
leaping the dimensions of inner life

(Fermyn Woods, Northamptonshire,
July 3rd 2011)

Savernake Forest

Only a forest could carry the name Savernake – or perhaps a venerable public school, or possibly a cathedral named after a canonised Anglo-Saxon bishop. The very word reeks of History, and also suggests somewhere deep, mysterious and utterly unique – which Savernake Forest certainly is. It is derived from a Saxon place name, Safernoc, for a forest of that title was known to exist around AD 934, in the far-off days of King Athelstan of Wessex. The fact that the forest's name has transmogrified only slightly over a millennium – from Safernoc to Savernake – is perhaps indicative of how strongly it relishes its sense of time, place and identity. There is over a thousand years of documented history here. Moreover, since William the Conqueror gave it to one of his knights as a hunting forest, Savernake has never been bought or sold, but has remained for 31 generations within the same family (including some female successions), though it has shrunk considerably in size and has effectively retreated to its core. Each generation of the family appoints a Warden of Savernake, who is charged with the stewardship of the forest's immense sense of place, its depth.

Essentially, Savernake Forest, which lies to the immediate east of the old borough town of Marlborough in Wiltshire, is a place apart. It is not of this age, but of Age itself, with numerous layers of history and much intrinsic mystery. It is pitted with archaeological features – old saw pits, and the like. Henry VIII wooed Jane

Seymour here, and enjoyed hunting within the forest's boundless acres. Jane, of course, was neither divorced nor beheaded, but died in childbirth. Later, towards the end of the eighteenth century, a 27-metre (90-foot) stone column was erected – a sycophantic excrescence – celebrating the return to health of 'mad' King George III. Then, Lancelot 'Capability' Brown imposed one of his designed landscapes on the forest, including the longest avenue in the UK – Grand Avenue, which is over 6 kilometres long and is fringed by Beech trees. During the Second World War the forest hosted a massive ammunition depot and a large number of Americans, who left behind much of the graffiti on the ancient Beech trunks. There are some seriously dark moments within Savernake's history, notably several murders, including the start of the horrific Hungerford massacre of August 1987. Either there is a dark side to this forest, or to some of the people attracted to it, or both. Humanity has certainly tainted its history. Or perhaps, as veteran tree expert Ted Green argues, forests are run by fungi, which are oblivious to humanity.

Edward Thomas picked up on this feel in his biography of his mentor, the great Victorian nature writer Richard Jefferies, whose heartland lies to the immediate north. Thomas visited Savernake with his wife Helen in August 1907. He writes that Jefferies was attracted to Savernake, 'liking the place for its beauty, its solitude, and its many uncertain memories.' Later he comments on 'the great depths below the forest roof that seem to be submerged in time.' Jefferies himself ventures deeper: in an essay entitled 'A Day in Savernake Forest', he states first that the forest 'beguiles us from the region of fact to the realms of fiction, and brings us face to face with Nature in some of her more witching aspects.' He then becomes even more profound:

> The silvery trunks and arching boughs more than realise all that poets and romance writers have ever said or sung of woodland naves and forest aisles, of which the noblest cathedrals offer so poor a copy.

Jefferies concludes by calling Savernake the 'loveliest forest in Britain', though to Jefferies 'loveliness' engenders love, and is way beyond mere visual beauty.

Savernake Forest lies on gently undulating plateau land, on Upper Chalk which is often covered with Clay-with-Flint deposits. Today, the main block of the forest totals about 1000 hectares, 904 of which are designated as SSSI. The SSSI was originally designated on account of the rich lichen flora of the forest's ancient oaks, but more recent surveys have found the fungi and saproxylic interest ('dead wood invertebrates') to be every bit as important, if not more so. Seemingly, this forest reveals its secrets only slowly, and is a place of ongoing discovery. It has many unique features; for example, other forests specialise in brambles and blackberries, but here the bramble cover has been inhibited by centuries of deer browsing, and instead Savernake specialises in luxurious Wild Raspberries.

Ted Green believes that Savernake Forest holds the largest number of ancient large-girth Pedunculate Oak and Beech trees anywhere in Europe, and perhaps also of Sweet Chestnut, and quite possibly sallows. Many of these ancient sentinels have names, like the Amity Oak, Duke's Vaunt Oak, King of Limbs and Saddle Oak. The best known is the Big Belly Oak, which is sited on the A346 which skirts Savernake's western flank. Other veterans stand close to the A4, an old coaching road that runs noisily through the forest's northern fringe.

For centuries, Savernake was pasture-woodland and/or a hunting forest – at one point with a deer fence (park pale) some 25 kilometres long. But silviculture gradually inveigled its way into the forest, initially through the activities of the 5th Marquess of Ailesbury during the nineteenth century. Then, in 1939, the Forestry Commission took on a 999-year lease from Savernake Estate for the timber rights. Rather predictably, large areas of Beech plantation were established, and the south-east sector of the forest was painfully coniferised, along with many of the outlying woods which were formerly part of the hunting forest. The long-term plan now, of course, is to restore native broad-leaved woodland, even pasture-woodland.

Butterfly-wise, Savernake supports a rather limited fauna (the moth fauna is far more impressive). Several of the more precious butterfly species have been lost from the forest in recent decades; as examples, the Pearl and Small Pearl-bordered Fritillaries both died out in the mid-1980s, the High Brown Fritillary a couple of decades earlier. The Brown Hairstreak was last recorded in 1982, just before the extensive stands of Blackthorn it frequented were cleared away. The White Admiral, so ubiquitous in many southern woods today, is decidedly scarce in Savernake, as Honeysuckle has been heavily browsed by a rampant Fallow Deer population, though it is stronger in some of the outlying woods that were formerly part of the forest. Even the Silver-washed Fritillary is distinctly localised, occurring around the main blocks of oak woodland. A scatter of surprisingly tall and healthy Wych Elms supports colonies of the White-letter Hairstreak.

Savernake Forest essentially specialises in one butterfly species, and one only – the Purple Emperor. Indeed, the Emperor is named in the SSSI citation. Strangely, and despite the long history of butterfly collecting in the Marlborough area, led by boys from Marlborough College, the Purple Emperor was not recorded in Savernake until 1947, and then not again until 1977. I R P Heslop considered the forest unsuitable – too open – in his 1964 book *Notes & Views of the Purple Emperor*. Since 1977, the butterfly has been seen annually in Savernake, mainly in the southern parts, around the Column. In some years the population seems quite reasonable, in others the butterfly is scarcely seen – but that's the Emperor all over. This is not the easiest or most sensible place in the country to see Purple Emperors, for here the males fly around unusually tall Beech trees and often appear as mere specks, which is misleading, as the Savernake race of *Apatura iris* is unusually large. There are nine male territories in regular, though not necessarily annual, use along Three Oak Hill Drive, the straight Brownian ride that leads off from Grand Avenue to the Column.

Butterfly enthusiasts, though, ignore these territories and gather only around the Column, simply because the butterfly regularly settles on this eighteenth-century folly, and can be photographed there, albeit through telephoto lenses. In 2013 one male was photographed perched on the part of the Column's inscription that reads 'their excellent and beloved Sovereign'. The butterfly may have a rosy future in Savernake, for in the early 2000s the Forestry Commission carried out extensive thinning and clearance works along Three Oak Hill Drive and the southern end of Grand Avenue, stimulating a considerable amount of sallow regeneration in the process. The butterfly started to breed in these sallows in 2013. Prior to then it was restricted to breeding on tall and often veteran sallows that occur locally in the forest, many of which are unusually large and are nearing the end of their natural lives. Clearly, Savernake Forest treasures its Purple Emperors.

Its next-best species are, curiously, the Green-veined White and Orange-tip. These are often profuse, as one of their main foodplants, Garlic Mustard, abounds in scrapings dumped along the edges of Grand Avenue and Three Oak Hill Drive when the avenues are resurfaced, as happens regularly, given their capacity to generate potholes.

Increasingly, Savernake is being invaded by the motor car. Traffic roars along its northern and western fringes, though the sound is muffled in summer by leaves. Under the open-access agreement established between the Forestry Commission and Savernake Estate back in 1939, people have the right to drive along Grand Avenue and Three Oak Hill Drive as far as the Column. Traffic seems to have driven away the Headless Horseman ghost that reputedly haunts Grand Avenue. The forest is becoming increasingly busy, subjected to modern-day recreation. Of course, when it is full of people it simply closes itself down. But in the gloaming, especially on still deep-winter days when the air is chill and the dog walkers have all but departed, the forest wakes, to play tricks of light on its few remaining visitors. A spectral white stag is reputed to appear occasionally at dusk, along with shadowy animated figures, some vaguely human, some distinctly animal, all primeval. And in a gale, it is its wildest self: an orderless elemental place, where wildness and meekness, dark and light, peace and anger are all one. Be careful, this place speaks in tongues.

Best of all, beneath aloof Beech trees off Three Oak Hill Drive lie a series of depressions, old clay workings, which fill up darkly with water and spent leaves in autumn. These have the feel of the pools described in C S Lewis's *The Magician's Nephew* – the pools that lead into other worlds, in a chapter entitled 'The Wood between the Worlds'. Savernake wishes to be that sort of forest. Jefferies was right: it is a cathedral, one of Nature's finest.

29   *It rained ...*

Chapter 9 of *Winnie-the-Pooh* begins: 'It rained and it rained and it rained. Piglet told himself that never in all his life, and *he* was goodness knows *how* old – three, was it, or four? – never had he seen so much rain. Days and days and days.' One wonders what poor Piglet would have made of 2012, which was so wet and miserable it was dubbed the Year of the Slug. It was *annus horribilis in extremis*.

Yet it all began so promisingly, with a dry and mild winter leading into a second consecutive superb March. Then, on April 5th the Environment Agency declared much of England to be in a state of drought, as far north as south Yorkshire. Hose-pipe bans were put in place. This plus the prospect of a Royal Jubilee summer and the London Olympics to come combined to produce the first effective rain dance devised by mankind. The jet stream immediately jumped south, to produce the wettest April and the wettest April-to-June period on record. The year deteriorated further, becoming the wettest for England, and for England and Wales combined. For the UK as a whole it was the second rainiest year on record, though that dataset only goes back to 1910.

In terms of a summer, UK-wide there were eight lovely days in late May, and southern Britain enjoyed a hot and sunny week in late July, whilst the rains continued unabated up north. There was also a scatter of pleasant days during August and September, and even the odd decent weekend. But that apart, it rained and it rained and it rained. It was a record year for summer floods, and widespread flooding also occurred during the autumn and again at

Christmas. The problem was that the jet stream was in the wrong place just about all year: too far north during the winter, leading to water shortages, and then too far south during the summer months – apart from in late May when the wretched thing briefly got its act together.

Dire as the year was, it was not a patch on the abominable summer of 1816, which must have been the worst recorded in Europe. It was known as the 'year without a summer', and was followed by two other bad summers. This trilogy of appalling summers is attributed to fall-out from the eruption of the Tambora volcano in faraway Indonesia in April 1815, the greatest volcanic eruption in recorded history. The gloom inspired Byron to write his apocalyptic poem, 'Darkness', quoted in Chapter 10. Widespread crop failure during the period 1816–1818 led to food riots in almost every European country. We were let off relatively lightly in 2012.

With the benefit of hindsight, the signs were ominous for 2012 from Day One, for heavy, persistent rain spread across the country during the afternoon – in stark contrast to the fine day that had been forecast. I started the year well, searching for the tiny hibernating larvae of the White Admiral in withered leaves of

Honeysuckle in the Straits Inclosure of Alice Holt Forest. These hibernacula, as they are known, are leaves folded down the mid rib and spun loosely together with caterpillar silk. The tiny grey-brown caterpillar hides within. Unfortunately, White Admiral hibernacula become harder to find with age, as spotting them requires keen, young eyes. The technique is to look for folded or withered leaves dangling down from Honeysuckle stems by silk strands, by shaking the bush lightly or blowing at it, to generate movement. But then the unforecast rains arrived, and soon became tumultuous.

Things got worse. White-letter Hairstreak eggs proved almost impossible to find that winter, at least in Gloucestershire and Wiltshire, even on known and trusted trees. The females prefer to place their eggs close to elm flower buds, into which the newly hatched larvae readily burrow, but the elm trees seemed to be having a year off from flowering. Even mature Wych Elms, which normally flower profusely, were bereft of flower buds. What did they know?

The wheels were coming off. At Strawberry Banks, the Marsh Fritillary population had crashed horrifically, from an estimated 25,000 larvae in March 2011 to a mere 52 twelve months later – and that paltry total was derived from four and a half hours of searching in ideal weather conditions. Only one of the eight larval webs found on the Banks in late August 2011 had survived the winter. Presumably the weather and associated environmental conditions were to blame.

The diary recalls that spring lifted off on March 10th, only I arrived late on site, having suffered *tediously slow shopping at Tesco in Tetbury, mislaid glasses and an irritating visit to the bank where the automatic paying-in machine maliciously chewed up my cheque.* Sometimes naturalists feel that the world is conspiring against them. But the diary continues: *There was a massive take-off of bumblebees at precisely 12.10.* Shortly afterwards the first butterflies appeared out of hibernation, Brimstone, Comma, Peacock and Small Tortoiseshell in that order, in one heady hour as spring broke through. Later, a Red Admiral graced the day. It seemed that winter was dead and buried.

From March 19th to 30th the weather was sublime. This proved to be the longest spell of warm sunny weather of the whole year. Later, one realised that spring and summer had swapped positions, and that Titania's warning in her 'forgeries of jealousy' speech in Act II scene I of *A Midsummer Night's Dream* was coming true. 'The seasons alter,' she states, 'The spring, the summer, The childing autumn, angry winter, change Their wonted liveries, and the mazed world, By their increase, now knows not which is which.' Even in Shakespeare's day the weather periodically lost the plot, but in 2012 it really lost it.

I narrowly failed to find Duke of Burgundy out in March, though Green Hairstreak proved to be well out at Rodborough Common on the 28th, the earliest I had recorded it there in twenty years. By the end of the month I had chalked up twelve species, a personal record for March, and could have managed one or two more. The most amazing record, though, was of Small Blues flying on the Isle of Wight on the 30th, five or six weeks earlier than usual.

Then Easter arrived early, which always tempts providence – and, sure enough, the weather collapsed. Snow fell in northern Britain on April 4th, Maundy Thursday, and the month became cold and increasingly wet, ending with over a hundred flood warnings in force. But April could be forgiven, as it had put on a definitive performance back in 2011, so we were due a poor one.

But May can hardly be forgiven. It was wet and cold – until it suddenly produced ten superb days late on. Those ten days were well used by the spring butterflies, and saved many a small colony from dying out. In Cirencester Park Woods the Pearl-bordered Fritillaries emerged in surprisingly good numbers, doubtless because the fine March had benefited the larvae and also because the adults managed to hold back from emerging until fine weather arrived. They wandered through almost every clearing in that extensive network of woods, and spread out onto limestone grassland slopes around Stroud, seemingly by using the railway line as a corridor. And, miracle of miracles, the Strawberry Banks Marsh Fritillaries made it through! Several of the 52 larvae found there in early March managed to emerge as butterflies, appearing first on May 23rd. I counted a dizzy nine there on the 26th. They had a mere eight days to make a go of things, before the Diamond Jubilee rains began.

At the start of June I was in a realistic, evidence-based mood:

Diary, June 1st 2012: *I have absolutely no confidence in this month whatsoever. The history of coronation and royal jubilee weather in this country is nothing short of appalling and, right on cue, a nasty little depression is set to sit on top of us. I still have nightmares about the Silver Jubilee rains of 1977, and this show's a Diamond Jubilee. The horror. The horror.*

Those fears were well grounded. The long Diamond Jubilee weekend suffered foul and abusive weather throughout, which was most unfair on Her Majesty. The Diamond Jubilee rains were followed by a fully fledged gale on the 7th and 8th, as the wettest June in the full UK dataset unveiled its horrors. It was also the second dullest June on record, after that of 1987. Incredibly, the far north-west of Scotland enjoyed relatively dry weather, which indicates just how far south the jet stream had jumped. Down south, there were seven reasonable days, mainly at the end of the month. The diary concludes, *All other days were Vile. I don't want a June next year.*

Yet some butterflies managed to do all right during the miserable June of 2012, notably our most neurotic aristocrat, the Large Blue. Somehow, it emerged in pleasing numbers at Collard Hill, in the Somerset Polden Hills, and made the most of the scatter of good days that occurred during the second half of June. This was all the more remarkable as the grass was far too long for it on the site. The problem was that the grass failed to grow during the dry March, necessitating the removal of the cattle, for there was no keep left on the slope for them. Then, as soon as the cattle had been taken off, the rains arrived and the grass grew madly, and it proved difficult to bring the cattle back. When I visited on June 17th Large Blue was the commonest butterfly on the site, not because it was genuinely numerous, but because all other species were in disappointingly low numbers. The Large Blue had been safely underground, as larvae and pupae, in ant nests during the worst of the weather. The poor midsummer weather seemed to spur it on, for it laid an impressive number of eggs.

The fine end to May meant that the high-summer butterflies were emerging on time, as their larvae had grown rapidly during warm weather then. The handsome White Admiral was even appearing in good numbers, at least in Alice Holt Forest, where they skimmed the woodland rides three or four at a time. And it was Emperor time again. Nationally, the first was seen at Bookham Common, Surrey, on June 28th, by Ken Willmott, whose duty it is to welcome the first Emperor of the year. My own appeared in most inauspicious circumstances, in Alice Holt on July 5th: I was being savagely barked at by a brace of bad-mannered dogs owned by an unapologetic man. That could not augur well.

On July 19th Neil Hulme and I recorded a programme on our passion for the Purple Emperor, with Brett Westwood, as part of a short series for Radio 4 under the intriguing title of *In Pursuit of the Ridiculous*. The series examined some of the strange natural history passions that individual devotees suffer – my colleague Andy Foster's irrational quest for a rare and totally obscure water beetle, a lady obsessed by slugs, whether it matters if rare orchids hybridise themselves out of existence or not, the virtues and vices of bird twitching and, of course, the Purple Emperor and the Sukebind. Hulme and Oates both came out wondrously during that final programme, openly confessing that the dimension this butterfly transports us to, in season, is actually the real world, and that the dimension we spend most of our lives in is an artificial construct. We also discussed what butterfly people are actually seeking, and the importance of heartlands, places of deep belonging. The Emperor loves to show off, of course, and duly put on a stupendous performance, not realising it was only radio. We even saw seven males together in a vista, a courting pair disappear into an oak tree together, and a terrified Nuthatch being pursued by an irate male. At the height of all this mayhem, a well-known lady butterfly enthusiast – named here only as 'P' – arrived, wearing a T-shirt embossed with large, brazen Swallowtails. She should have known better. 'Take it off!' we shouted at her, but too late. Insulted, the Emperors immediately stopped flying and hung up in the oak tops, until the lady covered up the offending garment, having declined the alternative.

It was time to visit Fermyn Woods, though not until after what turned out to be my last ever visit to Kingcombe, to run a butterflying weekend for a dozen needy souls. After a nightmare journey, when every road leading towards west Dorset proved almost impassable, I arrived to find that the place had run out of cake. Nothing could be more ominous, short of Ravens deserting the Tower of London. An evening walk around nearby meadows revealed a full-grown Peacock larva wandering off to pupate, 17 metres from the nettle patch where it and others had been feeding – quite a journey for a caterpillar some 4 centimetres long, assuming it had travelled in a straight line, which is unlikely. We also found an inter-species pairing, for a randy male Meadow Brown was mating with a freshly emerged Ringlet, mercifully a female. I must have seen a dozen or so similar occurrences over the years, mainly involving Meadow Browns. It is thought that any resultant eggs would be infertile.

On Sunday July 22nd the sun broke through, as an anticyclone at last moved in. Three species of Hairstreak were seen flying at Butterfly Conservation's delightful Alners Gorse reserve, a mosaic of scrub and old meadowland near King's Stag in north Dorset. For decades it was common land, where the local poor could gather gorse for winter fodder and fuel, for the stems burn hot and well and are good for bread making. Now it cares for poor and needy butterfly enthusiasts. Purple and White-letter Hairstreaks were joined by the first Brown Hairstreak of the year, which flew brazenly round a group of us. These three are rarely seen flying together – I had only managed it twice before, long ago at Noar Hill, and here at Alners Gorse in 2005.

That evening I left the paradise that is the Kingcombe valley in golden light that already seemed autumnal. The valley was alive and throbbing, but the Centre had seemingly lost itself – and me, for I never heard from it again. The truth is that our relationships with places can suddenly and inexplicably end, often just by accident. Perhaps it is natural.

The following day Fermyn Woods killed the fatted calf for me. Somehow I managed to drive through the first wood without disturbing any butterfly photographers, at 9.40 am, Emperor breakfast time, en route to staying again at Sudborough Green Lodge cottages. But beneath the line of poplars in Lady Wood Head I was stopped, dead, by a huge black butterfly descending to the ride some 75 metres ahead. It was obviously *iris*, and one sporting little if any white. The car door flew open, camera and binoculars were grabbed; then I had to freeze as the mighty insect flew towards me, and settled on the car number plate. At that moment my car, humbly known as LC61 YHE, became officially *Blessed* – at least as far as the Purple Emperor website was concerned. At that point I realised the vision was a pristine female. She soon settled to feed on the ride for ten minutes before a crowd started to gather, and frightened her off. She ascended to a nearby sallow tree, where she sat for precisely 42 minutes, wings closed, before suddenly making off at speed, up and away. She proved to be a standard ab. *lugenda*, possessing a few small white dots near her forewing upperside tips but lacking the typical bold white bands. She was seen again, nearby and briefly, at 12.41, laying eggs high up in the sub-canopy of a tall hybrid sallow. The vision haunts me still, and rightly so.

She was not the only Purple Emperor aberration seen that day, for a pristine male ab. *iolata* (formerly known as ab. *semi-iole*) appeared an hour later, settling briefly to feed along the East Ride before deciding to go off and search the sallows for females in need of male attention. Luckily, Doug Goddard photographed him before he was claimed by that pressing engagement.

The following day two other aberrant Purple Emperors were seen in Fermyn Woods, though not by me. This was the year in which the Purple Emperor varied: five distinct individuals were photographed in Fermyn Woods, and two others were reported from other districts. Why these aberrations appeared in one of the poorest butterfly years known is one of the many mysteries of butterflying. I was driving north, to visit Northumberland on business, stopping off at the Trowell service station on the M1 where a female White-letter Hairstreak was meandering blissfully over parked cars. 'Hello, Precious,' I said, much to the surprise of a family eating ice cream. In Yorkshire I drove into cloud, which persisted throughout my visit to northern England, whilst the south baked for a few precious days. Rothbury, in Northumberland, proved to be a hapless little town, bestialised by lorries that thundered through it all night, oblivious of its speed restrictions. Sleep evaded me, for my soul had been left behind in Fermyn Woods. What was I missing out on?

Northumberland, half-wild, empty, blessed by dark skies at night, and above all tranquil, was a veritable bog. But its bog-land butterfly, the Large Heath, was finishing a miserable season, having been all but washed away by persistent rains on the exposed blanket bogs it inhabits here. On the edge of Steng Moss, near Wallington, one of the best of the 158 Large Heath sites that Northumberland entomologist Harry Eales has surveyed, hangs a scarecrow man on an ancient gibbet, twisting and turning in the westing wind. It is called Winter's Gibbet, only Winter was not hanging there, Summer was. The mummy's gyrations seemed to summarise the entire summer. Yet strangely, I fell in love – again.

This was my first proper visit to Northumberland, and even in the direst of summers I fell under its spell, especially that of the brooding moors around Wallington. Here you can hear the Curlew call, and yourself think. Poetry could be written there, or even a novel, unhindered. I was there, at the birth of a new heartland. Part of me remained behind as I meandered the long, lonely Roman road that runs along Hadrian's Wall. This is one of the most enchanting roads in Britain, where driving is still a pleasure. It is probably wrong to travel the most magical stretch, from Walwick to Greenhead, without an archaeologist. Romans are everywhere – forts, turrets, a temple of Mithras and an ever-straight *vallum* (a fortified ditch). At any moment one could be ambushed by gerunds or gerundives. It is reputed to have been the worst posting in the Roman Empire, after Hardknott Fort over in Mountain Ringlet country in the western Lake District.

Eventually the Roman road ran out, and dumped me on the A69 (T) in the wake of a convoy of filthy lorries heading for the M6. They turned north, I turned south to visit Arnside Knott and its associated hills. It was late July, and the season was already ending. The trees were starting to turn, such had been the rains. The Olympics were starting, which meant the weather would surely pick up – as the entire population would be indoors watching TV – but it didn't. I fell asleep before the opening ceremony began on my hotel TV, having travelled 1600 kilometres (1000 miles) and seen 38 species of butterfly flying in a week (plus five other species found as immature stages). Only one of them had impressed, the Emperor, who had chosen this of all years to produce a number of acute colour forms – and claim Butterfly of the Year, uncontested.

Morecambe Bay was damp but impressive, especially the Cumbria Wildlife Trust's restoration of the raised bog at Foulshaw Moss, near Witherslack. Here 350 hectares of Scots Pine plantation and Rhododendron have been cleared from the bog, ditches blocked up and water levels raised. Ospreys were thinking about breeding. Meathop Moss, my old heartland by Witherslack, revealed its last Large Heaths of the year, two ragged females. The nature-reserve logbook indicated that the butterfly had started there on June 21st.

August limped in, but produced the odd good day and even two decent weekends, interspersed by more deluges. The Chalkhill Blue exploded on some downs, most notably at Friston Gallops at the back of the Seven Sisters in East Sussex. Here, in early August,

Neil Hulme estimated an on-the-day population of 150,000–200,000 individuals, based on an average of 5.2 per square metre over some 300,000 square metres. Another estimate, over a larger area, came up with a day figure of 827,897 butterflies (data per Butterfly Conservation Sussex Branch website). One visitor described the cloud of blue that rose up in front of him as being so in-the-face it was difficult to see ahead. This was put down to an unusual exuberance of the larval foodplant, Horseshoe Vetch. In the Cotswolds the Chalkhill Blue also put on some impressive displays, though of an order of magnitude less; again, seemingly because the larvae had benefited from unusually prolific growth of Horseshoe Vetch. But elsewhere the damage done by a wet and miserable summer was all too apparent. Marsh Fritillary larvae proved impossible to find in two independent surveys at Hod Hill, Dorset, one of its most renowned strongholds. Strawberry Banks fared no better, for a survey there also drew blank. The prospects for many species in 2013 were therefore ominous.

In late September the rains returned with renewed vigour, generating floods in northern England. The National Trust had arranged a meeting of its nature conservation staff in Upper Wharfedale, in the Yorkshire Dales. At the time Yorkshire and the North-east were being flooded by the remains of Tropical Storm Nadine.

> Diary, September 25th 2012: *After various detours we managed to get from Burnsall to Buckden in convoy, during persistent steady rain, with flooding in each dip, white lady waterfalls cascading down every hillside, and water gushing through limestone walls at the foot of every slope. The Wharfe had erupted and filled much of its valley bottom, where it sat, in tones of brown and grey depending on light angles. Sheep had huddled on hillocks, resigned to drowning. Interestingly, the locals had all stayed at home. We became trapped, in Yorkshire – in floating cars, for hours on roads that had become rivers.*

So the year sogged itself to a soggy conclusion. It rained, and it rained, and it rained.

30 *Fifty years on*

It had to be a cracker, my fiftieth summer of butterflying, yet the starting point was somewhere deep in the minuses, as butterfly populations entered the year at an unusually low ebb. Its predecessor had been so foul a summer that my 2013 diary began: *The previous year is proscribed and will never be named within these diaries. Where extreme necessity insists, it may be referred to as* That Year. 2013 was going to have to conquer a slope of Sisyphean proportions. Yet it began with a glimmer of hope, for the diary reads:

> *As the New Year came in, scudding shower clouds dissipated to reveal a dark night sky lit by a near-full moon and a host of dancing stars ... I could see the doom and gloom of* That Year *being physically pushed away by advancing brightness. Then the celebratory fireworks took over.*

There was promise in the New Year hour, and butterflies relish a challenge.

Down in Savernake Forest, on New Year's Day, things went backwards and then forwards. One of the Purple Emperor larvae I was following had been predated over Christmas – a shame, as it was particularly well concealed, and inappropriate Christmas fare – but I found, completely by accident, a replacement, elsewhere in the forest. Also, the hibernating female Brimstone I had been monitoring, perched low in a sparse bramble patch, had fallen off her leaf, and was lying comatose on oak litter below. I roused her gently, whispering sweet nothings to a spirit of the spring, and attached her to the underside of another bramble leaf. I felt happier as she returned to her slumbers.

Two weeks later Savernake excelled itself. On a visit to show the Reverend Prebendary John Woolmer hibernating Emperor larvae, the remains of one of the previous year's Emperor pupal cases was spotted, high up in a sallow tree. The basal half of the case was attached to the underside of a withered sallow leaf, which was still affixed to its twig by caterpillar silk. Never underestimate caterpillar silk, or chitin, the pupal case material. Incredibly, the silked-on leaf remained on its twig well into the autumn of 2013, some sixteen months after it had been attached, though by then only the stub of the old pupal case remained. In mid-February I found another of *That Year*'s pupal cases, by spotting a leaf spinning on loose strands of silk in the breeze, at Toy's Hill in west Kent. Of course! That's how to crack the mystery of where Purple Emperors pupate: look for the old pupal cases in late November or early December, after other leaves have fallen.

Then January, and indeed the entire year, decided to drag. Snow fell. Savernake's Brimstone was knocked off her bramble leaf and buried beneath several inches of snow. She was found lying horizontally on a beech leaf as the snow was melting. This time, I tilted her upright, stabilised the leaf she was resting on, and left her to it. Though asleep, she seemed to know what she was doing – butterflies are cannier than we think. She flew off during mild weather in mid-February, but was seen again on April 20th, dancing in a sunlit glade a kilometre away; I would have known her even if I had not marked her wing tips with indelible black felt-tip.

February allowed the land to dry out, as it so often does, but it was cold and spring was now running late. It got later, much later, then stalled altogether. We were due a poor March, and duly endured the second coldest March on record (after March 1962, and joint with 1947). In some districts it was the coldest March since 1892, the era of the late-Victorian mini ice age. The month produced one pleasant sunny day, the 5th, when Brimstones took to the air. I saw my first active butterfly of the year that day, a Small Tortoiseshell, in Coleridge's garden in Nether Stowey, which is a fair place to visit for a cup of tea and a piece of cake. To Coleridge it would have been a metaphor of things to come, but like Coleridge it was a will-o'-the-wisp spirit and immediately wandered away.

Easter arrived at the end of a bitter March. A hundred years earlier, during the Easter week of 1913, Edward Thomas had cycled from his parents' home in south London to the Quantocks in west Somerset, where he wished to encounter Coleridge. The weather was variable, typical of an early Easter. His account of the journey was published a year later under the beguiling title *In Pursuit of Spring*. The book is the jumping-off point for Thomas's greatly admired poetry, for much of the book's prose is on the very brink of poetry, though the developing poetic trance is frequently broken by moments of laconic humour and sojourns into human trivia. He was not pursuing spring, or anything; rather he was taking winter, and all the stuff and nonsense it represented to him, as far away as he could, and burying it. A hundred years on I broadcast a tribute to Thomas and *In Pursuit of Spring* on Radio 4. More importantly, one hundred years on to the day, on Easter Day, a small group of like-mindedness assembled on Cottlestone Hill in the Quantocks, where Thomas ended his journey and found winter's grave. There, in his memory, we raised the banner of *Poetic Nature*. We had little idea what that actually meant, but did it anyway; meaning can kick in later, if it wants. With butterflying experiences too, meaning often kicks in much later.

Back in 2013, winter lingered into April, but a slow, late spring is no bad thing, for good summers often come in on the back of late, poor springs. St George's Day dawned fair, as it should, for it is the traditional opening day of the butterfly season, when Orange-tips wander the wayside and woodland ways and put the world to rights. It was time for the first expedition of the year, and it had to be a biggie. A small number of Large Tortoiseshells had been seen in Walter's Copse near Newtown on the Isle of Wight the previous spring, and this supposedly extinct species had reappeared there this year. On April 20th Neil Hulme crossed over to the island and, as is his wont, cleaned up – photographing two worn males and nearly stepping on a third, larger specimen, presumably a female. I arrived by 10 am on the 23rd, to find several other butterfly folk already present, ensconced. Half an hour later one of them nearly trod on a Large Tortoiseshell, basking on the ground – it shot off in a huff. No more were seen until 1.15, when a male attempted to set up a territory where Neil had seen his. It had been disturbed by over-keen photographers, for this can be a decidedly wary beast. I arrived in time to witness its hurried departure, a tawny speck flying up into the tree canopy, with several people pointing towards it. Nonetheless, it constituted a sighting, and a tick, just.

At 1 pm I joined the ranks of those who have nearly trodden on a Large Tortoiseshell, by almost stepping on a giant of a butterfly, presumably female, basking below a hedge line in nearby Newtown Meadows. It flew off in a fury, high and into the sun. Such butterflies do not return. I had visited the meadows in hope of seeing the butterfly there, as elms and sallows, two likely larval food sources, were numerous in the hedges. Then, towards the end of the allotted time a battered male appeared in a coppice bay along one of the Walter's Copse rides, setting up territory there. He was last seen attacking a territorial Comma and the resident Peacock, with a degree of belligerence that a male Purple Emperor would have been proud of. Perhaps the males move from glade to glade, as male Commas do, setting up territory for a while before moving on, ceaselessly.

The main road back to the Yarmouth ferry terminal was closed at Shalfleet, necessitating a detour along narrow lanes. The inevitable happened – a major snarl-up, involving a stray bus, a tractor bearing a big bale on a spike, the obligatory horse box and several hopelessly lost cars. Gently weaving her way through this stasis was a female Large Tortoiseshell, as aloof from it all as the Purple Empress herself. Disdainfully, she hopped over a hedge of elm suckers, to fly on in my mind. Great individual butterflies do that: they fly on within us, as living memories.

I returned to the island in mid-June with Patrick Barkham, to search for the salient nests of Large Tortoiseshell larvae up in the elms, sallows, thorns and Aspens in the hedges and woods around Newtown. The stakes were high, as the butterfly has not been known to have bred anywhere in the UK since the early 1950s. (This is not strictly true, as in 1983 my former colleague Dr Keith Alexander, a leading entomologist, swept a full-grown larva from elm sucker growth at Cubert on the north Cornwall coast. It turned out to be parasitised.) Butterflies do not recognise limitations, which means that their followers and students must behave similarly. Patrick and I duly gave it our best shot, but without success. The fact that a gale was blowing at the time didn't help, but the truth is that there was simply too much seemingly suitable habitat for two people to search, extending far beyond National Trust boundaries. Without Hulme, our lucky talisman who had dipped out at the last minute – pleading daughter-issues – we were doomed to struggle. I believe, though, that this supposedly extinct butterfly is seeking to breed once more along our southern shores. It is trying to come home.

It was mid-June, and the season to date had been distinctly unmemorable, largely because spring had been dominated by cloud cover. There were, though, some rays of hope. Small and Large Whites had been out and about in relative plenty for a couple of weeks or so – 'relative' is the operative word here, for our cabbage whites never become numerous before late July. But it was clear that this year they were plotting something, and that a stupendous brood would start to emerge later, if and only if the weather permitted.

Despite the late spring, a cool, cloud-spoilt May and a stop–start June which at best only managed to stop the rot, I still had faith in the year: it was my fiftieth summer in heaven, and it would come true. The Emperor would turn things round. But July started ominously: a Purple Emperor pupa located in Savernake Forest on June 23rd had mysteriously vanished. The leaf it had been attached to was still there, but it and all its silk wadding had gone. I had followed that animal for ten months, only for it to vanish as an immobile pupa. A Grey Squirrel had been stripping bark off the trunk nearby – perhaps it was responsible? Curse and crush it!

But after four days of stagnant cloud, July and the summer of 2013 erupted: a massive anticyclone came over from the Azores, and sat overhead for three stupendous weeks, producing a sequence of fifteen hot and cloudless days which rendered the weather forecast redundant. Redemption was in the air, time itself was being redeemed. We and our butterfly spirits had been set free.

Rarely in Britain does one book annual leave, in this case to coincide with the Purple Emperor season, and actually find the weather clement. The only gremlin was that the butterfly season was running late and the Emperor was a few days off. White Admiral and Silver-washed Fritillary had scarcely started, and needed to be out in numbers before the Emperor would appear. The solution was simple – visit the Lake District and the Morecambe Bay limestone hills.

The season was running late on the Morecambe Bay hills too. Their chief denizen, the High Brown Fritillary, was not out, though imminent. Instead, pristine Dark Green Fritillaries were dashing about everywhere, feasting on thistle heads on the lonely hill above Witherslack, and breakfasting together one early morning on yellow composites, thistles and early bramble flowers on the lower slopes of Arnside Knott. The first pulse of females was emerging. They were being vigorously courted and purposefully mated.

On Sunday July 7th the vast expanse of raised bog at Meathop Moss, near Witherslack, was in oven-like mood. I had the place to myself, for the human populace was watching Andy Murray win at Wimbledon, and the myriad biting flies were hiding, torpid, in the narrow fringe of trees around the restored bog. Large Heath was at peak season, and for once was not being blown about in the wind, for it was dead calm. The only problem was that the weather was too hot for this northern insect: the females were largely inactive, shading tail-on to the sun in the lee of grass tussocks. One slumbered in the same spot for over an hour. I had hoped to watch them laying eggs, but it was far too hot for that. Every now and then one would be flushed out by a wandering male: she would rise up and then descend, finally rejecting male advances after much wing dithering in the grasses. Eventually a mating pair was located, but they were merely conked out together amongst the cottongrass. The males were wandering freely over the bog, nectaring occasionally on Cross-leaved Heath flowers. When two met in flight they would squabble. I re-taught myself how to sex Large Heath on the wing: the females have brighter, pinkish uppersides, the males duller grey hues. The problem with the Large Heath is that it is hard to see it doing anything other than bumbling about rather aimlessly, usually being blown downwind. Also, it settles only with closed wings, and is distinctly wary of humans – we've drained too many of its bogs, perhaps. The truth is that this is one butterfly you actually need to net, to appreciate the wonderful iridescent sheen on the wing uppersides, and also to check for aberrations in the underside hindwing spotting. But the days when one could wander freely on Meathop Moss with a butterfly net are long gone, and will not come again.

The following day, the Lakeland mountains stood aloof, in total calm, fringed with thin mountain-top cloud which permitted the palest of shadows. This is perfect weather for the Mountain Ringlet, another butterfly heavily prone to being blown about in the wind, or reduced to shading in grass tussocks during heatwaves. Today they were free and fully active, with the males indulging in unusually lengthy flights, before landing, as usual, rather randomly in the grasses. They were searching for females, and were attracted to any brown object, especially sheep dung. Imagine, mistaking a female of your own kind for sheep dung!

Insulted, though earnestly sought, the females were less active, basking for lengthy periods amongst the Mat-grass tussocks. Several were gunned down in flight by amorous males, and would drop to a tussock, to hide there, wings closed, until the all-clear was given. They were already mated. Two were watched laying eggs, placing them carefully on dead needle-like horizontal blades on the edge of Mat-grass tussocks. Then a text message came in from the far south: the first Purple Emperor of the year had been sighted. The reply was succinct: 'To *iris*, Emperor of the Woods, Monarch of all the Butterflies, from *Epiphron*, Lord of the Mountains, greetings Brother.' The true meaning was simple: I hear and obey.

Meanwhile, people marched by, keeping to the stony paths and not experiencing the soft cushion of fell-top grass all around them. I would like to say they were diligently studying Wordsworth, or better still Coleridge, but their conversations – which fog-horned across the fell sides in ever-stilling air – were dominated by IT issues, things they had recently bought, mortgage deals, and, more realistically, blisters. A company of teenage girls marched past, singing 'The Lonely Goat Herd', mercifully in ignorance of the actual words. In desperation, I visited Innominate Tarn, to pay tribute to Alfred Wainwright, who understood the profound nature of the high fells. This was his favourite place in all Lakeland, his spiritual home. He was there, and so was the Mountain Ringlet.

As Kevin Pietersen was being caught by Michael Clarke off the bowling of Peter Siddle for 14, in the first Test of the Ashes series, the high spirit of the midsummer trees, the Purple Emperor, appeared. Two males tussled together over the favoured Sweet Chestnut tree at the head end of Goose Green Inclosure in Alice Holt Forest. It was Emperor Time once more, and on July 10th too, the traditional starting date for the Emperor season. For a day or two they stuttered, emerging in paltry ones and twos in increasing heat, then they stormed the world. There is only one place to be during the Big Bang emergence period of the Emperor season, Fermyn Woods.

Oates's entrance to Fermyn Woods, late in the day on Sunday July 14th, was spectacular. He did well, managing to drive through the first block of woods without being accosted, en route to staying once more in the artists' community at Sudborough Green Lodge cottages. He was going to write a poem entitled 'Green Lady', exploring the physical, sensual side of our love of forests – sweat, limb ache, desire, and all. The butterfly photographers had long gone home, but a mighty ambush lay in wait at Lady Wood Head: a posse of Emperor males forced him to stop, to feast wantonly upon a disgustingly filthy car. They were desperate for any moisture, and a recently squirted car windscreen provided it. Four males instantly descended. Never clean your car in the weeks leading up to the Emperor season; in fact, spray it with shrimp-paste solution on arriving at an Emperor wood, and stand back and wait.

The following day was St Swithin's, but it was cloudless, calm and stupendously hot. St Swithin was clearly taking the year off. Perhaps he could be encouraged to take a lengthy sabbatical? For three days Fermyn provided a world apart, under azure skies and in intensifying heat. Emperors were emerging en masse, and were ardently seeking moisture along the woodland rides. The rides, of course, had been well baited by various folk, including a pair of eccentrics up from Sussex who were pedalling around the woods on cycles bearing jeroboams of shrimp-paste solution. Libations were poured, liberally, along various stretches of ride, to the gods of the summer forests. The Sukebind was splendidly in bloom, and the world had gone mad. At one point eight butterfly photographers were lying prostrate on the ground along a 30-metre stretch of ride, photographing breakfasting Emperors – much to the befuddlement of a stray dog woman who had inadvertently wandered into a different reality. 'It's Emperor time,' someone told her.

At 2.38 Fermyn Summer Time, a virgin Empress purposefully flew into a male territory high up amongst the Lady Wood Head poplars, and was instantly accosted by two males. Two other males launched themselves into the air, but decided to squabble amongst themselves instead, so the virgin led her two suitors to the upper spray of a Scots Pine, where she was instantly joined by the first male to arrive. The second male wasn't having that, though, and for the next 20 minutes tried to interrupt the copulating pair and muscle in instead. He eventually gave up and skulked off, terrorising an innocent Meadow Brown in a fit of pique. The successful pair, who still had not learnt each other's names, stayed together, mating, motionless, wings closed, for 2 hours and 45 minutes. This sounds epic but by Emperor standards is actually an hour short of the norm. They could perhaps be excused for under-performing in that heat.

Two insufferably hot days in Paradise followed, during which the temperature hovered around 30 degrees and the sky was blemished only by aircraft vapour trails. Emperors were flopping onto the ride surfaces, seeking any vestige of moisture, even sweaty human bodies. On three consecutive days I managed to clock up over a hundred individual Purple Emperors, peaking with 134 (a personal record) during a thirteen-hour marathon on Tuesday July 16th. That day was not without its tribulations, for I ran out of drinking water around 1 pm, having poured away much personal water to assuage thirsty Emperors – and carried on regardless. I was not the only centurion, for the Reverend Prebendary John Woolmer also notched up his maiden century, as did Gillian Thompson and Simon Primrose, who had driven over from the West Midlands for one stupendous and utterly exhausting day. They were last seen prostrate either side of a fresh pile of horse manure, photographing Emperors. It seemed the ideal situation in which a young man could propose to a young lady, so they were left to it. The Reverend Prebendary went on to write his customary letter to *The Times* on the state of the Purple Emperor season, but Oates failed to write more than a fragment of 'Green Lady'.

Leaving Fermyn Woods is never easy, especially with the Emperor at peak season and the weather set fair. Part of you remains behind, but it leaps to greet you when you return. The Emperor did not want me to go either, refusing to rise up from feeding on a fox scat along the woodland ride as I drove out on the Thursday evening – so I simply drove over him, avoiding him with the wheels, of course. He carried on feeding, regardless, as the vehicle passed carefully and dutifully over him. In the course of three heady days I had witnessed one pairing, three courting pairs, three rejection flights; I had seen a male of the *lugenda* colour form and a group of five males feeding together on a fresh fox scat;

England had won the first Test and my nose was starting to peel. But a major challenge had to be met.

One of the zanier members of Butterfly Conservation Sussex Branch is Dr Dan Danahar, a gangly schoolteacher from Brighton with a twinkle in his eye. He had come up with the idea of an annual butterflying contest, in which two teams battle to see how many species they can find in a single day, with points being awarded for each species and extra points for the difficult immature stages (egg, caterpillar, etc.). But each finding has to be witnessed by an independent judge, and the teams must cross over and operate on each others' patches. Some fool had decided that I would captain the Hampshire side, against Sussex, and being an even greater fool I had accepted. The situation was untenable, for I was leading one of my two favourite counties against the other. The teams gathered in the village car park at Bosham (pronounced Bossam). I had last visited Bosham as a choirboy, for a school choir competition, nearly fifty years previously. But this competition, on Friday July 19th 2013, was altogether more serious.

At 9 am, the Sussex team scuttled off into Hampshire. After giving them a head start the Hampshire team then set off into Sussex. Film crews from BBC South pursued both teams, eventually broadcasting a news piece that rendered butterflying seriously intriguing – and fun. The roads were busy: malevolent horse lorries abounded along the A272 and the tarmac was melting. The wretched A27, a dual carriageway designed by Descartes' Malicious Demon, was even bloodier. Friday was not a sensible day for this venture, but sense scarcely entered into it, certainly not common sense. Marlpost and Madgeland woods, bless them into eternity, welcomed the Hampshire Hogs, quickly presenting them with the Purple Emperor they needed, plus Silver-washed Fritillaries and White Admirals, and White Admiral eggs on dangly strands of shaded Honeysuckle. Meanwhile, the Sussex team invaded the inner sanctum of the Straits Inclosure, in Alice Holt Forest, Hampshire's Holy of Holies. Unwisely, the Straits revealed its secrets. The teams were running neck and neck.

Hampshire could be forgiven for wondering what connections Martin Warren and Nick Baker had with Sussex, men of Dorset and Devon respectively but batting for Sussex on the day, but Hampshire had managed to inveigle top field-craft ace Ken Willmott out of his native Surrey. There was some needle in all this. There had to be.

At the end of an exhausting and exhaustive day the two teams were level on points, and drinking together in the public bar of the Anchor Bleu, rehydrating and trying to recall a frenetic day that had rapidly hazed into a blur. The judges went into conclave, needing to reach a decision to satisfy BBC South Today. They made the wrong decision.

The silliness had to end. The Sukebind blossom was starting to go over, and it was time for my fiftieth season to reach up towards its zenith. 'It won't come down!' they complained – a couple of butterfly photographers in Madgeland Wood, determined to photograph a Purple Emperor. 'Of course it won't,' I grumbled back, as I headed out of the wood on to Marlpost Road. 'It's searching the sallow tops for a freshly emerged female – and neither would you descend from on high if you were on the trail of fresh crumpet.' People had so little idea of what these butterflies were actually doing. The silliness had to end.

There was only one place for the pilgrimage to begin, Marlpost Road; for Marlpost Road leads past Newbuildings woods, through Dragons Green, out on to the sacred road, the A272, the backbone of the Purple Empire, east and then south, to the Knepp Castle Estate's re-wilding lands, by Shipley windmill where Hilaire Belloc once lived.

No one had searched Knepp's re-wilding lands for Purple Emperors since my tentative explorations there in 2009, when the network of copses and hedge-lined fields recently taken out of arable or dairy farming was just becoming colonised. Neil Hulme had called in a few times, in passing, and had seen the odd Emperor there, but recent summers had been too dire, and Emperor numbers too low for systematic survey of a huge area of atypical habitat. But today, July 20th 2013, was the day to find out; the Emperor was fully out and in good numbers, for once. Neil and I anticipated seeing a dozen or so, maybe 20, but butterflies are extremely good at making one feel hopelessly wrong, particularly the Purple Emperor. In five hours we counted 84, within a relatively small area, and in rather cloudy weather. Clearly, the butterfly had erupted here. And they were not just numerous, but seriously violent too. We saw males attack a Chaffinch and a Blackbird, and loudly applauded a brace of females working together to extirpate a flock of young tits from a sallow stand – all to the accompanying sound of wedding bells drifting across from Shipley church. Up in the oak crowns, males were kicking each other's teeth in with gross regularity. We wound them up by singing skinhead football chants at them. At one point we saw five males hotly pursuing a female, and cheered them on.

Returning the following day, after a restless night, we added another 50, but the insects were less active and the habitat quality of the area we searched was not quite so high. Nonetheless, we had determined that within the space of a few years the huge southern block of Knepp Castle Estate, between Shipley and Dial Post, had developed what must be the second-largest Purple Emperor population in the country, after Fermyn Woods, and one that was destined to grow much larger. Never mind Birnam Wood moving to Dunsinane, Fermyn Wood was moving to Sussex; a new epicentre of the Purple Empire was developing, right where I started out fifty years ago, right in my heartland. Here, the butterfly was breeding in young sallow bushes, 2–4 metres tall at the most, which had developed after sallow seed had rained down on bare ground when arable fields were taken out of productivity about a decade back. No longer was the Purple Emperor a woodland butterfly at all, let alone the mysterious ancient-woodland creature it had long been assumed to be, but an opportunist deftly able to exploit the rural equivalent of a brownfield site. At Knepp it is a butterfly of scrubland, developing pasture-woodland and outgrown hedgerows. A particularly large penny had dropped. Poor Job must have felt rather like that when the Almighty explained it all to him at the end of his book.

The crescendo was building, even though the Emperor season was on the wane – albeit after conquering new and dizzy heights. If any other butterfly wanted to win Butterfly of the Year 2013 it would have to knock His Imperial Majesty off his perch, during one of his greatest seasons. Several were trying it on. As predicted, Small Whites and Large Whites were everywhere, and Peacocks and Small Tortoiseshells were emerging in excellent numbers, the latter having sprung from nowhere to fill almost every garden. Butterflies are amazingly good at coming from beyond the ninth gate of death, or however many gates there are.

Such was the paltry state of world news on August 6th, and so prominent were butterflies in the public eye, that the news release put out by the National Trust's Press Office then, celebrating my fifty years of butterflying, was taken up. No credit was due to me here, it was all down to the magnetism of butterflies, and the love and wonder they inspire. All I had done was take up butterflying fifty years previously, when given a copy of *The Observer's Book of Butterflies* and a net for my tenth birthday – and had never given up, but had become their vehicle.

We needed a venue with speedy access from London, and seriously good butterflies. Denbies Hillside, on the scarp slope of the North Downs just west of Dorking, offered just that. Moreover, the Chalkhill Blue population had erupted there, producing what is by far the greatest profusion of a single species of butterfly I have seen. The Denbies Chalkhills had done it before, as recently as 2006, but that year the peak count on the butterfly monitoring route there was a mere 832. This time it reached 3500. One must feel deeply for Gail Jeffcoate, who faithfully walks the butterfly transect route there each week. Normally the walk takes 45 minutes, this time it took two hours. There were massive aggregations of the Cambridge-blue males on every Marjoram clump, such that each patch glowed with iridescent blue. Earlier, in mid-morning, when the males were busy patrolling the breeding grounds in search of emerging females, whole expanses of short turf shimmered with sky blue. They also wandered far and wide, invading Dorking station and High Street. This wonder of the natural world was featured on Channel 4 News (we almost got it on the BBC1 main evening news bulletin). Sadly, photographs of such events sell the story badly short; only moving film depicts the true scale.

The following day, my sixtieth birthday, one of Christ's Hospital school's more prodigal sons returned, for the first time in decades, to conduct an interview with Patrick Barkham for a piece on butterflying for *The Guardian*. The place leapt to greet us. A Holly Blue met us at the entrance, and we found Purple Hairstreaks flying in the copse by Leigh Hunt house where I had begun butterflying. The school had intensified in beauty. Even then it could not hold me, for we ended the afternoon in Marlpost Wood. Once again, the forest closed around me and instilled its sense of deep belonging. A Jay's wing feather lay in the dust. At 4.45 pm one of the most majestic and memorable of female Purple Emperors ever seen flew lazily along the ride, to perch above us on an oak spray, basking in the glory of the day, before gliding effortlessly away. I knew *iris* would appear here, and that I did not even need to look for them – they would find me. The diary concludes: *Ended up with a sublime journey 'home' along the A272, into the sunset of the day and of life – only I'd just been Home.* And as for a party? That took place the following day in Savernake Forest, where a group of 25 friends and relations, adorned with picnic hampers and Pimms, were regaled by the last Purple Emperors of the season.

But great butterfly seasons do not go gentle into that good night, as Dylan Thomas put it. This one was by no means ready to bow out, and a dozen other species were preparing to do battle with the Emperor over the destiny of Butterfly of the Year 2013. Clouded Yellows invaded the UK in early August – and they seldom bother coming here in poor summers. More significantly, that most occasional of vagrants from the continent, the Long-tailed Blue, appeared – and meant business. On or just before my birthday, as a present to us all, what was probably the largest immigration of Long-tailed Blues in entomological history hit the south-east coast. They had hopped across the Channel on a fairly broad front.

By happy chance, I was destined to visit the Kent coast in mid-August, to run training events for National Trust staff there, and the weather was set fair. By then the butterfly had already been spotted in three or four places along the Kent coast, and a breeding colony had been discovered on Kingsdown Leas, a section of National Trust clifftop chalk grassland a few kilometres east of Dover. The initial discovery was made by birders, in pursuit of a rare bird there on August 9th, and was instantly put out on the birding grapevines. Given that the Long-tailed Blue is regarded as a once-in-a-lifetime experience for butterfly lovers in the UK, well over a hundred enthusiasts visited Kingsdown in search of the butterfly during the following weeks. The colony was breeding on the Broad-leaved Everlasting-pea (perennial sweet pea), which occurs in profusion along the cliff top there, and locally elsewhere in the district. This is a non-native species which frequently escapes from gardens and colonises rough or disturbed ground. It is rarely regarded as a nuisance, but on Kingsdown Leas it had benefited considerably from an autumn mowing regime, which had created myriad pockets of bare ground in which it could germinate, such that huge patches of the plant occurred all the way along the cliff top.

On August 14th at least three males and one female were present on Kingsdown Leas. These were old and tired butterflies, who merely wanted to sip nectar from their beloved pea flowers but would flit off at speed if disturbed. A systematic search of the Broad-leaved Everlasting-pea clumps revealed over 50 tiny pale-blue eggs, on the sepals of flowering sprays. These were found right the way along the cliff top, and so must have been laid by more than one female. They suggested that, weather permitting, a sizeable home-grown brood would emerge in early autumn, for the Long-tailed Blue is a fast breeder, going from egg to adult in half a dozen weeks in warm weather. It is one of the most widespread butterflies in the world, occurring in temperate zones of both hemispheres, breeding in the flowers and pods of a wide range of plants of the pea family. In some countries it is an agricultural pest. In Britain it is almost the ultimate butterfly twitch, though if our climate becomes warmer it could become a resident species in the deep south.

I also found eggs in Kingsdown village, where strands of the same Broad-leaved Everlasting-pea trailed down over a garden fence, and also in the nearby village of St Margaret's at Cliffe. However, there was no sign of butterfly or eggs on another, smaller type of perennial sweet pea, Narrow-leaved Everlasting-pea, which abounds at St Margaret's Leas cliffs. It seems that Long-tailed Blue adults fizzled out at Kingsdown in late August, with the last sighting being made on the 26th.

September started fair, then wobbled for two weeks. Fine weather returned on St Matthew's Day, the 23rd, when it so happened that I was destined to visit the Kent coast again. The home-grown brood of Long-tailed Blue was first noted at Kingsdown on September 18th, and a small emergence occurred on the 23rd, when at least six males and a female were observed by some twenty people. Twice that number of people appeared on the following day, which may have been too much for what can be a decidedly wary butterfly, for sightings were fewer and further between. Two males repeatedly attempted to establish a territory in a sheltered sunny hollow, but were quickly driven off by over-eager cameras. Long-tailed Blues lingered on at Kingsdown well into October, the final sighting being made on October 9th.

A number of other colonies were discovered along the coast of Kent and East Sussex, particularly on Thanet and around Newhaven and Brighton. Most were based on Broad-leaved Everlasting-pea. Fresh specimens were appearing until the autumn rains arrived with a vengeance around October 20th. Strangely, though, only a scatter of Long-tailed Blues was seen in West Sussex, and even fewer in Hampshire and on the Isle of Wight, where a few were seen at Ventnor in early October. Despite vigilance the butterfly was not recorded in Surrey, which meant that the drifts of Broad-leaved Everlasting-pea along the old coaching road at Denbies Hillside, near Dorking, which attracted the butterfly in 2003, went untenanted.

Like so much of the best of British wildlife the Long-tailed Blue looks too exotic to be British. The uppersides of freshly emerged males display an iridescence which hints at both the Large Blue and the Adonis Blue, whilst a fresh female can flash vivid turquoise at you. Conversely, a faded male could be mistaken for an old male Common Blue, albeit a large one, and a worn female for a female Chalkhill Blue – which makes one wonder whether it might have been overlooked, mistaken for commoner species. To make matters worse, Long-tailed Blues are active only intermittently, disappearing mysteriously for periods of time. With the males, they seem to hop from territory to territory, occupying several during a day on some sort of rota system. When two meet a vicious battle ensues, in which they spiral high up in a speeded-up version of Duke of Burgundy male combat. The females are even more intermittent in appearance. In flight, both sexes fly, or rather flit, more like a hairstreak than a blue, using a flight pattern reminiscent of that of the Brown Hairstreak. A great many UK butterfly enthusiasts made the effort to see this most lovely of butterflies in 2013, and so will know how to look for it should it grace our shores again – and it will. It has designs on the United Kingdom.

Eventually the great butterfly summer of 2013 was blasted away by the autumn rains, which arrived with a vengeance in late October. From humble origins it had become great and, more importantly, had set up its successor well, at least for most of our butterfly species. My fiftieth summer of butterflying had been like none of its predecessors; or rather, it had been like each one of them, in that it was, as all others had been, intrinsically unique.

Butterflies exist within a perpetual whirligig of change that prohibits repetition, and which ensures that those who study them remain forever entranced, dancing in the sunlight with them. For fifty years I have just been scraping the surface, dabbling in the shallow end. It is time to venture deeper. That may consist of giving up all butterflies bar one, and concentrating only on the one that matters most – His Imperial Majesty, the Emperor of the Woods, the one of whom the Nightingale sings, the Purple Emperor, *Apatura iris*, whose very name captivated a small boy half a century ago.

Go confidently in the direction of your dreams.
Live the life you imagined.

Henry David Thoreau

Towards some meaning

I want the inner meaning and the understanding of the wild
flowers in the meadow. Why are they? What end? What purpose?

Richard Jefferies, *Field and Hedgerow* (1889)

Nature has never been an easy path to follow, particularly in an
increasingly materialistic society run by increasingly convoluted
systems and forms of usury. It seems we seek perfection in (rather
than through) systems. Naturalists would rather pursue Nature's
wealth, and the freedom and depth of experience that Nature offers.
Many of them, perhaps those who feel most fulfilled, decide at an
early age that they would rather have time than money, realising of
course that one cannot have both, and that money does not buy
time. Time in Nature is what they seek.

Naturalists used to be loners, and were often regarded as odd
individuals. To many social strata they were at best eccentrics.
Certainly that is how it felt as a young person during the false
dawn of the hippy era, which opted for Flower Power when
Butterfly Power would have been more effective, then through
the mindless nihilism of punk and the hedonism of the Thatcher
years. But during the 1990s things changed, mercifully. It was
the birders – clothed in anoraks and bobble-hats, by reputation
only – who broke down the barriers of social inhibition, perhaps

by sheer weight of numbers and downright persistence. In parts of the country, notably along the north Norfolk coast and on the Isles of Scilly, servicing their needs became a significant part of the local economy, at least seasonally – even if what they were actually seeking was poorly understood, by others and perhaps by themselves.

Butterfly people are little different, now that they no longer carry nets and killing jars. Like birders, they stand around for ages in one spot, waiting. They loiter with intent. Above all else they are seeking glory moments, moments within Nature's glory; they seek discovery, and freedom – freedom to exist purely within the moment of being. They need patience, the ability to move without disturbing butterflies, to be able to read what is going on around them, phenomenal powers of visual observation, and they need to develop an intense, intuitive relationship with Nature. These essential skills are not easily learnt. Butterfly followers who have spent time fishing should be greatly advantaged.

Rather suddenly, and perhaps due largely to the focus and fellowship provided by the dynamic charity Butterfly Conservation, and the clear conservation messages the organisation has successfully conveyed to public and politicians alike, butterflies have become cool. Butterfly people, like birders, are no longer stigmatised outcasts. Without Butterfly Conservation, though, they might still be eccentric loners. With it, they can grow and make effective changes. Anyone who has read so far in this book is effectively a member of Butterfly Conservation, though some may not have paid their subscriptions yet.

Sublimation

The truth is that people rather yearn for Nature, and perhaps especially for one aspect of it, wildlife – or wilder life. At the very least we belong alongside Nature, though some of us would be happier actually living amongst her. The success of wildlife television owes much to this poorly recognised desire, this sense of belonging, and of current separation. Interestingly, wildlife TV is based on appreciating and understanding wildlife, rather than exploiting it – there are no TV programmes about country sports, except for occasional series on fishing. At the very least TV has provided a lifeline between an increasingly urbanised and acquisitive society and Nature. The problem, of course, is that direct experiences with wildlife are infinitely greater than remote, two-dimensional sublimations – but only to those who have experienced the real thing. Super slow-motion TV can show butterflies, not as they are, but as we might like them to be – nice and cooperative, our toys.

There is a danger of augmented or supplanted reality taking over here, particularly when computer screens, IT packages and sophisticated photographic equipment are brought into play. In this context the second verse of George Herbert's hymn 'Teach Me My God and King' is worthy of consideration:

> A man that looks on glass,
> On it may stay his eye;
> Or if he pleaseth, through it pass,
> And then the Heaven espy.

There is a friendly warning for butterflying here, as increasing use is made of digital photography – a great hobby, for sure, offering the thrill of the chase, the warm glow of satisfaction, clear memories, and great days out in Nature. But we must be careful that the camera does not dominate our relationship with these creatures, or we will revert to becoming butterfly collectors again in spirit (to practise what I preach, I have determined not to photograph butterflies on Sundays).

The message here is simple. With butterflying, do not settle for two-dimensional experiences – go the whole way, seek depth of experience; it is there on offer, even though the true meaning may not kick in until much later.

Psyche revisited

In the autumn of 2010 the National Trust website ran a competition asking people to write down what butterflies meant to them. Copies of Patrick Barkham's book *The Butterfly Isles* were offered as prizes. The volume and depth of the responses were nothing short of astounding. Clearly, a great many National Trust supporters value butterflies greatly, considering them vital to the health of the environment and to their own lives and wellbeing. The results were summarised in an article in the *National Trust Magazine* (summer 2011 edition).

Most readers had fallen under the spell of butterflies in childhood, and expressed a view that these winged creatures reminded them strongly of those halcyon days. One reader wrote: 'These fragile, winged beauties make me feel the enthusiasm and sheer joy that children know and adults forget.' So butterflies are symbols of something precious that has been lost, some much-missed part of ourselves, of yesterdays gone by. Perhaps some fall from grace has taken place? Perhaps our understanding of metaphor?

Several readers wrote in to report profound experiences involving butterflies, including at times of bereavement. One recalled encountering the exquisite Koh-i-noor Morpho whilst preparing to lead an infantry charge in the jungle. Others described how timely appearances of butterflies had helped them come to terms with the loss of a loved one. One lady reported two butterflies flying together high up in the church rafters during her grandfather's funeral service, where a single butterfly had flown there during her grandmother's funeral a year earlier. Another freed a red butterfly battering itself against her recently deceased red-haired mother's bedroom window. I had a comparable experience at my mother's funeral, as described in Chapter 24 – only I was expecting it.

Memory, heartland and loss

People collect memories, often inadvertently, so much so that some major industries are heavily reliant on this, notably tourism and recreation. Modern naturalists collect memories, as photographs, in diary accounts and, most notably, as after-images in the mind that coalesce to provide some curious warm glow of fulfilment, of belonging to the places they have experienced, of belonging in or at least with Nature. Butterflying is exceptionally good at providing such memories, as no two days out in the woods or fields are ever alike, for butterflies are grand masters of the art of constant change, even more so than the seasons and the places they inhabit. No two butterfly seasons are remotely alike, all are unique. Butterflies take us into the living pulse of spring, and far into the totality of summer, and then provide us with memories that become distilled and enhanced over time, gilded or silvered in sunshine and framed by green leaves.

Also, and more importantly, butterflies take us deep into many of the most wonderful landscapes in the British Isles, and when those places are at the very zenith of their annual cycles of natural beauty, on sublime days in spring and summer. They take us out of the material world in which we are entrapped. They take us to where the sense of spirit of place is so awesome that when we leave part of ourselves remains behind, and we take some microbe of the essence of that place away with us. Consequently, we are duty-bound to return, and the place leaps to greet us when, almost as prodigal children, we return. This experience is deeply poetic, spiritual and, for people who like the term, religious – and should be recognised and celebrated as such.

We do not merely fall in love with each other (something we may not be as good at as we think), but with places. Such places become our spiritual heartlands, places of treasured memories, of belonging and rootedness. The Welsh language recognises the concept of places of deep belonging through a conceptual term that does not readily translate. Strictly, *cynefin* means one's personal habitat – cultural, ecological, geographic, historic, social and spiritual. It translates poorly into English as heartland, only a deep and highly personal heartland. There is also a Welsh concept with which naturalists, especially birders, will readily identify – *y filltir sgwâr*, which translates as the square mile, or home patch. All my life I have sought to develop deep *cynefin*. At times I have almost got there – only to be forced out, obliged to move. I am now left with a vast amount of incipient *cynefin* (plural *cynefinoedd*) – modest spiritual homes, or loving heartlands, scattered throughout the British Isles. These range from the shores of Loch Arkaig in the north-west Highlands to the cliffs of Dover, from the Lake District high fells down to the limestone hills of Morecambe Bay and across the Irish Sea to Murlough Dunes and the Mountains of Mourne, from the Ceredigion coast, through the Malvern Hills and across to the Norfolk Broads, and too many to mention which are scattered across southern England. Eventually I will settle in one, and seek to grow my true *cynefin*. That single word needs to penetrate the English language, and take English culture by storm – but without losing its depth. Too many of us are rootless, and are searching for rootedness, as is suggested in much of today's new nature writing.

Conversely, Welsh culture and language also include the concept of *hiraeth* – a longing for home. This can be positive or negative, the latter equating readily to the homesickness felt by new pupils at boarding school. At its darkest, *hiraeth* is the spiritual sickness that develops when one's *cynefin* is broken by dramatic physical change to one's heartland, or by being forced to move away from where one's *cynefin* dwells. The life of John Clare (1793–1864), poet, superb self-taught naturalist and devout countryman, is worth examining through the perspectives of *cynefin* and *hiraeth*. The landscape of his homeland, around the village of Helpston in east Northamptonshire, was his heartland, his real and fantasy worlds combined. But that landscape was ruthlessly destroyed by Enclosure Acts early in his adult life. Furthermore, he was lured to London by his publisher, and by the bright lights – wine, women and song, which he liked. There, however, something fundamental was missing, so much so that he broke down and became confined to a mental asylum. Yet Home was calling him. He escaped and walked back to Helpston, starving, a beggar forced to eat grass. Only Home was no longer recognisable, beyond the village buildings; his deep *cynefin* lay shattered by agricultural changes. In such situations there may be no safe place to go this side of cloistered religion, or madness. Clare succumbed to the latter, and spent the last thirty years of his life confined to the asylum in Northampton, suffering from severe delusions. This interpretation should have resonance amongst environmental conservationists, and amongst people for whom the countryside is dear. His tale is perhaps a mighty metaphor for the present human predicament in the UK.

Fortunately, butterflies seldom take us to desecrated places. When they start to do that our relationship with them will break, for their heartlands will have been destroyed and they will be making last-ditch stands, their vital metapopulation structures shattered. Certainly, an increasing number of quality butterfly sites are devalued by traffic noise pollution which reduces the all-important sense of spirit of place – and is also a symptom of habitat fragmentation and isolation. Seeing the spring-flying fritillaries in young conifer plantations was always a struggle, knowing that those places had had their souls sold to the devil, and would develop into arboreal slums, and their joyous inhabitants – flowers, insects and songbirds – would all be lost. At times naturalists leave such places in a state of mourning.

Indeed, most of the older naturalists alive today have witnessed so much species loss and habitat destruction that they are traumatised by it, and are living in a state of unrecognised but profound grief – especially those who have worked in nature conservation and environmental conservation. Yet conservationists carry on, they have no other choice. They are Nature's spokespeople. Some may even be part of Nature itself.

Symbolism and beauty

Yet, as John Masefield so aptly puts it late on in his gipsy-land story-poem 'King Cole', butterflies are 'the souls of summer hours'. They help transport you into the vortex of spring and into the very epicentre of summer. They do not merely lead you into special places, but into special – ultra-special – time, time that is almost too virtuous and ecstatic to be of this earth. So the highs and lows, the weather-borne vicissitudes, of butterflying are massive. The problem for butterflyers in the UK is that spring and summer weather provides rather an imbalance between down-time and rapture. Also, the closer one lives to Nature, the more one exists under the thumb of the weather and the darker seasons.

If butterflies take you to special places in special times, then they are offering great depth of experience and immense freedom. Not for nothing are they forever seen as symbols of freedom, the freedom of the immortal soul, and the freedom of beauty. Butterflies can be viewed as keys to the freedom of Nature. However, their transience and vulnerability are such that they must not be regarded as symbols of perpetuity, especially as in Nature nothing persists indefinitely, everything occurs in successional phases, everything is Phase.

Those of us who are hard-wired to Beauty – which should be all of us – will find that butterflies have much to offer. This is not simply because of the beauty of their wings, and the grace of their flight, or their juxtaposition to and relationship with flowers, but because they exist in the most wonderful places, in the best of all weathers in the greatest of seasons – weather permitting, that is. Beauty will always win people over, providing it is communicated in appropriate language. The UK nature conservation movement desperately needs poets, and story tellers, to articulate this better; not least because the real battle for nature conservation lies not so much out there on the land but in the hearts and minds of people – win the people over, and the politicians will follow.

Knowledge, science and conservation

Perhaps above everything else butterflies feed a thirst for knowledge. This may well be the main reason why so many scientists, including some of the world's leading biologists and ecologists, are attracted to butterflies as objects of study. Metamorphosis does not over-excite scientists these days. They are more interested in butterfly interactions with climate, with habitat fragmentation, isolation, quality and quantity, the problem of habitat patches jumping in and out of suitability according to factors such as seasonal vegetation growth rates, as well as butterfly population structures and mobility, and with genetics. Predation, parasitism, viruses, pathogens and diseases are also on the research radar – and rightly so. One crucial area for research is the factors behind the long-term cycles of expansion and contraction, ebb and flow, rise and fall.

The more we learn about butterflies, the more we realise remains to be learnt about them. Despite the fact that British butterflies are amongst the best studied and most closely monitored taxonomic group in the world, their ability to surprise us seems infinite. They continually astound, and remain incredibly difficult to predict. What is not known about them must be more important than what is known, certainly in terms of practical conservation knowledge. Butterflies are changelings, continually moving the goal posts – including their own goal posts, by endeavouring to adapt to changing environmental situations and simply by pushing limits. Their main problem is that of keeping up with the increasing pace of environmental change. People with low boredom thresholds and a deep thirst for ecological knowledge and experience will find that butterflies will not let them down.

But what about conservation, you might well ask? Surely the whole purpose of spending fifty years recording and studying butterflies is to assist in their conservation? The answer is, well yes, of course – but not quite as you might think. Certainly, my middle thirty years of butterflying were concerned primarily with contributing effectively to their conservation, but then I began to question the meaning of conservation itself. In effect, I worked in nature conservation for some thirty years before I began to wonder what 'nature conservation' actually meant – and opened Pandora's box. Few of my colleagues were interested – they were too busy conserving biodiversity, setting up and attending meetings, or completing a grant application form or management plan on time. 'It's obvious!' they said, dismissively. It was not. Philosophical ponderings consequently took place, in places as diverse as traffic jams on the M25 and tree stumps in forest clearings.

Eventually, some truth dawned: nature conservation is essentially concerned with mending the relationship between people and Nature, and is an expression of love for, and an interaction with, the beauty and wonder of the natural world, and with belonging in Nature. This has been rather hijacked by ecology, in the vain hope that it might hold a panacea. Science provides some rationalisation and helps clarify priorities, and works alongside technology and resources to determine practicalities, but the whole show is essentially about Love. It matters not that love is scarcely rational.

And as for the conservation of butterflies, those shimmering, fickle creatures of change? In simplistic terms it is relatively easy to manage a place for a single well-studied species, such as a butterfly, for a while. Yet we are forever trying to manage small, isolated places for whole suites of species with diverse and even conflicting ecological requirements, and are continually trying to arrest successional change and freeze a place into a time capsule. Nature does not do time capsules, it runs in epochs, periodically moving on. Moreover, Nature does not recognise our targets: in Nature there is no agenda beyond the will of individual plants and animals to exist, and then only within the moment of being. The needs we attribute to Nature may actually be ours. Re-wilding is now being held up as a solution, but perhaps it is we who need re-wilding, not Nature.

And as for the butterflies themselves? Perhaps they are forever seeking to push limits – environmental limits, their own limits, our limits. After all, butterflies – led by the Purple Emperor, the ultimate butterfly – seek nothing short of world domination. Conservationists are there merely to help them realise that ambition.

> It is eternity now. I am in the midst of it. It is about me in the sunshine; I am in it as the butterfly in the light-laden air. Nothing has to come; it is now. Now is eternity.

Richard Jefferies, *The Story of My Heart* (1883)

Afterword: On Marlpost Road

And I rose up, and knew that I was tired;
And so continued my journey ...

> Inscription on the Edward Thomas Memorial Stone,
> Shoulder of Mutton Hill, Steep, Hampshire

In the forest the clay cracked, gaped and chasmed in awesome summer heat. Weeks of scorching drought had removed all moisture from the paths and rides, turning mud to earth, earth to dust, and dust to desiccation. Finally, the particles rose to hang low within pulsating air. At night the trees trapped the day's heat and held it close to the ground, threatening suffocation, only for the new day to add more. And so the heat accumulated and intensified, as if the summer was building towards some cataclysmic climax of intense power, and almost unnatural beauty. There may have been some grand purpose behind it all; it seemed almost so, but that remained hidden to man and was understood perhaps only by Nature. Each leaf strained for relief from the searing sun; some had fallen early, forming a carpet of crumpled Hazel and Silver Birch leaves upon the woodland floor. Beneath the shade of brooding oaks the Dog's Mercury had turned its leaves downwards, in abject surrender. The Honeysuckle leaves would follow, for they were yellowing and would soon turn brown and wither. The long hot summer had returned. Metaphor and reality had harmonised.

Somehow he had left himself behind. He had done this sort of thing before, though not always through the power of Nature, or through Psyche. Those early experiences now mattered little, being at best training exercises for the real thing. For now it was different, involving the truest reality, Faith. He had left himself staring up at some high tree, where something small and distant had flickered momentarily, once or twice, iteratively, perhaps calling from a different dimension of existence. Was it an Emperor, or an Admiral perhaps, or more? It mattered little, for the naming of something is only one small part of the experience of it. We can venture deeper than the meaning of words, as poets do; but, paradoxically, we can do this only through the medium of words, and words shimmer between their meanings.

The real him had wandered out of the wood and off down the oak-lined Marlpost Road; not quite as before, though still journeying from glade to glade, hurrying through the overhung sections where autumn lurked, and dallying in the sunlight glades where summer dwelt. Others had gone the other way, into the wood, bearing cameras and binoculars. Butterfly photographers – New Age collectors – seeking images, two-dimensional experiences; trophy hunters, collecting visual memories. But Nature would entrap them too, in time. The meaning of the experiences they were having now would kick in later, in ordained time. Psyche, the butterfly-winged goddess of the human soul, would entice them, further up and further in.

Now here, through the collective memory of place, some deeper, truer reality was being penetrated. The silliness had been left behind – a shame, as it was fun. Lucidity was breaking through, like shafts of sunlight in which hoverflies were dancing within the miasmic dust of endless summer days. It had been threatening to break through for some time, but had been resisted stubbornly, perhaps simply on account of innate humanity. There was no stopping it now, on Marlpost Road, where he had always been. He had never left the road he had taken as a schoolboy, though it had twisted and turned, perhaps trying to shake him off, and had never run straight as a Roman road, as now it did, calmly.

Some power had straightened it out. Through leaving himself behind, if only by mere *lapsus*, he had surrendered to that power. It had absorbed him. Nature had fulfilled its task with him. Nature was not his religion, and never had been, for though deeply fascinating it made no sense without a creator, and made most sense when given back its rightful name – Creation. Voltaire was right: a clock needs a clockmaker. Instead, Nature had been his mentor and had latterly become his cathedral, his place of spiritual development and, indeed, of ministry and worship. Of course, it had distracted him, but only as part of the teaching process. There was also a healing there, though from what and for what remained absurdly obtuse, and may not ultimately matter. He had failed worldly peer-pressure atheism rather splendidly – the myriad ecstatic experiences he had had in Nature had ensured that. Marlpost Road was his Road to Emmaus. In gratitude he had openly campaigned to give Nature back its meaning. Psyche, though, had proved to be a flibbertigibbet, a veritable minx, a green lady of the woods who flickered in and out of focus (mainly out), who practised beguilement and succeeded only in causing confusion. She was all too human. Metamorphosis was a doddle of a metaphor: we are caterpillars, we periodically change our skins; death is the pupal period, and then ... we are destined to fly!

Butterflies had long held his hand, for Nature is so vast, so utterly wondrous that we need a focus, we need to narrow it down. Send for the cameras and the binoculars, or even the dog lead! Butterflies had helped the development of his soul. He had long felt, as Keats most earnestly believed, that we are on this earth to grow our souls, whatever that may mean – it links to skin changing. Also, he had long suspected that butterflies, as members of the lower orders (not that any living thing is low), share some form of communal soul, as species. He did not need to understand any of this. Some things we are not meant to understand, but merely to believe. It is easier, though we consider it harder.

Then there is the small matter of ministry, of individual purpose on this earth. Many today do not believe in this. He did, eventually.

Iridescence

Scatter me, these living ashes, here
Within this forest, my cathedral,
For all I sought through ministry
Of place, was Nature's meaning,
Deep within the sanctum of a dream
That dreamt itself in wonderment,
And danced a wayward life
Along some woodland path
Before becoming, sudden, real,
Inside the calling of a summer day.
Spirit, on iridescent wings,
As words of life in living light
Descending, that all true dreams
May, through glory, be fulfilled.

Butterflies of the year

Memoria in aeterna…

Criterion: the butterfly species by which the individual year is best remembered. Occasionally two species cannot be separated and have to share the title.

1964   Clouded Yellow
1965   Orange-tip
1966   Painted Lady
1967   Red Admiral
1968   Pearl-bordered Fritillary
1969   White Admiral
1970   Holly Blue
1971   Purple Emperor
1972   Small Pearl-bordered Fritillary
1973   Purple Emperor
1974   Purple Hairstreak
1975   Purple Emperor
1976   Purple Emperor
1977   Brown Hairstreak
1978   Duke of Burgundy
1979   Purple Emperor
1980   Silver-spotted Skipper
1981   Wall Brown
1982   Duke of Burgundy
1983   Clouded Yellow & High Brown Fritillary
1984   Duke of Burgundy
1985   Dark Green Fritillary
1986   High Brown Fritillary
1987   Small Tortoiseshell
1988   Brimstone

1989	High Brown Fritillary
1990	Holly Blue
1991	Meadow Brown
1992	Peacock
1993	Green Hairstreak
1994	Marsh Fritillary
1995	Scotch Argus
1996	Painted Lady
1997	Mountain Ringlet
1998	Chalkhill Blue
1999	Heath Fritillary
2000	Clouded Yellow
2001	Purple Emperor
2002	Purple Emperor
2003	Purple Emperor
2004	Pearl-bordered Fritillary
2005	Brown Hairstreak
2006	Purple Emperor
2007	Purple Emperor
2008	Purple Emperor
2009	Purple Emperor
2010	Silver-washed Fritillary & White Admiral
2011	Marsh Fritillary
2012	Purple Emperor
2013	Long-tailed Blue

Bibliography

Barkham, Patrick. 2010. *The Butterfly Isles*. Granta, London.
'BB', illustrated by Denys Watkins-Pitchford. 1940. *Brendon Chase*.
    Hollis & Carter, London.
'BB', illustrated by Denys Watkins-Pitchford. 2013. *BB's Butterflies*,
    edited by Bryan Holden. Roseworld, Solihull.
Bright, P M & Leeds, H A. 1938. *A Monograph of the British
    Aberrations of the Chalk-Hill Blue Butterfly*. Richmond Hill, London.
Byron, George Gordon, Lord. 2008. *The Major Works*, edited by Jerome
    McGann (Oxford World's Classics). Oxford University Press, Oxford.
Castle Russell, S G. 1952. The New Forest in the 'nineties and after.
    Entomologist's Record 64, 138–144.
Chatfield, J. 1987. *F W Frohawk: his Life and Work*. Crowood Press,
    Marlborough.
Coleman, W S. 1860. *British Butterflies*. George Routledge & Sons, London.
Coleridge, Samuel Taylor. 2000. *The Major Works* (Oxford World's
    Classics). Oxford University Press, Oxford.
Emmet, A M. 1991. *The Scientific Names of the British Lepidoptera –
    their history & meaning*. Harley Books, Colchester.
Fowler, J. 1893. Notes from Ringwood. *Entomologist* 27, 142–144.
Gibbons, Stella. 1932. *Cold Comfort Farm*. Longmans, London.
Graves, Robert. 1955. *The Greek Myths*, vols 1 & 2. Penguin, London.
Heseltine, G. 1888. *Apatura iris* in Hants. *Entomologist* 21, 209–210.
Heslop, I R P, Hyde, G & Stockley, R E. 1964. *Notes & Views of the
    Purple Emperor*. Southern Publishing Co., Brighton.
Hudson, W H. 1903. *Hampshire Days*. Longman, Green & Co., London.
Hudson, W H. 1904. *Green Mansions*. Duckworth & Co., London.
Huxley, J & Carter, D J. 1981. A blue form of the Small Skipper, with
    comments on colour production. *Entomologist's Gazette* 32: 79–82.
Jefferies, R. 1883. *The Story of my Heart*. Longman, Green & Co., London.
Jefferies, R. 1889. *Field & Hedgerow*. Longman, Green & Co., London.
Kirkland, P. 2012. The enigmatic *Erebia* – the Scotch Argus in Britain.
    British Wildlife 23: 179–185.
Lascelles, G W. 1915. *Thirty-five Years in the New Forest*. Arnold. Reprinted
    by the New Forest Research & Publications Trust, Lyndhurst, 1998.

Lee, Laurie. 1969. *As I Walked Out One Midsummer Morning*. Andre Deutsch, London.

Masefield, John. 1923. *King Cole and other poems*. Heinemann, London.

Milne, A A. 1926. *Winnie-the-Pooh*. Methuen, London.

Mountain, Fiona. 2009. *Lady of the Butterflies*. Random House, London.

Oates, M R. 1996. The demise of butterflies in the New Forest. *British Wildlife* 7, 205–216.

Oates, M R. 2005. Extreme butterfly-collecting: a biography of I R P Heslop. *British Wildlife* 16, 164–171.

Oates, M R. 2011. Summer souls. *National Trust Magazine*, Summer 2011, 48–51.

Oates, M R & Warren, M S. 1990. *A Review of Butterfly Introductions in Britain & Ireland*. JCCBI/WWF.

Oates, M R, Taverner, J, Green, D, Fletcher, B & Thelwell, D. 2000. *The Butterflies of Hampshire*. Pisces, Newbury.

Pollard, E. 1979. Population ecology and change in range of the White Admiral *Ladoga Camilla* in England. *Ecological Entomology* 4, 61–64.

Sandars, E. 1939. *A Butterfly Book for the Pocket*. Oxford University Press, London.

South, R. 1906. *The Butterflies of the British Isles*. Frederick Warne, London.

Stokoe, W S. 1938. *The Observer's Book of British Butterflies*. Frederick Warne, London.

Thomas, Edward. 1897. *The Woodland Life*. Wm Blackwood, Edinburgh & London. Several subsequent reproductions.

Thomas, Edward. 1909. *Richard Jefferies: His Life and Work*. Hutchinson, London. Several subsequent reproductions.

Thomas, Edward. 1909. *The South Country*. J M Dent, London. Several subsequent reproductions.

Thomas, Edward. 1914. *In Pursuit of Spring*. Thomas Nelson & Sons, London. Several subsequent reproductions.

Thomas, Edward. 2008. *The Annotated Collected Poems*, edited by Edna Longley. Bloodaxe, Tarset, Northumberland.

Thoreau, Henry David. 2012. *The Natural History of Massachusetts*. In *The Portable Thoreau*, edited by J S Cramer. Penguin, London.

White, Gilbert. 1789. *The Natural History & Antiquities of Selborne*. White, Cochrane & Co., London. Over 300 editions issued.

Wordsworth, William. 1997. *The Prelude Book 13*. In *Selected Poetry*, edited by Stephen Gill & Duncan Wu. Oxford University Press, Oxford.

List of illustrations

Acknowledgements

Many friends, human and otherwise, have helped and inspired me over the years. In particular, two great and gloriously unique British institutions moulded me, somehow – Christ's Hospital school, in West Sussex, and the National Trust for Places of Historic Interest or Natural Beauty. Above all I must thank my late mother, Helen Oates, and my dear wife, Sally, for putting up with an awful lot for far too long. I also gratefully acknowledge the support of my lifelong friends Dr Nigel Fleming and Derek Longhurst, and of my close butterflying friends Dr Andy & Linda Barker, Dr Sue Clarke, Lynn Fomison, Doug Goddard, Dr Simon Grove, Neil Hulme, Gail and Stephen Jeffcoate, Caroline Steel and Ken Willmott, along with ecological mentoring support I have received from John Bacon, Alan Stubbs, Professor Jeremy Thomas and Dr Martin Warren. My friends and colleagues from the National Trust have helped more than they could possibly imagine, notably Dr David Bullock, Mike Collins and Katherine Hearn. I must thank Andrew Branson, founder of *British Wildlife*, for his unwavering belief in this venture, Patrick Barkham for opening the genre of imaginative writing on butterflies and for his enthusiastic encouragement, my artist and butterflying friend Tim Bernhard, copy-editor Hugh Brazier for his patient translation of gibberish into English, Abe Davies, Katy Roper and Nick Wright of British Wildlife Publishing, and Vicky Beddow, Jamie Criswell and Jim Martin of Bloomsbury. Brokenborough Poets commented helpfully on draft poems. Charlie Burrell and the Burrell family, Fermyn Woods Contemporary Art, the Religious Society of Friends (Quakers), Sufi Way and the *Test Match Special* commentary team have conspired, somehow, to keep me marginally on the right side of sanity.

Beyond all else, this book is the product of the profound fellowship provided by the charity Butterfly Conservation, its staff, branches and members. The places which have inspired, supported and tutored me are identified in this book, and are duly acknowledged here. At times the butterflies themselves obliged me, even some caterpillars.

I am grateful to Bryan Holden and the BB Society (www.bbsociety.co.uk), and Hollis & Carter for permission to quote from chapter 10 of *Brendon Chase* by 'BB'; to Peters, Fraser & Dunlop for permission to quote from Hilaire Belloc's *The Four Men*; to the Society of Authors as the Literary Representative of the Estate of John Masefield for permission to quote from Masefield's poem 'King Cole'; to the Trustees of the Pooh Properties for the quote from *Winnie-the-Pooh* by A A Milne, text copyright © 1926 published by Egmont UK Ltd London and used with permission; to Penguin Books Ltd for permission to quote 47 words (pp. 28–29) from *Finn Family Moomintroll* by Tove Jansson (Puffin, 2001), text and illustrations copyright © Tove Jansson, 1948, English translation copyright © Ernest Benn Ltd, 1950; and to Penguin Random House UK for permission to quote from the poem 'Spring goes, summer comes' from *Flower Fairies of the Summer* by Cicely Mary Barker, first published by Frederick Warne of London in 1925.

Matthew Oates
February 2015

Index of butterfly species

General index